# The Official History of Cri̇
# Justice in England and Wa

Volume III of *The Official History of Criminal Justice in England and Wales* draws on archival sources and individual accounts to offer a history of penal policymaking in England and Wales between 1959 and 1997.

The book studies the changes underlying penal policymaking in the period, from a belief in the rehabilitative potential of imprisonment to a reaffirmation in 1993 that 'Prison Works' as a deterrent to crime. A need to curb the rising prison population initially focussed on developing alternatives to prison and a new system of parole; however, their relative ineffectiveness led to sentencing becoming the key to penal reform. A slackening of faith in rehabilitation led to pressure for greater emphasis on humane containment and the rebalancing of security, order and justice in prison regimes. Thus, 1991 was the climactic year for what became largely unfulfilled hopes for lasting penal reform. Escapes, riots and prison occupations were prime catalysts for changes, often highly contentious, in penal policymaking. Notably, there was no simple equation between political party, minister and policy choice. Both Labour and Conservative governments had distinctly liberal Home Secretaries and, after 1992, both parties took a more punitive approach.

This book will be of much interest to students of criminology and British history, politics and law.

**David Downes** is Professor Emeritus of Social Policy and a member and former director of the Mannheim Centre for Criminology and Criminal Justice at the London School of Economics, UK.

# Whitehall Histories: Government Official History Series

ISSN: 1474–8398

The Government Official History series began in 1919 with wartime histories, and the peacetime series was inaugurated in 1966 by Harold Wilson. The aim of the series is to produce major histories in their own right, compiled by historians eminent in the field, who are afforded free access to all relevant material in the official archives. The Histories also provide a trusted secondary source for other historians and researchers while the official records are not in the public domain. The main criteria for selection of topics are that the histories should record important episodes or themes of British history while the official records can still be supplemented by the recollections of key players; and that they should be of general interest, and, preferably, involve the records of more than one government department.

**The Authorised History of British Defence Economic Intelligence**
A Cold War in Whitehall, 1929–90
*Peter Davies*

**The Official History of Criminal Justice in England and Wales**
Vol I: The 'Liberal Hour'
Vol II: Institution-Building
*Paul Rock*
Vol III: The Rise and Fall of Penal Hope
*David Downes*

**The Official History of the British Civil Service**
Reforming the Civil Service, Vol. I: The Fulton Years, 1966–1981
*Rodney Lowe*

Reforming the Civil Service, Vol. II: The Thatcher and Major
Revolutions, 1982–97
*Rodney Lowe and Hugh Pemberton*

For more information about this series, please visit: https://www.routledge.com/
Government-Official-History-Series/book-series/SE0789

# The Official History of Criminal Justice in England and Wales

Volume III: The Rise and Fall of Penal Hope

**David Downes**

Routledge
Taylor & Francis Group

LONDON AND NEW YORK

First published 2021
by Routledge
2 Park Square, Milton Park, Abingdon, Oxon OX14 4RN

and by Routledge
52 Vanderbilt Avenue, New York, NY 10017

*Routledge is an imprint of the Taylor & Francis Group, an informa business*

*British Library Cataloguing-in-Publication Data*
A catalogue record for this book is available from the British Library

*Library of Congress Cataloging-in-Publication Data*
A catalog record has been requested for this book

ISBN: 978-0-367-65395-8 (hbk)
ISBN: 978-0-367-65399-6 (pbk)
ISBN: 978-1-003-12927-1 (ebk)

Typeset in Times New Roman
by Apex CoVantage, LLC

# Contents

# Figures

# Preface

The title of this book, *The Rise and Fall of Penal Hope,* attempts to convey, for the period 1959–97, the continued unfolding of a set of aims and aspirations which had preoccupied policy-makers in the criminal justice field in England and Wales for a century or more – over and above the practical business of day-to-day administration and short-term planning – but which ultimately foundered on the rocks of the politicisation of law and order, the development of which is the subject of a separate volume by Tim Newburn and myself. This not to say that politics should somehow be excluded from issues of crime control, only that in this case its character hinged on what Professor Tony Bottoms termed 'populist punitiveness'.[1]

The great American sociologist C. Wright Mills defined the 'master aim of the historian' as 'to keep the human record straight'.[2] This implies that there is or should be such a record, and that it is possible to 'keep it straight', both of which assumptions would be challenged by many, especially post-modernist thinkers. Yet at the least the most egregious errors and misinterpretations can be challenged and, at best, historians can mediate to help resolve key differences between conflicting accounts. The very conception of an 'official' history is that such a record is possible, especially with the aid of access to documents normally withheld from public view. Thanks to freedom of information legislation, that access is less privileged than before 2000, but widening access has revealed the scale of the gaps in archival documentation. As Paul Rock has shown, in the course of his part in this overall project, much of what has been presumed to exist is simply not there, having been destroyed or lost in the process of relocating ministries or reducing storage costs.[3] Even so, the amount of material relevant to the task is still immense, and the amount of ground to be covered remains daunting. And some of the shortfall in documentation can be made good by interviews with people who had been directly engaged in the making or study of penal policy in this period and who may give access to personal papers that shed light on their character. .

My own response to the challenges involved was necessarily to be selective rather than comprehensive in analysis and coverage. The issues on which this history is based are those which demanded policy choices that had a decisive and lasting influence, for good or ill, on the penal system. Two such seminal developments were the Home Office acceptance in 1968 of the case made by the Advisory Council on the Penal System for the dispersal rather than concentration of category A prisoners, and the repeal of key sections of the 1991 Criminal Justice Act, which forms the taproot for the doubling of the size of the prison population, and the currently shameful state of many of our prisons, two to three decades on. In the words of the Chief Inspector of Prisons: "The recent history of many prisons in England and Wales has been deeply troubling. We saw once more in 2018–19 . . . that far too many of our jails have been plagued by drugs, violence, appalling living conditions and a lack of access to meaningful rehabilitative activity."[4]

This volume is part of a much larger project, two volumes of which, by Paul Rock, have already been published, on the liberal reforms of the 1960s and on the institutional creation of the Crown Court and the Crown Prosecution Service. A forthcoming book, co-authored with Tim Newburn, concerns the politics of law and order. Policing in this period will be the subject of a study by Tim Newburn.

## Notes

1 Anthony Bottoms, 1995, "The Philosophy and Politics of Punishment and Sentencing" in C.M.V.Clarkson and R. Morgan (eds.) *The Politics of Sentencing Reform*, Oxford: Clarendon Press.
2 C. Wright Mills, 1959, *The Sociological Imagination*, New York: Oxford University Press: 144.
3 Paul Rock, 2016, 'The Dreadful Flood of Documents': The 1958 Public Record Act and its Aftermath. Part 1: 'The Genesis of the Act', *Archives*, LI, no. 132–3, pp. 48–69; and Part 2: 'After-effects', *Archives*, LII, no. 134, pp. 26–50.
4 HM Chief Inspector of Prisons annual report, 2018–2019: 7.

# Acknowledgements

First and foremost, my thanks are owed to Professors Paul Rock and Tim Newburn, without whom the commission to write the official history of criminal justice policy 1959–97 could not have been undertaken at all. Their support, stimulus and informed criticism have been essential throughout. Thanks are also due to Tessa Stirling, Sally Falk and Roger Smethurst, of the Cabinet Office official histories team, who ensured a steady supply of helpful advice and archival files.

Invaluable help was given by David Faulkner, the erstwhile Deputy Under-Secretary of State and Head of the Criminal and Research and Statistical Departments at the Home Office between 1982 and 1990, not least by his generous loan of personal documents assembled over a period of time covering the 1980s until his retirement in the early 1990s. Such an archive is all too rare and constitutes a unique source of organisational memory, now under threat of evaporation in the age of the email and the internet. The late Sir Louis Blom-Cooper was immensely helpful in several ways, not least his enthusiastic support for the project. His was the longest term membership of the Advisory Council for the Penal System and his multiple roles as Chair of the Howard League for Penal Reform, Chair of numerous Public Enquiries and lifelong involvement in the campaign for the abolition of the death penalty and for penal reform in other respects, gave him an exceptional vantage-point in interviews about criminal justice matters. Professor Sir Anthony Bottoms was also exceptionally helpful, both in meetings and in providing us with both unpublished and source material gathered for his study, with Simon Stevenson, of criminal justice policy from 1945–1970.

As stressed in the Preface, interviews proved an essential part of the history, not just to fill myriad gaps in the archive, but mainly to convey the lived experience of active engagement with penal policy making and reform. Given that interviews not only take time and energy, but also are something of a hostage to fortune, not least to do with recalling events some two decades or more later, I am uncommonly grateful to those who agreed to be interviewed for this history: Kate Akester, legal practitioner with expertise on human rights; Professor Andrew Ashworth, author of *Sentencing and Penal Policy*, 1983; Lord Kenneth Baker*, Home Secretary, 1990–92; Anthony Brennan, Secretary to the Royal Commission on Capital Punishment, 1964–5; Kenneth Clarke, M.P.*, Home Secretary, 1992–93; John Croft*^, Director of the Home Office Research and Planning

Unit, 1972–1983; the late Sir Brian Cubbon*, Permanent Under-Secretary of State, Home Office, 1979–88; Brian Emes, HM Prison Service, Deputy Director-General during the Strangeways occupation by prisoners[1]; Arthur de Frisching, HM Prison Service; John Halliday*, Deputy Under-Secretary of State, Home Office, 1991–2001; Lord Michael Howard*, Home Secretary, 1993–1997; Lord Douglas Hurd*, Home Secretary 1985–89; Professor Roy King, co-author with Rod Morgan of *The Future of the Prison System*, 1980 and, with Kathleen McDermott, *The State of Our Prisons*, 1996; Anthony Langdon, Chair of the Control Review Committee, HM Prison Department, 1983–4; Professor Rod Morgan, Chief Inspector of the Probation Service 2001–4 and Chair of the Youth Justice Board, 2004–7; Robert Morris^, Secretary to the May Committee on the United Kingdom Prison Services, 1978–9; Anthony Pearson, HM Prison Department; Professor Andrew Rutherford*, Chair of the Howard League for Penal Reform, 1984–1999 and author of *Prisons and the Process of Justice*, 1984; Professor Mick Ryan, political scientist and analyst of penal pressure group politics; Barry Sheerman*, M.P., chair of the Labour Campaign for Criminal Justice, 1987–92; Baroness Vivien Stern, Director of NACRO, 1977–96 and Secretary-General, Penal Reform International, 1989–2006; Lord Woolf, author and co-author with Judge Stephen Tumim of Parts 1 and 2 respectively of the Report of the Inquiry *Prison Disturbances, April 1990*, 1991; and Martin Wright, Director of the Howard League for Penal Reform 1971–1981, and a pioneer of restorative justice.[2] I am most grateful to Joyce Lorinstein for her prompt and efficient transcription of the interviews.

Repeated requests for an interview with Roy Hattersley, shadow Home Secretary 1987–1992; with Tony Blair, shadow Home Secretary 1992–4, and Leader of the Opposition 1994–7; and with Jack Straw, shadow Home Secretary, 1994–7 went unanswered. John Patten, Minister of State, Home Office 1987–92, declined the request. Professor Terence Morris declined a formal interview but was unusually helpful in other ways. I am immensely grateful to Dr. Penelope Morris for access to an unpublished chapter of the classic study of prison life, *Pentonville*.[3]

My thanks also to Justine Rainbow, for advice on access to and the range of Home Office archives. I am grateful to the Ministry of Justice for access to the journals of the governor of HM Prison Wakefield 1974–5, and also to the Broadlands library of the University of Southampton for access to the papers of Lord Mountbatten relevant to his inquiry into prison escapes and security issues in the mid-1960s. I am also grateful to Margaret Clayton, Director of Services, Prison Department, Home Office, 1985–89; Professor Alison Liebling, Institute of Criminology at the University of Cambridge; and Dr. Sharon Shalev, Centre for Criminology of the University of Oxford, for timely help on critical points; and to Little, Brown Book Group Ltd for permission to quote from *Private Member* by Leo Abse.

British criminology affords a wealth of knowledge about the penal system and criminal justice in general over the period concerned. Apart from the numerous instances cited in the text, I would single out as particularly helpful successive editions of *The Penal System: An Introduction* by Michael Cavadino, James Dignan and, in the fifth edition, George Mair, and the four-volume history of *Responses to Crime* by Lord Windlesham, virtually an unofficial history in its own right.

Finally, my thanks to colleagues in the Mannheim Centre of Criminology and Criminal Justice at the London School of Economics for their unstinting help and encouragement; and to my son, Joshua, whose computer skills proved essential throughout.

## Notes

1 The interview with Brian Emes related to the control unit at Wakefield prison, not the events at Strangeways prison.
2 * indicates joint interview with Tim Newburn, ^ with Paul Rock.
3 Terence and Pauline Morris, 1963, *Pentonville: A Sociological Study of an English Prison*, London: Routledge & Kegan Paul.

# 1 The Rise of Penal Hope (1895–1967)

The first half of the 20th century was to prove an era of penal hope and liberal optimism about crime and punishment. Despite the logic of such contrasting theorists as Marx and Durkheim about inevitable rises in the crime rate in the late 19th century, assumptions echoed a century later by virtually all criminologists, the reality was, as also in the two decades 1995–2015, the reverse.[1] The late 19th and early 20th centuries also saw, though in this regard *unlike* the present day, a steady fall in the size of the prison population. From a rate per 100,000 of 108 in 1881, the daily average prison population fell more or less steadily to 60 in 1891, 55 in 1911, 32 in 1921, 29 in 1931, to a low point of 23 in 1940. It then commenced an upward trend during the Second World War, in contrast to the First, during which it had fallen quite steeply, to 50 in 1951, 63 in 1961, 81 in 1971, and 88 in 1981. It rose to the 1881 rate of 108 only in the late 1990s.[2] This long view of trends in imprisonment belies the belief that its increasing use is both inevitable and irreversible.

The falling rates of both crime and imprisonment no doubt assisted, consciously or not, the cause of penal reform. Not all of this presaged benign consequences for offenders. Eugenicist ideas combined with positivist theories of crime to envisage the selective breeding-out of inborn criminal tendencies.[3] While such ideas were not translated into actual programmes in Britain, they infused the debate with notions of moral defect and genetic inferiority.[4] Nevertheless, as Hood and Radzinowicz convincingly argue, such tendencies were substantially eclipsed by the 'widespread belief that, in the final analysis, far less could be achieved through penal repression than through advances in economic, political, social and moral spheres. It is for this last reason especially that these far-reaching changes in the weight of punishment, and more particularly in the deployment of incarceration, were not a transitory phenomenon . . . This set the pattern for the very optimistic approach towards crime and its control which flourished in the period between the two World Wars. The penal policy of England seemed at that time to be entering on a phase of new hopes and large expectations.'[5]

As a result, most reformism aimed to extend the philanthropy and welfare schemes which had begun to flourish in the earlier Victorian era. '. . . the official rhetoric and representations from the Gladstone Report[6] onwards cited "reform" as the central and organising aim of modern penal practice. This aim of reform or social readjustment was clearly the designated principle of the new institutions of Borstal, probation and state-funded after-care, but even the prison was now characterised more and more as a complex machinery of reform.'[7] For example, the Prisons Act of 1898, among a swathe of measures to implement the Gladstone Report, abolished the unproductive prison labour which had been so notorious a feature of penal servitude. The crank and the treadmill had been designed to calibrate hard labour, 'thereby promoting the goal of *uniformity* in this aspect of the prison regime as in all others.'[8] By contrast, the Gladstone Report gave primacy to the *individualisation* of the treatment of the prisoner and offenders in general.

This change of direction was to have profound repercussions for the prison service. 'The Report introduced confusion with its definition of "reformative" as a "manifest" task. The situation was made worse by its advocacy of *two* primary tasks, in the most frequently quoted statements in prison literature:

'We start from the principle that prison treatment should have as its primary and concurrent objects deterrence, and reformation.'

These proposals meant that somehow the prison service had to cope with two mutually exclusive tasks.[9] Reformation implies putting the needs of the prisoner first, with deterrence and security accorded lower priority. 'This was the crucial conflict which was to haunt the prison system until the post-Mountbatten developments established that the wishes of the community were to be paramount.'[10] However, reversing the priorities did not eliminate the conflict; attempts still had to be made to reconcile these seemingly incompatible tasks.

The innovations of probation and borstals came next, in the 1907 Probation of Offenders Act and the Prevention of Crime Act of 1908. Both added greatly to the upsurge of reformative measures, though not all sanctions in the 1908 Act were of that character, as it also introduced preventive detention. Borstals, so named after the village in Kent where the first such institution was located, were designed to provide a more educative and vocational regime for young offenders aged 16–21 than was available in adult prisons. A related aim was to separate the younger age group from more experienced adult offenders. Charles Russell, a leading pioneer of the boys' club movement, asserted:

'The Borstal system is without doubt an immense improvement upon anything that has previously been tried in this country. In many cases the discharged prisoner is hardly recognisable as the same young criminal who received the sentence. The habits of industry acquired in the workshops or on the farm, the improvement in intelligence and physique, are of incalculable advantage.'[11]

Borstal training involved a sentence of between one and three years for young offenders whose criminality was deemed serious but not irredeemable. The semi-determinate sentence allowed for release on licence when the Prison Commissioners judged enough reformative progress had been made. The growth of borstals and their high success rate in reducing reconvictions, at least in the pre-World War II period, prompted international interest. Borstals were introduced in several countries of the former British Empire, especially India.

The mood of questioning the morality of using imprisonment as a sentence for all but offences of the utmost seriousness reached its apogee in the celebrated speech by Winston Churchill on 20 July 1910.[12] In his brief tenure of office as Home Secretary 1910–11, Churchill decided to cut a swathe through what one might call the penal lumpenproletariat of petty, persistent offenders who composed the great bulk of the prison population. 'A principal feature of the English prison system in 1908 was the magnitude of throughput of prisoners, in excess, excluding remand prisoners, of 200,000 persons annually . . . Three out of every four prisoners received were either sentenced for a non-indictable offence or imprisoned as fine defaulters . . . Churchill displayed considerable scepticism as to what might be achieved through the prison system, and he quickly came to believe that imprisonment was greatly overused. He corresponded with John Galsworthy[13] on the need to reduce solitary confinement, he used his powers of executive clemency more frequently than was customary, and, of most significance, he set about framing legislative proposals to reduce severely the number of persons entering the prison system.

In a memorandum to the prime minister in September 1910, Churchill described the main problem as being 'the immense number of committals of petty offenders to prison on short sentences. He noted that two-thirds of sentenced prisoners were sentenced to two weeks or less . . . a terrible and purposeless waste of public money and human character'. Herbert Asquith, the prime minister, lent Churchill

**Average total prison population**

England & Wales, 1900-2016 (000s)

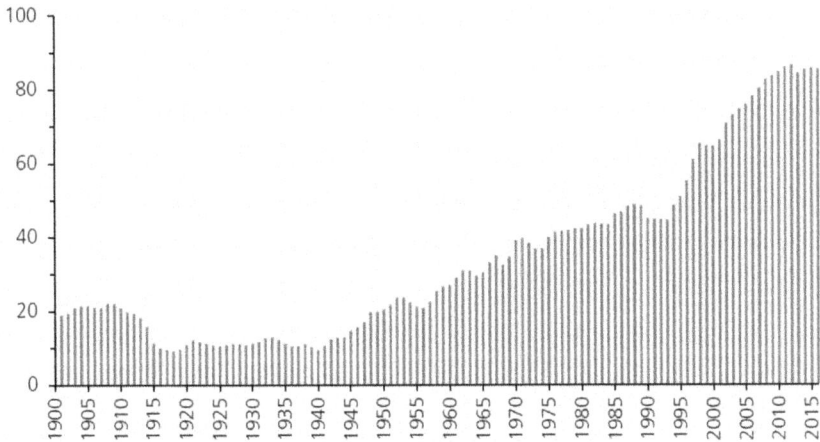

*Figure 1.1* Average total prison population, England and Wales, 1900–2016.

*Source:* MoJ, *Offender Management Statistics Quarterly,* various years

his support. Twelve months later, he was moved to the Admiralty, 'but left behind a momentum for reforming legislation.'[14] The much-quoted passage in his celebrated speech on imprisonment lifted humane penal philosophy to a height it has never surpassed:

> 'We must not forget that when every material improvement has been effected in prisons, when the temperature has been rightly adjusted, when the proper food to maintain health and strength have been given, when the doctors, chaplains, and prison visitors have been and gone, the convict stands deprived of everything that a free man calls life. We must not forget that all these improvements, which are sometimes salves to our consciences, do not change that position. The mood and temper of the public in regard to the treatment of crime and criminals is one of the most unfailing tests of the civilisation of any country. A calm and dispassionate recognition of the rights of the accused against the State, and even of convicted criminals against the State, a constant heart-searching by all charged with the duty of punishment, a desire and eagerness to rehabilitate in the world of industry all those who have paid their dues in the hard coinage of punishment, tireless efforts towards the discovery of curative and regenerating processes, and an unfaltering faith that there is a treasure, if you can only find it, in the heart of every man – these are the symbols which in the treatment of crime and criminals mark and measure the stored-up strength of a nation, and are the sign and proof of the living virtue in it.'

Churchill's strategy for the 'abatement of imprisonment' took both short- and longer-term forms: extra remission was extended to all prisoners on a novel *pro rata* basis; non-custodial disposals such as probation and the screening-out of imprisonment for mentally defective offenders, which were to be encouraged by the Prison Commissioners, were spelt out; and the extension of time for the payment of fines made substantial inroads on the size of the prison population[15]. The judiciary were clearly swayed by the force of the arguments against the overuse of imprisonment, especially excessively short-term measures for fine default, much of which emanated from 'drunk and disorderly' prosecutions. Due to these and other measures, the daily average prison population dropped from 20,291 in 1910 to 9,196 in 1918. It rose to 11,000 by 1920, but remained at or around that level until 1940 and beyond, a quite remarkable stability given that the crime rate doubled over the 20-year period, two decades which saw mass unemployment as a consequence of the Great Crash of 1929–31.[16] As David Wilson argues, in England and Wales the three decades between 1908 and the outbreak of the Second World War saw 'one of the world's longest sustained periods of decarceration in penal history, . . . partly prompted and promoted by the views Churchill expressed . . . In effect, our prison numbers halved, and as a result around twenty prisons had to close down, despite the fact that the crime rate in this period actually increased by around 160 per cent. By 1938 our prison population was among the smallest in Europe, and the reduction of our prison numbers was attracting the attention of American criminologists such as Edwin Sutherland, who wrote – almost in disbelief – that "prisons are being demolished and sold in England because the supply of prisoners is not large enough to fill them".[17] At the outbreak of the Second World War the prison system of England and Wales consisted of 22 prisons and seven borstals (institutions designed on a public-school model to house young people) with a total capacity of 19,600.'[18] The capacity was almost double the number of prisoners, an extraordinary development of *under*-crowding, the reverse of the situation that came to prevail in the second half of the 20th century. The reformist impetus was reinforced by two forms of political campaigning and resistance which emerged in this period. First, the Suffragettes' struggle for votes for women led them to challenge the authorities by symbolic acts of law violation. Imprisonment followed their refusal in many well-publicised cases to pay fines, and the harshness of prison conditions, and the suffering involved in hunger strikes, combined to strengthen unease about its scale and futility. The second group of largely middle-class, highly articulate people unexpectedly consigned to imprisonment were the conscientious objectors to conscription to the armed forces during the First World War 1914–18. Two of their number[19] later compiled a comprehensive survey of the conditions of imprisonment for different types of prisoner.

Following an exhaustive and severely critical survey of virtually all aspects of prison conditions, Hobhouse and Brockway concluded by making the case for 'the need to revise our penal theory'.[20] Far from acting as a deterrent or an agency of moral reformation, 'modern methods of punishment take the form of deprivation of liberty and the denial of intellectual, emotional and spiritual satisfactions. Stated in physiological terms, primitive forms of punishment consisted in the infliction of gross bodily hurt; modern penal methods are directed upon the higher functions of the central nervous system.'[21] Furthermore, '. . . much crime must be attributed to poverty, and its accompaniments and consequences; and imprisonment could in no such case help those who commit such crimes, since it merely makes it more difficult than before for them to live without crime. It must be recognised as an established fact that our principal punishment actually creates or perpetuates rather than abates crime in those upon whom it is inflicted.'[22] For young and petty offenders, community penalties such as probation 'give offenders opportunities to "make good" without withdrawal from ordinary life.'[23] For the more resistant, education and training should not be abandoned, but based on a more individualised approach: '. . . a drastic enquiry into the causes and antecedents of their offence; followed by a careful (though not minute) differentiation for purposes of re-education, by various kinds of curative treatment for mind and body, and by a thorough, and probably arduous, training for ordinary life and resumed liberty – a training which will involve wide opportunities for individual and corporate responsibility on the part of the delinquents.'[24] All of which, it was hoped, would be carried through by specially trained and motivated staff. Their vision was of a largely social and educative character, though harbouring – in its reference to 'curative treatment for mind and body' – the (doubtless unintended) potential for more aggressive "treatments" in the future, such as tranquillising drug medication. Overall, however, the Report made a thoroughly researched, scrupulous and reasoned case for widespread decarceration and liberal penal reform. The fashionable view that the 'feeble-minded' should be segregated, if not sterilised, that had almost come to prevail in the decade preceding the First World War, was now meeting increasingly formidable opposition.[25]

The main link between this kind of report, and other weighty yet reformist studies such as the Webbs' history of prisons and local government,[26] with its scathing attack on the Victorian prisons' 'fetish of uniformity',[27] and the more innovative thinking that came to inform the work of the Prison Commission, was embodied in the appointment as a new Commissioner, also in 1922 – an *annus mirabilis* for penal reform – of Alexander Paterson. Coming of age in the Edwardian heyday of liberal social reform, Paterson followed an Oxford education by going to live in Bermondsey 'and lived there not as a condescending visitor in a protected enclave, but as the folk in Bermondsey were themselves living, in a two-roomed tenement in one of the worst blocks on the river side. There he learnt what life at or below the poverty line meant to his neighbours and friends, and later communicated something of that knowledge in *Across the Bridges.*'[28] While it was not uncommon for members of the most advantaged classes to make forays into the East End, and the settlement houses started by Oxford and Cambridge colleges were bastions of what Gareth Stedman Jones termed an 'urban squirearchy',[29] the great exception to any hint of condescension had been Henry Mayhew's four-volume classic first-hand documentation, based on observation and interviews, of London labour and the London poor.[30] A few writers sought to convey or even share actual working-class living conditions. Jack London's *The People of the Abyss* (1903) contained photographic as well as vivid descriptions of the lives of the poor.[31]

Paterson's eloquence made him a formidable and lasting voice for liberal penal reform:

> '. . . it is the sentence of imprisonment, and not the treatment accorded in prison, that constitutes the punishment. Men come to prison as a punishment, not *for* punishment. It is doubtful whether any of the amenities granted in some modern prisons can in any way compensate for the punishment involved in the deprivation of liberty. It is the length of the sentence that measures the degree of punishment and not the conditions under which it is served.'[32]

'Prison can so easily become an unhealthy little cesspool. It is unnatural that men should live apart from women and children, unnatural that they should be solitary for so many hours in so small a space, that their movements should be so confined and their daily doings so minutely routined. In such an artificial surrounding it is difficult for men to develop or retain a normal social habit and attitude of mind. They may well become more hardened and anti-social, and return to the freedom that must come some day, firmly pledged to prey rather than co-operate.

'In some well-ordered prisons a more insidious process operates. The man who comes in as a criminal is made into a prisoner. All initiative and self-reliance are lost, obeying every order given him he comes in time to wait for an order. He develops a desire to please, which makes him furtive and sycophantic.'[33]

Paterson's impact on penal change was especially marked in relation to the borstal system, in which, in 1922, the 'penal element' was seen by Hobhouse and Brockway as 'still too dominant' compared with the educative and reformative. 'The military and disciplinary element is too obtrusive, particularly as expressed in the large numbers of warders on duty. It is indefensible that the vast majority of the personnel should be prison warders trained to administer the repressive regime of penal servitude and imprisonment.'[34] A note at the end of their chapter on the borstal system, headed 'Reforms at Borstal', states:

> 'Whilst this Report is in the Press, we hear that considerable reforms have been carried out at the Borstal Institutions, in part due, no doubt, to the appointment of Mr. Alec Paterson as a Prison Commissioner with special relation to Borstal.'[35]

By contrast with the early militaristic character of borstal, 'Paterson believed that the soundest method of training the young had been evolved in the public school system, with its conception of building up discipline from within, by encouraging the boys' social instincts of loyalty and *esprit de corps*, and stimulating their latent capacity for leadership. He believed also that the success of any organisation is dependent absolutely on the quality of the staff.

He therefore set about recruiting a new grade of prison officers – the Borstal housemaster, a grade which was to be "poorly paid and overworked",[36] but which offered almost infinite scope for powers of leadership and qualities of human understanding . . . A new type of subordinate officer was also enlisted, and a system of training inaugurated to give instruction in the new conception of discipline.'[37] This made possible the change to the 'open' borstal camp, where 'the safeguard against absconding was not high walls and iron bars, but the inner constraint bred of training and trust.' The principle was also then applied to 'star class' adult prisoners jailed for a first offence.

Paterson's faith in the public school ethos as inspiring a self-disciplined form of security through self-control did achieve some remarkable success stories. Young prisoners from Stafford prison marched across country to build North Sea Camp borstal. Paterson survived a foray into the Burmese jungle with young prisoners who their captors believed would finish him off. Even the young Brendan Behan, arrested in 1939 for possessing explosives as an Irish Republican Army recruit, described his experience in Hollesley Bay Borstal in positive rather than embittered terms.[38] After the Second World War, however, the borstal system gradually lost its lustre. The public school ethos was out of kilter with the less deferential times. Benedict Alper, an American criminologist, noted the change at Feltham Borstal some twenty-five years after he had first visited several borstals in 1939:

> 'With it all, I could not escape the feeling that a great change was reflected here . . . in the relationship between staff and boys. There was a freer attitude

between the two groups . . . At the same time I seemed to sense a note of greater truculence – or, at least, withdrawal – on the part of the boys themselves. Levity and enthusiasm are not generally the mark of persons in confinement anywhere . . . but the feeling of a public school which had been such a distinctive mark of Borstals as I knew them seems to have vanished . . . The former relationship, even at its best, smacked somewhat of the eleemosynary. In the other social welfare fields, this attitude is almost entirely gone. Why, indeed, should it linger on in correctional places for the young? Many of these view only with scorn the moral precepts and the religious training which was so integral a part of the Borstal idea – along with the influence it was expected would be exerted by the young men whom Alec Paterson had wooed from public school and University to dedicate themselves to helping the young offender.'[39]

The change was reflected in the declining borstal success rate, as measured by reconvictions, which fell steadily from 70 per cent in the 1930s to some 30 per cent in the 1960s. Other factors involved in the deteriorating success story were that 'we are getting many more lads of greater criminal sophistication, lengthier and more varied treatment experience and poorer prediction.'[40] Nor were the staff more professionally trained to cope with the tougher intake: 'Even though methods of group counselling are now being used, psychotherapy proper is still almost unknown in Borstal. The role of the housemaster has been described as analogous to that of the psychotherapist, but few have received any formal training in psychology or in casework techniques."[41] The fading hangover from the pre-war ethos was captured in the book and film *The Loneliness of the Long-Distance Runner*, in which a disaffected borstal boy spurns the opportunity afforded by a race against a team of public schoolboys by defiantly throwing away his chance to win.[42] 'Against the realisation of where he came from and what lies ahead for him, why should any Borstal lad want to win over a public school boy – or even compete with him? – asks *The Loneliness of the Long-Distance Runner*.'[43] Over a decade later, the film *Scum* (1979) portrayed borstal as a penal institution for adolescents as violent and repressive as any adult prison, with an inmate dominance hierarchy based on fear of the 'Daddy', the prisoner who most successfully vied for the toughest status.[44] The declension from the early hopes for borstal, however much they may have rested on a somewhat idealised imagery, was complete, with borstals renamed Youth Custody Centres in the Criminal Justice Act of 1982.

## Between the Wars: The 'golden age of penal reform'?

J.E. Thomas described the inter-war period as a 'golden age of penal reform'.[45] Though he was never Chairman of the Prison Commission, Alexander Paterson was clearly the dominant influence throughout the 1922–45 period: '. . . one of the giants of penal reform . . . Between the wars he became the most famous prison reformer of all time,'[46] though it is perhaps overstating the case to see his stature as exceeding that of John Howard. 'In this age of the 'anti-hero', it is difficult to understand . . . the very real veneration in which Paterson was held by Chairmen of the Commissioners, governors and borstal boys . . . But in the inter-war years, considerable numbers of people believed Paterson to be a great man because of his rare ability to translate penal theory into practice on a grand scale, and acclaimed him for it.'[47]

What did he and the Prison Commission achieve in this period? 'The first report after Paterson's appointment, for 1921–2, demonstrated that the reforms, already begun, were to be extended. The convict stage system was further modified, the convict "crop" was abolished,[48] prisoners were to be transferred in civilian clothes' – Oscar Wilde famously described the most humiliating moment of his prison experience as being transferred from Wandsworth prison to Reading gaol and taken in handcuffs and full convict garb via Clapham Junction station where he was surrounded by a jeering crowd[49] – 'the broad arrows were removed, visiting conditions were improved, talking was allowed at work . . . These changes heralded the golden age of penal reform. The "object in view" was defined as a "system of training such as will fit the prisoner to re-enter the world as a citizen".'[50] A symmetry was evolving between views of the causes of crime and delinquency and the appropriate modes of control and rehabilitation which – in principle – would surmount them. A critical mass of opinion and approach was forming around the work not only of Paterson, the Prison Commission, Hobhouse and Brockway and the Webbs but also such research as that of the psychologist Cyril Burt, who incorporated social and economic factors in his positivistic case studies of delinquency.[51] 'This view of delinquency, moreover, incorporated an understanding of the social and economic conditions which led to neglect and crime, and a faith in the contribution of investigation, classification and character-training to the promotion of "good citizenship".'[52]

'Good citizenship' was to be the touchstone of the development of what Garland termed the penal-welfare complex[53] over the era of criminal justice reform which lasted from the Gladstone Report of 1895 to the latter part of the twentieth century. 'The new, state-sponsored practices of probation, after-care and licensed supervision . . . share a common commitment to a mode of operation which might be termed *normalisation*. Each of these practices is concerned not just to prevent law-breaking, but also to inculcate specific norms and attitudes. By means of the personal influence of the probation or after-care officer, they attempt to straighten out characters and to reform the personality of their clients in accordance with the requirements of "good citizenship".'[54] This entailed the 'extension of the judicial power' to the offender's parents and family. 'As Herbert Samuel (Chairman of the 1909 Departmental Commission of probation) commented, "the home is put under probation" (Report on Probation 1909, p. 1087)'[55] However, 'this new apparatus was discreet, humane and relaxed by comparison [with the system it displaced], but promised at the same time to be more effective in operation.'[56] It was acknowledged by the start of World War II that 'one of the two main causes for the immense reduction in the prison population of today, compared with thirty years ago, is the operation of the Probation System.'[57] The percentage of adults convicted for indictable offences and placed on probation rose from 11 per cent in 1910 to 30 per cent in

1938. The inter-war period was notable for the growth of probation as the main 'creditable alternative to incarceration',[58] a role which waned after 1945, despite its growing professionalism.

At the deeper end of the penal complex are the 'correctional' institutions – borstals and reformatories in particular – and, for the most serious offenders, the 'segregative' institutions of the various forms of imprisonment. To Garland, the defining characteristics of twentieth century penality were thus forged in the 1895–1914 period. 'Many of these new sanctions, such as probation, or instalment fines, were conceived as direct alternatives to imprisonment, while others functioned to remove certain classes of offender out of the domain of the prison and into specialist institutions. The consequence was that the prison was *decentred* – shifted from its position as the central and predominant sanction to become one institution among many in an extended grid of penal sanctions.'[59] What came later was the development and elaboration of these alternatives into the professions of probation and social work, allied in key respects to the academic and applied subjects of criminology, psychology and psychiatry, much of which was crucially generated by the wider welfare services in the fields of health care, education, housing and income support.

Two fundamental tenets of the inter-war ideology of penal reform were all the more pronounced as the appeal of the eugenicist movement waned from its peak in late Victorian and Edwardian England. The first was that 'the key to the Prison Commission's aim of restricting the use of imprisonment in the 1920s was the Borstal training system.'[60] The demonstrable success of borstal training would, in Paterson's view in particular, sway the judiciary towards a progressive switch from prisons to borstal for young offenders aged 16–21. The second belief was that youth presented the best phase for steering offenders away from crime and into productive citizenship, an approach which genetic theories would have ruled out. Both tenets were substantially upheld in the inter-war period, though only in part. The use of imprisonment was indeed restricted, in the sense that the prison population, having halved from pre-war levels of 18–20,000, remained stable throughout the inter-war period, despite a doubling of the crime rate over the two decades. The popularity of probation played as large a role in this trend as that of borstals, whose expansion was financially constrained. But imprisonment itself remained extensively unreformed, a state of affairs reflected in the most dramatic event of the period, the so-called mutiny at Dartmoor Prison on Sunday 24 January 1932.

Morning exercise proved the occasion for a rampage which rapidly escalated into a riot and, for a brief hour and a half period, loss of control of the prison by the staff. In that time buildings were damaged and fires started. Control was reasserted only when police reinforcements arrived and armed force was used.[61] Such violent disorder was at odds with the tenor of penal policy. 'The Dartmoor "mutiny" was described by the Home Secretary as merely "somewhat serious". This tendency was also clear in official reluctance to use the word "riot" . . . a pejorative term that suggests "images of frenzied mob violence" and would reflect badly on any prison administration . . . The term "mutiny" suggested something more specific and organised than a riot – a betrayal of legitimate and rightful authority, usually in a military institution . . . Convicts themselves resisted such labelling and justified the initial outbreak as a "demonstration", "grievance" or "complaint" that deteriorated into a riot. For some convicts, the "mutiny" did have a logic – to challenge abuses made more visible by the reformative image of the 1930s prison.'[62] Nevertheless, the Home Office and Prison Commission chose to prosecute those involved with rioting rather than the more severe charge of "mutiny".

The underlying reasons for the riot seem inherently linked to the continuing harshness of conditions for adult prisoners. 'The vision of reform – the well-ordered prison of the 1920s and 1930s with its workshops and industries, libraries and lectures, prison visitors and more refined classification – was fragmented in its implementation and underfunded. Furthermore, it was wedged into systems and routines that had been developed largely in the first half of the nineteenth century and into buildings just as old.'[63] Notoriously remote and grim at the best of times, Dartmoor had also a convict population serving long terms of penal servitude. 'In many respects, its regime benefited little from reform that concentrated on younger and less hardened offenders and it maintained tough subcultures among both staff and prisoners. A new Governor – Stanley Norton Roberts – exacerbated these conditions. Roberts reduced the flexibility of prisoners to change their work details and, according to an ex-convict's account, curtailed educational classes and visits.'[64] However, such changes seem barely adequate to explain so signal a rebellion. More telling, in all likelihood, was the threat posed to prison officers by cuts in pay, manpower and prison closures – 29 of a total of 56 prisons had been closed since 1914 – and the fear that Dartmoor, a relatively costly prison, was being positioned for closure. Deteriorating staff-prisoner relations were the result of sharply declining officer morale in a prison whose inmates numbered, on the day of the riot, only 442 in a prison with 935 cells.[65] At the same time, it was generally acknowledged that prison conditions had become more humane, especially in terms of far greater association being allowed between prisoners, and time out of cell. Such relative freedom within walls presented officers with control dilemmas they had not previously been asked to face and resolve.[66] In a work praised by George Orwell as a 'very valuable and absorbingly interesting book',[67] Wilfred Macartney, who served his ten years of penal servitude at Parkhurst, a less inhumane prison than Dartmoor, argued that: 'As a beginning to a sane prison system the existing Standing Orders should be scrapped and new regulations compiled in which the maintenance of discipline takes a secondary place . . . Permit talking, allow smoking, abolish flogging and bread and water; maintain discipline by the deprivation of remission and of privileges – that is to say, permit a man to smoke, associate with his fellows from the beginning of the sentence, and, in the event of bad behaviour, take the privileges away . . .'[68]

It is doubtful if work and employment training improved markedly in the inter-war period. Having moved some way from the Victorian belief in hard labour as the means of instilling submission and discipline, industrial work was now seen as equipping prisoners for a useful life on release. Yet Hobhouse and Brockway had been characteristically scathing about the state of prison labour in the early post-war years: 'Prison industries are unsatisfactory from almost every point of view. They are of the most elementary character and are performed in a crude, amateur-ish way. Only in a very few instances are they of any educational value to the prisoner, whilst they are a serious economic loss to the nation. The "instructors" are rarely trained men, and efficient machinery and equipment are almost entirely lacking. The workshops are frequently poor, and the prisoners work under condi-tions which give them little interest in their labour and no incentive to do well.'[69] Compared with the numbers of prisoners employed in 'manufactures' in 1920–21, little had changed by 1932. With the daily population relatively unchanged, at c. 12,000, 2,736 were employed making mailbags in 1920–1, 3,189 in 1931–2.[70] Lionel Fox, a keen advocate of Paterson's ideas and ideals, and a fellow Com-missioner, stated some of the more pertinent difficulties involved: '. . . for the prisoners with short or even moderately long sentences, who form the mass of a local prison population, the most that can be hoped for by the prison authorities is to inculcate habits of industry and habitual work: there can be no question of teaching a useful trade. For all this large class therefore must be found forms of work which are useful and productive . . . and for the product of which there is a steady demand.'[71] Moreover, 'the sale of prison-made goods in competition with outside industry is liable to arouse so much opposition both by Trades Unions and by employers' organisations, that with trifling exceptions prison industries are limited to manufacturing for use by the prisons and by other Government Depart-ments . . .'[72] It was later argued by Hermann Mannheim that penal reform had to contend with the operation of the utilitarian principle of 'less eligibility', first enshrined in the 1832 Poor Law Amendment Act, in a particularly harsh form.[73] Like the Victorian workhouse, prison regimes should be less preferable, at least marginally worse, than the standards of living of the most disadvantaged in the larger society.

The 'Great Crash' and subsequent economic depression of 1929–33 proved a setback to improvements in the prison work sphere, limiting markets for the goods produced and limiting industrial options as a result. Even towards the end of the decade, 1938, Mark Benney, a highly articulate ex-prisoner, wrote: 'A cer-tain amount of work is done for Government departments. In the printing shop at Maidstone a great deal of work for H.M. Stationery Office and the Post Office is done. Tin-shops and Fitters'-shops at one or two prisons have now full-time work making various accessories under the rearmament plan. But mail-bag making and mending is still the greatest single industry, employing about a third of the entire prison population. If sewing-machines were used, the same amount of work could be done by a quarter of that number, yet prisoners engaged on this work frequently have the exasperating experience of seeing half-a-dozen Singers standing by idle, while they sew endless seams slowly and laboriously by hand. The fact is, as the Home Office Committee report puts it, "the root of all evil in the employment of prisoners is the definite shortage of work." The object of prison labour, therefore, is not production; the annual average output of a prisoner's labour is less than £5 12. 0d. Work is regarded as an expedient for keeping men out of mischief.'[74]

Penal reformers have long invested great hopes for the potential offered by imprisonment for the education of prisoners, most of whose offending careers were linked in the burgeoning literature on the causes of crime with educational disadvantage. The legacy of the first Chairman of the Prison Commission, Sir Edmund du Cane, had been dire from that standpoint. A former army officer, 'his views on crime and punishment were simple and severe; his conception of administration totally autocratic. Until his retirement three days after the report of the Gladstone Committee in 1895, which was a damning indictment of his regime, he ruled the prison system with a rod of iron and became increasingly pitiless towards inmates and subordinate staff alike.'[75] His successor, Sir Evelyn Ruggles-Brise, began to undo some of the most inhumane features of the system. His major innovation, the borstal system for young offenders, was to prove the lodestar for reform of the adult prisons. Nevertheless, little had been achieved by way of educational reform under his aegis. Hobhouse and Brockway summarised the 'principal defects' of prison education as 'seriously hampered by the punitive principles of the discipline and the silence rule'; the amount spent on education was too little and not subject to any inspection; prisoners aged over 25 were deemed incapable of benefiting from education; instruction was limited to the 3 'Rs' for five hours a week; teachers were untrained; no provision was made for further education or the learning of a craft; and the system was seen as part of the remit of already overburdened chaplains.[76]

The first real advance on this state of affairs occurred, again in 1922, with the introduction of adult education classes throughout local prisons, arranged in co-operation with the Adult Education Committee of the Board of Education.[77] Education was to be provided by voluntary teachers, but standards were to be raised by appointing educational advisers – who included professors, head teachers and directors of education – at each prison. By 1925 annual meetings were held of advisers and teachers at the Prison Commission in the Home Office. Though the basic provision centred on the 3 Rs, - reading, writing and arithmetic, particularly at remedial level – every effort was made to broaden the content and method, with the ultimate aim of building links to fuller citizenship after release. 'A prison syllabus is likely to show as many hours devoted to discussion groups, debates, play-readings and musical appreciation classes as to arithmetic, shorthand and French.'[78] The drawback to this form of provision was that it could only offer what voluntary teachers could muster at any given point, ruling out the cohesion and coherence of a regular curriculum.

'This scheme was virtually killed by the war'[79] After the war, the system was painfully redeveloped but along more professional lines, with Local Education Authorities playing a much greater role in expanding educational facilities in prisons, following a report in 1947 by the Education Advisory Committee. A route to degree work for longer-term prisoners was opened up by extension courses of the University of London, a pioneering venture which paved the way for degree work by prisoners when the Open University opened in 1971. In many ways its framework of teaching by a combination of radio, television and correspondence had great potential for prison education, overcoming the major problem of courses being interrupted by transfer. However, only a very small minority could take advantage of this provision. The main focus was on basic learning, with a special focus on illiteracy, a form of social and intellectual disadvantage strongly linked with recidivism. Even so, by 1948, only some 2,000 prisoners, roughly one in ten, entered courses. Overall, however, prisoners were to become, over the next few decades, more able to access links with the outside world via radio, libraries – all prisons had libraries linked to the local library service – and newspapers. Hobbies and craft work were in principle encouraged. In the era of post-war reconstruction, the way ahead for penal reform seemed all too clear: individual rehabilitation within and outside prisons via specialist services of social work, probation, education, work training and welfare.

The Criminal Justice Act of 1948 was in some respects a missed opportunity in relation to this approach. It continued the inter-war process of sweeping away 'the obsolete concepts of penal servitude, hard labour and the triple division of offenders. In line however with the widely held theory that long periods of imprisonment, giving time for training, discipline and reformation, were the only way to combat recidivism, the Act provided for a new sentence of corrective training for younger offenders, and variations in the arrangements for preventive detention (which led to an increase in the numbers serving this type of sentence).'[80] Thus, not without irony, the imperative of rehabilitation served to generate the very conditions of an expanding prison population which undermined its potential.

Nevertheless, under the chairmanship of Sir Lionel Fox from 1942–1961, the Prison Commission continued to apply the broad concepts of liberal reform in the penal sphere which Paterson had evolved. These crystallised into the concept of the 'treatment and training of convicted prisoners' which Fox incorporated into the Prison Rules of 1949. He went on 'to develop an organisational structure for the prison system within which training might be carried out on a more systematic basis.'[81] The well-intentioned but haphazard programme to improve the penal estate was faced by two important constraints, for which the penal history of the past half century had provided few pointers. First, the prison population rose sharply by some 50 per cent between 1946 and 1952, despite little change in the crime rate 1945–50. Secondly, resourcing the building and maintenance of training prisons was far more costly than that of local prisons, into which the surplus population was crammed and in which three prisoners to a cell increased markedly. The rise and rise of the prison population, even though it did not match that of the crime rate, at least until the 1990s, when it came to exceed it, was to prove the enduring problem confronting penal policy in the second half of the century.

Within this context, Fox and the Prison Commission, supported by the Advisory Council on the Treatment of Offenders, created in 1944 as an advisory committee on criminal justice policy whose reports were generally not published, continued to press for more humane regimes and conditions. For example, the growing demand by prison officers to play a more constructive role in relation to prisoners gave rise in 1956 to the Norwich system, so-called because it was started in Norwich prison. 'This had three main features: dining in association for all convicted prisoners, an increase in the hours of work from 26 to 35 without any increase in staff, and the allocation of groups of prisoners to specific officers. The Norwich system quickly spread and had generally good results.'[82]

The climax of this belief in the potential of the penal system both to cope with and to ameliorate recidivism came with the publication in 1959 of the White Paper *Penal Practice in a Changing Society.*[83] Whether mainly written or simply heavily influenced by Lionel Fox, it was a major attempt, the most substantial since the Gladstone Committee report, to produce a coherent strategy for penal policy, in both the short- and the long-term, along the lines evolved by Paterson, Fox and other notable Chairs of the Prison Commission, such as Maurice Waller. Rutherford noted a 'euphoric mood' about what he termed the 'Great Expectations' school of thought regarding penal policy throughout much of the Western world, including England.[84] Though the White Paper was hardly 'euphoric', it resonated a strongly optimistic belief in new concepts and methods of analysing crime and punishment.

It acknowledged the counter-intuitive nature of rising rates of crime despite post-war gains in affluence, welfare and employment.[85] While the causes of crime and its surprising growth since the war were little understood, rather more could be said about the prospects of success or failure of different methods of treating offenders. It was indeed the case that the rise in crime, rather than any increase in sentencing severity, 'had led to severe overcrowding in prisons and has strained the resources of other agencies such as borstals, approved schools and the probation service.'[86] Both sets of questions lent themselves to scientific research, and accordingly the Home Office 'has taken a lead. It has set up a Research Unit and assists from its vote research work being done elsewhere', in particular the financial backing for the establishment of an Institute of Criminology at the University of Cambridge, which would furnish a base for wide-ranging criminological research to complement that of the Home Office unit.[87] In an Appendix, 'current research on crime', lists 26 projects being conducted by the Home Office unit, nine being prediction studies stemming from the 1955 groundbreaking work *Prediction Methods in Borstal Training* by Hermann Mannheim and Leslie Wilkins; 15 projects at six universities were 'research assisted by Government grants', largely on different aspects of imprisonment and their effects; and 40 'independent research' projects, some of which were 'associated with' the Home Office, based mostly in universities and rather more wide-ranging. That at Bedford College (Department of Sociology) was described as 'Research on what the social sciences can say about people whose conduct is socially unacceptable, including research into popular hypotheses such as the theory that lack of maternal affection in infancy produces anti-social attitudes, or that problem families beget problem families.' The research was to be better known on publication as *Social Science and Social Pathology* by Barbara Wootton, a devastating critique of contemporary positivist theories of delinquency. By contrast, eleven studies being carried out at the Maudsley Institute of Psychiatry on such subjects as 'a comparison of

Approved School boys with maladjusted schoolboys' were much more characteristic of the approved research approach of the day. That over 80 projects of criminological research which fitted the Home Office model were in train gave backing to the confidence expressed in the White Paper about the gains to be made in explaining crime and optimal forms of treatment.

The second source of optimism lay in the prison building programme envisaged by the White Paper. A comprehensive plan was laid out covering the great majority of detainees. Only changes in provision for the under-16-year-olds were deferred, pending the long-awaited report of the Ingleby Committee[88] on juvenile justice. For young adults aged 17–21, the ongoing strategy was of replacing imprisonment for this group with training in borstals, detention centres and the non-institutional attendance centres. 'Borstal is essentially a remedial and educational system, based on personal training by a carefully selected staff.'[89] Classification to gauge the most appropriate form of training at the most suitable level of security was being developed by 'a skilled diagnostic team' in two reception centres at Latchmere House[90] and Wormwood Scrubs. The much shorter sentences of three to six months in detention centres were not only intended to inflict a short, sharp shock' on less serious offenders in the 14–16-year-old age group, but also to recognise that the elements of 'hard work, brisk tempo and strict discipline . . . should be used as part of a constructive reformative system in which the staff would make a real effort to find out what was wrong with a boy and put it right.'[91] Research by Dr. Max Grunhut added weight to the potential for senior detention centres to be developed alongside the junior model.

Taken together with proposals for remand centres and developments in post-release aftercare, the prospect of further restrictions on the imprisonment of young offenders could be realised. 'When the Secretary of State is satisfied that adequate alternatives to imprisonment are available to magistrates' courts, the imprisonment by such courts of persons under the age of 21 may be prohibited by Order in Council.'[92] The major problem constraining so radical a policy was that 'the system for the treatment of young adult offenders has been subjected to severe strains as a result of the great increase in crime in this age-group. Detention centres are full and courts have been prevented from committing offenders to a detention centre as an alternative to short-term imprisonment . . . Offenders sentenced to borstal training have frequently had to wait in local prisons for as long as 12 weeks before transfer to a borstal reception centre; and many young prisoners with sentences of three months or more, who are eligible for transfer to a young prisoners' centre, have had to serve the whole of their sentence in a local prison.'[93] Six borstals were hastily converted from local prisons and service camps. Accelerating the building of more detention centres and proposing an amalgamation of borstal and imprisonment 'into a single system' of custodial training with statutory supervision and aftercare were proposed as 'novel and far-reaching' but smacked of putting a brave face on stopgap measures.

The treatment of adult prisoners was aimed at fulfilling the principle established by the Gladstone Committee in 1895, to send the prisoners out 'better men and women, physically and morally, than they came in'. The Criminal Justice Act, 1948, endorsed this principle in Rule 6 of the Prison Rules:

> '6. The purposes of training and treatment of convicted prisoners shall be to establish in them the will to lead a good and useful life on discharge and to fit them to do so.'

Despite a rising population, and consequent overcrowding, shortages of staff, work for prisoners and resources for necessary infrastructure, much progress had been made since the war. The size of the service had grown from 40 establishments in 1946 to 73 in 1958. Despite this increase, a substantial programme of further building was needed if overcrowding was to be reined in and specialist provision was to be made for different prisoners' needs. The training prison concept was to be greatly expanded by the reorganisation of the local prisons and the development of a number along training prison lines.

'It might then be possible to reduce the population of the local prisons so as to allow one or more of them at a time to be emptied for reconstruction. Most of these buildings could then be turned into prisons which, while falling short of the ideal, would at least be reasonably well adapted to requirements, on the assumption that long sentences were no longer to be served there. The cells could be modernised, with larger windows such as are provided in the new prisons under construction. Ranges of classrooms for education and suitable rooms for dining and recreation could be provided. Workshop accommodation could be improved. Sanitation could be modernised, and modern facilities for family visits provided. This would be a long-term programme spread over many years, but very well worth while.'[94] In addition to a formidable current programme of building some 19 establishments and a thousand new homes for staff, a future programme amounting to eleven new institutions, including 'a security prison for dangerous prisoners serving long sentences' (i.e. 'Vectis', see chapter on the Mountbatten report below), the reconstruction of Dartmoor prison, enough security prisons to accommodate 1,800 long-term prisoners and 'such additional borstals, open and closed, as the needs disclose' was envisaged.[95] 2,000 new homes would be needed for staff.

This highly ambitious programme also acknowledged the need for staff of high calibre to implement it. The increasingly specialised division of labour among prison staff had been seen by prison officers as reducing them to a turnkey role. To the more traditional trade instructors, chaplains and doctors were now added, in many prisons, new staff roles. 'The psychologist, the tutor-organiser and the welfare-officer must all be thought of as part of the "training team".'[96] Prison officers, especially in local prisons, had become restive in the face of such competition for the claim to be enablers of prisoners to 'lead a good and useful life'. The Norwich system had been in part a response to such frustrations, 'an experiment . . . to see whether by changes of routine and method, coupled with a fresh approach by the staff to their relationship with the prisoners, two objects might be attained. First, a relaxation of these tensions [stemming from the traditional opposition between prisoners and staff], second a feeling among the whole of the staff that each of them had a personal and constructive part to play in the rehabilitation of the prisoners in their charge. With the full co-operation of the staff, these objects were achieved with no loss of fundamental discipline and control, and this system has now been extended to the smaller local prisons and is spreading upwards through the larger.'[97] To achieve these ends, three things were needed: first, pay and conditions of service must match the heightened standards involved; secondly, teamwork and common purpose are essential; and thirdly, 'the buildings, amenities, equipment and training' must be such as to enable them to work to the higher standards set.

## What Went Right?

The therapeutic prison, Grendon Underwood,[98] which opened in 1962, was the single principal embodiment of the policy expressed in *Penal Practice in a Changing Society*. Arguably the most progressive penal measure ever implemented in England – though not in Scotland, where the Barlinnie Special Unit could stake such a claim – Grendon, as Genders and Player emphasise, is not a 'psychiatric prison', a term which connotes a regime operating on 'the principles of a pure medical model',[99] with a pathological cast of determinative treatment. It runs, rather, on inter-disciplinary lines, giving psychiatrists a crucial but not exclusive role in deciding the reasons for and best course of treatment for the prisoner, whose own views on his offending behaviour are given real weight. 'The men who go to Grendon are typically in a state of distress: Grendon seeks to relieve their pain. That is the essence of its rehabilitative task.'[100]

After an initial period of positive appraisal,[101] 'for most of its thirty years of operation Grendon has inhabited an ideological wilderness, out of step with the prevailing ethos and marginal to mainstream penal practice.'[102] The onset of the 'Nothing Works' era in the early 1970s was especially bleak in its implications for the Grendon model, seemingly confirmed when rigorous research by leading psychiatrists found no grounds for optimism that the more expensive therapeutic regime paid off in terms of lower reconviction rates.[103] As Genders and Player stress, however, the whole debate about outcomes based on reconviction rates, though perfectly admissible, is bedevilled by the problematic nature of indices that rely on the hazards of detection and conviction. Their own research found more positive outcomes when allowance was made for prisoners' length of engagement with the therapeutic process.[104] Though the Control Review Committee argued in 1984 that Grendon was not the right model for the most violent and dangerous prisoners, Lord Woolf in his report on the riots at Strangeways Prison approved of the regimes and argued that a second such prison should be established in another part of the country. 'Post-Woolf . . . the tide has turned and Grendon now finds itself embraced by contemporary penal politics and feted as a prodigal son made good.'[105] This change of perspective was strongly enough based to last beyond the mid-1990s' 'tough on crime, tough on the causes of crime' ideology. In the view of David Ramsbotham, then recently retired as Chief Inspector of Prisons:

'Group therapy was pioneered at Grendon Underwood, where remarkable work with some of the worst sex offenders has taken place since the prison was opened in 1962. Group work is widely held to be the best method of treating sex offenders . . . The value of such therapy has been recognised by the Prison Service, which has now opened another similar institution, Dovegate, to provide a "Grendon in the North". Because such therapy is expensive it is best applied to the most serious offenders who need it most.'[106]

It is difficult to discern further tangible results of the particular brand of optimism inherent in *Penal Practice in a Changing Society*. But the outstanding liberal reforms of the 1960s (see Paul Rock's *The Liberal Hour*) were in tune with its ethos, though they were not anticipated or actively encouraged by it. The atmosphere of debate and discussion which it advocated was evident in the policy paper published in 1964 by a Labour Party group chaired by Lord Longford.[107] Though critical of the White Paper's focus on the individual offender as the author of his or her fate, and giving far more weight to the social and economic context as causally significant, the reforms it advocated were consonant with the 'treatment and training' approach. Its directives also went far to animate the work and approach of the Advisory Council on the Penal System, set up in 1967 to pursue the tasks abandoned by the abortive Royal Commission on the Penal System, which engineered its own demise barely a year after its formation in 1964. What could have been the main legacy of the White Paper, a thoroughly reorganised system of local and training prisons, borstals and detention centres, in practice substantially failed to materialise. Countervailing pressures were already under way: the resources needed to finance such an expansionary vista did indeed prove predictably scarce – the White Paper had made the case for resources as and when they became available – and the Home Secretary, 'Rab' Butler, had insisted on stressing how police methods and equipment were improving to match the increasing crime rates and the 'ingenuity of criminals', an early intimation of the need to reassure the public when introducing liberal penal reform.[108]

## What Went Wrong?

Bottoms and Stevenson, in their analysis of criminal justice policy in England and Wales from 1945 until 1970, see 'five central problems which together help to explain "what went wrong" for the optimistic hopes of the immediate post-war period. These problems were: the political climate created by, and the practical results of, the continuing growth of recorded crime; the strength of traditional values and affinities; problems of manpower for criminal justice agencies in a full employment economy; the beginnings of uncomfortable research results; and a series of individual incidents revealing underlying imperfections in the system.'[109] In relation to the penal policy agenda developed over the previous half century, which had found its apogee in *Penal Practice in a Changing Society*, by far the most important problems were those stemming from the growth of recorded crime, and events revealing underlying flaws in the system. Intimations that research results would not support the assumptions on which policy had been built were as yet of little significance.

'Serious' crime rates did not rise consistently until the mid-1950s, when the long and almost unbroken pattern of annual increases of five-six per cent began, a trend that was to last until the mid-1990s.[110] For ten years after 1945, except for a single year, 1950–51, crime rates were stable, a state of affairs which matched hopes that the burgeoning welfare state and post-war prosperity would lead to *reductions* in the level of crime. Counter-intuitively, the first post-war decade of austerity, rationing and the arduous tasks of reconstructing war-damaged infra-structure was accompanied by a stable crime rate. The sharp rise of 15 per cent in 1950–1 fell back by that amount the following year. As a result, the steady rise in crime after 1955 defied both common sense and informed expectations. The 1959 White Paper opened with the words:

> 'It is a disquieting feature of our society that, in the years since the war, rising standards in material prosperity, education and social welfare have brought no decrease in the high rate of crime reached during the war: on the contrary, crime has increased and is still increasing.'[111]

The next five years confirmed this pattern, crime having risen from its post-war rate of 1,134 per 100,000 in 1945, and the even lower figure of 1,034 in 1955, to 1,586 in 1959 and 2,463 – a rise of over 100 per cent overall – in 1964. Attempts were made,[112] notably by Leslie Wilkins, a leading Home Office statistician, to account for the trend at least in part in terms of the experience of growing up in families fractured by the exigencies of war-time: evacuation, fathers absent in the armed forces and the sense of endless crisis and suffering.[113] The force of this argument weakened with the continuing rise over decades after the key genera-tions were succeeded by others not so affected by war, but the study marked the first real grappling with the problems of explanation involved.

The impact of this trend on the prison system was substantially to throw the White Paper's policy off course. The daily average prison population in 1945 stood at 14,708, having risen throughout the war from 10,326 in 1939. By 1950, despite the level crime rate, it had risen to 20,474. Over the next five years, it first rose then fell back to 21,134. By 1960, however, after five years of rising crime, it reached 27,099. Ten years later, by 1970, and despite growing attempts to rein it in, it had reached 39,028. The White Paper in 1959 had stated: 'These increases do not, in the main, reflect any change in the sentencing practice of the courts. They are a direct result of the increase in the number of convictions and of the speed with which the increase has taken place.'[114] While this assumption hardly explains the sharp rise in the prison population 1945–50, at a time of a stable crime rate, it focused attention on the extent to which penal policy was now vulnerable to a rising crime rate, so much so that by the mid- to late-1960s, fresh measures of parole and the suspended sentence were introduced to staunch the process. 'A key element in the strategy of *Penal Practice in a Changing Society* was to reduce the prison overcrowding which had developed in post-war England by building more closed training prisons, and by acquiring more buildings suitable for conversion into open training prisons . . . But no-one in the Home Office realised the potential impact of further rises in crime on the future size of the prison population. Within a few years the whole of the extra accommodation provided by the building programme had been engulfed by the rising tide of prisoners . . . chronic overcrowding was to remain a feature of the English prison system for at least another twenty years. The optimistic paragraphs about the local prisons in *Penal Practice in a Changing Society* remained hopelessly unfulfilled, a text to mock the future.'[115]

It is conceivable that the 'liberal progressive' tradition in the Home Office, still upheld despite the transition in 1963 from the Prison Commission to the new, in-house Prison Department as the makers of penal policy on the ground, would have weathered the difficulties created by the stubborn rise in the prison population. However, the second and yet more significant problem analysed by Bottoms and Stevenson, emanating from what Harold Macmillan had termed 'events', fundamentally altered the penal system. The Prison Commissioners, in pursuit of their liberal 'treatment and training' agenda, had neglected the security implications of the change from a prison experience spent largely in cellular confinement to one which allowed prisoners increasing access to recreational and other forms of out-of-cell association. The results of this relative neglect of basic security, which should have been anticipated in the light of rising escape numbers, exploded in quite spectacular fashion in 1965–6 with the escapes of Ronald Biggs, of 'Great Train Robbery' notoriety, from Wandsworth Prison, and George Blake, a spy whose activities had allegedly led to the deaths of British agents in the 'Cold War' against Soviet Russia, from Wormwood Scrubs. Blake was by far the most damaging escapee in English history. But what arguably linked the two most strikingly, apart from the relative ease of their well-planned escapes, was the immense length of sentence they had incurred for non-capital offences: 30 years in the case of Biggs, 42 years in that of Blake.[116] Such sentences placed a premium for those so incarcerated on the possibilities of escape, and the prison system was increasingly obliged to contain increasing numbers of offenders whose convictions for armed robbery or, as in the case of the Krays, gangland murders, placed them in that situation.

The Prison Department became 'a public laughing-stock'[117] and predictably the response had to be dramatic. Roy Jenkins, the Home Secretary, immediately invited Earl Mountbatten to mount an inquiry into the escapes of Biggs and Blake. His report concluded that no prison in the country was secure enough to contain the most extreme escape risks. His recommendations for a system of security categories A-D, and for changes in the hierarchy of command in the Prison Service, were quickly accepted after a searching report that was completed in only six weeks. His main recommendation was to build a maximum security prison on the Isle of Wight which would be virtually escape proof due to new forms of perimeter security. This was not entirely novel. The White Paper in 1959 had envisaged 'a security prison for dangerous prisoners serving long sentences'. However, in the event, and despite the recommendation by Mountbatten being in line with that part of the Home Office programme, a subcommittee set up under the aegis of the newly created Advisory Council on the Penal System, and chaired by Professor Leon Radzinowicz, rejected that proposal in favour of such prisoners being 'dispersed' among several maximum security prisons holding other prisoners in a population more amenable to a liberal regime. The issues are dealt with in the chapter below.

## Conclusion

The Mountbatten Report was published in December 1966 and its conclusions and recommendations reverberated immediately throughout the prison system. As a result, it is possible to pinpoint 1967 as the year in which the long ascendancy of penal optimism began to tip over into a different set of priorities concerning security and control. 'The result was a sharp drop in the number of escapes, but also a definite change of priorities and mood in the Prison Service, which would never again treat the basic custodial task in as cavalier a fashion as it had begun to do in the post-war period. Indeed, so complete was the immediate change that Lord Mountbatten himself complained in 1971 that regime activities and rehabilitative programmes in higher-security prisons were being unduly restricted.[118] The policy line of the post-war Prison Commissioners and Prison Department had, unwittingly but unmistakably, been radically jolted by George Blake and his predecessors in escape.'[119]

None of which is to say that penal optimism evaporated overnight. It persists to this day in the belief that diverse forms and fashions in rehabilitation, from anger management to cognitive behaviour therapy, will see prisoners released to 'lead a good and useful life'. But the resources of buildings, equipment and trained personnel needed to provide such programmes across the board have never been remotely forthcoming. Instead, after 1967, attention came to be turned, far more than in the past, to reining in and even reducing the prison population as a precondition for lasting penal reform. Resources were increasingly devoted to security and control in the dispersal system of higher-security prisons and to ramping up security across the system, even in open prisons; and to coping with the seemingly endless rise in the prison population.

Under these changing circumstances, the persistence of a 'liberal progressive' culture in the Home Office seems all the more remarkable. It was sustained by the creation, following the failure of the Royal Commission on the Penal System to survive more than a year, of the Advisory Council on the Penal System, a wider-ranging body in membership terms than its predecessor the Advisory Council on the Treatment of Offenders. The reports on both custodial and non-custodial issues reinvigorated liberal hopes. The main example on this front has to be the subcommittee report, chaired by Barbara Wootton on the need to create Community Service Orders as a way of offenders tangibly compensating the community for their misdeeds.[120] CSOs came to be adopted on a wide scale internationally as well as domestically. The culture was strong enough for a young Home Office civil servant, later to hold an extremely senior post, to have regarded the Mountbatten Report at the time as 'dictatorial', a view which helps explain the rejection of its key recommendation of a single, total-security prison for the most dangerous offenders. 'There were elements in the philosophy behind the Mountbatten Report that were alien to ordinary Home Office civil servants' opinion. . . . The Borstal tradition didn't last, couldn't last. But it was still the apple of the eye of not just the prison staff and prison governors, but it extended into the Home Office . . .'[121] A paradox of penal policymaking still in dispute is how far that report would have been a means of perpetuating that culture rather than eroding it.

## Notes

1 See Lynn MacDonald, 1982, 'Theory and Evidence of Rising Crime in the Nineteenth Century', *British Journal of Sociology*, 33.3, 404–420.
2 Andrew Rutherford, (1986) *Prisons and the Process of Justice*, Oxford University Press edition: 189–192.
3 David Garland (1985) *Punishment and Welfare: A History of Penal Strategies*, Aldershot: Gower.
4 See especially John Macnicol, 1987, 'In Pursuit of the Underclass', *Journal of Social Policy*, 16.3, 293–318.
5 Leon Radzinowicz and Roger Hood, 1990, *The Emergence of Penal Policy in Victorian and Edwardian England*, Oxford: Clarendon Press: 777–8.
6 *Report of the Departmental Committee on Prisons* (1895) Parliamentary Papers, LVII. Herbert Gladstone, youngest son of William Ewart Gladstone, four times prime minister, went on to become Home Secretary 1905–1910.
7 Garland, ibid: 26.
8 Ibid: 13. Garland also notes that these devices had been abandoned in Scotland much earlier as 'improper instruments of punishment.' op. cit.: 34, note 9.
9 J.E. Thomas (1972) *The English Prison Officer Since 1850: A Study in Conflict*, London: Routledge & Kegan Paul: 117.
10 Ibid: 118.
11 Charles E.B. Russell and L.M. Rigby (1906) *The Making of the Criminal*, London: Macmillan: 129. Charles Russell (1866–1917) also wrote, with L.M. Rigby, *Working Lads' Clubs*, 1908, London: Macmillan. See Mark K. Smith, 2001, *The Encyclopedia of Informal Education*, www.infed.org/
12 H.C. Debates, 5th series, Vol. 19, cols. 1353–4, 20 July 1910.
13 A major novelist of the day, his sequence of novels known as *The Forsyte Saga* were bestsellers. His interest in penal conditions was exemplified in some of his highly successful plays. For example, *Justice* (1910) concerns a man driven to suicide by the harshness of his prison sentence. Both Churchill and Ruggles-Brise, Chairman of the Prison Commission, attended the play's first night on 21 February, 1910. According to Galsworthy's notebook, the former witnessed it 'with sympathy', the latter 'with a sinking sensation . . . His eyes were observed to start out of his head . . .' Leon Radzinowicz and Roger Hood *The Emergence of Penal Policy in Victorian and Edwardian England*, 1990, Oxford: Clarendon Press: 594.
14 Rutherford, op. cit.: 124–5.
15 The Mental Deficiency Act 1913; the Criminal Justice Administration Act 1914.
16 Rutherford, op.cit.: 125–6 and Appendix.
17 Edwin Sutherland, 'The Decreasing Prison Population of England', *Journal of Criminal Law and Criminology*, 1934, 24: 880.
18 David Wilson, 2014, *Pain and Retribution: A Short History of British Prisons, 1066 to the Present*, London, Reaktion Books: 89.

19  Stephen Hobhouse and A. Fenner Brockway (eds.), 1922, *English Prisons Today: Being the* Report *of the Prison System Enquiry Committee*, London: Longmans. After the Committee was established, in 1919, under the auspices of the Labour Party, 'the work was done in the teeth of Home Office opposition which included thinly veiled threats of prosecution. It had a major impact on penal reform.' Terence Morris, op. cit.: (1989): 85.
20  Ibid: 590–95.
21  Ibid: 580.
22  Ibid: 593.
23  Ibid: 594.
24  Ibid.
25  Leon Radzinowicz and Roger Hood, Ch. 10 'Eugenics Infiltrates the Penal Law: The Feeble-minded Offender' op.cit.: 316–338.
26  Sidney and Beatrice Webb (1922) *English Prisons Under Local Government*, London: Longmans. Published uniformly and simultaneously with, and intended as an historical introduction to *English Prisons Today*, it carried the preface by George Bernard Shaw, republished as *The Crime of Imprisonment*, 1946, New York: Philosophical Library.
27  Cited in David Garland, 1985, *Punishment and Welfare*, Aldershot: Gower: 13.
28  S.K. Ruck (ed.) (1951) *Paterson on Prisons: Being the Collected Papers of Sir Alexander Paterson, M.C., M.A.* London: Frederick Muller, Editor's Introduction: 10. *Across the Bridges: Life by the South London Riverside* (1911) London: Edwin Arnold, was Paterson's only book. His substantial work on prisons, many overseas, took the form of committee reports, conference papers and personal documents. He is not to be confused with Arthur Paterson, who wrote a book on imprisonment entitled *Our Prisons* (1911) London: Hugh Rees. Hobhouse and Brockway comment, somewhat sardonically, that this 'small volume, which may be regarded as a kind of semi-official *apologia* for our prison system, therein stated that the Commissioners, far from being hidebound by red-tape and tradition are "reformers of the keenest and most intrepid kind, . . ."' op. cit.: 65.
29  Gareth Stedman Jones, 1971, *Outcast London: A Study of the Relationship between Classes in Victorian London,* Oxford: Clarendon Press.
30  Henry Mayhew, 1851–61, *London Labour and the London Poor*, 4 vols, London: Office.
31  Jack London, 1903, *The People of the Abyss*, London: Isbister.
32  Ruck, op.cit.: 23. Ruck's editorial method makes it difficult to date quotations. The chapter from which this quotation is drawn is entitled 'Why Prisons?' and is compiled from four documents "printed for private circulation only": 'Italian Prisons' (1923), 'Prevention of Crime and the Treatment of Criminals in Burma' (1927), 'The Prison Population of America' (1931) and 'The Principles of the Borstal System' (1932). See p. 186, 'Sources and Acknowledgements'. These are not reprinted in their full original form.
33  Ibid: 24–5.
34  Op. cit.: 440.
35  Op. cit.: 439.
36  Reference is here made to Margery Fry on *'The Borstal System'* in *Penal Reform in England* (Macmillan, 1946).
37  Ruck, op. cit.: 13–14. See also Sydney A. Moseley, *The Truth About Borstal*, 1926, London: Cecil Palmer, a laudatory account which praises such features as the innovation of a 'house system' to borstals: 'The spirit of modern Borstal is as different from that of ten years ago as is the air of the mountain tops from the vapours of a city slum.' (p. 153).
38  Brendan Behan, *Borstal Boy*, 1958, London: Hutchinson.
39  Benedict S. Alper, 'Borstal Briefly Re-Visited: Recollections and Some Related Reflections', *British Journal of Criminology*, 1968, 8, 1, 6–19: 10.

40 Home Office, 1965, *Report on the Work of the Prison Department, 1964*, London: H.M.S.O. Cmnd. 2708. Cited in Alper, op. cit.: 11.

41 Roger Hood, 1965, *Borstal Re-Assessed*. London: Heinemann: 146. Cited in Alper, op. cit.: 12.

42 Alan Sillitoe, 1959, *The Loneliness of the Long-Distance Runner*. London: W.H. Allen. The film was released in 1962, directed by Tony Richardson, with Tom Courtenay as the runner.

43 Alper, op. cit.: 16–17.

44 *Scum*, directed by Alan Clarke, was originally made for the BBC *Play for Today* series in 1977, but banned due to its depiction of violence. The film version, also directed by Clarke, was released two years later.

45 J.E. Thomas,1972, *The English Prison Officer Since 1850: A Study in Conflict*, London: Routledge and Kegan Paul: 152. See especially Ch. 8: '1922–45: the Paterson initiative'. J.E. Thomas is one of the few criminologists to have worked in both the prison service, as an Assistant Governor and a staff tutor, and at universities, notably the Department of Adult Studies at the University of Hull. He co-authored, with Dick Pooley, 1980, *The Exploding Prison: Prison Riots and the Case of Hull,* London: PROP.

46 Ibid.

47 Ibid: 153.

48 The compulsory close-shaven haircut had been abolished for ordinary prisoners in 1899 but only progressively ended for those sentenced to penal servitude from 1922 onwards.

49 See the discussion of Wilde's prison experience, and the works it inspired – *De Profundis* and *The Ballad of Reading Gaol* – in David Wilson, 2014, op. cit.: 79–87.

50 Thomas, op. cit.:154.

51 Cyril Burt, 1925, *The Young Delinquent*, London: University of London Press. 'Psychologist to the Education Department of the London County Council, Burt combined case material and clinical insight with new statistical techniques in order to assess the existing theories of delinquency. His huge study . . . oiled the wheels of criminological debate for the rest of the inter-war period, and made a distinct impression upon the content of penal policy.' Bailey, op. cit. below: 13 et seq. His emphasis on the interplay of social disadvantage and psychological susceptibilities led him to emphasise the need for rehabilitative work with young offenders to be interdepartmental and interdisciplinary, a marked influence, albeit at several removes, on the much later stress on inter-agency co-operation in relation to young offenders.

52 Victor Bailey, 1987, *Delinquency and Citizenship: Reclaiming the Young Offender, 1914–1948.* Oxford: Clarendon Press: 63.

53 Garland, op. cit.

54 Ibid: 238.

55 Ibid.

56 Ibid: 239.

57 C.D. Rackham, 1940, 'The Probation System' in (eds.) L. Radzinowicz and J.W. Cecil Turner, *Penal Reform in England: Introductory Essays on some aspects of English Criminal Policy*, London: P.S. King: 121.

58 David Wilson, op. cit.: 94.

59 David Garland, op. cit.: 23

60 Bailey, op. cit.: 226.

61 Firearms were routinely issued to prison staff when supervising outside working parties on Dartmoor.

62 Alyson Brown, 'The Amazing Mutiny at Dartmoor Prison', *British Journal of Criminology*, 2007, 47: 277.

63 Ibid: 279.

64 Ibid.

65  Ibid: 280.

66  J.E. Thomas, op. cit.: 157–62.

67  George Orwell, review of W.F.R. Macartney, *Walls Have Mouths – Ten Years of Penal Servitude, with prologue, Epilogue and Comments on the Chapters by Compton Mackenzie*, The Adelphi, November 1936. Reprinted in Peter Davison (ed.), 2001, *Orwell's England*, Harmondsworth: Penguin: 44–47.

68  Macartney, op. cit.: 167.

69  Hobhouse and Brockway, op. cit.: 109.

70  Ibid: 110; and L.W. Fox, *The Modern English Prison*, 1934, London: Routledge: Appendix E, 246–48.

71  Fox, op. cit.: 89.

72  Ibid: 89–90.

73  Hermann Mannheim, *The Dilemma of Penal Reform*, 1939, London: Allen & Unwin.

74  Mark Benney, *The Truth about English Prisons*, FACT Number 12, March 1938, London: Kemp Hall Press: 23. The report to which he referred was *Report of the Departmental Committee on the Employment of Prisoners* (1935)

75  Terence Morris, 1989, *Crime and Criminal Justice since 1945,* Oxford: Blackwell: 72.

76  Hobhouse and Brockway, op. cit.: 170.

77  Lionel W. Fox, 1952, *The English Prison and Borstal Systems: An account of the prisons and Borstal systems in England and Wales after the Criminal Justice Act 1948, with a historical introduction and an examination of the principles of imprisonment as a legal punishment*, London: Routledge & Kegan Paul: 68–9.

78  Ibid: 209.

79  Ibid: 210.

80  Amy Edwards and Richard Hurley, 1997, 'Prisons Over Two Centuries', *Home Office, 1782–1982*, London: HMSO: 35.

81  Roy King and Rod Morgan, 1980, *The Future of the Prison System*, Farnborough: Gower: 2–3.

82  Edwards and Hurley, op. cit.: 5.

83  Home Office, February 1959, *Penal Practice in a Changing Society: Aspects of Future Development (England and Wales)*, London: HMSO, Cmnd. 645.

84  Rutherford, op.cit.: 23.

85  See also Paul Rock, Vol. 1, Ch.2, for a fuller analysis.

86  *Penal Practice in a Changing Society*: 2.

87  Ibid: 5–6.

88  Ingleby Report (Viscount Ingleby, Chairman) 1961, *Report of the Committee on Children and Young Persons*, Cmnd. 1191, London: HMSO. The Committee recommended, *inter alia,* that the age of criminal responsibility be raised from 8 to 12, and expressed the hope that it would later be raised to 14. In the event, it was raised to 10, where it remains. See David Downes and Rod Morgan, 2012, 'Waiting for Ingleby: The Minimum Age of Criminal Responsibility – A Red-line Issue?' in Jill Peay and Tim Newburn (eds.), *Policing: Politics, Culture and Control: Essays in Honour of Robert Reiner*, Oxford: Hart: 245–64.

89  *Penal Practice in a Changing Society*: 9.

90  Latchmere House, a former military hospital, was transferred to the Prison Service and became a young offender institution and remand centre in 1948. In 1992 it became a category D prison, much praised for its rehabilitative work. A prime site overlooking Ham Common in Richmond, Surrey, it was sold to the private property development sector in 2011.

91  Ibid: 8–9.

92  Ibid: 8.

93  Ibid:10.

94  Ibid: 14–15.

95  Ibid: 22.

96  Ibid: 23.
97  Ibid: 24.
98  Elaine Genders and Elaine Player (1995) *Grendon: A Study of a Therapeutic Prison*, Oxford: Clarendon Press.
99  Ibid: 12–13.
100 Ibid: 14.
101 See especially Tony Parker (1970) *The Frying Pan: A Prison and its Prisoners*, London: Hutchinson.
102 Genders and Player, op. cit.: 5.
103 Gunn, J., Robertson, G., Dell, S. and Way, C. (1978) *Psychiatric Aspects of Imprisonment*, London: Academic Press; also Gunn and Robertson (1987) 'A Ten Year Follow-Up of Men Discharged from Grendon Prison', *British Journal of Psychiatry*, 151, 674–78.
104 Genders and Player, op. cit.: 154–57.
105 Ibid: 5.
106 David Ramsbotham (2003) *Prisongate: The Shocking State of Britain's Prisons and the Need for Visionary Change*, London: The Free Press: 135–36.
107 Labour Party (June 1964) *Crime – A Challenge To Us All*, London: Labour Party.
108 Anthony E. Bottoms and Simon Stevenson, 1992, 'What Went Wrong? Criminal Justice Policy in England and Wales, 1945–70', in David Downes (ed.) *Unravelling Criminal Justice: Eleven British Studies*, London: Macmillan: 12.
109 Ibid: 10.
110 See the chapter in Paul Rock's *The Liberal Hour* on crime and criminal justice in the mid-1960s for a fuller picture.
111 Op. cit.: 1.
112 See Paul Rock, Vol. 1, Ch. 2 for a fuller account.
113 Leslie T. Wilkins, 1960, *Delinquent Generations*, London: HMSO. Home Office Research Unit Report, No. 3.
114 Op. cit.: 2.
115 Bottoms and Stevenson, op. cit.: 12.
116 For a fuller account of the escapes and their aftermath, see the chapter below entitled 'Dropping the Admiral'.
117 Bottoms and Stevenson, op. cit.: 25.
118 Speech at York University, April 1971: see *The Times*, 5 April 1971, and the *Prison Officers' Magazine,* May 1971.
119 Bottoms and Stevenson, op. cit.: 25.
120 Advisory Council on the Penal System, 1970, *Non-Custodial and Semi-Custodial Sentences*, London: HMSO. See also the fuller account of this measure's introduction in Ch. 7, 'The Pursuit of Innovation'.
121 Interview, 12 March, 2015.

# 2    Dropping the Admiral

## Changing Policy on Maximum Security Imprisonment 1965–8

The period from 1950 to 1965 was an era of penal optimism, a continuation of pre-war hopes for the comprehensive reform of adult prisons to benefit from the humane inspiration behind the borstal system and probation. 'Alexander Paterson (1884–1947), a Prison Commissioner, was undoubtedly the dominant influence on the penal system of the inter-war years, a period which had seen the progressive liberalisation of prison regimes and regulations. Since the same years had also seen a proportionate decline in the courts' use of custody, and neither policy had produced disastrous results, many informed people were inclined to believe that mercy could well temper penal severity without undue risk.'[1] Those 'informed people' formed a 'loose coalition' of 'liberal progressives'[2] whose post-war influence reached its pinnacle in 1959, with the publication of the White Paper, *Penal Practice in a Changing Society*; with the building in 1960–62 of the country's first (and only) therapeutic prison at Grendon;[3] and with the setting up of the (short-lived) Royal Commission on the Penal System in 1964. Prison conditions were steadily becoming less oppressive: training prisons and open prisons were tangible gains (though at some cost to local prisons); food and visiting conditions became better and more humane. 'Unfortunately, the years of liberalisation were also years of escape . . . They liberalised without increasing security precautions.'[4] The number of escapes rose sharply from 88 to a peak of 522 between 1955 and 1965.[5] Most were from open prisons, or from escorts and working parties, but 'it was certain spectacular escapes rather than an increase in the rate of escapes that triggered off the recent storm,'[6] The 'disastrous results' were, albeit belatedly, now mounting fast.

In the summer of 1965, the still relatively even tenor of penal policy was shaken by the dramatic escape of four prisoners from HMP Wandsworth in south London. This was the second instance of a member of the gang that had pulled off the 'most audacious robbery in the annals of British crime' (Morris 1989: 129) being 'sprung' from prison, the first case having been that of Charles Wilson in August 1964 from Winson Green Prison in Birmingham. 'The Prison Department managed successfully to avoid a public inquiry and the incident would have been forgotten but for the fact that the following year a second train robber, Ronald Biggs . . . made good his escape from Wandsworth in broad daylight . . . ' (ibid: 130) In his report on 'The Escape of Biggs and three others from Wandsworth prison, July 8th, 1965',[7] W.H. Kenyon, the Director of Prisons, described how the four escapees,[8] the most prominent of whom was the 'Great Train Robber', Ronald Biggs, had been among 14 men on the escape list on their one-hour period of exercise, supervised by four officers. In a phrase reminiscent of the Ealing comedies of the day, he stated:

> 'About 3 p.m., one of the officers saw a head appear above the wall.' Two ladders, one of rope and wood, one metal, were thrown over the wall. The four prisoners ran for the ladders, whilst the other prisoners obstructed staff. They escaped up the ladders and over the wall onto the roof of a van that came to within 10 feet of the top of the wall and that had been adapted for the escape. 'Aided by this vehicle the escape cleanly took place within a period of two or three minutes.' They then made off in waiting cars.

'This was a highly organised escape.' Yet staff had been fully aware of the high risk of escape by members of the 'Train Gang', who had in some cases been sentenced to the unprecedented term of 30 years' imprisonment for the sensational robbery of £2,500,000 in used notes from a mail train in 1962. Following Wilson's escape, they were on the alert for the possible springing of Ronald Biggs, one of the most high-profile members of the gang in custody. A key factor was Biggs's presence on the afternoon rather than the morning exercise in Yard D, one wall of which formed the perimeter, alongside which a side road led to ancillary parts of the prison complex. For outside assistance to work, knowledge of which exercise Biggs was on that particular day was essential – the allocation was deliberately random. This key fact was almost certainly conveyed to the outside team by a lawyer visiting a fellow escapee that morning, who would have known that Biggs, not being on the morning exercise, would be on that in the afternoon. Such visits by lawyers were out of the hearing of prison officers, which raised the issue of the 'implications of unsupervised visits'. Other issues raised by the escapes stemmed from the likelihood that the escape organisers had been armed; the lack of electronic aids to scan the walls; and the implications of leisure associations for high-risk prisoners. Kenyon's report thus raised issues that proved extremely germane to the subsequent inquiries leading to what came to be known as the Mountbatten and Radzinowicz Reports on the most suitable model for holding long-term prisoners under conditions of maximum security.

Despite the massive media coverage and Home Office embarrassment over the escapes from Wandsworth – all except Biggs were recaptured before long – reactions were negligible compared with the furore over the escape of the 'master spy' George Blake some 15 months later, on 22 October 1966, from HMP Wormwood Scrubs in north London. His escape made the Home Office a 'laughing stock' (Bottoms and Stevenson: 25). Quintin Hogg, the Shadow (Opposition) Home Secretary, demanded a statement,[9] to which Roy Jenkins, the Home Secretary, replied that whilst Blake had been held in Wormwood Scrubs since May 1961, following his sentence of 42 years' imprisonment for spying, he had been off the escape list since October 1961, though subject to restricted visiting conditions. Two steps had already been taken:

1.    An order for an immediate security review;
2.    The establishment of an independent inquiry into prison security to be directed by Lord Mountbatten, who had already accepted the role, which should take 'a few months'.

Jenkins resisted Hogg's demand for the inquiry to include the particulars of the escape itself. The Opposition overreached itself by proposing a motion of censure, which Jenkins defeated with style: 'It was by far the greatest parliamentary triumph that I ever achieved . . . The position was turned round by the debate. I, who had been against the ropes, was rampant. Heath and Hogg were flat on their backs. Yet nothing of substance had happened . . . Blake had still escaped and was as far as ever from being recaptured.'[10] Despite the *furore* occasioned by this and the escape a few weeks later of Frank Mitchell, the 'Mad Axe-man' from Dartmoor, which led to British prisons becoming, in Jenkins's words, 'something of an international joke',[11] no discussion took place in Cabinet of the escapes or the inquiry, on which a great deal now rested if the credibility of prison security was to be restored and indeed reinforced.

Outside the Cabinet room, the Prime Minister was kept informed of developments immediately after Blake's escape, which soon led to the tabling of a Motion of Censure by the Opposition two days later[12]: 'That this House deplores the refusal of the Secretary of State for the Home Department to set up a specific inquiry to report as a matter of urgency on the escape of George Blake from Wormwood Scrubs Prison.' The same day the terms of reference for the Mountbatten Inquiry were approved by the Prime Minister: 'To enquire into recent prison escapes with particular reference to that of George Blake and to make recommendations for the improvement of prison security.' Ironically on the same day, 24 October, a further breakout occurred, of three prisoners from Wandsworth Prison. The P.M. conveyed to both David Dowler, the Home Secretary's main aide, and the man who suggested to Jenkins that Mountbatten would be the prime candidate to head the inquiry, and to John Chilcot,[13] that he wished 'to be consulted in advance before any decisions are taken re the personnel of the Inquiry or any other major aspect of its activities.' Harold Wilson, as P.M., suggested that, 'if he [Mountbatten] agrees' - the announcement of the inquiry should refer to its 'very strong Chair'.

Why Mountbatten? 'Roy Jenkins . . . was quick to recognise the danger. It was not that the public was so much concerned with prison escapes as it was with spies, and from the late 1950s there had been a series of cases involving spies and double agents . . . Jenkins's period at the Home Office was characterised by both a commitment to liberal penal values and a realistic assessment of how far one could be casual about what might be the making of a political crisis. His reaction was to invite Admiral of the Fleet, Earl Mountbatten of Burma, to conduct a brief but searching inquiry into the escape of Blake and prison security generally.

It was an astute move for Mountbatten was not only a senior member of the Royal Family but also a man held in the highest public regard as a war hero. He had been last Viceroy of India and subsequently Chief of Defence Staff.'[14] It was an appointment designed to allay public anxiety and counter any political capital that the Conservative opposition might seek to make of it. But above all 'he [Jenkins] wanted a man of "public stature" to lead an inquiry into what was going wrong. A military man with excellent credentials both as a hero and a liberal must have seemed the ideal person to soothe the fears of the right without rousing the suspicions of the left.'

Mountbatten made it a condition of accepting the commission that it would be his personal report: he would be no mere figurehead.[15] His speed in producing the report is legendary. Appointed on 23 October, the inquiry's report[16] was not only completed but published less than two months later, on 22 December. In that time he and his team[17] interviewed previous Home Secretaries for the 1961–66 period; held meetings with 103 prison governors, representatives of the Prison Officers' Association, and some ex-prisoners; invited evidence from individuals and relevant agencies; and visited 17 prisons. It dealt with the escapes of Biggs, Blake, Mitchell, Wilson and others. Mountbatten's analysis of the system was scathing. Blake's escape, for example, revealed 'serious security defects' in Wormwood Scrubs. It occurred during a 'free association' period between 5–7p.m. on a Saturday when only two prison officers were supervising over 100 prisoners. Blake broke a window in a second-floor laundry, which gave access to a drop of 22 feet broken by two stages, in torrential rain and very poor visibility, with outside assistance (much later revealed to be two anti-nuclear activists)[18] who supplied rope ladders. But his intentions had been misread from the outset and he should have been transferred far earlier to a maximum-security block outside London.[19]

However, the flaws in the prison's security arrangements were simply one instance of systemic shortcomings. Lord Mountbatten said that: 'There is no really secure prison in existence in this country . . . I consider that the modern policy of humane liberal treatment aimed at rehabilitating prisoners rather than merely exacting punishment is right, and that escapes should be prevented by far better perimeter security.' (para. 14) The two most important recommendations flowed from this analysis of the problem. First, all prisoners should be classified into four categories, A-D, depending on the potential risk of their escaping and their dangerousness to the public and society should they succeed. 'Cat. As' as they came to be known are 'a hard core of prisoners who will take any opportunity to escape . . . who must be kept in really secure conditions.' (para 23) Others may be motivated to escape due to personal or domestic problems – that number should be reduced by more constructive regimes and welfare officers. Regular 24-hour home leaves would also help. But the policy of passing very long and, due to the abolition of capital punishment a year earlier, life sentences have introduced a 'new type of imprisonment, bringing with it human problems which have to be faced.' The proposed policy of categorisation was immediately accepted by the Home Secretary and acted upon.

The categories proposed by Mountbatten, with certain modifications, remain the basis for security classification to the present day.[20] Category A are 'those whose escape would be highly dangerous to the public or the police or to the security of the state'. They are to be placed in 'maximum security' conditions within an impregnable perimeter. Category B are 'those prisoners for whom the very highest conditions of security are not necessary, but for whom escape must be made very difficult'. Such prisoners should be housed in 'closed' but not necessarily 'maximum-security' conditions. Category C consists of 'prisoners who cannot be trusted in open conditions, but who do not have the ability or resources to make a determined escape bid'. Category D prisoners are 'those who can reasonably be entrusted to serve their sentences in open conditions' with minimal physical security. Secondly, having examined the nature of the escapes of Biggs, Blake, Mitchell and Wilson, from prisons as diverse as Wormwood Scrubs, Wandsworth, Dartmoor and Birmingham, as well as a group escape of 13 prisoners in transit from Parkhurst Prison on the Isle of Wight to Winchester Assizes, Mountbatten concluded that a new type of prison was needed to meet the needs of the 'new type of imprisonment'. Conditions in existing maximum security blocks at Parkhurst, Leicester and Durham were 'such as no country with a record of civilised behaviour ought to tolerate any longer than absolutely essential as a stop-gap measure.' (para. 212). 'A purpose-built prison is required at the earliest possible date to house those prisoners who must in no circumstances be allowed to get out', whether for reasons of national security or because of their likely violence. One such prison to hold 120 Category A prisoners should suffice, but another might be needed if the number of dangerous and violent prisoners continued to increase. An island site had real advantages but, with the disadvantages of Alcatraz in mind, it would need to be well populated, for reasons of staffing, resourcing and amenity. As Governor of the Isle of Wight, Mountbatten favoured its old Roman name of 'Vectis'.[21]

This recommendation was seemingly adopted in principle,[22] and the task of designing a regime for this 'new type of imprisonment' was allotted to the newly formed Advisory Council on the Penal System, which had been established in the wake of the dissolution of the Royal Commission on the Penal System in 1965. A subcommittee of four, chaired by Professor Leon Radzinowicz, of the Institute of Criminology, University of Cambridge, along with Leo Abse (Labour MP for Pontypool), R.C. Mortimer (the Bishop of Exeter, who held the Church of England's social affairs brief in the House of Lords) and Dr. Peter Scott, a leading psychiatrist at the Maudsley Hospital in London, was set up in February 1967 to carry out this task. It seemed a relatively straightforward if complicated project: to take Mountbatten's clear outline and elaborate in more detail what regime would best fit it. Mountbatten had commended 'as liberal and constructive a regime as possible' (para 226) whilst accepting that 'the chances of success in attempts at rehabilitation are likely to be slender.' Staff would accordingly face a depressingly demanding task, with little pay-off, and short tours of duty and higher pay would be essential as compensation. The four-prison system on the island[23] would facilitate that flexibility. The key to the

Vectis model was the prospect of a twofold gain: that greatly upgraded perimeter security would eliminate escape risks and enable the internal regime to focus on providing 'liberal and constructive measures'; by the same token, the rest of the system would be unburdened from coping with the demands of containing those prisoners deemed the most dangerous escape risks. It seemed a logically coherent solution to the problem that Mountbatten had been appointed to resolve. Mountbatten linked the categorisation and the purpose-built, maximum-security prison proposals to the need to re-energise staff morale, which was high 'but . . . not as high as it should be'. Another major recommendation was for a new rank of Senior Prison Officer to be created between the standard and Principal Officer levels, and for promotion to be based on merit as well as seniority. Upgrading was needed in relation to training, night patrols, inspection and a new post for the professional head of the Service – an Inspector General. In key respects Mountbatten anticipated the findings some 25 years later of Lord Justice Woolf in his report on the disturbances at Strangeways prison.[24] Prison regimes 'can also contribute greatly to the reduction of the kind of tensions that turn prisoners' minds towards escape. Worthwhile work, humane but firm governors and staff, constructive recreation are desirable in themselves *and* make for better security.' Closer staff-prisoner relations, 'and the more the majority of prisoners accept the fairness of their treatment, the easier it will be to detect symptoms of unrest which often indicate the planning of an escape attempt.'[25] These system-wide recommendations, which include the need for making a start in the new prison on decent sanitation, go far to explaining the popularity of Mountbatten with prison officers and the P.O.A.

## Concentration vs. Dispersal

Compared to the speed with which Mountbatten had produced his report, that of the Radzinowicz subcommittee was to prove much more protracted, although still fairly rapid by Whitehall standards. In order to fulfil their brief, they laid out a programme of prison visits, both here and abroad, and the hearing of expert and other forms of evidence, some of it commissioned, as the basis for evaluating the most appropriate regime. Their report, *The Regime for Long-Term Prisoners in Conditions of Maximum Security*, was presented to the fourth meeting of the full council some 12 months later, on 29 January 1968. It was only at that meeting that the rejection of the concentration model for that of dispersal was presented to all members present. Instead of being held in a single super maximum perimeter security prison, the Radzinowicz subcommittee recommended the dispersal of category A prisoners between four prisons with enhanced perimeter security. Two further meetings were held in February and March, at the second of which the report was unanimously adopted, save for the recommendation that perimeter guards in the dispersal prisons should be armed. It was a momentous rejection of Mountbatten's principal proposal. To some, especially Terence Morris (1970, 1971) and Roy King and Rod Morgan (1980), it contained the seeds of future penal discontents.

How and why had it been accomplished? To Radzinowicz, the immediate reactions to the concentration plan were very critical among penal 'insiders'[26] and the Home Office delayed action. But there was no implication in the referral of the task of detailing a suitable regime to the Advisory Council on the Penal System (ACPS) that the concentration principle was at that stage in question. Indeed, as early as 7 April, 1967, Sir Philip Allen replied to Radzinowicz about his view 'that it would be bound to take some months before their contribution would be forthcoming', by stating that 'Lord Mountbatten gave a suggested completion date in his report,[27] and the Government are pretty well committed to doing their best to build the prison by as near that date as can possibly be managed . . . [The Home Secretary] realises that this decision will be something of a disappointment to your Sub-Committee, but he is sure the members will understand the reasons for it and he will greatly value their advice in due course as to the nature of the regime to be provided within this maximum security prison.' Despite this emphatic endorsement of both Mountbatten's Vectis concept and the timetable for its realisation, in the event, that advice was to take far longer to deliver than this timescale implied, and was to reject the whole basis for its original brief. The report was to conclude that, while the arguments for concentration were very strong, they were counterweighed by the dangers of a very repressive regime developing where the 100–120 prisoners are labelled the 'worst' and where no possibility of transfer exists. Moreover, the strain on staff would be very corrosive.

Two questions that arise from the Mountbatten Report's recommendations and the context of its commissioning are:

1.   How accurate are depictions of the report as illiberal and oppressive in effect if not in intention and, insofar as these depictions are inaccurate, how did these images of the report gain prominence?
2.   On what grounds and by what means was so major a recommendation of the report rejected?

On the first point, the assumption that the Mountbatten Report led to a steep increase in the focus on security as *the* top priority in British prisons was exemplified in interview. Louis Blom-Cooper, a member of the ACPS from its inception to its final meeting in 1978, took it for granted that the adoption of the categorisation system had had a huge impact on penal policy and regimes, upgrading security and downgrading welfare and treatment goals. The May Committee Report commented: 'It is hard to evaluate just how much of a change in ethos the Mountbatten Report did initiate, but there is certainly a widespread belief that it ushered in an era in which concern with security became, and has remained, central to large parts of the system.'[28] Radical criminologists shared that view. Mike Fitzgerald, in his *Prisoners in Revolt* (1977) stated that the Mountbatten Report signalled the end of the 'treatment' era and ushered in the obsession with security and control which was soon to generate riots and disturbances in several prisons from 1969 and throughout the next decade.[29] Stan Cohen saw the classification system as ushering in an era of 'human warehousing'.[30] Yet the spate of high-profile escapes between 1964 and 1966 had been bound to provoke a high-profile response. Though the form it took could conceivably have been of a different character, enhanced security was inevitably the top priority.

Perhaps most significantly, Leo Abse M.P., a member of the ACPS subcommittee, saw the Mountbatten Report from the outset as a malignant force for prison regimes being designed on militaristic rather than therapeutic lines. Roy King[31] thought it had been anathema to Abse that a military man with no relevant experience should have been given the job of shaping the prison system. In short, the proposal for a single maximum-security prison to hold all Category A prisoners, to be constructed on the Isle of Wight, 'generated a storm of abuse so violent that it is hard for the outsider to understand. Mountbatten was condemned not merely for what he did suggest, but for the construction of maximum security wings within existing prisons . . . which his plan for one super-prison was intended to render unnecessary . . . He believed that in a single prison with an invulnerable perimeter it would be possible to allow the Cat. A prisoner far more liberty than was feasible when he was cooped up in a small section of a conventional prison . . . If the really dangerous men were removed, it would also be possible to ease restrictions and reduce the strain on the staff at the other prisons. He advocated improved security measures, but only as part of a package which, he believed, would liberalise the system as a whole . . . yet it is by these measures that his report is remembered; as Dr. Pauline Morris has pointed out, his name has become 'synonomous with the imposition of restriction and an almost obsessional concern with security'.[32] A contributory factor in this regard was that Mountbatten felt constrained by his status as a member of the royal family from defending his report in public debate. Had he felt free to do so, he would no doubt have entered powerful rebuttals of the false claims made about his report. As it was, he relied on sympathetic criminologists, such as Terence Morris, and husband to Pauline, to put his points across in *The Observer.*

The key argument that proved so damaging to the Mountbatten Report was by analogy: the comparison drawn in the Radzinowicz Report between 'Vectis' and Alcatraz. The most notorious prison in America, infamous for its costly and brutal regime, Alcatraz had recently been closed, in 1963, when the Radzinowicz committee visited the USA on their fact-finding mission in summer 1967 to examine how other countries dealt with their most dangerous long-term prisoners. The fact that the Federal Bureau of Prisons had abandoned Alcatraz gave the case against the Mountbatten proposal exceptional force. As Leo Abse put it in his autobiographical memoir,[33] the American prison scene allowed our committee to 'extrapolate considerable helpful evidence . . . that no satisfactory regime could ever be found for long-term maximum security prisoners concentrated in a fortress-like prison. The Alcatraz experience was usefully on our side, and the abandonment of that disastrous island prison, both on penal and financial grounds, and the successful dispersal of the inmates of Alcatraz throughout the American prisons reinforced our view.'

There were two major difficulties with the analogy thus drawn between Alcatraz and Vectis. First, the Vectis model was not a facsimile of Alcatraz. The plans for

Vectis envisaged a liberal regime within an impregnable perimeter, not the caging of prisoners on the Alcatraz model. One plan on file, not dated but c. November 1966, headed 'Special Security Block to be Built on the Isle of Wight',[34] contains a 'diagrammatic layout', roughly 2' by 3.5', with detailed specifications of security measures – floodlights, TV cameras, screens, barriers, chain link fences, concrete vehicle stubbs (sic), 9"-reinforced concrete walls, alarms, etc. A seven-page-long outline brief foresaw 80 prisoners serving longer periods 'than hitherto' as justified by the need for protection of the public. But 'punishment by deprivation' is deemed 'inappropriate', hence 'ample accommodation and as full a regime as is compatible with the establishment' are needed, cells with ample room for both sleeping and leisure and for 'a considerable volume of personal possessions and clothing', radio and TV provision, cooking facilities on each landing, an outdoor grassed area 70x40 yards and other amenities. Whether or not this plan was superseded by a later plan for Alvington, which the Radzinowicz committee disliked, is not known – the later plan may have been more meanly equipped. But this plan envisaged a regime that was hardly that of Alcatraz. It should also be stressed that Mountbatten was clearly aware of the defects of the Alcatraz model. While 'an island site has clear advantages', if uninhabited, as at Alcatraz, it would be prohibitively expensive – in part the reason for its closure – but the Isle of Wight is far enough from the mainland to retain the advantages without the major drawback of isolation. The dangers of the depressing effect on staff of working in such a prison would make short terms of duty and extra pay essential. But a four-prison system on the island would allow for that process.[35]

The second problem with the analogy is that it was, in all probability, based on a misinterpretation of what the American policy was. In an interview with Myrl Alexander, the then Director of the Federal Bureau of Prisons, in the late 1960s, Roy King[36] was told that the dispersal of the prisoners from Alcatraz to several penitentiaries had been an interim measure only, until a new maximum security prison was built at Marion four or five years later. 'Radzinowicz simply misunderstood the policy situation.' That said, the inference the committee drew from the dispersal of the former inmates of Alcatraz was that it had proved relatively problem free. There had been no rash of escapes. However, the reason for that state of affairs, as the committee was to register later in their deliberations, was the fact that escapes were in general on a negligible scale in American penitentiaries, due to the arming of guards in perimeter watchtowers. It should also be said that Marion was later, in 1983, to provide the genesis of the strongly repressive, super-maximum security prison system (King 1999; Shalev 2009),[37] a development which King accounts for as due to the US top security prisons being used to contain prisoners who present severe control problems rather than necessarily being escape risks.

Other factors militating against the Mountbatten Report, often unfairly, were the arguments that it had recommended arming prison guards, a policy explicitly rejected by Mountbatten but proposed by the Radzinowicz Committee (see below). Another recommendation by Mountbatten was for a new post to be created of Head or Director of the Prison Department, seen as an unwarranted intrusion into Home Office sovereignty. Also, just possibly, naming mattered. The term 'concentration' connoted the most appalling oppression, and two of the subcommittee, Abse and Radzinowicz, were Jewish. An alternative term, such as 'consolidation', would have avoided such negative associations.

Overall, though the appointment of Mountbatten may have been a most astute move politically, it was clearly at odds with the prevailing culture of the Home Office, so much so that the mindset of the day was strongly against its implementation. Looking back, a very senior civil servant, now retired but then a mid-career official in the ministry, said of the matter: 'I believe that the objections to Mountbatten stemmed from the strong Borstal tradition that still permeated those on the Governor grades who had a general influence on HO Prisons policy. It was simply not acceptable to run a prison on the view that security rather than rehabilitation dictated how *all* the prisoners should be treated. This view was shared by the administrative grades as well as the Governors.

The military approach and bearing of Mountbatten and Maunsell demonstrated that they were from a different culture.'[38] In interview, he had put it more strongly: '. . . it wasn't the views they held, it was the dictatorial way in which they pursued them . . . But it was a different, now that was a different culture. No, the Mountbatten Report, apart from the single prison on the Isle of Wight idea, was broadly acceptable . . . I think there were elements in the philosophy behind the Mountbatten Report that were alien to ordinary Home Office civil servants' opinion. The Borstal tradition didn't last, it couldn't last. But it was still the apple of the eye of not just the prison staff and prison governors, but it extended into the Home Office.'

The appointment of so potent an embodiment of military standing as Mountbatten was in effect a rebuff to the reformative liberal ethos of the Home Office, already under fire for its vulnerability to widespread criticism of security lapses and notorious escapees. A major irony is that the liberal core of Mountbatten's proposed solution came to be overlooked in the welter of upgraded security measures set in train by his report. 'The imposition of new security regimes had the effect of limiting freedom of movement within the prison buildings, in consequence of which the liberal and constructive programmes patiently built up over a period of 20 years were seriously eroded. Educational classes and hobby groups were among the first to suffer. The allotment gardens that Gilbert Hair had organised for the lifers at Wormwood Scrubs disappeared under the "dog track" of the steel-mesh inner perimeter fence. Prison reformers, voluntary workers in prisons, those who came in to teach evening classes and prison visitors began to complain about the changes. All too readily the prison authorities laid the blame at the door of the Mountbatten Report for which Mountbatten was held personally responsible.'[39] Despite having been, in Terence Morris's view, 'vilified', he felt constrained by his royal family status from entering the fray to defend his report. It was, however, strongly supported by the rank-and-file Prison Officers' Association, which maintained for well over a decade that 'Vectis' had been the best solution to the escape risk problem.

Turning to the second main question relating to the Vectis issue – by what processes did the 'dispersal' system come to be adopted as the alternative to that of 'concentration' – gaps in our knowledge remain. What does seem clear is that the small subcommittee of four, set up to examine the nature of the regime best suited to the containment of long-term prisoners under conditions of maximum security, contained one member convinced from the outset of the need to block 'concentration' and to argue for the alternative of 'dispersal'. Leo Abse was quite outspoken in his book *Private Member*, published several years later in 1973, about the strategy he employed in effect to sabotage the case for Vectis:

> 'Whatever openness of mind my colleagues may have had in their approach to this problem, I had none. I was totally prejudiced. To concentrate a group of evil men, who felt themselves finally rejected by society, in a repressive custodial atmosphere was to invite disaster . . . From the outset, I had one objective in mind: how to use our terms of reference to circumvent the implementation of the Mountbatten recommendations.'[40] To that end, he devised a strategy that deserves to be quoted at length:

'To thwart the Mountbatten Report, we were to affirm that we could not discharge the assignment set us by the Home Secretary without examining the framework of security within the intended fortress-like prison in which all maximum security prisoners were to be concentrated, and that, as a result of our examination, we were to assert that no satisfactory regime could possibly be established within such a prison and would proffer the alternative of these life-time prisoners being diverted to live with hundreds of other prisoners in three or four prisons, where a liberal regime could be introduced provided it was accompanied by a high degree of perimeter security.

But I knew that the community and the House of Commons would reject the real fact that insofar as prison security can be achieved at all it can come only from a regime that fosters good relationships between prisoners and an anticipatory prison staff. The public would want to know far more about the physical perimeter security: and I came to the conclusion that public anxiety about security would have to be allayed by some tangible and emphatic innovation, if we were to succeed in our aim of dispersing these category A prisoners into liberal prisons rather than concentrating them into an oppressive fortress that would cast a shadow over our whole prison system.

I cynically decided, therefore, to embark upon a diversionary tactic: to shift attention from the real issue of dispersal or concentration to another issue which would rouse the hostility of all the liberals, and place me on the side of the devils. It would provoke great controversy and, by diverting attention upon an irrelevancy, enable our sabotage of the main Mountbatten proposal to go unnoticed amidst the clamour. I put to my committee colleagues that perimeter security should be enforced by the use of guns.'[41]

There were of course strong arguments for this to be done, mainly that US gun towers make escape from Federal prisons 'almost unknown'. 'And there can be no doubt that confidence by prison officers in perimeter security does make possible a more relaxed regime within the walls.' Such arguments convinced Radzinowicz and the Bishop of Exeter of 'the need for armed tower watchers: and I would acquit them entirely of my political deviousness. I was pleased, however, to find that the kind psychiatrist who was the fourth member of our committee, refused to go along with us, and I knew he could be relied upon to write a fierce minority report against the use of guns that would precipitate the storm I knew would burst . . . Radzinowicz, . . . the Bishop and I would be dubbed as toughies: and indeed it was not long before leaks occurred in the press stigmatising me as gun-mad.

It was an easy martyrdom to endure, for I knew that only by a compensating show of toughness would our real aims be achieved. The full Advisory Council on the Penal System, on receiving our report, divided almost down the middle on the silly issue of guns, with the present Lord Chief Justice [Widgery] supporting us . . . Most of my friends on the committee fortunately opposed me. Almost the whole Council, however, agreed on dispersal and rejected Mountbatten. I was even more shamelessly pleased with my misbehaviour when I saw the press concurring in our view of dispersal and, with the ambivalent Prison Officers Association, demurring against our reactionary plea for guns. The Home Secretary, by now Jim Callaghan, ever with sensitive antennae to majority opinion, accepted most of our report, except the guns. Not for the first time in politics, wickedness triumphed. Painfully slowly . . . the grim temporary maximum security blocks are being closed down and their inmates dispersed to new prisons like Albany and Long Martin (sic) where, hopefully, if reformers are vigilant, our recommended liberal regimes can be implemented no less effectively than our security suggestions. Mountbatten's fury that his plan was rejected was evidently boundless: even four years later, at a conference in 1971, in a highly publicised attempt to re-write history, he was still attacking the Radzinowicz Report and seeking to minimise his earlier obsession with security. In subsequent public exchanges with him I bluntly accused him of responsibility for putting back penal reform in this country by a decade. Doubtless Mountbatten's arrogance is his strength . . .'[42]

Despite the extraordinary nature of Abse's account, in which he claims to have duped not only the subcommittee, the full ACPS, the Home Office and the world, reactions have been muted. There is no critique of his account of the shortcomings of the Mountbatten Report by two of its main academic supporters, Roy King and Rod Morgan, in their detailed and otherwise comprehensive criticism of the dispersal system in their evidence to the May Committee in 1979, or in their subsequent book *The Future of the Prison System* (1980). Terence Morris does not refer to Abse's account in his history of post-war criminal justice policy[43] which contains a chapter on the 'penal crisis 1960–1988'. Lord Windlesham, in his four-volume history of criminal justice policymaking since 1945, alludes only briefly to the issue. Only Andrew Rutherford gives serious consideration to Abse's 'curious account' and comments: 'Abse's liberal instincts on this occasion may have been misplaced. Once the principle of dispersal was accepted it was not long before prison system administrators concluded that three or four dispersal prisons were insufficient. By 1970 there were five dispersal prisons, and by 1980 there were seven . . . The policy of dispersing high security prisoners . . . has fuelled the pressures towards relentless expansion of the prison system.'[44]

The view of Radzinowicz himself about the veracity of Abse's memoir is not on record. In his autobiography, he somewhat pointedly avoids any reference to it, indeed any positive reference to Abse himself. 'There were three other members of the committee: the Bishop of Exeter (The Right Revd. R.C. Mortimer, DD), Dr. Peter Scott, the distinguished psychiatrist, and Mr. Leo Abse, MP. I found my collaboration with the first two unassailably fruitful and trustworthy. Our two assessors, Mr. H.J. Taylor (the Chief Inspector of Prisons) and Mr. W.N. Hyde of the Prison Department, were of inestimable value to us. Their readiness to help and their tact could not have been excelled. Furthermore, Mr. Hyde's draft of the report could not be improved on, and Major L. Snowden proved to be a most diligent Secretary.'[45] This silence is eloquent testimony to what in all probability was Radzinowicz's distinct displeasure about, if not disbelief in Abse's version of events.[46]

Radzinowicz's account in his autobiographical *Adventures in Criminology*[47] is far more circumspect. Reactions to the Mountbatten Report were, he states, very critical from the outset among penal 'insiders' and the Home Office delayed action, Roy Jenkins giving the task of drawing up the most appropriate regime for Category A prisoners to the newly formed Advisory Council on the Penal System, chaired by Sir Kenneth Younger, who asked Radzinowicz to chair the subcommittee formed to address the issue. They took immense pains to visit top-security prisons both here and abroad, one each in Denmark, Sweden, Germany, France and six in the USA. They held numerous hearings with experts and solicited 199 papers of evidence. Dispersal emerged as the key recommendation and was unanimously agreed by the full council. Armed guards in watchtowers was the main point of contention and divided the full committee. The Home Secretary, by then James Callaghan, wrote to Younger on 24 July 1968 that he accepted the recommendation on dispersal and that policy was announced in Parliament the next day. The move towards a British Alcatraz was thereby halted, and with it the dangers of rushing into a momentous new development, such as had occurred with the penitentiary phase of the early 19th century adoption of static, 'thoroughly repressive' institutions, that cost a fortune to build. Mountbatten's admiration for the 'mechanical oppressiveness' of Kumla Prison in Sweden was not shared by the subcommittee, who were more impressed by the fact that the dispersal of prisoners following the closure of Alcatraz rarely led to security risks. Sadly, Mountbatten 'never lost his sense of betrayal' about the fate of his key recommendation. On a point of historical record, Radzinowicz was strongly critical of the view expressed by Rod Morgan[48] in his analysis of the work of the ACPS, that the subcommittee had 'worked in seclusion' from the rest of the council until the Final Report stage. The assertion that 'the full Council was suddenly presented with the final report is particularly hurtful'.[49] Two meetings of the full council copiously discussed it.[50]

Several points in these accounts bear fuller examination. First, Radzinowicz's rejection of Morgan's contention that the subcommittee 'worked in seclusion' is not borne out by Louis Blom-Cooper[51] who stated that 'we [members of the full council] had no idea what Radzinowicz was thinking, because if they took any minutes of the sub-committee's meetings, they weren't circulated in advance of the final report of the sub-committee, which was a practice that other sub-committees had adopted.' He went on to say, however, 'I think one ought to add that even if we had had intimation that the sub-committee was going to turn its back on Mountbatten and recommend dispersal, I'm not sure that it would have changed things.'

Secondly, Radzinowicz's assertion that the dispersal policy was 'unanimously agreed by Council', though formally correct, glosses over the evident unhappiness of several members, albeit a minority, about the move away from this major recommendation. Louis Blom-Cooper, in interview, in effect endorsed the success of the strategy of Leo Abse: 'That divided the Council . . . Looking back, I think the fierce contentiousness of arming prison officers distracted from perhaps the more important issue, concentration or dispersal.' The point made by Blom-Cooper and Morgan is not that the final report was not discussed by council, on three rather than two occasions. It is that the airing of key issues and the process of deliberation in earlier subcommittee meetings had not been shared with other council members. Yet the subcommittee were clearly aware of the importance of the shift in policy that their thinking implied. They wrote to the Home Secretary on 23 September 1967 from New York: 'Since we last wrote to you we have taken further evidence and visited institutions in Europe and the United States. The result has been that we are now gravely doubtful whether the creation of a small unit for a relatively restricted category of prisoners, in conditions of maximum security, and serving long sentences, is the right solution.

Even if we were to come to the conclusion that a small unit is the right solution – and we repeat that we are gravely doubtful that it is – we are absolutely certain that the concept and design at present envisaged are totally wrong, and would be widely regarded as retrograde.' The 'concept and design' referred to were presumably those flowing from the 'concentration' principle, but the alternative of dispersal had become coupled in the subcommittee's minds with the arming of perimeter guards. Thus, the minutes of their meeting on 19 September 1967 in the Albert Pick Motel, Terre Haute, Indiana, record: 'The Sub-Committee met, after visiting three State prisons and two Federal penitentiaries . . . The American prison authorities had complete confidence in their perimeter security, of which towers were an integral part and everything else flowed from this . . . The towers had armed guards inside, and if that was the price to be paid for a liberal regime within, the sub-committee were not prepared to reject the idea out of hand . . . The members of prison administration and staff of prisons . . . felt that many prisoners required security but that these were better handled if spread over a number of establishments. They would not want to have one small prison to contain all these prisoners. This they felt had been tried at Alcatraz and had failed.'

The letter of 23 September closed with the words: 'We therefore regard it as our duty to inform you that no irrevocable decision should be taken to proceed with the creation of this proposed unit until you have our report in front of you.' The letter sent reverberations around senior Home Office policymakers. Brian Cubbon wrote to Sir Philip Allen six days later (29/9/67) conveying Mr. Younger's concern 'as Chairman of the Council, about the possibility of serious embarrassment arising between the Home Office and the Council on this issue. By 3 October, W.D. Pile was writing to Philip Woodfield to delay telling the Ministry of Public Building and Works about suspending work at Alvington (formerly Vectis) as 'they might well disband the design team and it might take considerable time to reassemble them when we did want to proceed.' The tone and timing of these concerns – 'serious embarrassment' is very high on the list of Home Office anathemata – do indirectly bear out Terence Morris's view that dispersal 'was undoubtedly the preferred solution of the Home Office which was concerned not only with the prospect of how to organise a regime for prisoners all of whom presented potential problems of intractability but with the cost of adapting the design of Albany for the purpose. Supporters of the Mountbatten proposal considered that the Home Office had made its wishes abundantly clear to the Radzinowicz Committee in advance, though whether the Home Office would have gone ahead if the Committee had recommended in favour of concentration is by no means certain'.[52] In support of that view, Stevenson stated the situation as more or less settled at this point in favour of dispersal: 'Though we know that the expense of the plan for an English Alcatraz (Alvington or 'Vectis') made its delay more or less imperative as of January 1968, all the important discussions that would lead to its final demise had already occurred in the mid-September of 1967. As W.D. Pile, a new Deputy Undersecretary of State for Health, noted for Private Office on 15 September: 'The cost per place at Alvington is, I understand, of the order of £25,000. This inevitably gives pause to one brought up on a cost per school place of £140 (primary) and £250 (secondary) and, more recently, of a complete hospital bed . . . of about £10,000.'[53] Most conclusively, in a Cabinet meeting on 9 January 1968, in a discussion of public expenditure post-devaluation, the Home Secretary stated he 'can cancel new maximum security prison at Alvington; and cancel start on 2 other prisons, although no. of prisoners increasing.'[54]

Behind the scenes, cost considerations were from the outset to bedevil the implementation of Mountbatten's proposals, though Vectis was not the main, immediate concern, given its exceptional status as requiring its own planning programme. For example, even before Jenkins's ringing endorsement of Mountbatten in the key debate on the report, on 16 February 1967, concerns about the costs of improving the effectiveness of security measures across the system in general began to be raised in the Treasury, along with anxieties about rapid increases in the prison population, mainly of male adult prisoners. In a Home Office letter to the Treasury of 10 February 1967 the new category B prisoners who, according to Mountbatten, 'ought to be kept in very secure conditions', were first estimated to number 16,000, of an overall total of 26,080. The six prisons initially assigned to category B prisoners were clearly insufficient, so all local and many closed prisons would need to be brought up to category B standard, 'a large and difficult problem'. Such measures were needed as floodlighting of walls, improved communication systems with local police, clearing perimeter walls of adjoining insecure hostels and sheds, replacing working-out schemes, added to which would be secure transport, better sanitation through electronic locking, and staff housing for the extra staff needed to cope with the expected increase of 5,500 prisoners by 1970/71. An internal Treasury letter demurred from the full Home Office estimate of the costs of security upgrades, recommending the position be reserved until the Civil Review in the summer.[55]

Mountbatten was later, in his only public utterance on the subject, at the 1971 NACRO AGM,[56] to deplore the overestimated security costs involved in what he saw as a misinterpretation of his analysis: 'The effect of dispersal, when combined with the introduction of security categories, has produced a level of security in every closed prison which bears no relation to the category of the majority of inmates. 50% of men fall into category (C) but the security provided is normally much higher and in fact is upgraded to category (B). What a waste of resources!'

Following three more months of attempts by the Treasury to prune Home Office bids to implement the recommendations on security in the Mountbatten report, Jenkins suggested a meeting with the Chancellor, James Callaghan, to discuss with him direct Home Office expenditure bids for the 1967 Public Expenditure Survey Committee (PESC). £2.4 million was being requested for Mountbatten as an increase on 1966 figures.[57] A draft reply was requested to Roy Jenkins from the Chancellor. In the event, John Diamond, Chief Secretary to the Treasury, signed a draft reply, dated 11 May 1967, stating that over the three-year period 1967–8 to 1970–1, forecasts equalled £39.8 million while the corresponding 1966 forecast had been £24.7 million. 'You are therefore asking for an extra £15 million over the next three years for prison building work, in addition to the substantial increase (nearly £12 million) in the forecasts on current expenditure on staff, etc., over the same three years.

I recognise the difficulties that confront you because of higher forecasts of prison population and the Mountbatten proposals, and I have already agreed to some additional expenditure in this financial year on this account. But for future years the size of the proposed increases in expenditure are such that, at this stage, I can only note what you are asking for, while fully reserving my own position. We must wait until we have looked at public expenditure as a whole before making decisions on particular fields.' In short, there was no basis for a meeting. How Callaghan phrased his actual reply – or whether he sent one – has not been found on file. Nor is Jenkins at all revealing in his autobiography about the matter, not even mentioning the outcome of the proposed Category A prison in the Mountbatten report.[58] Can one assume that the policy had been effectively abandoned by the time Jenkins and Callaghan exchanged roles in November 1967, Jenkins becoming Chancellor of the Exchequer and Callaghan Home Secretary? It is plausible to assume that the costs of the substantial security enhancement programme were, by the time of the summer expenditure reviews, so marked that building a new top-security prison was shelved until the subcommittee of the ACPS, chaired by Radzinowicz, reported. Nevertheless, in a letter of 23 June 1967 from G. Emerson of the Home Office to J.D. Skinner, Treasury, to justify an extra £1.5 million added to earlier estimates: 'Initially a high standard of security must be provided at a limited number of prisons where high-risk category B (and until Alvington is built some category A) prisoners are to be held. Albany, Gartree, Hull, Chelmsford and Wandsworth have been selected.'[59] Further references to Alvington have yet to be found until Callaghan's announcement in Cabinet on 9 January 1968 that it was to be dropped. In a letter to Callaghan dated 4 February 1968, Mountbatten expressed his disappointment: 'It was, of course, a bitter blow when Alvington had to be postponed but I for one would regard this as acceptable as a temporary measure provided the other points I have made are faithfully carried out.'[60] Indeed, he never abandoned his hope that the concept would be revived, writing to the May Committee and to Merlyn Rees, then Home Secretary, a decade later. To Rees he wrote: 'I fully realise that as my idea was not adopted when the money was available in the 1960's, it will be far more difficult to find the money now. But surely if the policy were now to be accepted, plans could be prepared in slow time and thoroughly investigated with a view to implementation when the money can be made available?' Mountbatten clearly held the view that it was not the Treasury, but the Radzinowicz subcommittee, that had been the decisive voice against the proposal for a single totally secure prison for the worst-case escape risks, Roy Jenkins having assured him that, ten years on, 'gossiping about old times and our long standing friendship, he admitted that the only thing he felt unhappy about was his failure to adopt my maximum security prison suggestion, . . .'[61]

By March 1968, a combination of cost and the inferences drawn by James Callaghan as Home Secretary from disturbances by Cat. A prisoners in E Wing at Durham prison 'alerted me to the dangers of putting all our eggs in one basket. Their combined presence forming an elite in an ordinary prison unsettled the rest of the inmates, and strengthened Mountbatten's case for separating them completely . . . in a secure, fortress-type gaol. On the other hand, there was a potential danger in aggregating the most dangerous of the prison population of young, vigorous professional criminals . . . In April 1968, I paid visits to Durham, Parkhurst and Leicester . . . and saw for myself the living conditions of some of Britain's most dangerous prisoners in their security wings . . . I returned to the Home Office convinced that the best solution was not to build a special prison, but to disperse these particularly dangerous men in penny packets to a large number of gaols where their numbers would be too small to dominate the life of the institution.'[62]

Even at the earlier point, no more was done to acquaint members of the committee with the subcommittee's antipathy to the Vectis/Alvington model. On 16 October, Younger wrote to Sir Philip Allen, who had succeeded Sir Charles Cunningham as the Permanent Undersecretary of State, Home Office, in 1966, that having spoken to Radzinowicz on his return from America, and been told that he 'had had a few words with the Home Secretary in New York', that 'if the Home Secretary is going to take a fresh decision about the new prison . . . it seemed to me very important that the Report itself should be a well-balanced document, taking all of the various arguments into account . . . It seemed to me, and Radzinowicz agrees with this, that it would be a pity if the Report were to seem like a confrontation between the Sub-Committee and the Prison Department or, for that matter, Mountbatten.' There could be embarrassment if any leaks occurred or even a Parliamentary Question, before the full Report appeared. Secrecy was indeed the order of the day, and it was not until four months later, on 29 January 1968, that the full council met to discuss the report for the first time.

The fourth plenary meeting of the council began with Radzinowicz's summary of the six main reasons why 'the Sub-Committee had rejected the solution of concentration.'[63] Of these, as later critiques would argue, only (2) arguably weighed heavily in favour of dispersal rather than concentration: the capacity to transfer unusually recalcitrant prisoners from one maximum security prison to another. The regime that was then outlined by Radzinowicz was certainly a liberal system, but it could equally as well have been compatible with concentration. Security was especially important, as it emphasised the need for 'the provision of observation towers manned by armed guards. With the exception of Dr. Scott, who had dissociated himself from that part of the Sub-Committee's report, the Sub-Committee felt that armed guards would be essential if a more relaxed internal regime were to be instituted.' (para 7/8).

In discussion, four members of Council voiced opposition to or doubts about dispersal: Mr. Millard; Lord Delacourt-Smith; Barbara Wootton; and Louis Blom-Cooper. More were opposed to the arming of perimeter security guards. The discussion was wound up by the ACPS Chair, Kenneth Younger, stating that the absence of five (out of 18) members precluded definite conclusions and that a further meeting would be needed. The Home Secretary would be given 'a short covering report . . . reflecting the differing views and making some assessment of the various alternatives.' (para. 18).

The fifth plenary meeting of the ACPS was held at the Home Office on 15 February, just over two weeks later. Members unable to attend had made their views known to the chairman or the secretary. More assented to the dispersal model than not, though not necessarily to the arming of perimeter guards. Lord Sandford pointed out that the 'shift of policy from that advocated in the Mountbatten Report . . . would present the Home Secretary with a difficult problem if these recommendations were not strongly supported . . . there was little prospect of their being implemented if the Council was not all of one mind.' (Minutes, para. 7). It was agreed that those dissenting from the arming of guards should sign a note of reservation associating themselves with Dr. Scott's views. However, a distinct prospect of even wider discussion was raised by Louis Blom-Cooper. In a lengthy statement, he found himself 'compelled to append a separate note of reservation on the use of guns and to explain why I lean in favour of concentration of Category A prisoners either in a separate establishment or in association with another existing penal institution. This would provide the necessary object of flexibility in treating this and other categories of prisoners . . . I entirely accept the argument in favour of perimeter security – of taking a good deal of the security out of the prison and onto the walls . . . The Sub-Committee was, to my mind, too concerned with the risk of escapes organised with outside help.' The location of the prison, with perimeter defences designed to forestall escapees being sprung, are essential. 'But the use of guns is not only alien to the spirit of the English penal system – and their introduction a wholly retrogressive step; their use would also add little or nothing to the quality of security . . . If security must be geared to those who need it, it follows that Category A prisoners need the greatest degree of security . . . To disperse Category A prisoners among the prison population is to lead to the provision of a higher degree of security for all prisoners confined with them because of the presence of a minority only who really need it. That would militate against the potential for reformative aspects of the regime for the majority. The idea that segregation units will solve the problem of recalcitrant Category A prisoners in dispersal prisons is to revive the problems of existing special security wings in which "the most intractable and unresponsive prisoners might well be confined . . . almost indefinitely.

The Sub-Committee was evidently struck by the fortress-like appearance of Alvington and was very unfavourably impressed with the detailed internal planning. This judgement is fully accepted. But concentration does not necessarily mean adopting a plan along the lines of Alvington.' Quotations from the Proposed Note of Reservation by Mr. Blom-Cooper.

The sixth and final plenary meeting of the Council on this issue took place on 7 March 1968:[64]

> 'Mr. Blom-Cooper said that he wished to apologise to the Council for putting forward a proposed note of reservation at such a late stage . . . He appreciated that the Council could not now delay further the submission of the Sub-Committee's report, and that if in the light of discussion it was decided to add a further note of reservation it would be necessary in consulting the whole Council about this development to ask them to reply as a matter of urgency so that the report might be submitted the following week.'

Lady Serota added her basic agreement with Mr. Blom-Cooper.

'Professor Radzinowicz said that he was disappointed that the Council was taking so long to decide on its attitude to his Sub-Committee's report. He was himself subjected to a good deal of pressure by the Press and if there were to be any further delay he would feel obliged to make a public statement that the Sub-Committee had forwarded its report to the Council and that the matter was no longer in his hands.'

Lady Wootton 'also had doubts about the policy of dispersal and that these had been adequately expressed in the original draft of the covering letter. She was unwilling to accept without qualification a report which unequivocally supported a policy of dispersal.' She too shared the view that dispersal would mean that over-rigorous control would be exerted on less dangerous prisoners.

'After further discussion the Council decided that the situation should be met by adding to the draft letter a statement to the effect that some members of the Council were not entirely convinced that some form of concentration might not be the right solution . . . Mr. Blom-Cooper said that in these circumstances he would be quite content to withdraw his note of reservation. It was agreed that the report should be submitted to the Home Secretary . . . together with the revised covering letter and the Minutes of the Council's 4th and 5th meetings.'

The revised covering letter referred to a 'balance of advantage lying with dispersal' rather than a minority of members [five out of 18] favouring 'some form of concentration'. However, the revised version was accepted by members without demur. The report was submitted to the Home Secretary that day, 7 March, and was accepted by him in a letter to the Chairman on 24 July. The arming of guards was rejected, but the report was otherwise accepted. The change in policy was announced in response to a Parliamentary Question the next day, 25 July 1968. A month earlier, on 18 June, Callaghan had addressed the Council at its 7th meeting. Echoing the financial estimates of almost a year before, he said: 'One important consideration was that of the enormous cost of the Alvington project which amounted to £25,000 for each prisoner: it might seem paradoxical to devote a large proportion of resources to the needs of some 150 prisoners while 30,000 others were detained in conditions which ought to be improved. He wished to take a little longer to consider the matter but had to announce his decision before the Summer Recess. The Council's valuable recommendations about the regime for long-term prisoners were in the meantime being carefully studied by the Prison Department.'[65] So it was that the policy of dispersal came to be the basis for long-term imprisonment under conditions of maximum security in England and Wales.

## Aftermath

Writing some three decades after the event, Alison Liebling[66] concluded that 'If Radzinowicz were here today, I suspect he would approve of the current dispersal prison system', even though some key elements of a liberal regime have been sacrificed, or reined in, to enable the prison service to win the 'control and security war' after over twenty years of precarious stability. Regime variation and generous home leave and visiting entitlements are still lacking. However, the size of the maximum-security estate has been brought down to five prisons, at the cost of allowing the proportion of Cat. As to reach 30 per cent in some cases, higher than Radzinowicz envisaged. To Roy King, the system as a result looks far more like that which Mountbatten envisaged. Mountbatten had made the case for Cat. As to be 'concentrated' in one impregnable prison, but had foreseen the need for two if the population of more serious offenders, in the aftermath of the abolition of capital punishment, led to an increasing proportion of that category of prisoner. That was when the daily average prison population numbered 33,000. It is now 85,000, and five prisons for Cat. A prisoners is much in line with Mountbatten's projections, even if they are mixed with Category B prisoners, defined by Mountbatten as those for whom escape must be made 'extremely difficult' even though it would pose no threat to national security or constitute a major public danger. In short, we have evolved a system of maximum security imprisonment that is a hybrid of the principles of concentration and dispersal, rather than a pure dispersal system.

How could this be? The main answer must lie in the similarities rather than the differences between the Mountbatten and Radzinowicz Reports. Both aimed to provide a 'liberal regime within a secure perimeter'. They simply had different ideas as to how that could best be attained. Both aimed to provide generous welfare and rehabilitative resourcing. Both aimed to relax internal constraints to the minimum to allow much more freedom of movement and association within walls. Both aspired to minimise the pains of long-term imprisonment by generous home leave and visiting arrangements that would ultimately include conjugal visiting. Both saw education and work as staple needs to be met by trained staffing. Though the road to the present system has been hard, with developments in political terrorism and drug-related crime making for even more difficulties than were foreseen at the time of their writing, their joint impact has arguably made possible a system which has, thus far, been resistant to the growth of 'supermax' forms of imprisonment that have proved so contagious across the USA and have taken root in even so liberal a system as that of the Netherlands.[67] Avoiding what must be seen as a system of extreme penal repression is, however, to set the bar far too low.

## Notes

1  Bottoms and Stevenson, '"What Went Wrong?": Criminal Justice Policy in England and Wales, 1945–1970' in Downes (ed.) *Unravelling Criminal Justice: Eleven British Studies*, 1992, Macmillan: 7.

2  The term is Victor Bailey's (see his *Delinquency and Citizenship: Reclaiming the Young Offender, 1918–1948*, Oxford 1987: 266).

3  See Elaine Genders and Elaine Player, *Grendon: A Study of a Therapeutic Prison*, 1995, Oxford; and the *Howard Journal of Criminal Justice*, Special Issue '50 Years of HMP Grendon', December 2010, 49, 5.

4  Terence Morris, 'Humanity <u>and</u> security', *Observer*, 1 March 1970. Terence Morris (1931–2013) was one of the leading criminologists of his generation. In the 1960s, his role as a public criminologist complemented his academic career at the London School of Economics. He was a key member of the Labour Party inquiry, chaired by Lord Longford, on criminal justice policy which, in 1964, produced the influential report *Crime – A Challenge to Us All* (see Paul Rock, Vol. 1 this series). His joint research with his first wife, Pauline Morris, *Pentonville – A Sociological Study of an English Prison*, (1963, London: Routledge & Kegan Paul) was the first study of its kind in Britain. His articles on crime and penal policy were a regular feature of the Observer in the 1960s. Throughout his life, he was a notable proponent, with Louis Blom-Cooper, of both the abolition of capital punishment and its replacement by the mandatory life sentence.

5  S.J. Stevenson, 'Official responses to escapes from and crises of control in British prisons, 1945–1974', 1996, mimeo., table, p.4.

6  Advisory Council on the Penal System, *The Regime for Long-Term Prisoners in Conditions of Maximum Security*, 1968, HMSO: 18.

7  HO 278/10; P.E.8; IPE 100/1/15.

8  The 'other three' escapees, soon recaptured, were Eric Flower, Robert Anderson and Anthony Jenkins. By contrast, Biggs accomplished the perfect escape 'to celebrated (and non-extraditable) exile in Brazil.' (Bottoms and Stevenson: 25)

9  HC 24 October 1966, Hansard Vol. 734, cc 649–56.

10 Roy Jenkins, *A Life at the Centre*, 1991, Macmillan: 203. The Opposition, led by Edward Heath, proposed 'That this House deplores the refusal of the Secretary of State for the Home Department to set up a specific inquiry to report as a matter of urgency on the escape of George Blake from Wormwood Scrubs Prison.' Quintin Hogg as Shadow Home Secretary repeated the charge, inter alia, that Blake should have been moved to a more secure location. Jenkins replied that at several points during his imprisonment in 1961 that issue had been discussed and rejected by both Butler and Brooke as the then Home Secretaries, had imposed no special restrictions on him despite earlier allegations of a plot to spring Blake and despite several successful escape attempts by other prisoners in 1961 to early 1964. Moreover, the overall rate of prison escapes had fallen under Labour and the specific matter of Blake's escape had been written into the terms of reference of the Mountbatten Inquiry, whose coverage of the wider issue of prison security was vital. As Hogg had agreed the terms of reference in the immediate aftermath of the escape, Jenkins criticised scathingly the Leader of the Opposition for 'insisting on tabling this Motion which . . . is about as much of a vote of censure on his own Shadow Home Secretary as it is upon me.' This 'trumped up Motion' should be rejected, as indeed it was, by 331 votes to 230. Hansard, HC Debates, 31 October 1966, Vol. 735, cc. 115–70.

11 Ibid: 204.

12 Prem. 13/952; 1966 – Home Affairs.

13 (Sir) John Chilcot served as Permanent Undersecretary of State at the Northern Ireland Office, as Deputy Undersecretary at the Home Office in charge of the Police Department and various posts both in the Home Office and in the Cabinet Office, including Private Secretary to Home Secretaries Roy Jenkins, Merlyn Rees and William Whitelaw. Knighted in 1994, he was appointed in 2009 to chair the inquiry into the British involvement in the 2003 invasion of Iraq. His 2016 report gained immense coverage for its conclusion, *inter alia*, that such a war in 2003 was both unnecessary and damaging to the authority of the United Nations.

14 Terence Morris, *Crime and Criminal Justice Since 1945*, 1989, Oxford: Blackwell: 130–1.

15 Philip Ziegler, *Mountbatten: The Official Biography*, 1985, Collins: 649–52.

16 *Report of the Inquiry into Prison Escapes and Security*, HMSO, Cmnd. 3175. The largely standard practice of the report being substantially written by the Secretary to the Inquiry, Philip Woodfield, was followed, but the tone and content were Mountbatten's.

17 Apart from the Secretary, three assessors were chosen for their varied expertise and experience: J.R.G. Bantock, a former Governor of Brixton and Manchester Prisons; R.J. Lees, Deputy Director of the Royal Aircraft Establishment at Farnborough; and Robert Mark, Chief Constable of Leicester (and later of the Metropolitan Police). Mountbatten rejected the P.M.'s suggestion of Sir Roger Hollis as an assessor for the inquiry as he had no expertise in prison security and 'it might be embarrassing for him to be too closely connected with the Blake part of the inquiry since to some extent the conduct of the Security Service during his term of office, and in particular their alleged wish that Blake should be kept in a London prison, is bound to be called in question . . .' It is therefore difficult 'to force him on Mountbatten'. (Letter from Jenkins to the P.M., 26/10/66: Prem 13/952).

18 Michael Randle and Pat Pottle who, with Sean Bourke, had met Blake in prison and regarded his 42-year sentence as 'inhuman'. See their *The Blake Escape: How We Freed George Blake and Why*, 1989, London: Harrap. Blake's sentence of 42 years comprised three 14-year sentences of imprisonment to run consecutively for a spying career that was held to have involved the death of at least one British agent and the disabling of MI6 networks in Eastern Europe.

19 Despite the recommendations of the governor, Leslie Newcomb, 'who had warned that it was improper, dangerous and stupid to keep Blake in Wormwood Scrubs from

which people, ten people a year, escaped.' (Brian Emes, senior civil servant and former prison governor at Wakefield, interview 2012). 'Leslie was within three to four weeks of retirement and Roy Jenkins decided that he needed a new governor for political reasons. So Leslie got early retirement and this was a man who'd had a long and distinguished career . . . It was very hurtful for him."

20  For a critical analysis of its longevity, see David Price (2000) 'The Origins and Durability of Security Categorisation: A Study in Penological Pragmatism *or* Spies, Dickie and Prison Security' in G. Mair and R. Tarling (eds.) *British Criminology Conference [1999]: Selected Proceedings, Vol. 3.*

21  Local traders also using that name objected to its association with imprisonment and the Home Office renamed it 'Alvington'.

22  See, for example, the letter by Sir Philip Allen of 7 April 1967, p. 7 below.

23  Consisting of Albany, Parkhurst and Camp Hill prisons, to be supplemented by Vectis/ Alvington.

24  Lord Justice Woolf (Parts I and II) and Judge Stephen Tumim (Part II) *Prison Disturbances April 1990: Report of an Inquiry*, February 1991, London: HMSO. Cm 1456. See also Ch. 6 below: 'The Woolf Report and After'.

25  Mountbatten report, op. cit.: paras. 17 and 318 et seq.

26  No examples are given by Radzinowicz as to whom he is referring but Terence Morris (op. cit.: 1970), a leading proponent of the model which Mountbatten came to adopt (Morris: 1966) argues that the senior Prison Department administrators, steeped in the liberal reform era of Alexander Paterson, 'scorned American watch towers and searchlights', ironically the very measures advocated by Radzinowicz's committee, as well as by Mountbatten. As a result, 'they liberalised without increasing security precautions.' (Morris: 1970). See Terence Morris, 'How to stop jailbreaks, *The Observer*, 12 June 1966; 'Humanity and security', *The Observer,* 1 March 1970, and 'Mountbatten betrayed', *The Observer*, 28 March 1971; see also Roy King and Rod Morgan, *The Future of the Prison System*, 1980, Farnborough: Gower; and David Price, op. cit.

27  The date by which the prison 'must' and 'could' be built was stated as June 1969 (para 15).

28  *Committee of Inquiry into the United Kingdom Prison Service Report,* 1979, London: HMSO, Cmnd. 7673: 20.

29  Mike Fitzgerald, 1977, *Prisoners in Revolt*, Harmondsworth, Penguin: 49–52.

30  Stan Cohen, 'Human Warehouses: The Future of Our Prisons?' *New Society*, Vol. 30, no. 632, 14 November 1974: 407–11.

31  Interview, 25 March 2010.

32  Philip Ziegler, op. cit.: 650–51.

33  Leo Abse, *Private Member*, 1973, Macdonald: 129–30.

34  HO 278/36.

35  Mountbatten Report: para 217.

36  Roy King, Professor Emeritus of Criminology, University of Wales at Bangor, interviewed 25 March 2010, by DMD.

37  Roy King, 'The rise and rise of supermax: an American solution in search of a problem', *Punishment and Society,* 1999, 1 (2), 163–86; Sharon Shalev, *Supermax: Controlling risk through solitary confinement*, 2009, Willan.

38  Email extract, 24 March 2015, following questions arising from his interview on 12 March with DMD and TN. The Mountbatten Report had recommended the establishment of a new post to provide leadership for the Prison Service, termed 'Inspector-General'. 'This "high-level and vital post" needed unusual ability, "and the first may have to come from outside the prison service". Existing expertise was passed over . . . Prison officers approved of the establishment of the post, and of the reappointment of Brigadier M.S.K. Maunsell to fill it.' J.E. Thomas, *The English Prison Officer Since 1850: A Study in* Conflict, London: Routledge & Kegan Paul, 1972: 215, 231. Maunsell had been the previous Inspector of Prisons, a less authoritative post.

39 Terence Morris, op. cit.: 134–5.
40 Leo Abse, op. cit.: 124–5. The Advisory Council's terms of reference were 'to consider the regime for long-term prisoners detained in conditions of maximum security and to make recommendations.'
41 The relevant Minutes do not provide a basis for testing this claim.
42 Abse, op. cit.: 130–35. Mountbatten's opinion of Abse's account is expressed in a letter dated 29 April 1975 to the Rev. Dr. Bolt, an active penal reformer who had sent him 'extracts from Leo Abse's book "Private Member" which referred to my Prison Report . . . I am sure I do not need to tell you how far "off beam" Leo Abse is. The last thing I wanted to do was to put back the clock as far as rehabilitation of prisoners was concerned. All I ever wanted to do was to get the minute percentage of really vicious hardened criminals who should on no account be allowed to escape put in a place where they would not be able to escape because of secure perimeter control but would have a reasonable life to live in prison.' Mountbatten Archive, University of Southampton: MB1/N84A.
43 *Crime and Criminal Justice since 1945*, 1989, Blackwell: (Institute of Contemporary British History series).
44 Andrew Rutherford, 1986, *Prisons and the Process of Justice*, Oxford: Oxford University Press: 79–81.
45 Sir Leon Radzinowicz, 1999, *Adventures in Criminology*, London: Routledge & Kegan Paul: 304.
46 The psychoanalytical musings of Abse in the book about Radzinowicz's character could hardly have been welcome.
47 Op. cit.: 1999. See especially Ch. 12 'A Prison System in Crisis', pp. 294–321.
48 In his *Formulating Penal Policy*, 1979, NACRO.
49 Radzinowicz, op.cit: 319.
50 On this point reference is made to the minutes of the 4th and 6th meetings: ACPS (M) 29/1/68 and 7/3/68.
51 Interviewed by DMD on 9 March 2010.
52 Op. cit.: 133–4.
53 Stevenson, op. cit.: 27–8.
54 CAB/195/29 Cabinet Notebook 30/11/67–20/6/68.
55 Treasury T 353/8, File No. 2HG 28/66/04, 'Prisons: Measures to arise from the Mountbatten Report on Prison Security and from the increase in numbers of prisoners'.
56 Earl Mountbatten of Burma, 'Prison: A Human Problem', Speech at the Annual General meeting of the National Association for the Care and Resettlement of Offenders, York University, 3 April 1971. Mountbatten Archive, University of Southampton, MB1/N84A: 3.
57 Internal Treasury letter from J. Anson to J.D. Skinner.
58 Roy Jenkins, 1991, op. cit.: See also Paul Rock, Vol. 1, where he reports an absence of material on criminal justice policy in Jenkins's archives at the Bodleian Library.
59 File 2 HG 28/66/04 E, '
60 Mountbatten Archive, loc. cit., MB1/N84A.
61 Letter to Robert Armstrong, Permanent Undersecretary of State, Home Office, 14 November 1977, Mountbatten Archive: loc. cit.
62 James Callaghan, *Time and Chance*, 1987, Collins: 241–9.
63 Minutes of the fourth meeting of the ACPS, 29/1/68, para 5, (1)-(6).
64 Quotations are from the Minutes of the meeting.
65 Advisory Council on the Penal System, Minutes of the Seventh Meeting, held at the Home Office, 18 June 1968. The 'enormous' estimated cost of £3.75 million would soon be overtaken by those incurred in building seven suitably secure 'dispersal' prisons. See especially King and Morgan, 1980, op. cit.: 78–9. The figure of 150 Category A prisoners differs from Mountbatten's estimate of 120, though he had envisaged a possible second such prison if the prison population continued to increase.

66 'A "liberal regime within a secure perimeter"?: dispersal prisons and penal practice in the late 20th century' in A. Bottoms and M. Tonry (eds.) *Ideology, Crime and Criminal Justice: A symposium in honour of Sir Leon Radzinowicz*, 2002, Willan: 97–152.
67 Roy. D. King and Sandra L. Resodihardjo, 'To max or not to max: Dealing with high risk prisoners in the Netherlands and England and Wales', *Punishment and Society*, 2010, 12, 65–84.

# 3    Forcing the Issue;
## The making of the dispersal
## system, 1968–79

## Introduction: Setting the Scene

Both 'concentration' and 'dispersal' policies of managing long-term prisoners, under conditions of maximum security, had been in embryo before the crisis of prison security occasioned by the escapes of 1964–66. The White Paper *Penal Practice in a Changing Society* had envisaged a single prison of heightened 'maximum security' to hold the most dangerous and violent prisoners. Pending that innovation, a number of prisons were to be designated as of heightened security, some of which would have Special Security wings. These were planned as temporary stopgaps by the former Prison Commissioners such as Duncan Fairn but, in the words of the Mountbatten report, were 'such as no civilised society should tolerate'. The escape crisis of 1966, which led to that inquiry, meant that the choice between concentration and dispersal could no longer be deferred. The two policies could no longer be subject to piecemeal development in parallel.

Once the issue had been settled in early 1968 in favour of dispersal, planning had to proceed more systematically to provide enough prisons suitably equipped to handle the mixture of categories A, B and C envisaged by the Radzinowicz Committee as the necessary basis for a liberal regime within a secure perimeter. Hopes for the success of dispersal prisons were reasonably high, if not unmixed. For example, an undated note by W.N. Hyde of the Prisons Board in mid-1968[1] takes dispersal as a *fait accompli* – it was not formally announced by James Callaghan, the Home Secretary, until 25 July 1968 – and raises the question of how the recommendations of the Radzinowicz Report were to be implemented. It needs careful thought on 'the effect of what the Advisory Council regarded as a "liberal" report may be the opposite of what was intended'. The recommendations were 'not easy to implement' within existing resources. An earlier note (29 April 1968)[2] about night sanitation stated that an experiment with electronic locking had been running successfully at Albany for six weeks. The aim was to do the same at two other dispersal prisons, Coldingley and Long Lartin. It was also planned to provide a lavatory and wash basin in each cell at the local prison at Lockwood, but 'the Treasury are being tiresome about this – and, indeed, about night sanitation generally – but I hope the end of the battle is in sight.' This was hardly the case, as in-cell sanitation had to await the implementation of the Report of the Woolf

Committee over 20 years later. Even relatively minor innovations were scoured for possibly adverse side-effects. Electric shavers were preferable to the then current system of officers issuing and collecting razor blades daily, but the issue needed to be handled with care, as it might lead to accusations of providing 'luxuries'. In comment (29 April 1968) Hyde wrote to Woodfield that both electric locking and lavatories in cells 'are to be found in almost all the overseas prisons visited.' Senior Home Office administrators were thus constantly subject in the policy process to a frame of reference formed by the Treasury, public opinion and – to a far lesser extent – foreign examples of what was possible. Moreover, Hyde was reminded[3] of the need to keep in view, in the light of the report, the needs of female, remand and long-term prisoners.

Hence the Prisons Board needed to set up a project group under the Governor of one of the prisons concerned, Long Lartin, due to open in 1969/70. The committee should represent all relevant sections – PD2, PD3, the Prison Directorate, DPMS, DIS and Estates II.[4] The Radzinowicz Report recommendations were divided into those already in hand, and those to be referred to the project group. On 27 July 1968 that programme was agreed by the Prisons Board. The transition to dispersal prisons was now under way.

## The Disturbances at HMP Albany

The first test of dispersal policy occurred unexpectedly soon after its implementation at HMP Albany in the Isle of Wight. By chance, from its origins as a medium-secure training prison, Albany was studied by two criminologists, Roy King and Kenneth Elliott. Their book, *Albany: birth of a prison – end of an era*, published in 1977,[5] came to the unequivocal conclusion that dispersal policy was a failure, albeit well-intentioned, and should be abandoned in favour of a somewhat modified version of Vectis, the linchpin of Mountbatten's concentration policy. However, by the time drafts of their study and its conclusions were sent to the Home Office for comment, the decision to persist with the policy of dispersal had been taken on a seemingly irreversible basis. It was a policy that could not be allowed to fail.

Albany was opened by Lord Stonham in April 1967 and was at first hailed as a 'breakthrough' providing a 'more dynamic and personal training' for recidivists. Just over five years later, 'after an increasingly stormy series of incidents culminating in an alleged mass escape and a riot', it was by then known as a 'jail of fear' in which 'mafia groups' were said to '"terrorise" staff and prisoners alike' (ibid: iv). How had this transformation been wrought?

Albany was seen by King and Elliott as embodying all the changes in English penal policy 'in microcosm'. The prison was originally conceived in 1961 as part of the post-war building programme that would enable the Prison Commission to give up Dartmoor – the sixth secure prison, planned to hold 480 long-term prisoners. In 1962 it became linked with the embryo of the maximum-security prison envisaged in *Penal Practice in a Changing Society*. Commission files were minuted with 'the need to provide a small, entirely separate prison for between

30 and 60 inmates somewhere in this area.' The Ministry of Public Buildings and Works were to explore 'building a specially secure block to the W or S of the main block on the Albany site' for 'lifers' (ibid: 24). Estimates for 1963–4 included the figure of £2 million for Albany, plus 'the only Treasury-approved estimate we have been able to discover for the special security block of £270,000.' Its design was referred to the newly formed Prison Department Working Party. A £1.65 million tender for Albany was accepted in November 1963. Site work began in 1964 with a completion date of October 1966. By November 1965 an 'outline brief' had been developed for a maximum security block to hold 80 prisoners in security 'as complete as can be contrived'. In the post-Blake and Biggs era, the main security was to be provided by a 30' high concrete wall, with overhangs, surrounded by 'dead ground planted with anti-tank blocks' and with an underground entrance. Internally, 'humane standards of accommodation' in terms of both space and amenities were envisaged – large cells, with adjacent toilet facilities, accommodation for 'conjugal visits' and a heated swimming pool. In mid-December, Sir Frank Soskice, the Home Secretary, urged the Ministry of Public Building and Works to get on with it. A later meeting dropped plans for conjugal visits and assigned the swimming pool to review.

In 1966, Mountbatten visited Albany on 7 December and deemed existing plans for it too insecure for Vectis in the post-Blake era. It now became due to open in April 1967 for 'difficult recidivists' but, until perimeter security was improved, the selection of inmates would need 'great care'. After its opening, Stonham still expressed the hope that the maximum security block, now renamed Alvington, would be completed by 1970. In July, the Eleventh Report of the Estimates Committee (HC 599) endorsed the proposal. In October and November, Albany gained highly favourable publicity as a 'revolutionary prison' for its emphasis on security combined with liberal treatment and training.[6]

The regime was initially largely home-grown rather than imposed from on high. Albany, along with Gartree and Blundeston prisons, were products of the 1959 White Paper which gave priority to treatment and training as reformative instruments to change criminals into non-criminals, as incarnated in Prison Rule 1. But the Prison Commission was 'too set in its ways' (ibid: 76) to manage such innovation effectively. Albany therefore evolved its own agenda to give effect to 'humane' management, initially and most distinctively under its first Governor, David Gould. The 'emergent blueprint' consisted of two major components: social training and industrial training. Social training aimed to build on what the Governor called 'controlled and therapeutic anxiety' to effect 'behaviour changes from criminal to non-criminal'. What it boiled down to was 'a nudge in the right direction'. Social training was based on training plans drawn up for each prisoner (two-thirds of whom were category Cs at this point) under the general supervision of the principal psychologist (ibid: 109). Case officers for up to eight prisoners each were to monitor progress. But the preparation of the file for each prisoner was soon routinised to the point where monitoring boards made little headway. Industrial training was based on a two-shift system of industrial work, tailoring and allied trades and, later on, carpentry, which was the cornerstone of the regime.

The two-shift system provided both a certain choice and – crucially – time for other aspects of social training: social, educational and welfare. Yet despite the staff's immense efforts, never more than 58% of prisoners were so employed in workshops: the rest were occupied by routine service and administrative tasks. Nevertheless, and despite severe shortfalls in meeting 'revolutionary' expectations, 'Albany came close to solving some of the managerial problems that had been posed for it, and might have succeeded had it not been for the implementation of the dispersal policy.' (ibid: 90).

On 28 October 1968 the Home Secretary announced[7] that Albany would operate as a dispersal prison receiving category A prisoners from December 1969. From that point on a sequence of security upgrades went in parallel with a deteriorating state of discipline and internal control. Though Cat. As did not start to arrive until October 1970, Cat. Bs had been moving in in increasing numbers from March 1969. By 1970, security upgrades included a second fence, dogs, an administrative control unit and a segregation unit which 'Provided the fail-safe which finally transformed Albany from a Cat. C to a Cat. A dispersal prison.' (ibid: 29). In December 1970, arson incidents occurred and numbers placed on Rule 43 started to rise due to fears of intimidation. In April 1971, the prison's second Governor, Brian Howden, left a note for his successor predicting a 'definite bid for power' by some prisoners. In May 1971, the POA representatives complained of frequent alarms and searches for firebombs. Nine 'subversive' prisoners were in the segregation unit. In September two notorious prisoners were placed in segregation only after a struggle, leading to a 'Kray gang's men in prison battle' headline in the *Daily Telegraph* for 8 September 1971. The prison was locked down for two days, several transfers resulted and a new low point in staff-prisoner relations had been reached. 1972 began with a sequence of confrontations and incidents of intimidation, and when in May the Preservation of the Rights of Prisoners (PROP) movement was launched, it was shortly followed by an in-cell demonstration for PROP by 100 prisoners. There was 100 per cent backing for the national prisoner strike call by PROP in August, but it ended peacefully.[8] However, when the Home Office agreed to talk to PROP about the prisoners' complaints, Albany officers led the POA to adopt militant demands of their own: 'work to rule' unless stricter action was taken against 'subversives'. Escape gear was found at Albany leading to a complete security search that triggered a riot lasting two days and nights and extensive damage. The media's extensive coverage meant that Albany was 'now the most notorious prison in the country' (ibid: 31). Prison officers' wives picketed wives visiting prisoners, provoking a 'Jail of Fear' headline in the *Daily Mirror* (28 August 1972). Demonstrations followed 'in Parkhurst, Chelmsford, Gartree, Dartmoor, Maidstone, Liverpool, Cardiff and even Peterhead' (ibid: 297). But no evidence of a mass escape plot or anything else of significance was unearthed in the great search. Nevertheless, 158 prisoners were dealt with on 654 counts involving damage (ibid: 298).

Following this assertion of staff power, the main upshot for penal policy was the announcement by the Home Secretary, Robert Carr, on 6 September 1972, of a review of dispersal policy. The Working Party on Dispersal and Control (WPDC) reported the following May (11 May 1973), reaffirming the wisdom of the dispersal principle and recommending its further development by an increase in the number of dispersal prisons from seven to nine; tighter controls over freedom of association between different categories of prisoner; and the creation of two new 'special control units' to deal with especially recalcitrant prisoners of the 'subversive' type. Calls for the concentration policy of Mountbatten to be belatedly adopted, by the POA in particular, were emphatically rejected.

How far did this conclusion fly in the face of what King and Elliott regarded as a series of events at Albany which could clearly be attributed to the effects of dispersal policy? Though their analysis was not available for the review called for by Robert Carr, criticism of dispersal policy was all too evident, both from the POA, from academic criminologists such as Terence Morris and, in a rare speech on the subject at the NACRO AGM at York University on 3 April 1971, from Lord Mountbatten himself.[9] Having restated his case for a Vectis-type prison on the Isle of Wight, where staffing tensions could be handled by a rotation of staff from the other three prisons there, he stated: 'The effect of dispersal, when combined with the introduction of security categories has produced a level of security in every closed prison which bears no relation to the category of the majority of inmates.' This was not only a waste of resources, but a source of regime tightening and the curtailment of rehabilitative measures.

The interpretation of King and Elliott of the events at Albany (ibid: 305–27) was that a clear distinction needed to be drawn between violent disturbances at Albany in 1971 'which recurred and spread to other dispersal prisons in 1972 and 1973' and the normally peaceful demonstrations organised by PROP. The former concerned long-term prisoners' specific conditions of custody; the latter were more broadly based and to do with conditions for *all* prisoners. Moreover, PROP aspired to be a radical movement to link prisoners' rights issues with wider radical politics. The POA were much more worried by the former and yet linked the two in pursuit of their opposition to PROP, the case for better conditions for their members and their advocacy of the Mountbatten proposals. For different reasons, the Home Office also blurred the distinction between the two types of disturbance.

Nor was it the case that the main troublemakers in the dispersal prisons were category As. They were just as, if not more likely to be Bs or even Cs – the 'young toughs' of press notoriety. The 'Big Men' were the Cat. As but not all were involved, as the press implied, in the incidents. 'All this is not to say that the troubles at Albany were not directly attributable to the implementation of the dispersal policy, because we believe that they were. But it is to say that there is a vitally important distinction to be made between prisoners who constitute a threat to security and prisoners who constitute a threat to the good order and discipline in the prison.' (ibid: 309). Some are both but many more are in either and vastly more are in neither.

If dispersal policy was to blame, what exactly did the damage? In 1969, even after 'tightening', Albany was still a 'flexible and humane' establishment. Association across the halls of the prison lasted from morning till night. But as the raising of the 'coefficient of security' demanded by the Radzinowicz subcommittee took place, so the population changed. In 1971 compared with 1969, significantly more prisoners were in Albany for serious violence (up from 8 to 24%) and with significantly longer sentences (nine months or less, down from 69 to 34%; 22 months or more, up from 12 to 36% (ibid: Tables 9:1 and 9:2, 311–12).

The attempt was made by Howden to keep the 'spirit of the dispersal prison' alive by spreading the long-termers throughout the four halls; and, to maintain the liberal regime, 'Prisoners are in constant association from 6.30 a.m. to nearly 9.00 p.m. We do not restrict them from going into each other's cells, it would be futile to try to do this. They do gamble, they do play cards, in fact they do a lot of things which perhaps are, technically speaking, against the rules, but which we know about and try and keep a reasonable measure of control on.' [10] 'But there is no doubt in our minds that the implementation of such a policy in the conditions prevailing at Albany was a recipe for disaster.' (ibid: 312–13). It 'actually contrived to make a subversive, manipulative response more likely than it might otherwise have been. Thus, the allocation of both long- and short-term prisoners to the same halls only served to remind the long-sentence men just how long they still had to do.' (ibid: 310). Also, far from approving of the facilities they found on arrival, dispersal prisoners resented that "they did not get the same privileges they had enjoyed in the special wings'. To be told, in effect, that they were *not* 'special' went against the fact that they *were* special: 'it was for people like them that the whole elaborate machinery of security had been set up.' (ibid: 315). And as the restrictive realities of heightened security started to take effect, they were imposed on all categories of prisoner alike, the basis for Cat. B and Cat C. prisoners' resentment at the loss of privileges and entitlements they would have received in Cat. B and Cat. C prisons.

Could the troubles have been averted? A host of special factors operated at Albany to lessen the probability that they could have been forestalled: hall management could have been better and stronger; more experienced staff could have been deployed; the POA pursuit of a five-day week might have been postponed, thus making joint working arrangements more effective. 'When all is said and done, however, the real causes of the troubles at Albany must be sought not just in the special circumstances of implementing the dispersal policy there, but in the inherent problems of the dispersal policy itself.' (ibid: 324–25). Leon Radzinowicz had argued for dispersal as absorbing the majority of Cat. As into the general population. Failing that, Rule 43[11] and segregation units would cope. Albany did just that, but it still broke down, and ended by overturning the two key principles of dispersal: that of absorbing difficult prisoners and of maintaining a liberal regime. By May 1973, following the separation of short- and long-termers and the far greater compartmentalisation of prison life, 'the prison was quiet, but the spirit of dispersal had gone' (ibid: 327).

Since the commitment to dispersal took place in 1968, Home Office administrators had been steadfast in its defence.[12] Their response to the draft report of the study by King and Elliott in 1976 was that Albany had been exceptional in having to undergo transformation from semi-secure to maximum security status in the space of a few years. And King and Elliott had to acknowledge that the better planning of Coldingley went far more smoothly. However, Albany was not to prove an isolated case. The problems arising from its evolution were also rife in the case of the abortive control units that emerged from the report of the Working Party on Dispersal and Control set up by Robert Carr; and also re-emerged in starker form in the Hull Prison riot of 1976.

## The Control Unit Fiasco

On 20 March 1973 W.R. Cox wrote to Mr. Angel of the Home Office Prison Department that two major reports were almost ready – one on rewards and punishments, the second on dispersal and control. The latter was the report of the Working Party on Dispersal and Control which Cox had chaired in response to the Home Secretary's call for a review of dispersal policy on 6 September 1972, following the disturbances at Albany and other dispersal prisons. A handwritten note dated 20 March 1973 by 'DC' says these must be dealt with as a 'matter of urgency – we must not allow them to gather dust while Ministers take too long to find time to deal with them.'[13]

The reason for the urgency was that dispersal prisons were proving both more costly and less secure than anticipated, and their sustainability was being questioned by the POA in particular. The Regional Director concerned had made recommendations following disturbances at Gartree which were the basis for a draft submission to the Home Secretary by the Prison Department (letter from Hornsby to Clark). They were: (1) perimeter security had been 'far too easily breached', so that both walls *and* fences were needed, despite Treasury reluctance, for all dispersals. (2) search procedures therefore need to be tightened, especially more rigorous cell searches, which are 'intensely unpopular and 'destructive of staff/inmate relationship'. As a result, more staffing was needed, probably 20 more staff at an estimated £34,000 a year plus capital of £132,000 for housing. (3) Cell walls needed strengthening both internally and externally – at Gartree, prisoners were able to breach them 'without very great difficulty . . . This is essentially a control problem: but there are security implications also' due to potential mass escape attempts. The total cost for existing prisons would be c. £120,000[14] over two-three years (i.e. £120 per place) and costs for two new prisons. (4) Movement control should be more restrictive on a wing basis, needing c. 120/130 more staff at a cost of 250,000 p.a. plus £800,000 for housing.

The costs of dispersal were mounting up, but 'a reasonably relaxed regime' is inevitably costly. Nevertheless, in a letter from Cox to Hewlings about a letter to the POA on dispersal policy, it was emphasised that the Home Secretary was 'not persuaded that there was anything wrong with dispersal policy . . . Indeed, he considers that the course of concentrating the most troublesome prisoners (in a single prison) would create more problems than it would solve.' Such a course had not, in point of fact, been recommended by Mountbatten, whose report had focused entirely on security and not control risks. However, the entire concentration vs. dispersal debate thus far had tended to conflate the two quite distinct sets of problems: the danger of escape from, as distinct from disruption to prison regimes.

The Home Secretary went on to defend the dispersal system as not yet fully in operation. 'Teething troubles' flowed from the fact that the system 'is not yet large enough'. However, three prisons were about to come on stream; segregation units were not yet available in all dispersals and would be provided; and 'two small special control units should be set up' to provide a 'spare but not Spartan regime' for 'persistent troublemakers'. A handwritten note added that '. . . the new units are to be seen as a transitional facilities (sic) which it is to be hoped that the system will be eventually able to do without . . .'

The overall strategy for penal policy was more optimistically set out in a draft document entitled 'Prisons – The New Approach', which noted that it was prompted by Lord Colville to contextualise current changes. This nine-page-long draft, sent from W.R. Cox to Weiler, Hewlings and Miss Owen on 12 April 1973, listed ten points couched in terms of a coherent strategy for a leaner, more efficient and 'humane' prison system. For example, the first 'big moves' to reduce prison numbers were set out in the 1972 Criminal Justice Act, reference mainly to the new system of community service and reparation that ensued from the ACPS subcommittee reports chaired by Barbara Wootton and L.C.J. Widgery. Recent improvements were listed, such as 'more on education, including the "Open University": higher pay; better shoes and clothing; more food, etc.' Dietary punishments had been abolished i.e. 'bread and water does not conform with modern penal philosophy'.

Nevertheless, there remained the problem of containing 'violent and dangerous men':

'12. There has been a certain amount of confusion in public discussion of this problem. There are some prisoners whose character and offences are such that the most stringent possible measures should be taken to prevent their escape; there are others who by their nature actively create trouble in the prisons. These groups overlap, but they are not identical. The Mountbatten Report recommended that the first group (the so-called category A men) should be contained in a single fortress prison. Successive Home Secretaries, while accepting all Lord Mountbatten's other recommendations, have been persuaded that to do this would produce an "end of the road" situation which would be oppressive for prisoners and staff alike. They have instead pursued a policy of more limited concentration under which these men are placed in a limited number of prisons with very high perimeter security (the dispersal prisons). So far as security is concerned, this policy is working reasonably well . . .

13. The problem which came out very clearly in last year's disturbances is that it was a rather different group of men who were at the bottom of most of the trouble. These are men who are not simply troublesome; they are the troublemakers who organise and stir up violence and disorder in prisons. It is tempting to suggest that all these men should be taken out of the dispersal

prisons and put into a single establishment, but the disadvantages of doing this are even more evident than the disadvantages of putting all the high security risk men together. To do this would be to create a highly explosive situation . . .

14. One part of the solution, therefore, lies in pressing on with the bringing into operation of more high security prisons so that the pressure points can be eased. In addition, all these prisons need proper segregation units for the temporary containment of men who are creating trouble, and this is being got on with.

15. But a new type of outlet is required, and it is accordingly proposed to set up two special control units within existing dispersal prisons to which inveterate troublemakers can be sent. These will not be the "end of the road" for these men; the units will be run under a spare but not Spartan regime which will give the staff of the units the opportunity to lead these men [*pencil underlining in text, with "too positive?" in the margin*] through their problems to a frame of mind in which they can return to more normal conditions, as soon as possible. The location of these units within dispersal prisons will allow for a regular and frequent interchange of staff and will give the Governor the opportunity of testing out informally a man who is showing progress by transferring him to the main part of the prison. It has to be recognised, however, that for a certain minority the stay in a special control unit may prove to be a long one.'

From this point on, the nature of the 'Special Control Units' (SCUs) was to preoccupy the Home Office Prison Department for over a year in seeking to solve a problem it had not as yet had to contend with: a form of sanction more severe than segregation units or solitary confinement, but yet which was not 'the end of the road'[15] for this newly defined group of arch troublemakers. It proved to be a solution that foundered on the rocks of fears that staff would be 'subverted' by manipulative troublemakers into colluding with prisoners working the system for their own benefit. But it was only gradually that those fears came to dominate potentially more constructive aspects of the unit's regime.

In a slightly revised version of the WPDC Report for consultation with staff associations, including the POA, sent by Cox to Sir Arthur Peterson and other senior policymakers in the Prison Department, it was specified that SCUs should be small but big enough for 'positive treatment and work', to hold a maximum of 40 prisoners.[16] 'These will by definition be concentrations of exceptionally violent, manipulative and unco-operative men.' To offset the risk of the regime succumbing to 'oppressive bias', the essential ingredient is that 'the staff should themselves see the need of the prisoner for help and tolerance . . . and the prisoners as individuals and in some depth.' The SCUs must be in existing dispersal prisons to ensure Cat. A security, even though not all would be Cat. A prisoners. A trial period to assess progress in the main prison was envisaged but placement in the SCU was to be an HQ decision. The units must be separated from the main prison. The staff would need support, special training and frequent rotation. Psychiatric cover was essential and at least two units would be needed for flexibility. By definition, prisoners may be in the unit for a long time. But, for effective control, 'it is of paramount importance that they should be able to see that there is hope of progress and of movement and that this can be achieved by their own choice and effort'. 'To incorporate a positive treatment element, the atmosphere must be sufficiently relaxed to encourage' constructive staff-inmate relations; a regime that is 'spare but not Spartan', flexible enough 'to enable progress to be tested' and 'where real progress is rewarded by movement out of the unit rather than by special privileges.' Virtually all of these components of a relatively humane regime were to be eviscerated in the course of the next twelve months.

The response of the Prison and Borstal Governors came on 7 May 1973 in a letter from R.S. Llewellyn, Chair of the Committee. He stated, without elaboration, their broad support for the need for 'concentration' or 'qualified concentration' but argued that both will inevitably be seen as 'the end of the road'. They objected to the term 'Special' as an incentive to misbehave. The number of troublemakers in the system had been underestimated: they 'could be as high as 300' and 20 should be the maximum number in any one CU – more would be 'dangerous' and even 'explosive' if numbers were allowed to rise. Nine dispersal prisons were the minimum needed and ten or more were recommended. Each unit should contain 'full hospital services . . . including padded cells and hospital cells.' Staffing and training were top priorities with a Class I Governor in charge of all dispersals. This counsel of perfection in resource terms was mainly ignored in the event, as was the Governors' view that the units should be housed in Victorian local prisons, because their location in a dispersal prison would be 'paramount to installing a human time bomb'.

The 1973 POA AGM was addressed by the Home Secretary, who reiterated his intention to retain dispersal policy but strengthened by upgraded security and the two Special Control Units. The POA Chief Officer, Sidney Powell, responded by reiterating their preference for a 'special prison for dealing with Cat. A and other intractables' as the key to long-term imprisonment planning. In bracketing the two together, the POA repeated the error of imputing to the Mountbatten concept a policy of concentrating *control* risk prisoners that he had never proposed. At an earlier meeting on 9 May between the Home Secretary and the POA, Powell went so far as to state: 'The Association did not wish to see a policy of concentration to the extent that was recommended by the Mountbatten enquiry, but they did see advantage in all the most difficult people being retained in one institution with a regime designed for them.' The Home Secretary countered this suggestion, a distinctly novel one, by suggesting such a prison would be 'demoralising' for staff. At the AGM, Powell took the opportunity to mount attacks on both the ACPS and 'woolly thinking armchair penologists' on the one hand, and PROP and 'outsiders' who encouraged 'violent and turbulent demonstrations', on the other. Since the adoption of the dispersal policy the prison service had to face and contain major incidents involving escape attempts and riot situations at several prisons, including Parkhurst, Albany, Chelmsford, Hull and Gartree. The same nucleus cropped up 'with monotonous regularity . . . They were aggressive psychopaths being allowed to mix with other long-termers as a result of dispersal.' (*Daily Telegraph*, 16 May 1973). The need to convince the POA to accept the reality of dispersal as 'here to stay' was increasingly stressed in Home Office documents. The significance of the control units as part of this process was evidently pressing. The POA had expressed concern at their AGM that control units would be seen as a relatively privileged sanction, resented by other prisoners as had been the case with special wings. They were reassured that this would not be the case with Special Control Units.

Between April and October 1973, as various policymakers grappled with the nature of the regime Control Units should operate, it became increasingly obvious that they experienced severe difficulties in defining rewards and punishments for which the prisoners could 'opt' as ways of assuring staff they were ready to rejoin 'normal prison life'[17] For example, Mr. K.H. Dawson of P2 Division wrote to Hewlings, Head of Operations, on 11 April 1973, suggesting his Division take the lead in drawing up a regime, chairing a Steering Committee with representatives from other sections. 'In general, the emphasis should be towards pitching the standard just below but not too far below that enjoyed by the population of the main prison.' A marginal question mark suggested doubt from Hewlings. For example, cooking facilities, normally available 'at local discretion' should not be allowed in SCUs. This attracted a marginal tick. There should be some provision for work in association, though education should be in-cell or very small groups. It is intriguing to chart the steps whereby this relatively innocuous regime proposal became in reality, little more than a year later, the basis for accusations of sensory deprivation sufficiently potent to bring about the closure of the only such unit in operation, at Wakefield Prison.

A note by GSG Chambers of P5 Division[18] stated that provision for 'very intractable prisoners' should be made in Wakefield F Wing (the whole) and Wormwood Scrubs A Wing (part). He recommended that 'we play down the setting up of the two units from the beginning and as a start drop the word "special" . . . We must not allow the units to become notorious as Special Security Wings became notorious five years ago . . .' The units 'must not become a dumping ground for just any awkward prisoner' nor should they replace segregation units. They are for those unaffected by segregation units and/or adversely affecting the rest of the population as an 'influential troublemaker'. Hence the regime should be 'extremely simple and based strictly on what a prisoner has legally to be provided with under the Prison Rules.' It should be a 'barren existence' but *not* a 'physically taxing and repressive regime of the old "glasshouse" variety but rather the reverse – in his cell, working if he chose and being paid for so doing, but not otherwise, with no demands being made upon him and largely ignored by staff – the thing which troublesome and attention-seeking prisoners can bear least of all. I would suggest that such a regime strictly followed out would prove successful in most cases in a matter of months.' (para. 6). Protest against so 'sterile' a regime could be anticipated 'in the form of petitions and letters to MPs on the part of the prisoners undergoing it.' But these could be rebutted as due to the fault of the prisoner 'who may return to the normal life of a dispersal prison as soon as he gives any indication of mending his ways.' In the event, this analysis could hardly have been more flawed.

A ten-page proposal by Arthur de Frisching of P2 Division on 11 May prepared for a Working Party meeting on Control Units a week later (18 May) had the potential to tilt the regime away from 'sterility' and towards a more constructive approach. Experience in the USA suggested that men who have proved resistant to solitary confinement and allied punishments are over 30, have had several prison sentences, and are often both violent and litigious. Hence the regime must be constructive and not punitive. 'Experience suggests that a punitive regime cannot be sustained successfully over long periods.' Therefore 'the primary elements of control should be based on separation from other prisoners *and a high level of contact with staff.*' (emphasis added). Prisoners should be based on Rule 43 to ensure the safeguard of monthly review. In relation to 'progress . . . The broad philosophy should be one of self-help followed by staff support.'

This document introduced the notion of phases, perhaps for the first time. In Phase I, the prisoner should be separate from other prisoners but in 'regular and frequent contact with staff'. There should be opportunities for paid work, education and training in cell. They should be allowed personal radios, books and games. In Phase II, the transition to 'controlled association' takes place. Short periods of association should be allowed. But it is 'unlikely that any prisoner sent to a Special Control Unit, as opposed to a segregation unit, will be ready for Phase II in less than 6 months.' Opportunities were to be sought proactively by the prisoner rather than routinely laid on. Leisure should be strictly time controlled, not flexible regarding activities. The prisoner needed to show achievement in all three areas of work, education and leisure to progress to Phase III. This phase should be a more restrictive and controlled version of a normal prison routine, e.g. no cooking facilities allowed in the unit. Visits could be one two-hour visit per month in open but closely supervised conditions. Though less than for long-term prisoners at Wakefield and Wormwood Scrubs, this 'still represents a considerable increase on the statutory minimum.' For adult male prisoners that stood at one half-hour visit every four weeks.

These proposals were discussed by the Inter-divisional Working Party on Control Units on 18 May 1973, with representatives from P2, P3, P5, P6, P7 and the Chief Psychologist. They could not agree on the average length of time the average prisoner would spend in the units. But there should be two units with one 'philosophy'. Talk of 'phasing' should be dropped – though it was later reinstated as two phases. Too much onus was seen as resting on staff to 'recognise change of heart'.

Paragraphs 5–7 of the Minutes seem to indicate a key point of slippage from the earlier emphasis on 'regular and frequent contact with staff'. It was now proposed that 'staff should take a cool, professional attitude and encouragement would be by checks and controls in the system, rather than by oral persuasion . . . Any sign of trouble would be interpreted as his choice to regress from that area in which he had misbehaved. In a sense this would be a sort of phasing within the individual: it was to be hoped that each inmate as he tired of the sparseness of the control unit would sooner or later show that he meant to conform, with an expectation of eventual return to dispersal conditions.' (para. 5).

'Paragraphs 6–20 would all need re-casting omitting talk of "phases" and misleading words like "progress" . . . It was important that there should be no onus on the staff to "mark', and that the range of alternatives did not shift themselves into a progression towards a goal of "virtue", deserving transfer out of the control unit. This would mean that if a man conformed, won the right to return to a dispersal prison and promptly made trouble on return, *it would look as if the unit staff had been duped* [emphasis added] . . . The period in the unit should in some way be related to the original period of troublemaking in the main prison; and that a control unit need not be "duped" twice: a second stretch there would be a long one.' (para. 7)

Paragraph 8, headed 'Arrival at the Unit', went on to make it clear that the regime precluded association, wireless and any work except mailbag sewing. An hour's exercise was a statutory right. 'The problem of a man refusing to exercise would be followed up by P3 Division: it was undesirable to have any point on which a control unit inmate could make trouble by disobeying a rule.' Later it was in principle permissible for the regime to allow work, recreation and education in association – but the possibilities here were very restrictive, e.g. 'no television and wireless restricted to a speaker in one room controlled in the staff office'. Space limitations were severe at both Wakefield and Wormwood Scrubs. The Working Party acknowledged that the two locations were 'far from ideal . . . for example, at Wakefield, the exercise space was no more than a dark corridor.'

No great changes were made in the next few months, beyond a decision not to compel prisoners in the units to work, due to the 'kind of confrontation' to which this can lead, and the danger of the 'creation of martyrs'. The onus is on the prisoner to activate the process. On 13 August, D.G. Hewlings (Controller – Operations) compiled a further paper based on earlier drafts which stated that, due to the constraints of staffing and location, 'the regime may be a shade more bleak than originally intended.' However, this was not a problem as 'We do not want prisoners to find that they want to remain in control units.' There was expressed sensitivity to liberal opinion in a handwritten note from Sir Arthur Peterson (15 August 1973): 'I agree with these proposals, and in particular with the conclusion that work should not be made compulsory. This would certainly be regarded by the Howard League and such bodies as a very retrograde step.' On 24 August, Lord Colville agreed: 'I also agree. We can start on this well thought out basis, and learn as we go on.' The Home Secretary, Robert Carr, concurred: his Assistant Private Secretary wrote to Hewlings: 'Before he went on leave, the Home Secretary had an opportunity to see your note of 13 August and minuted: 'I was most interested to read this outstanding report. When we can do this sort of thing so well and so quickly – as indeed we, of course, did the review leading to the new policies on dispersal and rewards and punishments – I wonder why we need to put out so much policy work to Advisory Committees which take so long to produce results.' Such confidence was to prove misplaced.

By 21 September, a Security and Control Measures Implementation Committee (SCMIC) had been set up[19] to draw up detailed plans for staffing the units at Wakefield and Wormwood Scrubs and to organise training schedules. Criteria for *entry* were to be that a prisoner should be demonstrably an 'inveterate trouble-maker' bent on 'challenging authority' and capable of persuading others to do the same, causing persistent disruption to the system and for whom segregation units and transfer have failed to work. Criteria for *discharge* should be 'demonstrable and sustained good behaviour and constructive effort'. Timetables were mapped out and routines sketched in.

On 10 October 1973, Sub-Committee B of the SCMIC held their first meeting,[20] chaired by Miss G.M.B. Owen of P5 Division. It was agreed that, as the major aim of the control units was to relieve the dispersal prison concerned, three months 'might be too short'. The normal minimum stay should be six months, three months on 'basic' and three on the 'associated' regime. Though this was in total shorter than earlier drafts of the time to be spent in this form of solitary confinement, passage through the unit was now to be conditional, perhaps even longer than in previous conceptions. If at any time a prisoner did not conform, he would normally start again at the very beginning. Difficulties might arise 'if persistent misbehaviour led to "protracting" the "basic" period. "Such cases would require careful examination. This pointed to the need for close monitoring so that the system could be modified and developed as necessary." This somewhat fateful set of decisions set the system on the course which would lead to its early termination. It was also agreed that the discretion given to the Governor of the control unit prison to allow a "trial period" back to his main prison, following improvement in his behaviour, should be abandoned. "If the idea was retained (and it was now of doubtful value) decisions regarding transfer would be for the central authority and not the governors concerned."'

The SCMIC also produced a document entitled 'The Philosophy of Control Units' on 30 October 1973.[21] 'It is part of the philosophy of control units that they will neutralise potential troublemakers by virtue of the fact that men sent to them are thereby out of circulation within the normal prison community for an appreciable period of time. The regime will be austere, lacking the comparatively relaxed atmosphere and varied amenities of dispersal prisons . . . The extent to which the custody and control of highly manipulative prisoners (as these will necessarily be) imposes strain on staff has been recognised. The regime is accordingly structured so as to reduce the occasion for confrontation with staff or manipulation of staff by prisoners to the minimum . . . The regime must not be harsh – we do not want to create martyrs – but neither must the units be seen in any sense as "soft options" and the regime must not degenerate into the sort of relaxed, indulgent yet pointless existence which special wings have now come to offer.'

A meeting on 1 November 1973,[22] to discuss the operation of CUs, considered the view that less than six months might suffice if a prisoner made good progress. This idea was quickly squashed: prison equilibrium needed six months to be recovered if 'severely disrupted'. Moreover, a 'more flexible policy . . . would necessarily introduce subjective judgements as to reformation of character which it was the aim of the regime to avoid.' The nature of the documentation required for discharge 'had yet to be considered'. Perhaps more ominously, consultations with the POA were still to come.

Presciently, the Wormwood Scrubs Principal Medical Officer pointed out that 'the lack of visual stimuli . . . could cause mental stress necessitating hospital treatment.' Prisoners would need to be 'watched carefully'. Nevertheless, the austere regime demanded that even attendance at church services was not to be permitted. 'The routine provided for religious instruction to be brought to them in control units.' Visits should not take place in the units, as prisoners may 'provoke officers' to use physical constraint in front of visitors. Further scrutiny was needed on this point. Opening of the Wakefield Unit was deferred until April 1974.

The gaps still to be filled in planning and co-ordination are evident in a letter of 28 January 1974 from Governor III Development Training Department to the P5 Principal, asking for guidance on points in the staff manual relating to Control Units. With regard to cell furniture, would pets and pin-ups be allowed? Would weight training, remedial or otherwise? How long should visits be, and how many visitors at a time? 'May children sit upon father's knee? (It may seem silly, but up to what age may a child sit upon father's knee?) May sweets be offered? . . . What is an "embrace" and for what period of time may it continue?' On work and pay – 'will tea breaks be allowed' It is striking that such questions should be raised as late as January 1974. The Staff College Principal at Wakefield wrote on the same day stressing the need for a circular to cover *all* aspects of control unit administration and management. At least three weeks' training would be needed for staff before the opening of a unit.

It took six weeks for the Head of P5 to reply to these letters, with a draft Circular Instruction sent also to the POA and the governors of Wakefield and Wormwood Scrubs. Cell furniture should be restricted to 'issue items only' – no personal possessions. Visits were to be one hour per 28 days. No physical contact and no food allowed. On work, no tea breaks or Thermos flasks allowed. Discipline was 'a difficult area'. 'The stronger sanction (than loss of pay or remission) will be the administrative one of requiring the prisoner to remain in or revert to Stage 1, which will not of course be dependent upon disciplinary proceedings. A Review Board would be needed, to review each prisoner after the 10th week of Stage I or the ninth of Stage II, or at any time there was 'cause for concern' for deferral of Stage 2 or reversion to Stage I.

Control Unit staff training was eventually to take place at Wakefield from 15–31 July 1974. The syllabus would cover the philosophy, ethos, aims, tasks and methods devised for the units. The first few days included sessions on key topics, such as types of inmate for admission; psychiatric aspects; and even 'problems of the total institution' – one wonders whether Cohen and Taylor's *Psychological Survival*[23] was on the reading list. But thereafter the content peters out somewhat, with whole days such as Friday 19 July taken up with 'Open Session', 'coffee', 'Open Session continues' to '12.00 terminates'. There is nothing on file about how far these training schedules were followed and what trainees were issued by way of material. Certainly the other key matter on file is the drafting of the Manual for Control Units. But this was not available for trainees. On 10 September 1974, Miss Owen, the Head of P5, wrote somewhat frostily to Mr. Towndrow, the Head of P6[24]: 'After taking a month to produce our revision of this first draft, I hesitate to press you for early comments. But as you know, we already have prisoners in the unit and since we none of us know exactly what staff were told on their training course . . . it is extremely important to get this staff manual out as soon as possible before we find that irreversible errors of practice have crept into the regime . . .' How far the precipitate closure of the regime was the result of following or ignorance of the manual is not on file.

Six months later, on 3 March 1975, Owen again wrote to Towndrow with what, in her view, was a final draft of the manual. She went on to say: 'I should doubt myself if it is now worth issuing it to the staff since the last of the prisoners is due out at the end of this month, if all goes well. But the manual should presumably be retained for issue if and when we get any more prisoners allocated to the control unit.' A further six months later, on 21 October 1975, Mr. R.M. Morris chaired a meeting on the 'Closure of the Control Unit', which would now hold Rule 43 prisoners. An announcement would be made in Parliament on 23 October to that effect. The three prisoners still held there would be transferred to Manchester, Durham and Liverpool.

What had happened to bring this experiment in the control of 'persistent troublemakers' to so abortive a conclusion? Nothing has so far been found on file in the National Archives or in the files retained at the Home Office and the Ministry of Justice to fill in the major gap of what actually happened to the prisoners in the only unit to have been operative, at Wakefield, to demand its closure.[25] The only material on this crucial matter is a report from *The Sunday Times* Insight team on 6 October 1974, entitled 'The grim secret of Wakefield prison'. The control unit regime had been held responsible for a deterioration in the condition of a prisoner, Michael Williams, so severe that his sister felt the need to write in protest to the new Home Secretary, Roy Jenkins, the prison governor and the Bishop of Wakefield. Martin Wright, then Director of the Howard League, was contacted by the families of two prisoners in the unit and played a crucial role in its publicisation by putting them in touch with Peter Watson of *The Sunday Times*. The nature of the regime, with its emphasis on lack of contact between staff and prisoner in an unusually intensive form of solitary confinement, thus 'saw the light of day'.[26] Concern was expressed by criminologists and penal reformers as well as by lawyers for the prisoner that the regime was not only extremely austere but that transfer to the unit was an administrative, not an adjudicatory decision by Home Office officials. As such, it was not subject to regular review, or appeal, and was indefinitely extendible on any breach of any rule. Accusations of the practice of sensory deprivation as a control technique permeated rising concern.

The unit had opened on 1 August 1974 and was closed little more than a year later, having held only a few prisoners instead of the 20 or so for whom it had been intended. The story as a whole is one of lack of informed preparation and awareness of the likely effects of so punishing a regime. Yet the planning had not, at the outset, been intent on designing so harsh a system. That had evolved in successive planning sessions, despite warnings along the way, as the result of ceding overriding importance to two considerations: first, that staff should at all costs be protected from any possible manipulation by prisoners labelled 'subversive' and 'intractable'; and secondly, that the key decisions regarding punishment, phasing and discharge should be taken centrally, not locally or regionally, and by administrative not judicial procedures. The regime had been developed in the kind of official secrecy that logically led to accusations of Home Office cover-ups when the 'inside story' did not so much leak out as emerge as a full-blown scandal, due to the evident integrity of the family member who first broke it, and the dramatic impact of the reportage for which the Insight team became justly renowned. It was the nadir of the Home Office's attempt to bolster dispersal policy in the context of widespread disturbances increasingly linked with the infliction of maximum security on far more prisoners than Category A escape risks.

One document on file in the Control Unit folders relates to the escape attempt by three prisoners at Inverness Prison in 1972, which was prevented at the cost of an officer being blinded in one eye. One of the prisoners involved was James ('Jimmy') Boyle, later to become widely known as the epitome of the success of the Barlinnie Special Unit at Glasgow's main prison.[27] The document is included presumably as an example of relevant evidence sought by the Home Office from its Scottish counterpart. It records the incident in detail and had clear bearing on the escape attempts from Gartree, showing the lengths to which prisoners can go to pursue the means of escape. But in Scotland, the aftermath a few years later, and perhaps with the failure of the Wakefield unit in mind, was the willingness at all levels to experiment at Barlinnie Prison with a unit based on the principles of rehabilitation and self-government by inmates drawn from the most violent prisoners in Scottish jails. By contrast, the aftermath of Gartree in England was the infamous and short-lived Control Unit at Wakefield Prison.

Five years later, the still largely secret nature of the development of the unit was substantially disclosed, and its notoriety reinforced, in the course of the action brought by Michael Williams against the Home Office for false imprisonment (see coda below). Leaked documents by the plaintiff's solicitor, Harriet Harman, formed the basis for a detailed, full-page article by David Leigh in *The Guardian* which excoriated the Prison Department of the Home Office for implementing a plan, drawn up in secrecy, for a unit which violated human rights and rehabilitative principles.[28]

The article presented a vivid picture of the defenders of liberal and welfare oriented policies in the Home Office defeated by the upholders of unyielding punishment. Thus, the Cox Report was 'thoughtful and humane . . . Yet the reality, over the following year, turned into something very different – an attempt to punish into final submission prisoners on whom punishment had already failed . . . It is the story of how the Home Office invented special "control units" for prisons; set one up amid bureaucratic infighting; swept aside all protests; hastily altered it when its apparently harsh and pointless regime was exposed; and finally abandoned the whole notion, admitting its ineffectiveness.' It is 'a story of muddle and recriminations . . . No-one could study the original report: it was kept secret, even from prison governors.' And, one might add, from future historians, another instance of record management amounting to record destruction.

The core of the article is the breakdown of the victory of P5 over P2 in the course of formulating the most appropriate control unit regime.[29] Leigh quoted a note by K.H. Dawson: 'P2 should take the lead on this'. P2 favoured 'a relaxed and purposive regime' with 'communal activities of all kinds pitched to a standard just below that of the main prison.' The Head of the Home Office, Sir Arthur Peterson, accepted the plan as being 'spare but not Spartan' providing 'positive treatment and work in an atmosphere sufficiently relaxed to encourage worthwhile relationships between staff and inmates.' He was anxious to avoid 'an oppressive bias' and wanted a constructive regime in which 'the staff can see the prisoners as individuals needing help and therefore deserving of some special tolerance.'

Mr. Chambers of P5 was quoted as having very different plans: advocating realism and a disbelief in troublemakers as capable of being influenced by 'any kind of treatment and training, call it what you will . . . I advocate that the regime should be extremely simple and based strictly on what a prisoner has to be legally provided under the Prison Rules.' He recommended 'sterility . . . seclusion and anonymity . . . a barren existence more likely to persuade him to behave . . . largely ignored by the staff. Such a regime strictly followed would prove successful in most cases in a matter of months . . . From then till the year's end, a bureaucratic battle raged, between members of P2 trying to implement the original scheme and the authoritarians in P5. As a later minute tried to explain: 'P5 prevailed.' The crucial components of the regime – the silent treatment, reversion to day one, stage one if any rule was violated, two phases of 90 days, with association allowed only in stage 2, no radio and minimal visiting – were assembled in harsher form.

The article was unsparing in its depiction of the Home Office as dominated by authoritarian officials who were secretive, incompetent and resistant to informed criticism both from within and without. It 'summarised the efforts made by officials to reduce public knowledge of control units. For example, ". . . the circular to governors setting up the regime was to be kept secret, even from MPs. A draft circular warned governors that there were bound to be pressures to modify its severities and censorship must be rigid." An official is quoted as observing: "Only circular instructions which modify standing orders are sent to the House of Commons Library. This one will not, therefore, go to the House of Commons."[30] Harriet Harman was subsequently held to be in contempt of court for making available to the press documents which were read out in open court, with costs awarded against her. In dismissing her appeal, Lord Denning stated: "I can see no public interest whatever in having these highly confidential documents made public . . . It was in the public interest that these documents should be kept confidential. They should not be exposed to the ravages of outsiders." '[31]

## The riot at Hull Prison

With the closure of the control unit at Wakefield Prison in 1975, and the decision against opening that at Wormwood Scrubs, a key element of penal policy stemming from the WPDC Report of 1973 was abandoned. The Home Office now aimed to make dispersal policy work by extending the number of such prisons and by upgrading the training of staff to run them. The elements that combined to make the prison system an estate in seemingly endless crisis were continuing to grow in scale and intensity: the steady growth in the overall prison population, due to rising rates of crime and the apparent ineffectiveness of alternative measures to imprisonment, including the newly created Community Service Orders; the growth in particular of the number of long-term prisoners, due to the abolition of capital punishment; the increase in those convicted of more serious crimes, such as armed robbery; the rise of other crimes of serious violence, in particular IRA terrorism; the emergence of PROP as a political wing of prisoner revolt; and the backdrop of persistent reluctance by the POA to accept the reality of dispersal, and the refusal to adopt concentration policy, by senior Home Office policymakers and by ministers. All these elements were to surface in the riot at Hull Prison that began on 31 August 1976.

There were subsequently to be three reports on the riot: the official inquiry led by G.W. Fowler, the Chief Inspector of Prisons; a local inquiry by the Labour MP for Hull, Mr. (now Lord) John Prescott; and an inquiry set up by PROP and chaired by John Platt-Mills QC.[32] The latter report by PROP published its evidence gathered in public and criticised the official inquiry for not publishing its evidence in full, though at least the inquiry report was published, unlike that into several earlier prison disturbances. All three reports agreed on the basic sequence of events, though not on the crucial matter of their initial causation. In brief, the spark for the riot was the alleged beating up of a prisoner in the segregation unit, rumours of which spread rapidly throughout the prison in the early evening of 31 August. The reports differ on whether or not the prisoner had in fact been a victim of staff violence. The official report, drawing on medical, staff and some prisoners' accounts, concludes that no such assault took place. On the contrary, the prisoner concerned had himself assaulted four members of staff, having refused to obey an order to return to his cell, and resisting staff physically moving him there. That offence was subsequently upheld by the Board of Visitors and the prisoner punished by the loss of 120 days' remission and 56 days' stoppage of earnings. On repeating the charge, he received a further 90 days' loss of remission. By contrast, in the view of Thomas and Pooley,[33] there is substantial evidence to the contrary gathered by the PROP Inquiry two years later. The fact that some prisoners saw no evidence of injury to the prisoner was due to the 'Don't Mark his Face' strategy of his assailants. It was also due to the severe penalties attached to any prisoner who committed the offence of giving 'false and malicious' testimony against prison officers. Simply finding any allegations against a prison officer unfounded was deemed proof of this offence, which carried severe penalties. The loss of remission, earnings and recreation can amount to months if not years of extra imprisonment or loss of privileges. The Prescott Report (not seen, and not published, though privately circulated at the time) is non-committal on this point.

The next development was that 70 or so prisoners assembled in the Emergency Control centre and demanded to speak to the allegedly victimised prisoner. At this point, the absence of the governor, a recent appointee, was clearly critical, as the Assistant Governor Class II, the person left in charge of the prison, refused their request, a decision which the governor endorsed by phone. Major James, a witness at the subsequent trial of several prison officers, and a member of the official inquiry, stated in the magistrates' court that 'it was a totally wrong decision and a calamitous decision to put an Assistant Governor Class II in charge of B Wing on the Friday night and Saturday morning.' He was subsequently charged, and acquitted, of failing to prevent the beatings inflicted on prisoners after the riot by the prison officers who were so convicted.[34] Even the official report was critical of this decision, citing an earlier incident when just such a situation had arisen and a delegation of prisoners had been allowed to speak to the alleged victim, had established that no victimisation had occurred, and potential trouble had been forestalled. In this instance, the refusal may be explained by the acting governor's fear, or even knowledge, that an assault on the prisoner had indeed occurred. The result of the refusal was a rapid escalation of the prisoners' action. They proceeded to occupy three of the four wings of the prison, one of which, C Wing, they re-entered via the roof after prison staff had retaken it.

In the early hours of the morning of 1 September, a further escalation occurred when the prisoners discovered files relating to their cases. The riot really erupted when records and reports were read. In the words of one prisoner at the scene: 'As a result one must look at the extensive damage to the prison. Since the age of 13, and I am now 26, I have been sentenced to a total of 20 years in institutions[35] but in that time I have never come across such unified hatred owing to the reading of words. What was written by 'unqualified amateur psychologists' was sickening to say the least . . . The demonstration just erupted into a riot, I don't think it was premeditated. In my opinion, it wasn't an escape attempt.'[36] The Fowler Inquiry report also stated that the reading of the files was 'the real trigger to the devastation' (para. 149). What prisoners resented in particular was the bandying about of terms like 'psychopath', 'misfit' etc., and the ascribing of evil intent to every friendship between prisoners.[37] Fowler enters a defence of such 'frank' record keeping as essential for parole and disciplinary matters.

What was unleashed was a bout of sustained fury in which, over the next two days, prisoners left the prison 'very badly wrecked' (para. 175). By the late evening of 31 August, all risk of escape, whether mass or individual, had been forestalled by police securing the perimeter, prison staff drafted in from Leeds and Wakefield, and all available Hull staff recalled to the prison. Some officers were released from having been trapped in D Wing for 24 hours. Damage was so extensive that the repair estimates amounted to £750,000.[38] However, despite some injuries, and the risk of fatalities from prisoners hurling slates from the roofs, no serious injuries were sustained by staff, prisoners or onlookers. Surrender began on Day 4 and was completed by 4.00 p.m. 235 prisoners, not all of whom had been active in the riot, were transferred to 13 other prisons. 75 remained in B Wing, 'which was, of course, the only habitable wing' (para 211).

The aftermath of the riot took several forms and phases. The immediate result was the calling for an official inquiry and the disciplining of prisoners allegedly most involved in causing the riot and leading it on. Some two years later came the trial, the first one for two centuries, of prison officers, 12 in all, eight of whom were convicted of assaulting prisoners. They received suspended prison sentences of between four and ten months. From the outset also came the debate and rancour on causes and how far, if at all, the nature of the dispersal system could be held responsible for so devastating a sequence of hostilities. It is on this point that we shall now focus.

The Chief Inspector of Prison Services could be in no doubt about the weight of opinion in the prison services themselves against the dispersal system and its responsibility for the turmoil in dispersal prisons. The POA wrote to him on 8 October 1976 listing the grievances arising from the riot. The catalogue of salient issues to be discussed included, along with 'the scale of provision of riot gear', the possible reintroduction of the control units and a review of policy relating to Cat. A and long-term imprisonment, with special reference to 'any residual build-up of subversive inmates in dispersal prisons.'[39]

Evidence by the Prison and Borstal Governors Branch (of the Society of Civil and Public Servants) on the Hull riot was even more explicit. 'From the outset governors have had doubts about the wisdom of accepting the dispersal of high risk prisoners. The presence of a serving governor on the ACPS may have aided a better solution . . . The Hull riot was a dramatic example of the wholesale chaos created when one part of the system gets out of control. It would be less worrying if the Hull riot was an isolated instance of severe disorder. But the sad fact is that Hull represents only the tip of the iceberg, as events at other dispersal prisons have shown . . . The ill-fated control units were not given a real chance to prove or disprove their worth, and the manner of their hasty demise casts serious doubt on the Department's resolve to tackle the problem fearlessly. We are therefore persuaded that the time has come for the dispersal policy to be subject to a fundamental review.

We do not view concentration as the only alternative and a mixture of concentration and a better managed dispersal appeals to us as a possible solution.'[40]

The official report, nevertheless, came down firmly for the dispersal system to be retained, whilst conceding the case for a review of its administration. In the process of exonerating dispersal, blame had to be allocated elsewhere and, in Fowler's view, that pointed to the changing nature of society, reflected in changes relating to staff and prisoners in the deepest end of the system. Part IV of the Report, 'The Dispersal System and the Causes of the Riot', whilst arguing uncontentiously that 'no single cause but a number of contributory and predisposing factors' led to the riot (para 249), placed a potentially damaging stress on the core elements of the principles of dispersal: '. . . the more sophisticated prisoner of today comes into prison armed with formidable knowledge concerning the law, civil rights and the legislation touching on imprisonment. He challenges every-thing that smacks of restriction and now realises that he has powerful allies among the pressure groups outside who believe that prison is an anachronism and should be replaced by non-custodial forms of treatment . . . The widely held view within the Prison Service is that if the present trend towards liberalisation continues it will become increasingly difficult to attract men and women of the right calibre into the Service.' Moreover, 'the pecking order' in a dispersal prison means that 'enlisting the co-operation of the prisoner can result, in consequence, in appeasing the "big boys" to the detriment of the smaller fry who are exploited within their own culture.' (para 258). Yet the mixing of prisoners of differing security catego-ries was the hallmark of dispersal policy.

Such problems had been magnified at Hull where, in the words of the Chief Inspector, 'the previous Governor may have contributed to the instability of the Hull population for the best of reasons. He felt that Hull had achieved a tolerable *modus vivendi* in accordance with the Radzinowicz recommendations – a liberal regime within a secure perimeter. Thus, when he was asked to take some of the most difficult men in the system – prisoners who had been "turned away" from other dispersal prisons – he accepted them without demur in the belief that the staff at Hull could cope. At the same time, however, the Governor's ability to transfer difficult and dangerous men away from Hull was severely limited. In any event, transfer to where? Hull was seen by staff and prisoners as the end of the road . . .' Yet the capacity to transfer prisoners cast as 'subversives' was the major asset of the dispersal system compared with that of concentration. By placing his main emphasis on the need to review the *administration* of the dispersal system and its regime, Fowler – whose opinion carried the weight of his status as Chief Inspector of Prisons – was in key respects by-passing problems inherent in the policy itself.

This was the major criticism levelled at the official inquiry report by J.E. Thomas and Dick Pooley. Both had played roles, albeit minor and off-stage, in the events at Hull. Thomas, a former assistant prison governor and now a lec-turer at the University of Hull, was a close observer of events,[41] and Pooley, a founder member of PROP, had been an active onlooker of the riot from a nearby block of flats. His role was much castigated by Home Office officials and even seen as contributing to the trouble by encouraging rioters in the process of sur-render to persist in their protest. The post-riot inquiry by PROP was regarded with irritation by Home Office staff and in particular incensed the POA, who regarded any dealings with PROP as tantamount to a betrayal of their own position.

Their account and analysis of the riot finds the official report seriously want-ing for its exoneration of the dispersal system in generating the conditions which sparked the riot off. The major criticism, that dispersal spread the tensions associ-ated with maximum security conditions over 4,000 rather than 400 prisoners, was consistently brushed aside in official responses, as was the cost of such measures compared with that of a single, or even two Alvingtons. For the secure perimeter did not permit the degree of liberalisation for which the Radzinowicz subcommit-tee had argued. At both Albany and Hull, the tightening of restrictions consequent

upon the mixing of different categories of prisoner was the prelude to disturbances and riot. The disturbances did not necessarily, in either case, emanate from
the Cat. A prisoners or the terrorists – it was the 'smaller fry' who were as much
involved as the 'big boys'. Thomas and Pooley indeed express much sympathy
for prison officers in their attempt to square the circle of liberal policies within
a perimeter so secure that escape is ruled out. Prisoners undergo goal displacement, pushing the boundaries within the prison itself. Security measures come
to be pursued with a zeal that militates against the welfare role liberal reformers
upheld in principle. Such arguments were to be made against dispersal, yet again,
to the May Committee, but were again to be firmly rejected. The Home Office was
determined to adhere to it, come what may.

## Coda

Following his release from prison in 1979, Michael Williams brought an action
against the Home Office,[42] claiming damages from the ministry for, *inter alia,*
false imprisonment and the infliction of 'cruel and unusual punishment'. He was
encouraged to do so, notably by PROP, the radical penal reform group,[43] and by
the National Council for Civil Liberties, whose legal officer, Harriet Harman,[44]
acted on Williams's behalf. Though the action was dismissed, the wide and critical coverage of the case raised concerns which went far to ensure that in future
units to deal with 'difficult' prisoners would be set up to avoid so illiberal a
regime.[45]

The first hearing, on 17 and 29 January 1980, under Judge McNeill, was taken
up with the plaintiff's claim for disclosure of 23 documents, a small part of a total
of 6,800 pages that were disclosed, withheld by the Home Office on grounds relating to the formulation of policy, and therefore subject to public interest privilege.
The judge held that six documents should be released as sufficiently germane to
the plaintiff's case for inspection despite being related at different points to communication by and with ministers on the formulation of policy. The remaining 17
should not be disclosed, including a note from the Parliamentary Undersecretary
of State, Dr. Shirley Summerskill, to the Secretary of State, Roy Jenkins, dated
6 November 1974, and detailing her visit to the unit at Wakefield Prison and her
meeting with the prisoner. This should be withheld on grounds of 'freedom of
expression between ministers at all times' (p. 1155).

The main hearing on 25–29 February, March and 9 May 1980, under Judge
Tudor Evans, ended with his dismissal of the array of claims made by Michael
Williams against the Home Office as lacking substance and harbouring the potential, if upheld, to render the prison system unworkable. Thus, for example, the
claim for damages for false imprisonment in respect of the 180-day period he
spent in the unit was based on rule 43 (2) which required a review at the end of
one month and monthly thereafter. 'The fact that the control unit committee had
not complied with r 43 (2) did not affect the lawfulness of the plaintiff's detention
in the unit.' (p. 1212) In other words, a technical breach had occurred due to the
automatic renewal of the prisoner's detention in the control unit but this did not

amount to rendering it 'unlawful'. In sum, the judge argued that the system, but not the rights of the prisoner, had been abused!

A second instance concerned the charge that the regime imposed on Michael Williams (and the other two prisoners in the unit) was 'cruel and unusual', as staff were deliberately remote and impersonal in their relations with him; no association with the other prisoners in the unit was allowed during the first 90-day period; and monthly visits (half the normal allowance) were vitiated by overly intrusive staff surveillance. These charges were rebutted on the written evidence of staff and by Brian Emes, on behalf of the Home Office, that conditions in the control unit were no worse than those in segregation units[46]; that not only prison staff but also Boards of Visitors and medical staff interacted frequently with him; and that in the second 90-day period in the unit, when association with the two other prisoners was allowed, Williams 'forewent the opportunity' to mix with them.[47] 'History sheets' (not yet discovered in the course of this research) kept by staff recorded Williams as 'laughing and joking' with warders, an image redolent of the 'holiday camp' stereotype of prisons beloved of the tabloid press: '24.12.74 The usual Williams today, always a laugh and a joke. Declined assoc. 21.1.75. Continues to amble his way through his time here . . .'[48]

A quite separate account by John Masterson, a prisoner in the unit at the same time as Williams, stated that a change in the unit's regime did occur, which helps explain some of the seeming inconsistencies in accounts of prisoner/staff relations.[49] Masterson had been transferred in 1974 from Hull Prison to Strangeways Prison, Manchester, and then to the new control unit in Wakefield Prison, without having been told why or where he was being transferred. The regime was 'quite unlike anything Masterson had experienced . . . What made the unit different were the "head game tricks" used on the inmates: the constant presence of numbers of officers, their silence, their stance, their harassing tactics.

If you did ask a question, they just blanked you, as if you were mad. Just stared past you or went into the Home Office stance as I call it – sticking their chests out, heavy breathing, legs apart. This was all for the psychological effect when you got back in the cell. Then you started tearing your mind apart.

The first sign that adverse criticism was having an effect on the prison authorities was a relaxation of the rules.

Before it was exposed, before the back-pedalling began, and after it was exposed – in a way it was like two different worlds. Take an instance: they used to strip-search us, never less than three times a week they used to come in, strip us bollock-naked, touch your toes, search your body, right? . . . once it had been mentioned in the newspapers, they done it once and then finished it, no more strip-searches the rest of our stay there. When the papers caused all that stink, then a few people started coming around taking a bit of interest. Then we were allowed to talk.'

The first to visit the unit was Shirley Summerskill, at that time Parliamentary Undersecretary of State at the Home Office. The unit had been spruced up for her visit, including a toilet door fitting, with staff now showing every sign of a relaxation of the atmosphere to offset press reports of sensory deprivation. But the underlying reality was still, in Masterson's view, as that of Williams, to practise a new methodology of mind control.

The governor's journals for the period of the control unit's operation,[50] though completely unrevealing about the actual operation of the regime and its effects on the prisoners, confirm a growing sense of urgency in dealing with adverse publicity and demonstrations outside the prison gates. The first intimation of outside interest was on 2 October 1974: 'Saw Mrs. Whittaker,[51] who had been contacted by the Howard League over Williams in the Control Unit. I advised her not to get involved directly with the Howard League, but to inform them that the Home Office was dealing with the matter.' On 8 October, two days after the Insight team report, he records: 'General paper work in the afternoon and discussion about the Control Unit which has recently received publicity and ill-founded criticism in the Sunday Times and, to a lesser extent, Guardian.' A flurry of activity followed. On 10 October, he took part in an interview with a Sunday Times team. 'Their visit is in connection with a forthcoming article on long-term prisoners' and a press visit to the Control Unit was discussed with the Press Office. Two days later 'Mr. R. Dauncey, Deputy Regional Director visited the prison in the morning to see the new Control Unit'. On 23 October 'Asst. Gov. I.D. Allum addressed the Board about the Control Unit. Phone call from H.Q. stating that Dr. Shirley Summerskill will visit the prison on November 1st.' The visit duly took place: 'She was accompanied by Mr. Hewlings (Controller Operations), her private secretary and a principal information officer. We toured most parts of the prison including the control unit where the Minister interviewed all three prisoners individually.' This phase culminated in the entry for 14 November: '. . . morning mail contained copy of Parliamentary Written Answer by Home Secretary on modifications to certain administrative procedures in the Control Unit. I brought this to the attention of local P.O.A. and Senior Officer Glenville, in charge of the Control Unit today . . .'. Five days later he discussed 'proposed alterations in the control unit with the Deputy Governor – These were concerned with disciplinary awards and reversion in stage. Proposals went to the Regional Director . . .'

It would, however, be a mistake to assume that the control unit dominated the agenda day by day. The governor also had a maximum security prison to run, with a segregation unit containing many more prisoners than the control unit. Such events arose as that, also on 14 November, in which 'Today's Yorkshire Post carried a prominent front page article on Miss Ashe, a former part-time tutor at this prison: the article was headed "Jail Tutor Sacked Over I.R.A. Leaflet Smuggling". This article sparked off a hum of activity with the National Press and Press Office and I spent most of the day intermittently on the phone with the Press Office discussing how to deal with the incident . . .'. No such heightened activity appeared in his journal concerning control unit coverage.

On Thursday 12 December came 'a phone call from H.Q. advising that there is likely to be a demonstration by R.A.P.[52] outside the prison on Saturday. Local police and security informed to take usual measures.' There was no mention of the control unit as the target for protest but it seems the most likely reason. However, two days later '. . . The projected R.A.P. demonstration proved to be a non-event. Five students from Sheffield University arrived at about 12.30 p.m. but left immediately.'

Further demonstrations were to take place some months later. On 2 April 1975, a small group of Scientologists handed in a letter 'at the end of their half hour vigil. It was a very peaceful affair.' On 19 July, two demonstrators 'stood outside the prison entrance and the woman hurled abuse at members of staff as they left or entered the prison. This was the expected demonstration against the CU.' On 26 July, a larger demonstration was mounted by R.A.P. 'About 30 persons attended, some with banners. They handed out . . . leaflets protesting about the CU . . . entirely peaceful and dispersed at about 2.15 p.m . . . No sign of any internal demonstration.'

Such demonstrations could be brushed aside, but criticisms in the press clearly posed more of a challenge. By mid-April, the original three prisoners had been released from the unit and a hiatus occurred before three more were assigned to it in mid-July. It appeared that the unit's survival was no longer in doubt. However, on 11 September, the governor recorded a visit by Mr. W.A. Brister, Assistant Controller of P5 Division [responsible for security policy]. The Control Unit 'appears yet again in the National Press in critical terms and I spent a long time on the telephone with the Press Office correcting the usual inaccuracies in reporting.' On Monday 15 September, '. . . Discussed with Tilbury of the Press Office another article on the CU in the Guardian – these articles become more bizarre as the weeks go by!'[53] A month later, on 16 October, the governor recorded 'A scurrilous article in today's Guardian on CU's.' The following day, he discussed with governor grades 'the implications of a particularly scurrilous letter in the Guardian on the CU.' That letter was signed by several doctors and psychiatrists. A week later, on 24 October, he recorded '. . . the Home Secretary will announce in the House this afternoon his decision to close the Control Unit . . .'.

Another criterion of the concern fuelling the adverse publicity was the range of visits to the Control Unit by M.P.s, academic criminologists and penal reformers. Thus, for example, on 10 January 1975, '. . . in the afternoon a party of visitors came to see the Control Unit. They were Mrs. A. Morris, Cambridge Institute of Criminology, Mr. Wright, Director, Howard League, and Mrs. M. Jones and Miss A. Wood of the Penal Affairs Committee, Society of Friends. The Regional Director was present throughout the visit.' Nothing at all, however, is recorded about their questions and concerns. On 22 January, the deputy governor discussed with D.R.D.'s secretary certain observations made by Martin Wright following his visit to the CU . . .' but no record is made of their substance. On 31 January, a week-long inspection of the prison ended with a meeting between the Chief Inspector and his team with the senior staff of the prison, though nothing of the discussion is recorded in the journal. On 7 April, Mr. R. Cryer, M.P. and Mr. M. Madden, M.P. visited the unit and spent the morning there. On 8 October, Dr. Shieler, Director of the Herstedvester Clinic in Denmark and Dr. Nigel Walker, Cambridge Institute of Criminology, visited the unit and discussed 'various points which they raised after a tour of the prison with the P.M.O. [Prison Medical Officer]'.

On 21 October, 'visited CU and spoke to Dr. Roger Hood, Mrs. McCabe and Mr. Steer, who were visiting the Unit from Oxford.' Again, no mention of what was discussed is recorded. Three days later, and with little prior warning, the Unit's immediate closure was announced by the Home Secretary.

As a liberal Home Secretary, Roy Jenkins had to field several awkward Parliamentary Questions in the course of the year's existence of the unit. Having made two changes to the original regime, namely to stipulate that the board of visitors of the holding prison should authorise any prisoner's transfer to the unit, unless overruled by him personally, and that automatic reversion could be waived by the governor and board of visitors at Wakefield prison, his answer to PQs was to refer back to those changes. Thus he replied on 21 November 1974, to Bob Cryer, M.P.,[54] who had asked if reviews of the control unit were planned. But Cryer persisted by raising the issues of the length of solitary confinement in the unit, possible breach of the 1964 Prison Regulations, and damage to any prospect of rehabilitation. The latter point was taken up also by Leo Abse, M.P., a formidable voice on penal affairs due to his membership of the Advisory Council on the Penal System subcommittee, chaired by Professor Leon Radzinowicz, which had recommended the dispersal system policy in 1968. Other Labour M.P.s later to attack the unit's regime or to call for its termination included Christopher Price[55] and Gerald Hooley and the Liberal M.P. Alan Beith. On 17 July, Bob Cryer pressed for its termination. Though its rationale, to insulate the prison system from the most 'disruptive' prisoners, was defended by the Home Secretary and other M.P.s, mostly Conservative, the regime was not.

Throughout the Unit's existence, and in the later action for damages brought by Michael Williams, the Home Office response to the welter of criticism of its regime was to rebut any such charge. Thus, control units were intended as 'regulatory' rather than 'punitive'. The regime was no more austere than that of segregation units, so could be designated neither 'cruel' nor 'unusual'. The 1688 Bill of Rights was not breached by lawful imprisonment, and imprisonment conferred the right on the part of the state to effect transfers and regime changes without explanation or reasons being given, insistence on which would render prisons unworkable. The comparison drawn in evidence with comparable regimes in Canada and the USA by Professor (Laurie) Taylor and Dr. J.E. Thomas were inappropriate due to differences in sentence lengths which were far greater in that country. 'But above all, they [the comparable North American prisoners] were in the unit, on the whole, for very much longer periods. The plaintiff *McCann* spent a total of 1,471 days in the unit, of which the longest continuous period was 754 days. Another plaintiff, named Oag, spent 682 days in the unit, of which 573 were continuous. The prisoners were locked in their cells for twenty-three and a half hours a day'.[56] Such units had now been outlawed as constituting unacceptably inhumane regimes. Nevertheless, the judge deemed the Wakefield unit regime 'was not cruel' by comparison.[57] Claims for damages due to the plaintiff were therefore rejected.

In a further argument against the plaintiff's case, the judge cited what he regarded as a contradiction between Dr. J.E. Thomas's support for the 'fortress' prison proposed by the Mountbatten report for the detention of long-term, dangerous prisoners, which was not adopted due to its 'inevitably repressive nature', and his opposition to the regime of the control unit. 'Presumably, therefore, Dr. Thomas would not regard the rejected regime of the "fortress" as cruel, and yet he condemns the regime at Wakefield.'[58] The judge's equation of the liberal regime envisaged by Mountbatten with that of the demonstrably harsh control unit was not only highly contentious but showed the enduring importance of the 'concentration' versus 'dispersal' issue.

It was, however, the charge that the control unit rationale entailed sensory deprivation that went furthest to discrediting the regime so dramatically that its existence was limited to barely one year, and only three prisoners at any time in the only such unit, no more than six in all throughout its duration, instead of the 20 or so envisaged for each of several units. To Brian Emes,[59] the unit's closure was due not only to sustained adverse publicity, but also to the disproportionately high cost of maintaining so expensive a facility for far fewer prisoners than planned. The reason for that, he believed, was the need, which he himself had emphasised as director of P5 division, to screen out psychologically disturbed prisoners as unsuitable for so austere a regime.

Sensory deprivation is difficult to quantify, but in all likelihood the regime fell just short of its full implementation. The withholding of information and the constant threat of reversion to stage one, day one, in the event of some ill-defined rule violation, were probably the most unsettling and, over time, psychologically corrosive components. The judge and Home Office witnesses made much of the refusal of Michael Williams to associate with his fellow prisoners in stage 2, when such association became permissible. But Williams's explanation for that, that he had by then been rendered too paranoid to face such interaction, was arguably dismissed too readily by Judge Tudor Evans. All in all, the irony was that the control unit fiasco had been founded, and foundered, on a fallacy: that good order in prisons is best accomplished and sustained by an extreme form of solitary confinement.[60] It is at least to the credit of senior Home Office staff that that lesson began to be acted on in the next two decades.

## Conclusion

Events in the 1970s belied the hopes of both Home Office ministers and reform-minded civil servants that the liberal developments of the 1960s would work to good effect, whether to stem the rise in the prison population, or to manage the problem of those prisoners who presented either control and/or security risks, or both. The high expectations about 'dispersal' had run into difficulties some had foreseen due to imposing maximum security conditions on ten times as many prisoners as the 'concentration' alternative would have allowed. Adopting that alternative was, however, steadfastly rejected by the Home Office and by the May Committee, set up in 1978 to inquire, in effect, into the state of the penal realm, whose report is discussed in the next chapter. This is not to say that adoption of the Mountbatten alternative would have fared substantially better. The so-called 'fortress' prison would not have been designed to cope with high-risk 'control' rather than 'security' prisoners, though it would have removed the problems of 'over-security' for non-Category A prisoners held in dispersals. Also, the emergence of problems that arose only after the Mountbatten and Radzinowicz reports, especially the issue of containing those convicted of Irish 'terrorist' crimes on the mainland, was seen as a strong argument for dispersal. '. . . he (Radzinowicz) was sufficiently influential in the Home Office and fortunately people were prepared to buck Mountbatten . . . Just you think what it would have been like when the Troubles started if we'd only had one establishment to put all the IRA' was the verdict of a senior Home Office official and former prison governor, Brian Emes.[61] King and Morgan, by contrast, saw IRA prisoners, who were self-styled 'political' prisoners, as presenting – for that very reason – both control *and* security problems that made them more suitable for being held in 'special security' wings, rather than either dispersal or a single 'fortress' prison.[62]

The major effect of the control unit fiasco – 'Well, probably worse than a fiasco', according to a senior Home Office member of that time, Anthony Langdon[63] – and especially the case brought by Williams for damages, despite its rejection in the High Court, was to strengthen the hand of those within the Home Office who sought a radical change of direction in penal policy in general, and specialist units in particular. As King and Morgan stated presciently[64]: '. . . the very fact that the case was brought, and the nature of the evidence admitted, is bound to affect future Prison Department policy. First, the Home Office has been forced to reveal documents, including memoranda prepared for ministers by senior civil servants, connected with the planning of control units. The secrecy with which the Home Office has typically shrouded its activities has been dealt a major blow. Secondly, the evidence has called into question whether the day-to-day operation of the Wakefield control unit was in accordance with directions formulated by headquarters. Matters relating to the accountability of institutional staff, and what kinds of watchdog bodies are appropriate, have thus been brought to the fore.' One might go further and see, in the travails of the prison riots and abortive programmes to resolve them of the 1970s, the elements of a new era in the making of penal policy. But what emerged was to be not so much notional 'positive treatment' called for by the May Committee as an agenda for basic decency in the character of imprisonment. Foremost in that agenda was the creation of the May Committee's most important recommendation, a truly independent prison inspectorate.[65]

## Notes

1 HO391/147 [P.B. (68) 14].
2 From G. Emerson to Philip Woodfield, copied to Hyde and the D.P.A., Philip Woodfield had been secretary of the Mountbatten Inquiry. Mountbatten wrote that he did 'a superlative job as the Secretary of my Commission, ably assisted by Dick Jones. These two know more about the appalling state of the Prison Service than anybody else in the Home Office today.' (letter to Sir James Mackay, Deputy Undersecretary of State, Home Office, 28 December 1966 – Mountbatten Papers, Prison Security correspondence 1966–71, University of Southampton. MB1/N 84 A).

3  by K.J.Neale, 23 March 1968.

4  The terms stood for Prison Department 2 (treatment and training), Prison Department 3 (convicted adult male prisoners, and hence those needing high security), the Directorate of Prison Medical Services, and the Directorate of Industries and Supply.

5  R. King and K. Elliott, 1977, *Albany: birth of a prison –ß end of an era,* London: Routledge & Kegan Paul.

6  Isle of Wight *County Press*, 11 November 1967, repr. In the *Prison Service Journal*, cited ibid: 24.

7  Hansard, Vol. 770, cols. 333–4.

8  Formed largely by ex-offenders and former prisoners to act as a trade union for prisoners, the strike 'was the high point of PROP's visibility . . . around this time, PROP faded away as a cohesive national union.' Mick Ryan, 2003, *Penal Policy and Political Culture in England and Wales*, Winchester: Waterside: 52. It went on to develop a significant role as a penal lobby throughout the 1970s. To Arthur de Frisching, a former prison governor and Home Office Prison Department member, it influenced the field 'hugely. I mean the whole notion that, you know, prisons were no longer able to be run as wholly autocratic institutions in which the staff were in charge, the prisoners were entirely passive and would do what they were told, was open to question.' Interview, 6 January 2012.

9  'Prison, A Human Problem', Mountbatten Papers, University of Southampton.

10  From *Some Notes on Albany Prison* left by Brian Howden for his successor as governor, Gifford Footer.

11  Rule 43 could be invoked to segregate two quite distinct categories of prisoner: first, those deemed a threat to 'good order and discipline' (GOAD), and/or secondly, those seen as in need of protection for their own good. The Woolf Report (discussed in Ch. 6) in particular criticised its application to two such different categories of prisoner. See S. Livingstone and T. Owen, 1999, *Prison Law*, 2nd edition: Ch. 10, note 6.

12  Confirmed by Robert Morris in interview, 10 August 2010: 'Nothing that happened in the riots . . . shook the policy on dispersal because it was quite clear that the view in the Prison Department then was that dispersal was the right policy. And certainly I agree with that wholly. It did seem to me you were asking for a lot of trouble if you put all your bad eggs you could identify in one place. And that it was one of the dottier proposals that came out of the Mountbatten Committee and somehow or other it had to be seen off and it was seen off, right, before anybody spent treasure on Vectis, what it was going to be called.' Robert Morris was secretary to the UK Prisons Inquiry (May Committee) 1978–9. His career at the Home Office 1961–97 included periods as Principal Private Secretary to the Home Secretary 1976–8 and Head of the Crime Policy Planning Unit 1979–81.

13  HO 391/228 [PDG 68 174/4/58]. No copy of the original report has yet been traced.

14  The equivalent would be £1,383,096 in 2014 prices.

15  'The end of the road' concept seems to have been used throughout, especially in relation to the Mountbatten proposal for an impregnable 'fortress' to hold the highest escape risks, to signify incontestably oppressive and self-defeating consequences for both prisoners and staff. Alternative images, such as the relatively 'safe haven' such a terminus could represent in a liberal yet well-controlled regime, was never raised. One possible model would have been the Barlinnie Special Unit (see p. 16 and Ch. 4 below). And Mountbatten explicitly factored in the need for key staff to be rotated between the Isle of Wight prisons.

16  HO 391/228 Doc. 9, WPDC Report, paras. 123–8.

17  HO 391/227 Cat. A Prisons – Dispersal – Control Units Regime.

18  Control Units – Wakefield and Wormwood Scrubs/P5 Div./25/4/73 PDG/68 174/4/55.

19  PDG/68 174/4/78

20  SCMIC (Subcommittee B) (73/3)

21  P5 GMBO PDG/68 174/4/78

22 HO 391/444.

23 Stanley Cohen and Laurie Taylor's *Psychological Survival: The Experience of Long-Term Imprisonment*, a study of long-term prisoners in the H Wing of Durham Prison, was highly critical of its regime and conditions, and censured by the Home Office for publication without official permission. It had been published by Penguin Books in 1972.

24 PDG/74 197/1/2.

25 A search was made of the relevant governor's journals in the Wakefield prison archive held at the Ministry of Justice.

26 Interview with Martin Wright, 6 June 2014.

27 Jimmy Boyle, 1977, *A Sense of Freedom*, Edinburgh, Canongate; 1984, *The Pain of Confinement: Prison Diaries*, Edinburgh, Canongate. Boyle's artistic status was based on his sculpture as well as his books.

28 David Leigh, 'How Ministry hardliners had their way over control units', The Guardian, 8 April 1980. Cited in Andrew Rutherford (1986) *Prisons and the Process of Justice,* Oxford University Press: 111.

29 P2 Division concerned treatment and training, P5 security and discipline.

30 Andrew Rutherford (1986) *Prisons and the Process of Justice*, Oxford University Press: 111.

31 Quoted in Rutherford, loc. cit. She successfully appealed against the verdict at the European Court of Human Rights.

32 *Report of an Inquiry by the Chief Inspector of the Prison Service into the cause and circumstances of the events at H.M. Prison Hull during the period 31 August to 3 September 1976*, 13 July 1977, HMSO 453; J. Prescott *Hull Prison Riot: Submissions, Observations and Recommendations of Mr. John Prescott, M.P., Hull East. Presented to Mr. G.W. Fowler, Chief Inspector of Prison Services*, unpubl.; *The Public Inquiry into the Hull Prison Riot*, PROP: 97 Caledonian Road, London N1, 1978.

33 J.E. Thomas and Richard Pooley (1980) *The Exploding Prison: Prison Riots and the Case of Hull*, London: Junction Books. The Preservation of the Rights of Prisoners (PROP) was founded jointly by a group of ex-prisoners and radical criminologists in 1972 to act as a trade union on behalf of prisoners.

34 Ibid: 110–11.

35 Some were presumably still to be served.

36 Extract number 28 from prisoners' statements to the official inquiry.

37 Thomas and Pooley: 60.

38 According to P7 (Division of Works) the damage would have been far worse but for the sheer solidity of the Victorian building. P7 and Prescott both recommended materials *other than* slates for reroofing.

39 Document 15, HO 413/39.

40 Document 32, ibid: December 1976: 3–4.

41 J.E. Thomas was also the author of the only significant study, at that point, of the history, character and culture of prison staff, which he saw as a 'study in alienation', due to the role conflict they experienced between their duties of care for and control of prisoners. See his *The English Prison Officer Since 1850: A Study in Conflict*, 1972, London: Routledge & Kegan Paul. See also Alison Liebling and David Price, *The Prison Officer*, 2001, Leyhill: Prison Service Journal, for an 'arguably less pessimistic' analysis of the modern prison officer's role, due to intervening changes.

42 Williams v Home Office, *All England Law Reports*, 1981, Queen's Bench Division, 1151–1161 and 1211–1248.

43 Brian Emes, who gave evidence on behalf of the Home Office at the hearings, commented in interview that 'Williams was a stalking horse for PROP'.

44 Harriet Harman subsequently became Labour MP for Peckham from 1982 onwards and Deputy Leader of the Labour Party in 2007.

45 See the chapter below, 'Getting to Grips'.

46 'Although segregation under Rule 43 is an administrative procedure, and is not (officially) intended as a punishment, this is nevertheless how it is viewed by those on the receiving end.' J. Cavadino and J. Dignan, (1992) *The Penal System*, London: Sage: 135.

47 Williams v Home Office, op. cit.: 1238.

48 Ibid.: 1239.

49 'Prison Control Unit Terror' in *Britain's State Within the State: A News Line Investigation,* 1982, London: New Park Publications: 106–114. *News Line* was the daily newspaper of the Workers Revolutionary Party.

50 The Governor's Journal for Wakefield Prison, Book Number 35 for 1/8/71 to 25/11/74, and Book Number 36 for 25/11/74 to 25/3/77 are held in store by the Ministry of Justice and not by the National Archive. The appointment of the incoming Governor, Major Oldfield, coincided with preparations for the new Control Unit.

51 A member of the Board of Visitors at the prison.

52 Radical Alternatives to Prison (RAP) was a British movement launched in 1970 committed to the abolition of imprisonment. Mainly a group of academics and practitioners, they were strongly influenced by the work of Louk Hulsman in the Netherlands and the Norwegian organisation KROM. See Thomas Mathiesen (1973) *The Politics of Abolition*, Oxford: Martin Robertson; and Mick Ryan (1978) *The Acceptable Pressure Group: Inequality in the Penal Lobby, a case study of the Howard League and Radical Alternatives to Prison*, Farnborough: Saxon House.

53 The article in question was on the front page of The Guardian, 15 September 1975: 'Fear on prison control units' by Gareth Parry. It reported a meeting agreed between eminent psychiatrists and prison medical authorities to discuss the implications of prison medical officers passing a prisoner as 'mentally and physically fit' before allocation to the unit. A comparison was drawn to Soviet abuses of psychiatry, and opened the question of the Royal College of Psychiatrists recommending against their members having anything to do with the running of the units. In that event, prison medical officers faced the prospect of losing their licence, leading to the inevitable closure of the units. Two prisoners, David Anslow and Walter Probyn, had reported traumatic experiences in the units, the latter at Wormwood Scrubs where the unit was somewhat misleadingly, 'said to have been dismantled'. Two leading psychiatrists, Dr. Harold Meraskey of the National Hospital and Professor Alex Jenner of Sheffield University were to meet the director of prison medical services, Dr. Ian Pickering and the medical officer for Wakefield. Pickering was quoted as saying 'There has been a deal of misunderstanding about the units.' Nevertheless, the report's most salient point was that 'Many leading psychiatrists now believe that there is evidence indicating the possibility of real sensory deprivation of a degree which could do serious harm, precipitating psychotic symptoms in previously sane individuals.'

54 Robert Cryer, (1934–1994), Labour MP for Keighley, 1974–83 and a notable left-libertarian campaigner. See the obituary by Tam Dalyell, *The Independent*, 13 April 1994.

55 Christopher Price, Labour MP for Lewisham West 1974–83, was notable for his role in reopening the Maxwell Confait case which proved influential in the creation of the Crown Prosecution Service. See Paul Rock, Vol. II, of this history.

56 Williams v Home Office (No 2), op. cit.: 1246.

57 Ibid.

58 Ibid.

59 In interview, 12 July 2012.

60 For a succinct analysis of the history and effects of solitary confinement, see Sharon Shalev (2008) *A Sourcebook on Solitary Confinement*, London: Mannheim Centre of Criminology, London School of Economics, who comments (personal communication, 29 December 2014): 'Michael Williams's refusal to associate when offered

the opportunity to do so may be indicative of his deteriorated state of mind. I have recently interviewed several prisoners who have spent long stretches in segregation/ close supervision units who are similarly reluctant to associate when given the opportunity. A number of 'old school' guys explained that refusing to associate (with some even refusing to take outdoor exercise) is also to do with regaining some control where they otherwise have precious little control and that they prefer not to have anything which can then be taken away from them . . .' The Wakefield control unit in its original state seems to have conformed most closely to the concept of 'impoverished solitary confinement regimes' op.cit: 47–49; or 'reduced sensory input', about which see her *Supermax: Controlling Risk through Solitary Confinement*, Willan, 2009: 193–95. The Wakefield regime lacked such features as masking, hooding or 'white noise' that characterise regimes based on sensory deprivation.

61  In interview with DMD, 12 July 2012.
62  King and Morgan, 1980, op. cit.: 92–94.
63  Interview with Anthony Langdon and Tony Pearson, 15 November 2011.
64  1980, op. cit.: 207.
65  See Chapter 7 below.

# 4 Getting to Grips

## Penal policy from May to Langdon

### Introduction

The 1970s proved another turbulent decade for the prison service, the background to which was that the average daily prison population had climbed steeply by a third, from 30,421 in 1965 to 39,028 in 1970. A study by Richard Sparks published in 1971 was entitled *The Crisis in Local Prisons,* the sector under growing stress due to numbers increasingly outstripping capacity. His study of the case of Birmingham prison exemplified that of local prisons as a whole:

> 'In one sense, then, the men who make up the resident population of the general locals[1] . . . are thus the *lumpenproletariat* of the whole English penal system . . . Indeed . . . for many prisoners the general local prison *is* the English prison system . . . Yet the general local prisons are also the most neglected sector (as well as the biggest) of the English penal system.' Sparks 1971: 90).

The neglect largely stemmed from the extent to which the numbers of prisoners exceeded prison capacity, the deficit being entirely laid at the gates of the locals, where overcrowding (two or three to a cell intended for single occupancy) had been allowed to proliferate for well over a decade.[2] For example, in 1967 a Certified Normal Accommodation (CNA) of 23,247 in the locals held 26,909 adult male prisoners, a shortfall of 3,662 places, and masking a *surplus* of several hundred places in the rest of the system: the shortfall in the locals was well over 4,000 (Sparks, Table II. 1: 10). Moreover, that spelt steadily increasing overcrowding in the local prisons over the relatively recent past, lending weight to the experience of prison officers that their role was increasingly custodial and less welfare-oriented than had then seemed imminent. From 1967 to 1979, the general prison population rose from 35,009 to 42,210, a slower rate of rise than in the 1960s but in the face of substantial attempts to reduce it: parole and suspended sentences, the new Community Service Orders and warnings from Roy Jenkins in particular who, as Home Secretary for a second term, said in 1975: 'The prison population now stands at over 40,500. It has never been higher. If it should rise to, say, 42,000, conditions in the system would approach the intolerable, and drastic action to relieve the position would be inescapable. We are perilously close to that position now. We must not just sit back and wait for it to happen. If we can prevent it, we must do so.'[3]

Overcrowding, however, was the apparent rather than the principal cause of the industrial disputes which came to plague the prison service in the 1970s. Staffing had kept pace with the rise in the prison population, and cell sharing was not necessarily unwelcome to prisoners. What had changed was the growing militancy of prison officers and their union, the Prison Officers Association (POA).[4] The growth in militancy was fuelled by several developments.[5] First, the paramilitary tradition which animated prison officers' working lives, and which emphasised discipline, hierarchy and the acceptance of authority, became increasingly out of kilter with the growth of industrial and political militancy in the larger society. Secondly, the paramilitary tradition was seen by penal reformers and administrators alike as having been an obstacle to the adoption of reformative goals from the Gladstone Committee of 1895 onwards. That tradition had been weakened by the conflicting and confusing demands on prison officers to become more welfare-oriented without becoming overfamiliar with prisoners, due to the perceived risks of corruption and manipulation. 'But the vague aim of making prison officers quasi-social workers had an especially dysfunctional effect. For the attack on para-militarism led to its demise and there was no effective code of behaviour put in its place.' (Thomas in King and Morgan 1980: 147).

A source of both anxiety and resentment to prison officers was the emergence in 1972 of the embryonic prisoners' union Preservation of the Rights of Prisoners (PROP), an alliance between radical reformers, including academics, and prisoners. Two new movements combined to lend credibility to the PROP cause. First, the upsurge of concern for human rights in general[6] was taken up by campaigners in relation to prisoners. Secondly, radical criminologists, such as Ian Taylor, Paul Walton and Jock Young, authors of *The New Criminology* (1973),[7] saw prisoners as a key constituency for political mobilisation. The sequence of prison disturbances that took place in the early 1970s took the Prison Department by surprise: 'They had no policy to deal with it' (Arthur de Frisching).[8] As a result, things were left to the governors and staff locally. The staff reaction was therefore very assertive, with the POA calling for a more concerted Home Office response. This led to the establishment of a 'rewards and punishments' subcommittee in the Prison Department, The Home Secretary, Robert Carr, set up a working party on Control and Disturbances, chaired by Robert Cox. It was out of the latter group that the concept of Special Control Units took shape in what was to prove an extreme and short-lived form. (See Ch. 3 above)

Thus motivated to respond to the PROP phenomenon, the POA mounted a series of demands and strategies with which the Home Office contended somewhat irresolutely. The POA were especially infuriated whenever the Home Office seemed to give credence and credibility to the demands of PROP. A firmer line had come to be taken by 1976 when the Home Office vetoed a request by PROP for material for their own inquiry into the riot of Hull Prison. POA militancy had by then come to extend to an even wider range of issues and tactics, not least extensive resort to work to rule. For example: 'Prisoners have not been produced in court . . . new or repaired units of accommodation have not been manned, so accentuating overcrowding elsewhere.' (Thomas, in King and

Morgan, op.cit.: 149). By 1978, POA discontents had crystallised into a series of demands for better pay and conditions. The government could no longer react only 'on the hoof' to the deteriorating state of industrial relations in the prisons. On 17 November 1978, the Home Secretary, Merlyn Rees, appointed Mr. Justice May to head a wide-ranging inquiry into the prison services not only of England and Wales, but of the United Kingdom as a whole.

## A. The May Committee

The terms of reference of the May Committee were unusually wide, nothing less than into 'the state of the prison services in the United Kingdom', from the 'size and nature of the prison population and the capacity of the prison services to accommodate it' to 'the effectiveness of the industrial relations machinery . . . within the prison services'; 'the remuneration and conditions of service of prison officers, governors and other grades working only in the prison services, including the claim put forward by the Prison Officers' Association for certain "continuous duty credit" payments and the date from which any such payments should be made.' In interpreting their terms of reference, the Committee argued that 'although . . . we should concentrate on the organisational, resources, pay and industrial relations issues, it was equally plain we could not ignore wider criminal justice matters, despite the fact that our terms of reference did not ask us to make recommendations upon them.' (May Committee: 2). They were inextricably intertwined. Given that the Committee's brief included Northern Ireland and Scotland as well as England and Wales, it is not surprising that the report took about a year to complete, as distinct from the four and a half months which the Home Secretary, Merlyn Rees, had hoped for in view of the urgency of the pay dispute within the service. This had the effect of the report being delivered to the new Conservative government in 1979.

The bulk of the meticulous 337-page-long report is taken up by an analysis and suggested resolution of the pay and conditions of service issues which had plagued the prison service for a decade. A reasonable though not over-generous settlement resulted. But most attention was paid to the way in which the Committee came to its conclusions in three other respects. First, it argued against the idea, put most persuasively by Roy King and Rod Morgan,[9] that the opportunity should be seized to revert to the Mountbatten Report's proposal for concentration as distinct from dispersal as the way of dealing with the top security risk prisoners classified as category As. Secondly, it concluded, again *contra* King and Morgan, that 'treatment and training' should not be replaced by 'humane containment' as the fundamental principle governing regimes. The Committee made the case for prisons to be run on lines of 'positive custody', a modified version of 'treatment and training' but without undue expectations about what it might achieve. Thirdly, they recommended a truly independent inspectorate should be created which reported to the Home Secretary and, through him, to Parliament, as before. But the reports should be published and the appointment of Her Majesty's Chief Inspector of Prisons should be opened up to outside candidates. This recommendation was arguably the most important. The independence of the inspectorate became a crucial point of principle which underlay the growing importance of the published reports as a source of knowledge in public debate on the state of the prisons.

The independent inspectorate proposal was generally welcomed as an important and overdue recommendation, and was quickly implemented. Otherwise, the May Report was widely seen as disappointingly conservative, arguing for more of the same rather than for bold new initiatives. To penal reformers, 'positive custody' in particular was seen as a somewhat nebulous compromise between the rehabilitative principle that underlay 'treatment and training' and the case for a more radical interpretation of 'humane containment', to be based on the explicit recognition of rights rather than privileges and accountability in open rather than closed terms.[10] On somewhat different grounds, the POA saw the report as a great disappointment.[11]

This somewhat negative response did the May Report an injustice, for it broke new ground in distinct respects. First, it focused, for the first time in an official report of this kind, and endorsing the ACPS report on sentencing in 1978,[12] on the need to reduce the prison population not simply by providing more mechanisms for early release or community sentences, but by tackling the complex problems presented by 'petty persistent offenders' who were imprisoned in large numbers more for the persistence rather than the seriousness of their crimes. Secondly, it voiced the need, again for the first time in an official report of this character, to examine why and how comparable societies, such as Sweden and the Netherlands, managed to flourish despite a prison population far lower than that of the UK. Sentencing policy in a far broader sense than hitherto was pushed centre stage by a set of recommendations which set the scene for what, in the 1980s, became a central preoccupation of policymakers and penal reformers – how to reduce the prison population by a co-ordinated set of policies in relation not only to sentencing but also to crime prevention in both its situational and social forms.

### Concentration versus dispersal revisited

The most formidable evidence to the May Committee was that of Dr. Roy King, whose research into the dispersal prison at Albany, on the Isle of Wight, was discussed above (Ch. 2). King had long defended the Mountbatten proposal for a single maximum security prison, originally known as 'Vectis', with the possibility of a second such prison should numbers grow, as the best response to the acknowledged problems of some 250 prisoners, out of a total of over 40,000, in 1978, who held the potential for serious danger should they escape. The deferral and then rejection of that policy by the ACPS subcommittee chaired by Sir Leon Radzinowicz., in favour of a policy of dispersing Category A prisoners around several high security prisons which also held Categories B and C prisoners was mistaken in its conception but made even worse in practice by expanding the dispersal system and tightening security at every crisis. Yet the Prison Department 'seems determined to persevere.' (Dispersal Policy: Evidence from

Dr. King, para. 10, PSI (79) 46). The *economic* cost of dispersal, ostensibly an argument against 'Vectis' in 1967–8, has 'proved vastly more expensive' due to the growth of the dispersal system (seven dispersal prisons plus a dispersal wing and an eighth prison in the process of being built at a cost of £11.9 million), has been 'beyond all expectation'. 'Vectis' at the point of its abandonment was costed at £2.6 million (Hansard, Vol. 935, col. 184). By 1976 the Albany upgrade alone had cost £2 million. (Hansard Vol. 918, col. 523).

The *human* cost stemmed from the infliction of top security conditions on those Category B and C prisoners for whom it was not needed. The aim of dispersal was to achieve a liberal regime within a secure perimeter, but as the problem of control had grown, so the liberal regime 'has been whittled away' (King, para 19). In effect, there were now seven 'fortress' prisons instead of the one-two envisaged by Mountbatten. Dispersal in practice made a nonsense of classification, as 'once a prisoner is assigned to the dispersal system, he is subject to the same high degree of security and the same basic regime . . . as all others in the system.' (para. 21). Yet the growth of dispersal cannot be accounted for by the increase in the prison population as a whole, or of 'lifers' (following the abolition of the death penalty) or of long-term prisoners. The changes that have occurred have not been nearly enough to justify the over-use of maximum security, which has had the effect of heightening security throughout the system. Ironically, responsibility for this 'exaggerated concern' about security, caused by dispersal policy, has been 'wrongfully levelled against Mountbatten's proposal for concentration.' (para. 33). The system's failure to maintain discipline and control is demonstrable: the fact that 'the most serious eruptions of indiscipline in recent prison history have all occurred in the dispersal prisons – Parkhurst, Albany, Gartree and Hull – is surely no coincidence.' (para. 39).

The key problem to King was that neither Mountbatten nor Radzinowicz had adequately recognised the distinction between 'dangerous' prisoners, who embodied high escape potential, and those whose threat stemmed from their 'subversive' character. Radzinowicz had treated the latter as a 'residual' problem to be dealt with *ad hoc* by segregation units. The two groups overlap but are basically distinct. However defined, they are very small in number. Dispersal prisons, however, heightened the risk of 'subversive' control problems, mainly because the maximum security regime repressed all prisoners in them regardless of their categorisation, and because the 'small fry' short-termers had little, therefore, to lose by acting up to impress the 'big boys', 'hard men' etc. The Prison Department response to the riots amounted to tightening regimes even further; expanding the dispersal system even more, in part to allow more scope for transfers; and, *in extremis*, devising the 'infamous control units'. Category C prisoners were taken out of the system almost completely, thus negating the whole logic of the dispersal principle. All of which was contrary to the advice of the POA, who were by now resigned to the Prison Department 'persevering with their mistakes', but who nevertheless were more subjected, as were the prisoners, to the 'aggravated conditions' of high security prisons, than would have been the case under a policy of concentration.

The only defensible policy, even at this late stage, was to revert to a policy of concentration for the 'dangerous' escape risks and to what would have been, in effect, a policy of dispersal for the dangerous 'subversives'. This latter group should be classified during their initial allocation and sent to wings, halls or cells based on their 'subversive-enforcement quotient' (para 61). Thus troublesome prisoners could be separated from the rest without need for solitary confinement, segregation units, or a sanction-based regime unless their actual offence (within prison) demanded it. That framework would enable the escape risks to be accommodated in two Mountbatten standard prisons – without the anti-tank and underground passages he envisaged – which could be upgraded versions of two existing dispersals. King recommended Albany and Long Lartin as the best prospects. The rest could revert to being local prisons or for non-Category A lifers. The two Mountbatten prisons could hold all the existing 257 category A prisoners, as at January 1979, but could hold up to 400 if category Bs were in some cases reclassified in view of the policy change.

In its evidence to the May Committee, the Home Office reacted strongly to this frontal assault on its policy for high security risk and 'subversive' prisoners.[13] In reviewing the state of dispersal policy, 'our approach is to ask how the assets represented by the dispersal prisons can best be used for the future, rather than to engage, as does Dr. King, in a highly speculative and essentially historical assessment of what might have happened and what might have been the cost had a different decision been taken in 1968.' (p. 1). In a point by point rebuttal, it was argued that:

-   'The view that the history of the dispersal system is one of remarkable, unpredicted and unintended growth is erroneous.' All but one of the dispersal prisons had been planned from the acceptance of dispersal policy in 1968.' (p. 3).
-   'Security precautions in dispersal prisons are less expensive and extensive than Lord Mountbatten envisaged [for a single maximum security prison] yet have succeeded in preventing escapes'. [parenthesis added].
-   The number in dispersal prisons are less than Dr. King estimated, due to only one wing at Wormwood Scrubs being a dispersal prison. In February 1979, the CNA in the seven dispersal prisons was, therefore, 2,684, with an actual population of 2,255, not Dr. King's higher figures.
-   Allocation to Category A had become 'more selective over the years' despite the large number of IRA and UDA prisoners convicted of serious violence since 1973 and rising convictions in general for serious crime. *Contra* Dr. King's fear of grade inflation, the total number of Cat. As had 'remained reasonably stable at around the 240/250 mark' (pp. 8–9).
-   One 'fortress' prison would necessitate any surplus Category A prisoners being kept under very restrictive conditions in other prisons (p. 11).
-   *Contra* Dr. King, there were no grounds for thinking that Category Cs were part of the dispersal population.
-   It was not true that Category B prisoners alone could be housed in less secure accommodation. 'The security measures and the high staff/inmate ratio in the dispersal prisons are as necessary for many of the Category B prisoners as

for the category As. The record of the dispersal prisons in avoiding escapes has been extremely good, but there have been enough near misses involving Category B prisoners as well as Category A prisoners to make it abundantly clear that the security provision is not excessive for the kind of regime that is being operated.' (12–13)

- Dr. King's separation of escape risks from troublemakers in itself lends no support for his case, for problems of dealing with 'subversives' would remain in that case too. (19)
- King's cost argument is queried and rejected as 1968 costs are not applicable to the 1970s; also, the riots at Gartree and other dispersal prisons were not necessarily due to the presence of Category As. Therefore his whole argument is speculative and 'sterile'. (20–22)
- 'Regimes in dispersal prisons are in many ways better than those in non-dispersals, so they cannot be regarded as unduly repressive, and are often over-lenient in regard to personal possessions, work discipline and privileges as a result.'
- The lack of transfer possibilities is the clinching argument against a policy of concentration, especially as [since the Mountbatten Report was published][14] one-third of Category A prisoners are IRA, UDA or Arab terrorists, whose highly dangerous character would be heightened if held together. Dr. King is too dismissive of the risks involved, especially of an attack from *outside* the prison to assist escape.

These and other points against those put by Dr. King were in their turn subjected to a weighty critique in his response, submitted as further evidence to the Inquiry[15]:-

- The withdrawal of all but 40 Category C prisoners from dispersal prisons weakens the 'normalising' role, which was their chief justification originally;
- The inconsistencies involved in the numbers of Category Bs who are held to need maximum security conditions, yet are not seen as meriting Category A status;
- The fact that the original, potent imagery of concentration as equal to creating an 'Alcatraz' was now outdated in the USA itself, as Marion Prison in Illinois had now been built to take its place;
- The greater economy in adopting a policy of concentration in two prisons, which would be 'amply served' by adapting two existing dispersal prisons, e.g. Albany and Long Lartin, rather than its currently expanded state of having seven dispersal prisons, not three-four as originally envisaged;
- The inability of the system to cope with IRA and other terrorist prisoners under *either* policy framework led to the need to retain four Special Security Wings;
- The Home Office is effectively in denial about the need, even at this stage, to return to the Mountbatten proposal, which would not need to equate to an Alvington 'fortress-like' prison, but could be as suggested above;

- Dispersal prisons have been the site of the worst rioting 1970–73, though Category As were not the prime movers. 'This is especially ironic because the chief reason for adopting dispersal was because it was feared that the control problems under a concentration policy for high security risk prisoners would be insuperable.' (p. 13)
- However great the economic costs of dispersal, they are beside the point, which is 'the human costs of dispersal – regime restrictions, unwarrantable labelling effects, and knock-on effects throughout the prison system whereby security gets greater emphasis than it deserves." (1'3). This relates to an earlier point. 'The provision of maximum security accommodation, with its double perimeter, geophonic devices, electronic surveillance, alsatian dogs, high mast floodlighting and all the rest exercises a dominating all-embracing influence that far outweighs any fine distinctions that might apply to particular categories of prisoner within it.' (Pp. 5 and 4).
- All in all, he said, 'I am amazed at the complacent way in which the Home Office dismisses unpalatable arguments as speculative while it accepts others which are in no way less speculative, and at the way in which the Home Office ignores real evidence from research which it has itself funded.' (p. 1')

Despite this withering verdict on the existing system, the May Committee nevertheless on balance accepted the Home Office arguments for retaining the *status quo*, albeit for reasons to do with the strength of the case *against* concentration rather than those *for* dispersal. 'We have therefore concluded that the balance of argument is in favour of continuing with the present dispersal policy. Whatever the arguments in favour of concentration – and we acknowledge some raise important issues which no prison system should ignore – they do not in present operational conditions add up to justifying either a partial or a total reversal of dispersal policy (May Report, p. 137).

## B. The Control Review Committee

The next significant attempt to resolve the outstanding issues of security and control in the prison service was the report of the Control Review Committee (CRC),[16] set up in September 1983. Chaired by the Director of Operational Policy, Anthony Langdon, the committee had been appointed by the Home Secretary, Leon Brittan, probably in anticipation of disturbances following his changes to parole policy, which expanded parole for less serious offenders but restricted it, even retrospectively, for offenders imprisoned for serious violence. 'Very crudely, come the next riot, he might not get a very good press if it was alleged that he'd toughened the parole criteria and nobody had thought about the consequences. I've got no sort of evidence of that. I always just assumed that was the reason.' [Anthony Langdon].[17] That said, 'it came at a time of enormous uncertainty in the dispersal system . . . There had been a number of serious disturbances. And the dispersal system was a fairly fragile beast, actually, at that stage.' [Tony Pearson]

The continuing uncertainty about the wisdom of dispersal policy had not been resolved by the report of the May Committee. Arthur de Frisching, a member of the Control Review Committee and both a former prison governor and member of the Home Office Prison Department, commented 'the general point about May was that it was very badly received by the Prison Service . . . The contrast between the May Report and the Woolf Report was just chalk and cheese. So the May Report was perceived as not really having done anything hugely helpful . . . The May concept of positive custody fell completely flat.'[18] He went on to say that 'the whole question of control and security in the dispersal prisons remained a kind of running problem all the way through the 70s, right up into the 80s . . . But it was the Albany riot,[19] I think, that triggered Anthony Langdon saying, we need to have a much more deep-seated policy review, . . . think about how we deal with these difficult prisoners, particularly in dispersal prisons'. [ibid: 12].

This sharper focus led to a set of recommendations which began the process of reducing the size of the dispersal system while proposing ways of handling long-term prisoners presenting the most difficult problems as 'troublemakers'. Those ways built on past experience of what to conserve and what to avoid. It also opened the door to a return to the principle of concentration whilst settling the immediate cast of policy in favour of retaining a leaner dispersal system.

The committee addressed both immediate and longer-term issues with the combined hard-won experience of prison governors and seasoned administrators. The issue of what later would be termed 'perverse incentives' was exemplified by Tony Pearson (interview: 31): 'We were driven by frustration that all the negatives were negative incentives. You behaved badly, and you were rewarded, is principally what it was about.' The goal of a consistent progression of rewards and punishments became a chief recommendation, a primacy justified also by the experience gathered on a field visit to America, where Norman Carlson, the Director of the Federal Prisons, had instituted a system of 'earned privileges' which provided a model for 'a consistent progression or regression. But the uniform professional advice was that it would not be possible, given the constraints on the system, the huge population pressure no doubt was a significant factor, to behave with that consistency.' (Langdon interview, pp. 36–7). The committee nevertheless had recommended that 'there should be a clear connection between a prisoner's behaviour and the course of his prison career'.[20] Ironically, the American system did not forestall the rise of the 'supermax' prison, set up to deal with hard-core disruptive prisoners.[21] Nor did the future Director General of the Prison Service, Derek Lewis, realise that Langdon, Pearson and the CRC had recommended far more than 'some vague general principles allowing individual governors to retain their discretion' in any 'overhaul of the system of privileges for prisoners.'[22]

Other key recommendations were:

-   As a 'long-term possibility', for the dispersal system, that 'the "new generation" of prison designs in use in the USA appear to avoid many of the dangers which led the Radzinowicz and May committees to advise against a policy of concentration' and merit urgent examination. (paras. 18–20, recommendation 1, p. 100)

- 'Sentence planning units' should be established for lifers and long-term prisoners serving five or more years, to ensure thorough assessment is given, in their first year or so, to their most appropriate individual sentence plans. (paras. 31–2, and p. 100)
- 'The therapeutic regime at Grendon has much to offer the rest of the system.' (paras. 59, and p. 101). However, whilst an enlarged or even second version of the psychiatric prison at Grendon seemingly had 'much to offer', on closer examination the kind of prisoner deemed a 'troublemaker' was exactly the kind that Grendon wished to avoid. Its regime rested on prisoners of above average intelligence who could cope with group psychotherapy. Any violence led to rapid transfer. 'The contribution which Grendon is able to make to the long-term management of highly disturbed prisoners is, therefore, greatly restricted.'
- 'C Wing at Parkhurst should be re-established' (paras. 60–62, and p. 101). This wing for prisoners presenting control problems had operated with some success from 1970 until 1979, when it was closed due to disturbances in the main prison which had rendered it inoperative. It had proved a valuable, 'open' system, with a high (1:1.5) staff-inmate ratio but with a flexible staff deployment. The philosophy of the wing was not to 'cure', as at Grendon, but its record led it to be very strongly supported by the Prison Service and by outside scrutineers such as, for example, the House of Commons Expenditure Committee Report for 1980, *The Reduction of Pressure on the Penal System.*[23] Two such units were recommended.
- 'A number of small units, operating a variety of regimes, should be established to cater for other prisoners who are identified as presenting control problems' (para. 65 and p. 101) as well as the mentally ill and Rule 43 prisoners needing special facilities. (paras. 57–8, 71–2, and p. 101)
- 'The categorisation system should be reviewed in the light of developments in other penal systems.' (paras. 82–5 and p. 101)
- Incentives to progress to C and D categories should be enhanced by exploring increases in home leave, relaxed censorship and phone use. (paras. 102–4 and p. 102)
- Overall, 'these measures should enable the present dispersal system to be reduced in size.' (para. 129 and p. 102).

The coherence of the report was due to the realignment of the concentration versus dispersal debate and the clarity of the distinction drawn between security and control problems. On the first issue, a strong steer was given towards reviving and reinterpreting the concentration principle, as the American 'new generation' architecture would open up ways of meeting the objections against it. Architecture was thus given a higher priority than in the past century since the *panopticon* model fell from favour. On the second issue, control problem prisoners were seen as needing to be handled in a variety of ways. The concentration principle was to be rejected in their case. The fact that in the USA such control problem prisoners were so concentrated, the very reverse of the Mountbatten principle, had proved a key factor in the resort to 'supermax' prisons. All in all, the CRC report set the seal on humane management as preferable to coercion as the way forward in regime change. And the key to that form of management is that 'relations between staff and prisoners are at the heart of the whole prison system and that control and security flow from getting that relationship right . . .' (para. 16). The Woolf Report was to build on that insight several years later.

The main conflict overlooked by the May Committee in relation to the governance of prisoners was their growing sense of injustice in the era of burgeoning human rights consciousness. A host of measures designed to enhance security and control operated counter-productively to heighten the very problems they were meant to resolve, a contradiction exposed most cogently by the Woolf Report in 1991. For example, as recalled by Kate Akester,[24] a human rights lawyer, the 'simultaneous ventilation' rule 'was in operation then so you had to ventilate your complaints internally. The prison authorities would then examine it. As likely as not, I don't know any example when they didn't do this, they would say, no, we don't believe you, you've made this up. Now we're going to do you for making false allegations and you'll have a board of visitors hearing and we'll take remission from you. So there was a kind of vicious circle going on.' In 1983, having heard from a prisoner that he wanted advice on how to take his case, alleging being beaten up by prison officers in the course of riots, to the European Court, she made an appointment to see him. 'And then Wormwood Scrubs rang up and they said we're cancelling your appointment . . . You can't see him. He's got to ventilate this inside the prison first. . . . And I thought, no, I'm not going to go along with this. It must be challengeable. . . . So we then challenged the simultaneous ventilation rule and we got leave to apply for judicial review.' The European Court increasingly became not so much the last as the only resort for those prisoners denied access to courts in England and Wales, a development which hastened the demise of the simultaneous ventilation rule.

Other examples of procedures which caused simmering resentments were the 'ghosting' of prisoners who were regarded as very disruptive and difficult around the country, repeatedly transferring them every 28 days from one prison to another in what they used to call the merry-go-round. 'So they never knew where they were, they never knew what was happening, they never knew whether they'd be able to get their visits. And it was terribly inhumane . . . Another aspect of ghosting was that because these prisoners were going around the country all the time, they had an unrivalled opportunity, if you like, to pass messages on, to communicate. There was a sort of prison grapevine which was fed by the movement of these prisoners, usually . . . from one segregation unit to another. And I think that helped to build up the consciousness that something had to give.' Akester also regarded the roles of Boards of Visitors as not only conflicted, combining both adjudicative and pastoral responsibilities, but also flawed by lack of training. Following riots at Albany in 1983, a number of cases entailed a 'poverty of proceedings' which, in a context where prisoners were charged with prison mutiny, included such instances as a request to call nine witnesses being allowed only three, and one not allowed to give a defence. Her main criticism was that boards of visitors 'didn't know what the burden of proof was . . .' and, once prisoners' right to legal representation was granted, it revealed 'such a shambles that they rather quickly got rid of boards of visitors' adjudicatory role altogether.'

The building up of resentment of and resistance by prisoners to such flagrant inconsistencies, which increasingly involved Irish prisoners as a complicating factor, underscored the need for the kind of rethinking pursued by the Control Review Committee, though their framework of reform did not extend to the need for radical reform of the injustices that still prevailed. It would take the riot and occupation at Strangeways and the consequent Woolf Inquiry Report to achieve that goal.

## C. Roads Not Travelled

The May and Langdon reports, taken together and despite their differences, set the scene for the management of security and control risk prisoners for over a decade, if not to the present day. Three possible directions for the future came, in the process, to be ruled out: first, the development of 'new generation'-design prisons on the US model for top security risks – despite their advocacy by the CRC report; secondly, the creation for England and Wales of a unit based on the Barlinnie Special Unit in Scotland; and thirdly, the development of 'supermaximum' security prisons along American lines. Though there are clearly limits to the extent to which any history can explore counterfactual possibilities, the rejection or avoidance of what might be construed as salient policy options stands in need of explanation as much as policies that came to be adopted.

## 1. 'New Generation' Prisons

The first recommendation of the CRC was headed 'Long-term possibilities for the dispersal system, and stated: "The "new generation" of prison designs in use in the USA appear to avoid many of the dangers which led the Radzinowicz and May committees to advise against a policy of concentration. Their possibilities should be urgently examined." (paras. 18–20, and p. 100) What was it about these prison designs which so encouraged the Committee to advocate exploring their potential in such glowing terms? The key feature was the achievement of "decentralised unit management" for small (30–100) groups of prisoners, whose cells were clustered around a "central multi-use area" rather than along long corridors." (CRC report, para. 18; and see diagram, Annexe F, p. 87). This made possible better control via the "development of good interpersonal relations" (para. 19) and therefore undermined the central argument against a policy of concentration. "We think that our requirement for very high security accommodation is unlikely to be more than 300–400, and it would appear that, if "new generation" prison designs are indeed successful, the number could be held in two small prisons of the new kind without incurring the disadvantages that we have noted as being inherent in dispersal policy.'

In the event, this amounted to a missed opportunity rather than a decisive switch towards concentration and away from dispersal. To examine the possibilities, a working party was set up, chaired by Terence Platt, Director of Regimes and Services in the Prison Department, which in effect repeated the positive view of 'new generation' prisons expressed by the CRC, but failed to suggest how these designs should be taken forward.[25] Excessive caution rather than any ideological or institutional bias seems the reason for the report's low-key recommendations and conclusions. However, signs of a lack of affinity for the subject are to be found in the view of the chairman, expressed two years later, that 'they discovered an almost complete absence of relevant research reports or other analytical material."[26] On the contrary, argued David Canter,[27] the working party ignored some highly relevant material: studies by Farbstein and Wener (1982), and by Wener and Olsen (1980) and what is described as a major study by Canter and Ambrose (1980),[28] even though the latter had been commissioned by the Home Office. The American federal prison system under Carlson had achieved a degree of coherence between the character of the regime and its architectural embodiment which had in general not occurred in Britain. The size and, no doubt, the cost of the task proved too daunting. Thus, 'it is clear from the Platt Report on prison design . . . that such management systems would, if introduced in England, involve far-reaching changes: "The flexibility required of staff under the particular Unit Management model which has been developed by the Federal Bureau would represent a radical change for the prison system in England and Wales, raising considerations that go far beyond the scope of this report"' (Platt Report: 74, in Bottoms and Light, op. cit.: 16). Hence the head of steam generated by the Langdon Committee about 'new generation' prisons was all too soon dissipated, never to be revived in a comprehensive form.

Nevertheless, a legacy of sorts did materialise. The Platt Report was arguably more positive than the above criticisms allow, though its impact was decidedly muted, despite its colour illustrated examples of NGP design in the USA. The passage from p. 74 of the report quoted above continues: 'We do not however believe that the benefits accruing from the "new generation" design thinking are necessarily dependent on accepting the Bureau's own approach to staffing and management issues, and we consider that, provided questions of regime and operation are clearly addressed, and staff understand their role and what is expected of them, there is no reason why a design based on some of the "new generation" thinking should not equally be able to accommodate and indeed assist the operation of a different type of management structure.' Though hardly a clarion call to action, this is a clear pointer to the "new direction for prison design" intended by the committee. The riots of 1986–7 then brought a sense of urgency to the task. "The House of Commons 25th Report of the Committee of Public Acounts was severely critical of the current prison systems and buildings and insisted that the costly mistakes of the 1960s and 1970s had to be avoided in future. In 1987 the Prison Building Board was set up, and a start was made on producing the Prison Design Briefing System (PDBS) . . .'[29] The stage seemed set for radical change.

What explains this 'road not taken' is not so much that the NGP idea ran out of steam as that it ran up against upholders of reversion to a more traditional style of prison building. Margaret Clayton, Director of Services in the Prison Department 1985–89, disliked the American design as far too expensive[30] and she blocked the model after the only example to be based on it, Woodhill Prison in Milton Keynes, had been commissioned.[31] She preferred adaptations of the traditional Victorian 'galleried' prison design, which had been displaced by the 'corridor' model greatly disliked by staff as a threat to security, as tried and tested in terms of safety and control. As Stephen Shaw put it: 'Fashions change, and with the refurbishment programme, which has ended slopping out and made all prisons lighter, cleaner and airier, Victorian galleried designs are now regarded with much greater favour and form the basis of many new prisons and houseblocks.'[32] She was unaware of the case made by King and Morgan for the use of NGP design for Category A prisoners nor of the Mountbatten report on the case for concentration vs. dispersal. Her brief, as she saw it, was to implement the large prison building programme agreed in 1982, which had been expanded to include 21 new prisons for completion by 1994, to contain the burgeoning prison population.[33] This was accomplished by accelerating the prison building process, notably by securing Treasury agreement to advance purchase of sites, a measure which reduced the time scale by up to three years.

What could have been a breakthrough in English prison design, a synthesis of the Control Review Committee report, the priority newly accorded the staff-prisoner relationship in key practitioner circles,[34] and the 1985 Home Office Working Group inquiry on the American 'new generation' design principles (the Platt Report), consequently failed to materialise. Extolled by Leslie Fairweather as the way ahead, 'the term "new generation" does not refer to design as such, but to new ways of *managing* prisons, to which design must respond.'[35] 'Emphasis is on achieving as "normal" an environment as is consistent with security; on encouraging interrelationships between prisoners and staff; and on understanding the activities which go on in prisons.' In 1987, a 'dedicated design team,' under John Lynch, was set up in the Prison Department to produce design briefs incorporating such principles, which led to the publication in 1987 of the *Prison Design Briefing System*. A Prison Building Board was set up in December 1987, chaired by Margaret Clayton, to supervise delivery of the building programme. The design to match these principles was realised in only a limited number of cases.

The other main factor in the marginalisation of 'new generation' thinking was the entry of the private sector to the realm of penal policy. 'The involvement of the private sector security industry in the prison system has been the largest recent organisational change in the prison world. Will the gap between penal ideas and prison design widen still further? Because of their financial regime and speed of construction, private prisons are very relevant to the rate at which the prison system can be expanded; however, this also means that prison design is now almost entirely for outside contractors to decide . . . With the advent of privately funded and built prisons, it is possible that the good work springing from new generation principles could come to naught.'[36] Sir Andrew Derbyshire goes further to regard the UK adoption of the private route as almost wholly malign: "The effect on architectural quality of the PFI [Private Finance Initiative] approach is potentially extremely serious. The UK seems to be unique in using a device that actually drives a wedge between users and designers. Other countries employ private finance on terms that still leave the designer answerable to the Prison Service rather than to the funder.

Secret competitive tendering prohibits the dialogue between designers and the Prison Service that is the essential pre-requisite of a good design. It is well nigh impossible for the authorities to resist the pressure to award the contract to the bidder who offers the greatest number of cells at the lowest price.'[37]

The trend in penal architecture and design became, as a consequence, a move towards large-scale, even 'titan' prisons.[38] The new generation ideal on which to base much smaller prisons, and more humane regimes, reflecting the thinking both of the Control Review Committee on Category A prisoners and the Woolf Report on prisons in general, was in effect abandoned. The Prison Department decided, soon after the Platt Report, that whilst it would introduce new generation design principles into the design of new prisons, it 'decided not to proceed with the building of any new-generation prisons specifically to house long term maximum security inmates; and it has in any case decided, following the Gartree escape of 1987, to retain and remodel the dispersal system (though using a smaller number of prisons (six), and incorporating a distinction between institutions that can hold only 'standard risk' Category A prisoners and those that can hold both 'standard' and 'high-risk' Category A's.) In the light of these developments, CRC's vision of all or most Category A prisoners in England being held in two new-generation prisons is clearly dead.'[39]

The move away from the new generation design seems to have been set in the Home Office just as substantial comparative evidence was published confirming its effectiveness. In a comparative study of an American new generation high-security prison, Oak Park Heights in Minnesota, and Gartree, an English dispersal prison, 'using similar research strategies and instruments', Roy King concluded that 'Oak Park Heights is perceived to be safer, more secure, and more trouble-free; it also offers a much fuller and more highly rated programme of treatment, industry, and education, and provides better contact with the outside world . . . It is possible that the rejection by the British prison service of new generation design in the high-security context has been premature.'[40] Though the study in the USA was carried out in 1984, only two years after the opening of Oak Park Heights, six years later there had been no serious incidents of violence or escapes. It is a tragic irony that, despite this success story, so many states in the USA have adopted the far more inhumane model of supermax imprisonment.

## 2. The Barlinnie Special Unit

England and Scotland had, by 1970, come to face similar problems of prison violence, but chose to adopt strikingly dissimilar solutions to them. The Scottish equivalent to the disastrous control unit experiment of 1974–5 in Wakefield

Prison was arguably the resort to extreme coercion in the 'cages' at Porterfield Prison at Inverness, which in the post-war period held Scotland's most disruptive long-term prisoners, very small in number but immensely costly and difficult to control. The 'cages' came close to epitomising sensory deprivation: 'Your bed, on the cold bare stone floor, is a solid four-inch high fixed board in the corner. Only at nights do you get a mattress, pillow and army-type blankets. In the opposite corner is a fixed white bollard seat in front of a small angled table fixed onto the walls and cage bars. In the other corner a plastic baby-sized potty with the considerate touch of a plastic lid for overnight use. And that's it . . . Someone locked in the cage can pace up and down to pass the time. Four steps from side wall to side wall, three steps from bars to back wall . . . up and down, back and forward.'[41] Added to which was the way in which 'human contact is made three times a day when the "screws" enter to search the body of the prisoner. His mouth, armpits, anus and the soles of his feet are searched each time, even though he could not have left the cell between searches. This humiliation and degradation takes place daily.' (Jimmy Boyle, who had been held in the cages, cited in Fitzgerald and Sim: 106–7.)

Such measures provoked rather than deterred prisoners from further disruption. The use of the cages was suspended after December 1972, after a riot in the segregation unit at Inverness entailed serious injuries to several staff and prisoners. That they were reopened in 1978 after public pressure from Scottish prison officers is a testimony to the belief that coercion pays, despite all evidence to the contrary. However, 'when the prison regime itself is questioned, the logic of control is sometimes challenged. This happened in the early 1970s, and led to the opening of the Special Unit at Barlinnie Prison'[42] in February 1973.

The Barlinnie Special Unit was to prove unique. The most distinctive element to be evolved by its members was a self-governing, democratic community, in which both staff and prisoners participated, with weekly meetings to decide on how to resolve any problems. The prisoners wore their own clothes, visiting arrangements ensured privacy and were far more generous than the norm elsewhere, mail was uncensored, and prisoners could decorate their own cells and cook for themselves with food bought with their own money. In these and other ways the unit allowed far more freedom and scope for personal responsibility than the traditional system. Above all, inmates were allowed the freedom to create works of art, which led to a remarkable flowering of talent in painting, drawing, sculpture, ceramics and photography.[43] The price was the need to maintain good order, and anyone infringing the rules would face taking the 'hot seat' for criticism and chastisement from fellow prisoners and staff. This process of censure was reportedly far more effective than traditional punishment measures. (See MacDonald and Sim for a fuller description of the Unit and Coyle for its character in relation to other units in the Scottish system).[44]

The chief drawback to the Unit was its cost. Staffing levels were very high, due to the prisoners' prior records of violence, though the very high costs thus incurred should be offset against those of the Unit. The Unit was also a victim of its own success, and became subject to what Bottoms and Light termed 'slippage' and 'siltage'.[45] That is, over time the criteria for entry into the Unit became more diffuse and proved so popular with prisoners serving very long terms that they stayed on indefinitely. This combination of problems ultimately led to its closure in 1995. The fact that the Unit 'worked', in the sense that the prisoners' extreme violence was greatly curtailed,[46] was overridden by its stark contrast with the rest of the system and became politically insupportable.

The interest aroused both nationally and internationally by the Barlinnie Special Unit, and its most celebrated inmate, Jimmy Boyle,[47] led the May Committee to include it in their visits to other systems than that in England and Wales. It received short shrift in their assessment of its potential as a model for dealing with prisoners presenting the most severe control problems. Several members of the May Committee visited Barlinnie Prison in Glasgow on 4 January 1979. With over 1,000 prisoners, Barlinnie was, and still is, the largest prison in Scotland, largely for short-term prisoners. The Note of the Visit[48] stressed the extent to which overcrowding was much less of a problem in Scotland than in England and Wales. Its large site 'enabled Barlinnie to run regimes of association generous in comparison with anything available in local prisons in England and Wales.'

The Special Unit was visited briefly and dealt with in a single paragraph of the report of the visit to Barlinnie Prison as a whole. Its self-contained character and purpose were described in two sentences. Slightly more space was given to describing the cell of Jimmy Boyle, who acted as their guide: 'Mr. Boyle's cell was tastefully papered and had ceiling to floor curtains in a John Lewis fabric. It had a number of tastefully framed and chosen prints on the walls, a carpeted floor, a four-drawer filing cabinet, a substantial library in a wall-shelf unit, television, an easy chair, a stereo record player and a large number of cassettes.' The precise cataloguing of such desiderata conveys a sense of affront that the core penal principle of less eligibility[49] had been so grievously breached. The paragraph proceeds unequivocally: 'The special unit is, of course, unique not only in the United Kingdom prison services but in practice anywhere else. Its special situation is, although of interest, not perhaps of direct relevance to the Inquiry.'

This verdict, which made no reference to the contents of an updated background note of 29 November 1978, or to a considered appraisal of the Special Unit by Kenneth Murray, a Principal Nurse Officer with six years' experience of its operation, put paid to any attempt to distil ideas for security and control from its history. A committee member explicitly voiced his disapproval of the domination of the Unit by Jimmy Boyle. The conclusion drawn overall, however, was that a variety of units were needed to provide difficult prisoners with different needs scope for their better provision (see Coyle, op. cit.) but there would be no English Barlinnie as part of the picture. This strongly one-sided judgement on the Unit forestalled any real attempt to distil the lessons of its largely successful operation.

Misgivings were also expressed by Anthony Bottoms[50] who, as a member of the Research and Advisory Group (RAG) on the long-term prison system, set up following the CRC Report, in 1986, was sympathetic to the idea of possibly creating an English version of Barlinnie, 'which I was quite keen on but which the Prison Service was absolutely not keen on. I was keen on it with reservations, because we went and visited Barlinnie quite a lot and I thought that Barlinnie had become too liberal. So, for example, people, girlfriends and so on, were allowed to visit for hours at a time and one afternoon . . . this guy was complaining that his girlfriend had to leave the prison at night and come back in the morning. Wouldn't it be much simpler if she was allowed to stay the night and so on? I said well, hang on, this is actually supposed to be a prison, right? . . . So that they had let it drift too far but I also thought that there was a lot going for the Barlinnie model . . . and the evidence supports that from David Cooke's research and so on . . . There is a tentative model of "this is what it would look like if we had one" kind of stuff in the RAG report,[51] but it was never going to fly.' The report had argued: 'We anticipate that such a regime would have a low degree of structure, though there should be a requirement for prisoners to engage in collective discussion. We anticipate also that there would be a very high degree of staff involvement with prisoners, a high degree of prisoner participation in decisions about the way in which the unit operates, and a high degree of involvement by prisoners in finding ways of modifying their own problem behaviour.' (para 131).

The obvious problems with Barlinnie's difference in kind from all other forms of imprisonment had nevertheless been faced. For example, 'one of the early difficulties was that some prisoners elsewhere in the system regarded the unit as a soft option and took the view that if they created maximum unrest, often by assaulting staff, they were more likely to be transferred to the unit. The method of assessment and selection has attempted to exclude such motives for transfer and has been generally successful in doing so.' (Coyle, op. cit.: 240). The prisoners in the Unit appreciated their privileged status and on the whole kept their side of the bargain. This was not to be so in cases such as the Unit at Whitemoor where, in the 1990s, IRA prisoners extracted privileges and concessions from staff which enabled three of them to escape, one of a series of major security lapses which cost the Director General, Derek Lewis, his job.[52] The Barlinnie Special Unit was not a case of disruptive prisoners gaining the upper hand. It provided a different basis for the governance of the prison, and as such it offered what was ultimately too radical a model of democratic power relations for it to be politically sustainable.

## C 'Supermax' Prisons

The third 'road not travelled' represents something of a triumph for the liberal tradition within English penal policymaking. By contrast, the rejection of or indifference towards new generation prison design and the Barlinnie Special Unit reflected an aversion to the spirit of radical innovation that had created Grendon. Or it may, on the other hand, mainly reflect a pragmatic avoidance of high-risk costs. Paradoxically, the inspiration for super-maximum security ('supermax') prisons, developed originally in the early 1980s in the USA, stemmed from the very 'new generation' design which had realised, especially at Oak Park Heights prison in Minnesota, the architectural potential for a 'liberal regime within a secure perimeter' upheld by both Mountbatten and Radzinowicz.

'These new generation prisons are constituted of small housing units ("pods") which are arranged around a communal area where most activities take place. Prisoners are directly supervised by guards who mingle with them in the communal area. The small unit design enables the provision of specific environments for defined groups of prisoners, while maintaining close and direct staff supervision . . . The "new generation" concept also emphasises "deliberate manipulation of symbolic features of the environment so that the reduced opportunity physical design does not feel oppressive to inmates". (Bottoms 1999: 243)' (Shalev 2009:101).

As Shalev goes on to argue: ". . . supermax prisons typically utilise some of these new design principles, but not quite for the purpose for which they were intended. Instead of direct staff supervision and increased contact between staff and prisoners, the small unit layout and new technologies are used to reduce staff numbers, to support total separation of staff and prisoners, and to enable a regime based on remote surveillance and command." (Shalev, op. cit.: 102). Following a series of prison riots in the USA in the 1970s, and the resort by prisoners to litigation in cases brought against the prison authorities for breaches of human rights law, penal administrators cast around for ways of designing such potential for litigation out. Supermaxes came to be justified as "end of the line" institutions, "prisons within prisons", used to accommodate "the worst of the worst", prisoners who need to be removed from the general prison population and subjected to the highest degree of control. The chosen method for managing the prisoners is solitary confinement, coupled with restricted movement under tight control and enhanced security measures . . . In supermax prisons, architecture's power is demonstrated with rare bluntness; every detail of the design, materials and colours is carefully and, quite overtly, calculated to achieve maximum control of prisoners . . . This vision represents a sharp break with traditional segregation units, where isolation was a short-term punishment, to a carefully designed system of prolonged isolation as a tool of long-term prisoner management.' (ibid: 102). It is as if, echoing transportation, the germ of the idea behind the abortive Wakefield control unit of 1974–5 had been transplanted and greatly elaborated to inspire an entire sub-system of imprisonment in the New World.

As it happens, this inversion of the ideals behind 'new generation' prison design has proved highly exportable from the USA and has counter-intuitively influenced even so liberal a penal system as that of the Netherlands. At Vught, a special segregation unit reproduces the key features of the total isolation of staff from prisoners and of prisoners from each other, save in very limited and heavily controlled circumstances. Yet, despite a rash of escapes from maximum security prisons in the early to mid-1990s in England, the supermax option was ruled out. Why should this have been so?

The main attempt at an explanation has been offered by Roy King and Sandra Resodihardjo.[53] One key difference between the two situations was the frequency with which escape attempts in the Netherlands involved hostage-taking. This threat to the lives of prison staff left the government and the prison authorities very little 'leeway' to moderate their preventive measures, and therefore a supermax option for the highest risk prisoners was taken up. Ironically, even in the Netherlands, the Mountbatten case for a liberal regime within a totally secure perimeter was not explored, the major reason for which is the fear of prison staff that they could be taken as hostages. Another reason given by King and Resodihardjo is that 'learning' how to deal with these situations had a much longer history in England than in the Netherlands. The latter had evolved a very liberal system in the post-war period[54] which, until the mid-1980s, had had little adverse experience of escapes of an extreme and damaging character. In England and Wales, decades of turbulence in the prisons culminated in the 25-day-long occupation and large-scale damage to Strangeways Prison in 1990, and the series of escapes from maximum security prisons in the Isle of Wight. The Learmont report on the latter went so far as to recommend a supermax solution, but this was rejected by the working party set up to evaluate that proposal. It judged the network of special segregation units, set up in the wake of the 1984 CRC report, a sufficient basis for tighter security and control. Derek Lewis, as Director General of the Prison Service, had visited the supermax prison at Florence, in the USA. He found it a dehumanised environment where the very chairs in the cells were made of concrete. Despite the fact that it was 'horribly effective', he refrained from advocating its importation into England and Wales.

## Conclusion

The CRC report was to prove a more decisive influence than that of its main predecessor, the May Committee, in settling the future shape of regimes for high-risk prisoners in English gaols. The dispersal system was to be both retained yet restrained, a bow to the powerful arguments of those who criticised the overuse of maximum security for prisoners who posed no serious risk of escape. Humane management, not coercion, was to be the central principle underlying the regimes for even the most disruptive prisoners, and a network of units of varied character was to be established to meet their highly differentiated needs. Existing institutions were to be adapted rather than new ones created on 'new generation' lines. Regimes would be neither too liberal nor over-controlling. This settled the most outstanding matter of how the dispersal system should be developed for the highest risk of both escape and/or disruption presented by a small minority of prisoners. It was now acknowledged that those presenting the two types of risk were in general quite distinct, though overlap could occur in a very small number of cases, and needed quite distinct regimes. A shift towards concentration was envisaged for the most escape-prone, but should not be the basis for controlling disruptive prisoners. That was the road to supermax prisons along American lines.

By the mid-1990s, it had become clear that Special Units had proved a less comprehensive solution to the problems posed by the very small minority of the most persistently 'difficult' or 'intractable' prisoners than the Control Review

Committee had assumed, or at least hoped. The CRC had set out four principles on which Special Units should be founded: they should not be punitive, nor viewed as places of last resort; they should be diverse and complementary in their structure and function; and they should be open and accountable in their mode of operation. The spectre of the Control Unit fiasco of the mid-1970s, and the need to avoid a similar disaster, clearly hung over this formulation, which proved next to impossible to realise in practice. In particular, the criteria and processes for the selection of prisoners to Special Units (understandably) took so long that Governors came to rely far more on transfer within their own or to other prisons on grounds, for example, of Rule 43 (GOAD) application.[55] 'There is a danger that the whole small-unit strategy might overstate, by implication, the extent to which "control problems" in dispersal prisons are *simply* the product of "difficult individuals". We are not denying that some individual prisoners are habitually more troublesome than others . . . What we are saying is that the social and situational contexts in which these "troublesome individuals" live are *also* very important in the generation of the phenomenon known as "control problems": and that the small units strategy, *precisely because it is about "selecting out" difficult individuals for special treatment*, runs the danger of institutionally obscuring this important fact.'[56]

Nor do these points apply only to dispersal prisons for long-term prisoners. The majority of prisoners in the overcrowded and under-resourced local prisons, also have needs which had been unduly neglected in the process of focusing on the most problematic. That was to prove a recipe for the most devastating event in the history of imprisonment in Britain – the occupation and substantial destruction of Strangeway Prison in Manchester, and several others around the country, in 1990. The response to that violent protest was, in the shape of the Woolf Report, to prove a landmark in prison administration and penal policy.

## Notes

1  So-called to distinguish them from a few 'special' locals.
2  The classic study of a local prison, *Pentonville* by Terence and Pauline Morris (1963) documented the pattern of three rather than two to a cell.
3  Roy Jenkins, unpublished speech to NACRO, 21 July 1975, draft p. 13. Cited in Andrew Rutherford, *Prisons and the Process of Justice*, 1986 ed.: 56.
4  The Prison Officers Association was formed in 1939 as a staff association, in effect a trade union, from the Prison Officers Representative Board, a largely compliant body 'which the [Prison] Commission regarded as satisfactory and the officers as unsatisfactory'. J.E. Thomas, 1972, *The English Prison Officer Since 1850: A Study in Conflict*, London: Routledge & Kegan Paul: 171.
5  See Thomas (1976, 1980 and 1987) for an excellent analysis.
6  See in particular Geoffrey Robertson, 1999, *Crimes Against Humanity: The Struggle for Global Justice*, London: Allen Lane, and Anastasia Karamalidou, 2017, *Embedding Human Rights in Prison: English and Dutch Perspectives*, London: Palgrave Macmillan.
7  I. Taylor, P. Walton and J. Young, 1973, *The New Criminology: For a Social Theory of Deviance*, London: Routledge & Kegan Paul. See also the seminal work of the Norwegian criminologist Thomas Mathiesen, 1974, *The Politics of Abolition: Essays in Political Action Theory*, London: Martin Robertson.

8 Arthur de Frisching served both as a Prison Governor and a member of the Prison Department, Home Office, between the 1960s and the 1990s. He was also a member of the Control Review Committee (see below). Interviewed 6 January 2012.

9 In both their evidence to the Committee and their subsequent book *The Future of the Penal System* (1980). In their earlier book *A Taste of Prison: Custodial conditions for trial and remand prisoners* (1976), their 'advocacy for humane custody was in very large measure based on the fact that "treatment and training" led to a gross injustice – namely the concentration of overcrowding in the local prisons and remand centres where remand prisoners, implicitly, were not deemed eligible for "treatment and training".' (Rod Morgan, personal communication).

10 An exceptional case of a successful outcome in the system, despite its limitations, is that of Erwin James, who records his rehabilitation in Wakefield Prison due to the psychologist Joan Branton. See his *Redeemable: A Memoir of Darkness and Hope*, 2016, London: Bloomsbury Circus.

11 Arthur de Frisching, interview 6 January 2012, confirmed this point.

12 Advisory Council on the Penal System, *Sentences of Imprisonment: A Review of Maximum Penalties*, 1978, London: HMSO.

13 PSJ (79) 141 III (9).

14 Parenthesis added.

15 PSI (79) 171 and HO 263/42.

16 Home Office, 1984, *Managing the Long Term Prison System: the Report of the Control Review Committee*, London: HMSO.

17 Interview with Anthony Langdon and Tony Pearson, 15 November 2011. Langdon had chaired the Control Review Committee, of which Pearson had been a member.

18 Interview with Arthur de Frisching, 6 January 2012.

19 The riot at Albany lasted from 19–25 May, 1983. Despite the regaining of control, after a short time, in most of the prison by the MUFTI [Minimum Use of Force Tactical Intervention] squad from Parkhurst, 10 prisoners refused to give up their rooftop occupation until 25 May. Extreme damage caused to B and C wings put them out of action till early 1984. (Annexe D, CRC report, 'Dispersal Prisons: Major disturbances since 1969'].

20 Recommendation iii, Control Review Committee report, p. 100. The basic idea was pioneered in penal terms by Alexander Maconochie at Norfolk Island prison in the 1840s, where he developed the idea of earned release by a 'marks' system. See especially Robert Hughes, 1987, *The Fatal Shore: A History of the Transportation of Convicts to Australia, 1787–1868*, London: Collins Harvill: 499–509.

21 See below, and Sharon Shalev 2009, especially chapter 6.

22 Derek Lewis, 1997, *Hidden Agendas: Politics, Law and Disorder*, London: Hamish Hamilton: 79.

23 HMSO, Cmnd 7948, June 1980.

24 In interview, 17 March 2015. Kate Akester worked as a solicitor for Benedict Birnberg 1983–92, Justice 1992–2002 and as a sentencing advisor in the House of Commons 2004–7.

25 *New Directions in Prison Design*. Report of a Home Office Working Party on American New Generation Prisons. 1985 (The Platt Report) HMSO.

26 Terence C. Platt, 'New Directions in Prison Design' in Bottoms and Light, 1987, in A. Bottoms and R. Light (eds.), *Problems of Long-Term Imprisonment*, Aldershot: Gower: 140.

27 David Canter, 'Implications for "new generation" prisons of existing psychological research into prison design and use', in Bottoms and Light, 1987, op. cit.: 214–227.

28 J. Farbstein and R.E. Wener, 1982, 'Evaluation of Correctional Environments' *Environment and Behavior*, 14, 671–94; R.E. Wener and R. Olsen, 1980, 'Innovative Correctional Environments: a User Assessment' *Environment and Behavior*, 12, 478–93;

D. Canter and I. Ambrose, 1980, *Prison Design and Use Study: Final Report*, Guild-ford: Department of Psychology, University of Surrey (mimeo).

29  Ian Dunbar and Leslie Fairweather, 'English Prison Design' in Leslie Fairweather and Sean McConville (eds.) *Prison Architecture: Policy, Design and Experience*, 2000, London: Architectural Press: 25.

30  By contrast, Sir Andrew Derbyshire, President of the RMJM group – a multi-disciplinary practice of 500 architects, engineers and planners with experience of inno-vative prison design – argued: 'The new generation of prisons promoted originally by the PSA [Prison Services Administration, of which he was a member 1975–79] and the Prison Department has been dismissed as too expensive, although no evidence has been presented of even a rudimentary cost-benefit study.' From his article 'Architects and the Prison Experience" in Leslie Fairweather and Sean McConville (eds.) op. cit.: 56.

31  Interview by phone, 27 November 2012. See also Margaret Clayton 'Managing the Prison Building Programme' *Prison Service Journal*, No. 76 New Series, October 1989: 9–12. In fact, two more prisons built on new generation lines were completed – Lancaster Farms, a YOI for males in 1993, and Doncaster, a male local in 1994.

32  Stephen Shaw, 'Prison architecture and the politics of reform' in Fairweather and McConville, op. cit.: 151. Stephen Shaw was secretary of the Prison Reform Trust 1981–99 and Prisons Ombudsman 1999–2010.

33  Ian Dunbar and Leslie Fairweather, 'English prison design' in L. Fairweather and S. McConville, op. cit.: 24.

34  See especially Ian Dunbar, *A Sense of Direction*, HM Prison Service, 1985. A former prison governor, he was then director of prisons in the South-West region.

35  Leslie Fairweather, 'Prisons: A New Generation', *Prison Service Journal*, No. 76, October 1989: 26–31.

36  Ian Dunbar and Leslie Fairweather, op. cit.: 28 and 30.

37  Sir Andrew Derbyshire, op. cit.: 57.

38  Proposed in 2007 by the Home Secretary, Jack Straw, following the report *Securing the Future*, by Lord Carter of Coles. Though the idea was dropped in 2009, the thinking underlying the proposal was not.

39  A.E. Bottoms, 1991, "The Control of Long Term Prisoners in England: Beyond the CRC Report" in Keith Bottomley and Will Hay (eds.) *Special Units for Difficult Pris-oners*, University of Hull: Centre for Criminology and Criminal Justice: 2.

40  Roy D. King, 'Maximum-Security Custody in Britain and the USA: A Study of Gartree and Oak Park Heights' *British Journal of Criminology*, Spring 1991, 31, 2, 126–52: p. 149.

41  *Daily Record*, 15 November 1978, quoted in Fitzgerald and Sim, 1979: 106.

42  Fitzgerald and Sim, op.cit: 107.

43  Documented in Christopher Carrell and Joyce Laing (eds.) *The Special Unit, Barlin-nie Prison: Its Evolution through its Art*, 1982, Glasgow: Third Eye Centre. 'Yet the attention paid to their artworks could well have blinded some to the Unit's primary aim, which is not acclaim for the art but therapy for the artist.' Ludovic Kennedy, Foreword, p. 6.

44  See D. MacDonald and J. Sim, 1977, *Scottish Prisons and the Special Unit*, Edinburgh: Scottish Council for Civil Liberties; and Andrew Coyle 'The Scottish experience with small units' in Bottoms and Light, op.cit.: 228–248.

45  "Introduction: Problems of long-term imprisonment" op. cit.:, 1987: 33.

46  See especially David J. Cooke, 'Containing violent prisoners: an analysis of the Bar-linnie Special Unit' *British Journal of Criminology*, 1989, 29(2): 129–143. 'Since its establishment only 2 assaults have occurred (expected frequency = 105) and 7 serious incidents (expected frequency = 49). It is argued that these changes can be attributed to features of the regime, including the quality of staff-prisoner communication, the use of group meetings for the ventilation of aggressive feelings, and mechanisms whereby grievances can be dealt with rapidly.' (Abstract)

47 Jimmy Boyle had by 1979 gained repute for his sculpture, a talent he had discovered whilst in the Unit, and as an author. *A Sense of Freedom*, 1977, Edinburgh: Canongate, is his autobiography until that point.

48 HO 263/389.

49 As discussed, for example, in Herman Mannheim, *The Dilemma of Penal Reform*, 1939, London: Allen & Unwin.

50 Anthony Bottoms, Emeritus Professor of Criminology and former Director of the Institute of Criminology at the University of Cambridge. Interviewed on 3 December 2015.

51 Home Office (1987) *Special Units for Long-term Prisoners: Regimes, Management and Research.* A Report by the Research and Advisory Group on the Long-term Prison System. London: HMSO: paras. 131–2. See also Keith Bottomley and Will Hay (eds.) (1991) *Special Units for Difficult Prisoners.* University of Hull: Centre for Criminology and Criminal Justice; and John Ditchfield (1990) *Control in Prisons: A Review of the Literature.* Home Office Research Study 118. London: HMSO.

52 See Derek Lewis, *Hidden Agendas,* 1997, chapters 11 and 12.

53 'To max or not to max: dealing with high-risk prisoners in the Netherlands and England and Wales' *Punishment and Society,* 2010, 12 (1): 65–84.

54 See David Downes, *Contrasts in Tolerance: Post-war penal policy in the Netherlands and England and Wales,* 1988, Oxford University Press; and 1998, 'The Buckling of the Shields: Dutch Penal Policy 1985–1995' in R. Weiss and N. South (eds.) *Comparing Prison Systems*, Amsterdam: Gordon and Breach: 143–74.

55 GOAD is the acronym for Good Order and Discipline as the basis for transfer to Rule 43, protective segregation, status.

56 Sparks, R., Bottoms, A.E. and Hay, W. (1996) *Prisons and the Problem of Order*, Oxford: Clarendon Press: 296–7. A passage from evidence by the authors submitted to and quoted by the Woolf Report, 1991. Italics in the originals.

# 5    The Making of the Criminal Justice Act 1991

The Criminal Justice Act 1991 represented in many ways the culmination of decades of thought and effort by several Home Secretaries, senior Home Office civil servants and penal reformers in and out of Parliament to evolve a means of accomplishing penal moderation in the face of a steadily rising prison population and instability in the prisons themselves. The Act had a long gestation period during which several preconditions for its enactment came to be assembled by accident or design. This chapter begins by analysing some key such elements and then examines the processes whereby the Act was passed in February 1991. The Act in the event proved the anticlimax rather than the climax of a fascinating attempt at sustainable sentencing and penal reform.

## i. *Overcrowding and the sense of growing crisis*

In 1979, the prison system was generally recognised to be in a sorry state. The bare facts were of an increase in what later came to be termed, by Andrew Rutherford,[2] 'high cost squalor', the outcome of rising prison numbers outstripping capacity, despite a growth in the number of cells available. Between 1969 and 1979, the prison population rose from 34,667 to 42,210, with increases in capacity failing to make good the gap between numbers of prisoners and cell space: overcrowding was the logical and inevitable outcome. While prisoners, as the May Committee noted, did not necessarily find cell sharing objectionable, what made it intolerable was the lack of integral sanitation and the stench of human faeces before the 'slopping out' ritual could be performed twice daily. Yet not all prisons were overcrowded. The 'training prisons', holding roughly 40 per cent of the overall population, were protected at the expense of the more congested 'local prisons', which held remand as well as convicted prisoners. This situation was based on longstanding policy, designed to favour the notionally more rehabilitative part of the system. Critics such as the criminologists King and Morgan found little empirical justification for this divide, and pressed the May Committee to distribute prisoners more evenly across the whole estate. And though May objected to the 'localisation' of all prisons, due to what they felt would be a corresponding loss of rehabilitative character, the Committee were emphatic that the 'worst prisons are very bad indeed.'[3]

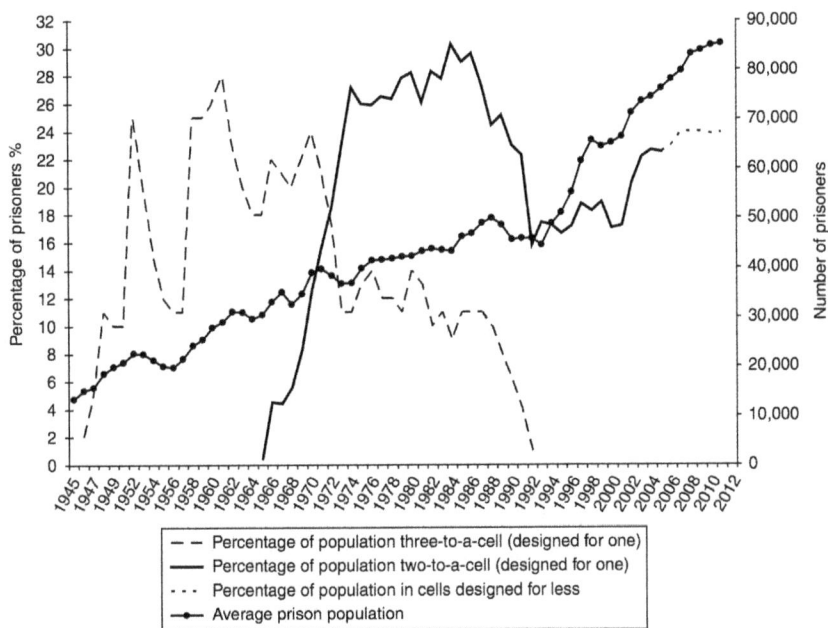

*Figure 5.1* Prison overcrowding, 1945–2012

*Source:* Hansard electronic archive of written parliamentary answers, and subsequently Ministry of Justice data 2011.[1]

The sense of drift and growing pressure of population had led in the 1970s to a plethora of industrial disputes in the prison system, the primary reason for the establishment of the May Committee of Inquiry in the first place. As King and McDermott put it, in their authoritative study of the prison estate several years later:[5] 'Security had already impinged on the notions of treatment and training with the implementation of parts of the Mountbatten (1966) and Radzinowicz (1968) reports . . . Its implications for regimes, and especially for staffing, however, had hardly been realised. By the 1970s, the main concerns of the prison system were directed at questions of control', initially of prisoners. 'But later there were as many difficulties in the control of staff, as the long-standing problems of a service which had been allowed to become dependent on the large-scale overtime of hourly paid officers disintegrated into a situation of perpetual disputes over manning levels, pay, and allowances.'

King and McDermott's research indicated the scale of the task that had to be surmounted. In 1986–7 they conducted a survey of five prisons of different types in one region, a sample designed to match a similar grouping of prisons studied in 1970–72 by Roy King. These data provided the material by which to measure

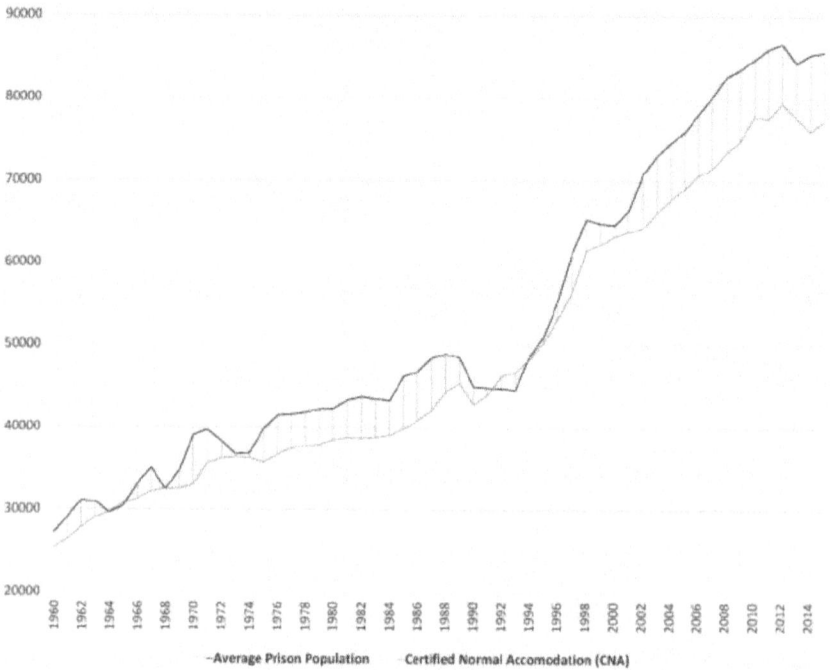

*Figure 5.2* Average prison population and Certified Normal Accommodation (CNA), England and Wales, 1960–2015.[4]

the trend in standards over a decade and a half. The expectation was that, given the substantial increases in resourcing over the period, some changes for the better would have occurred, albeit of a minor kind. The results were a devastating blow to any such complacency and provided ample support for those who had advocated more radical measures to reduce the prison population.

By five indicators on which to evaluate the direction of change, the results revealed 'consistently worse regimes' than the earlier study. Crowding was significantly worse within and between sample prisons. For example, Birmingham, a local prison, the site of Richard Sparks's warning of 'the crisis in local prisons' 18 years earlier, had an occupancy rate, gauged by comparing its actual daily population (ADP) with its certified normal accommodation (CNA) of 155% in 1971–2 and 190 in 1986–7. Its comparator prison, Winchester, had improved its occupancy rate somewhat, from 160 to 140, but was still seriously crowded. The other four comparator prisons were all more crowded in 1986–7 than in 1971–2.[6] On other indicators, marginal improvements in space per prisoner and 'signs of genuine and hard-won' improvements in facilities for personal hygiene were evident.[7]

But these gains both depended on and were offset by longer periods spent 'banged up' in cells than in 1971–2: '. . . the differences are so large, and so consistent, that it is hard to resist the conclusion that there has been a massive deterioration over the period. The changes are most marked at the higher end of the security spectrum. Prisoners in Gartree dispersal prison, intended to have a relaxed regime within a secure perimeter, spend five and a quarter hours more each day locked in cells than did their predecessors at Albany . . . Perhaps the most dramatic finding here is that the hours locked and unlocked in the training prisons at Gartree and Nottingham today almost exactly mirror those for convicted prisoners in the local at Winchester over 15 years ago.'[8]

It was no great surprise, therefore, when the data revealed that 'in every instance less time was spent in work in our study prisons than was the case fifteen years ago'[9] and that 'proportionately fewer prisoners today participate in education than formerly'.[10] This 'gloomy picture' is not 'wholly unrelieved by brighter spots', especially in the areas of facilities for sanitation and personal hygiene.[11] But overall the indices of 'ever-deepening crisis' were undeniable. How could that have occurred? King and McDermott rejected the (then) standard explanation that overcrowding, especially in local prisons, had outstripped resources of staff and facilities. Investment in both had outstripped, particularly in the case of staffing, any rise in numbers of prisoners. Staff: prisoner ratios had improved from 3.48 in 1971 to 2.47 in 1986–7, an increase of 71.0 per cent. One reason for the deterioration despite this increase is that 'rightly or wrongly, the quest for greater security and control in the dispersal system has led to massive increases in staff and major curtailments in regimes.'[12] The data confirmed that 'the crisis in the prison system is not simply a problem of overcrowding and poor sanitation in the local prisons'[13] but time out of cell restrictions having increased to the point where even 'hard won' gains in provision and facilities had been obviated. A few years later, in 1990, the eruption of the prisoners' revolt at Strangeways Prison in Manchester dramatically confirmed this analysis. If, as is now the case, up-to-date information on such variables as 'time out of cell' had been available, this underlying problem could have been addressed far sooner. As it was, the data of King and McDermott came as a shock to the system of the Prison Department.

## ii. *Alternatives to alternatives?*

Frank Soskice and Roy Jenkins as Home Secretaries in the mid-1960s had mapped out what looked like a viable policy for stabilising, if not reducing, the prison population, then growing year on year in response to rising and, in some respects, such as the increase in armed robbery, more serious crime rates. The 1967 Criminal Justice Act introduced both parole and the suspended sentence as ways of tackling rising prison numbers as well as being defensible measures in their own right. Parole had both pragmatic and rehabilitative appeal:[14] '. . . the White Paper which announced the government's intention to introduce parole asserted (without any actual evidence) that a 'considerable number of long-term prisoners reach a recognisable peak in their training at which they may respond to generous treatment, but after which, if kept in prison, they may go downhill' (Home Office, 1965: para. 5). Thus the focus was on long-term prisoners only. The Act stipulated that only those who had served at least one-third of their sentence, or 12 months, whichever is the longer, would be eligible for parole, i.e. only those with sentences of three years or more. This tended to imply that no such 'peak' was obtained for shorter-term prisoners. The treatment model, of a group of experts deciding on a prisoner's suitability for release by such criteria, fitted the high expectations of a science-based system that were to come under challenge in the early 1970s. But though the 'collapse of rehabilitative optimism' undermined parole's 'original positivistic rationale', it survived and was greatly expanded as a 'safety valve' for reducing prison numbers.

Parole had come to be referred to, in the Home Office discussion papers on penal reform in the 1960s, as 'an idea whose time had come'. 'Parole gave administrative expression to prevailing support for indeterminate sentences and the personalisation of punishment."[15] It had a long and diffuse history. Its roots lay in 'tickets of leave' which, beginning in 1801, granted convicts of good character freedom to work and travel in the colonies to which they had been transported; in the release on licence of those serving sentences of penal servitude after the decline of transportation led to the Penal Servitude Act of 1853; and in the innovation of remission for ordinary prisoners in 1898 following the Gladstone Committee Report three years earlier. Remission became for over half a century the main form of early release, increasing from one-sixth of the sentence in 1907 to one-third in 1940 due to the pressing need for accommodation in wartime. The key difference between remission and parole was that the latter was release on licence, subject to recall and supervision by the probation service. Remission was automatic and subject only to deferment due to offences within the prison. The likely adverse side effects on the prison population meant that the decision was taken to add parole to remission rather than convert the whole early release system to that of parole.

Limiting parole eligibility to offenders serving sentences of 18 months or more 'was a conscious decision to curtail the scope of the system' to those serving long enough sentences to benefit from 'an effective programme of rehabilitation'.[16] Frank Soskice in cabinet emphasised the importance of the 'distinctive contribution to the reform of the penal system' such a principle would make. He saw it as a match for the White Paper on young offenders.[17] Despite ill-health forcing his resignation after barely eighteen months in office, Soskice's determination to put two key recommendations of the 1964 Longford Committee into legislative shape, as well as to facilitate the abolition of capital punishment, set the scene for Roy Jenkins to succeed him in December 1965, belying the latter's description of him as 'a remarkably bad Home Secretary',[18] and ushering in a period of pathbreaking liberal reforms in the criminal justice sphere.[19]

In his second term as Home Secretary, from 1974–76, Roy Jenkins encouraged the granting of parole without excessive caution. Along with the suspended sentence and limitations on the power of the magistrates courts, parole was now to signify what he declared to be 'an overarching policy objective, *"that of keeping out of prison those who need not be there". '*[20] 'By 1981, parole was being granted at double the rate it had been a decade earlier – in 55 per cent of cases considered compared with 27 per cent in 1969. But even this was not sufficient to 'abate the prison numbers crisis'[21] Further expansion occurred in 1983, when Home Secretary Leon Brittan introduced a bifurcatory[22] element into the parole system by increasing its availability for shorter-term prisoners and simultaneously, and retrospectively, reducing it for such long-term prisoners as those convicted of more serious violent offences. These changes tended to cancel each other out, as far as reining in the prison population was intended, and also heightened concerns about the legitimacy of the system, in terms of its secretive decision-making, lack of any chance of appeal, and its impact in terms of intensifying bifurcation. The Carlisle Report of 1988 addressed some of these concerns and implied the need for greater parsimony in sentencing. But the net effect of parole on the prison population over this period was that at best it operated as a safety valve and at worst that it indirectly facilitated sterner sentencing. However, the judiciary accepted a need to dissociate the two processes and no evidence has emerged to imply any such facilitation.

By contrast, the suspended sentence of imprisonment has been called into question as a reductionist measure that seemingly failed to achieve its intended effect. Its introduction in the 1967 Criminal Justice Act by Roy Jenkins was unambiguously linked by him to devising new ways of maintaining deterrence yet avoiding the resort to immediate imprisonment: 'Whichever way the outcome goes in an individual case, I do not believe that society can lose. If no further offence is committed, the deterrent has worked, prison space has been saved, and the offender has not been made used to prison conditions. If a further offence is committed, the offender will be punished certainly and surely, for both the earlier and the subsequent offences.'[23] The clear intention was that only where custody would have been the sentence, and only then, could the sentence be suspended for between one to two years, to be activated if a further offence was committed. The idea that the suspended sentence should also be used as an alternative to other noncustodial sentences, termed by Bottoms 'special deterrent theory', was clearly rejected by the Home Secretary, a position upheld by the Court of Appeal in R. v O'Keefe (1969).[24]

Scepticism about the impact of the suspended sentence arose soon after its implementation on 1 January 1968. Sparks in 1971 summarised the evidence on the first few years of its operation as follows: 'It is clear . . . that about two-thirds of those given suspended sentences in 1968 and 1969, at both magistrates' courts and the higher courts, would have been dealt with by something other than imprisonment if the suspended sentence had not been available: it seems likely that about half would have been fined, and one-sixth put on probation. Even if this does not continue to happen, the net effect of the suspended sentence may well be to increase the prison population rather than reducing it. And if it does continue to happen, the suspended sentence could well turn out to be the most counter-productive penal reform ever enacted.'[25] Another unwanted side-effect was to convert short-term prisoners most likely to serve their time in open prisons – the most under-crowded sector – into longer-term prisoners most likely to serve it in the locals – the most over-crowded, by virtue of the activation of the double sentence requirement following a further offence. That effect mainly stemmed from the suspended sentence having been mandatory for most offences that would have attracted a sentence of six months' imprisonment or less in any court. Magistrates found this objectionable as a constraint on their powers and that component of the suspended sentence provision was abolished in the 1972 Criminal Justice Act. Its scope was thereby greatly narrowed and its impact on imprisonment correspondingly reduced. Though it and other diversionary meas-ures, such as the introduction of Community Service Orders in 1972, provided an array of alternatives to custody, greater than any comparable criminal justice system, their use as alternatives to each other and not to prison, whatever the legislative intent, had become all too apparent by the end of the 1970s. The May Committee were all too aware of the dangers: 'In the face of this experience, there is bound to be caution about the case either for activating section 47 [of the 1977 Criminal Law Act creating the power to partially suspend sentences] or any variants of expanding suspension . . . The difficulty is that the judiciary might, on the lines of what happened originally with suspended sentences, impose the immediate sentence of imprisonment they would have imposed anyway and add a suspended portion to that. Over time the result would be to increase rather than diminish the prison population.'[26]

By the mid-1980s, scepticism about the potential for decarceration to be achieved by devising yet more 'alternatives to prison' was deepening. In a key summary article in 1987, 'Limiting Prison Use: Experience in England and Wales',[27] Bottoms convincingly showed that measures designed, since 1965, to avoid the imposition of imprisonment had had 'little success' in that endeavour. Measures designed to reduce time served had 'had more impact on the size of the population but at the cost of several anomalies', all of which amounted to pessimism about the then government policy of 'improving the recent rather dismal track record of attempts to limit prison use in England.'[28] In the first case, measures aimed at avoiding custody altogether, neither suspended sentences, introduced in 1967; nor Community Service Orders, introduced in 1972; nor Probation with special conditions, introduced in a number of areas following the Criminal Justice Act 1972, were without successes, but the overall balance of evidence showed that in about half of all cases, such sentences had been used as 'alternatives to alternatives' rather than to prison sentences. Modes of shortening prison sentences, parole, introduced in 1968; partly suspended prison sentences, introduced by the Criminal Law Act 1977 but only brought into force, for adult offenders only, in 1982; and judicial advice, mainly guideline judge-ments by the Court of Appeal, from 1980, are seen as having a mixed success but as generating 'severe difficulties' of various kinds. For example, changes in parole thresholds to extend the scope of parole had entailed such complexity of assessing sentence lengths as, in the words of David Thomas, the academic doyen of judicial training, to 'having reduced the process of custodial sentencing in the Crown Court to a complete farce.'[29] At this juncture the route that had seemed the most obvious remedy for too marked an expansion of imprisonment now appeared not only to have failed to work but also to have generated undue problems of both principle and practice.

### iii. *The Resort to Restrictive Criteria*

By the end of the 1970s, it was clearly the case that the legislative reforms of the 1960s onwards had failed to stem the rise in the prison population. Parole, the suspended sentence and the failed attempt in the 1973 Powers of Criminal Courts Act to curb custodial sentences for young offenders aged 17 to 21 all combined seemingly to confirm that a 'carceral society' (in Foucault's phrase)[30] had come into being, which converted all measures, even the most apparently anti-custodial, into ever greater recourse to imprisonment. A good example, quoted by Lord Windlesham,[31] and cited in debate in the House of Lords by Lord Hutchinson of Lullington QC, concerned the ease with which supposedly restrictive criteria in the 1973 Act were rendered inoperative. The court was required to avoid a sentence of imprisonment 'unless it was of the opinion that no other method of dealing with him was appropriate . . . What happens in magistrates' courts very often is that the clerk, after the magistrate has sentenced the person to imprisonment of some kind, looks up and simply says: "No other method appropriate?" The magistrate nods and then that is entered on the record. It becomes a pure formality. Exactly the same thing has happened with not sentencing first offenders to prison. Again you have to state your reasons and once again off goes the person to prison and the clerk says: "Seriousness of offence?" and the magistrate nods, and down goes "seriousness of offence".'[32]

Another example of well-intentioned restrictive criteria being ignored, bypassed or watered down concerned the use of 'care' orders for juveniles aged 14–16. Custodial sentences for males in this age-group rose by over four times the rate at which the number of offences rose, as measured by court convictions or cautions:

|  | Young Offenders aged 14–16 | | | | | |
|  | Guilty or cautioned | | | Receptions under sentence | | |
|  | Male | Female | Total | Male | Female | Total |
| 1971 | 69,000 | 11,700 | 80,700 | 3,032 | 34 | 3,066 |
| 1981 | 94,900 | 18,800 | 113,700 | 7,535 | 52 | 7,587 |
| % change | +36 | +69 | +41 | +149 | +53 | +147 |

*Figure 5.3* Young offenders aged 14–16, 1971 and 1981

[*Sources:* CS 1981: 107; PS 1981: 61]

Why and how did this occur despite the best intentions of the 1969 Children and Young Persons Act to divert young offenders from punishment to welfare measures? Part of the explanation lies in the way custodial sentences for juvenile offenders were boosted in the 1970s by the adverse jostling of welfare and punitive aims.[33] 'Care' orders played a prominent role in the unanticipated increase in custody for this age-group, since the breach of a 'care' order led all too often to detention centre or borstal, and 'care' orders were made too readily too low down the 'tariff'.[34] The three criteria used for research into such orders – danger to self and others; homelessness; and special educational and/or psychiatric needs – were shown in a study of six areas to have applied to only 14 per cent of 537 cases – that is, by any one criterion. In sum, well-intentioned legislation, confusingly implemented, had led to a classic net-widening effect (Cohen, op. cit.). Indeed, research, especially by the 'Lancaster Group', played such a key role in effecting changes in the recognition of these unwanted side-effects that legislators accomplished a remarkable shift in policy towards juvenile offenders in the early to mid-1980s.[35]

In sum, 'the steady decline in the number of young male offenders sentenced to custody which occurred throughout the 1980s is one of the most remarkable post-war achievements of deliberate legislative enactment. That it owed so little to the government, and so much to independent-minded members of both Houses of Parliament, was later acknowledged in a generous tribute to Baroness Faithfull by Elton'.[36] Fully aware of the pitfalls affecting restrictive criteria in practice, Baroness Faithfull had argued for, and tabled, amendments to the Criminal Justice Bill 1982 which passed in the Lords and was then unopposed by the government on its return to the House of Commons. The fact that the All Party Parliamentary Penal Affairs Group was genuinely non-partisan proved a key factor but, as a Conservative peer, Baroness Faithfull had succeeded where the original proponents of the amendments, Sam Silkin and Robert Kilroy-Silk, both opposition Labour MPs, had failed. The key addition to the criteria, that the offence was 'so serious that a non-custodial sentence cannot be justified', and that the reasons had to be set out in written form, was added to the other two – the failure of previous non-custodial penalties and the need to protect the public – to resharpen the focus of the restrictive criteria. Most importantly, 'a succession of judgements enforcing the statutory criteria by the Court of Appeal from 1983 onwards bore out the accuracy of his [Elton's] prediction' (that the judiciary would not object to being given such guidelines).[37]

Also crucial to the aim of reining in the resort to custody for juvenile offenders was the very practical grant of £15 million for the provision of Intermediate Treatment schemes in 1983. Scope for such measures had been enacted a decade earlier, but it was only with the 'publication of a circular by the then Department of Health and Social Security, which stressed the importance of multi-agency approaches to the management of serious and persistent offenders, and made available £15 million of seedcorn money to develop I.T. projects as alternatives to custody and care"[38] that real fruit materialised. 110 projects offering 3,389 places were set up by voluntary bodies in 62 local authority areas 1983–87.[39] The results were momentous:

| Young Male Offenders Sentenced to Immediate Custody 1982–90 | | |
|---|---|---|
| | Aged 14–16 | % reduction from 1982 |
| 1983 | 6,900 | −5.5 |
| 1987 | 4,000 | −45.2 |
| 1990 | 1,700 | −76.7 |
| | Aged 17–20 | |
| 1983 | 23,500 | +1.3 |
| 1987 | 21,600 | −6.9 |
| 1990 | 14,100 | −39.2 |

*Figure 5.4*  Young male offenders sentenced to custody, 1982–1990.

[*source:* Home Office, Crime Statistics. Cited in Windlesham, ibid: 171]

For the first time in the post-war period, tangible proof existed to encourage reformers to persist in pressing the case for legislation to rein in the resort to custody, not only for juveniles but also for adult offenders. Five years on, the ministerial meeting on Home Office policy at Leeds Castle, a crucial step towards what became the 1991 Act, recognised that 'Restrictive criteria of the kind which the Criminal Justice Act 1982 had successfully introduced for young offenders could be extended to adults.'[40]

## iv. *The Conversion to Crime Prevention*

In the 1970s, in the wake of 'Nothing Works' disillusionment with the goals of the treatment and rehabilitation of offenders that had so animated penal policymaking after World War II, the business of how to run the prison system seemed bereft of ideas. Crisis management was the order of the day, as prison overcrowding and problems of security and control loomed ever larger with the growth of the prison population. More prisons could be built, and escapes from high-security prisons staunched, but at an exceedingly high cost. The report of the May Committee grappled with these problems but without offering any clear alternative strategy. 'Positive custody' appeared to be the last gasp of the former 'treatment and training' outlook. Unsurprisingly, therefore, the 1980s began with a policy of 'more of the same' – young offenders would be taught to respect authority, and William Whitelaw, the new Home Secretary following the 1979 victory of the Conservative Party led by Margaret Thatcher, announced, inter alia, a tougher experimental version of detention centres, to be tested out in two new institutions. The first Cabinet meeting of the newly elected Tory government accepted in full the generous terms of the Edmund-Davies report on police pay, following the recommendations of a Committee set up by the outgoing Labour government. Police and prisons were to remain the mainstay of the criminal justice system in the fight against crime, a crusade which the Conservative Party had pursued to great electoral effect at the expense of Labour. A 'punitive turn' seemed inevitable in the decade to come.

That this did not occur was due to a confluence of factors, among which crime prevention came to play a substantial role, offering, at least for a time, a different 'direction of travel' from ever-increasing investment in policing and prisons. These had been the taken-for-granted staples of traditional crime prevention, linked by sentencing which, in its turn, was becoming steadily more punitive. New forms of crime prevention were partly technologically driven, as in the case of electronic surveillance. The first outdoor CCTV cameras in the UK were installed as late as 1985, credit cards beginning far earlier, in 1966. But the major developments took the form of social and more extensive modes of situational crime prevention. 'Social' forms of crime prevention were to be taken up and developed in the 1980s by such programmes as Safer Cities[41] which funded, for example, local job training and work placement schemes for young offenders. Neighbourhood Watch schemes proliferated and were, for a time, assumed to have some effect in crime prevention.[42] 'Situational' crime prevention took such forms as enhancing surveillance and reduced opportunities in relation to likely targets for theft, vehicle crime and domestic burglary. Better sight lines in housing estate design and 'target hardening' by strengthening locks, doors and windows, were aimed at reducing opportunistic offending which, in the influential work of Ron Clarke, of the Home Office Research Unit, accounted for much volume crime.[43] Both approaches could be combined via such concepts as 'defensible space', a theory developed by Oscar Newman, an American architect, in a book so entitled in 1972.[44] His major insight was that architectural form served either to facilitate or obstruct the skein of social relationships which constrain people from crime commission. Spatial configuration may, as in high rise flats, prevent parents from observing their children at play. Though open to criticism on empirical grounds,[45] the approach has proved seminal in encouraging ways of 'designing out crime'.[46]

Overall, developments in new forms of crime prevention, or in new ways of activating older forms, such as enabling parents to see what their children are up to in street and playground, have borne out the classical insights of Cesare Beccaria over two centuries ago. It was his analysis in *Dei Delitte e delle Pene* (On Crimes and Punishments) (1764) that first argued for the certainty of conviction as a far more important deterrent to crime than the severity of punishment. That assertion is now seen to have been astonishingly prescient, and has generated a neoclassical wave of research and policymaking.

In the 1970s, the Home Office Research Unit criminologists began to explore such approaches more actively. Pat Mayhew's *Crime as Opportunity* in 1976 built on such seemingly banal and 'obvious' findings as that rates of vandalism were far higher on the top deck of buses, rather than the lower deck that was much more observable by the driver. Ron Clarke in 1980[47] summarised the central axiom of situational crime prevention as stemming from the criminogenic nature of the crime situation itself, rather than the 'dispositions' of offenders, whether shaped by social, psychological, cultural or economic variables. As he stressed, the situational elements in offending had been greatly neglected by criminologists, to the detriment of workable policies. After all, strengthening locks and hardening targets, on the one hand, and enhancing surveillance on the other, were far more doable than engineering revolution or psychic transformation.

This approach fed rapidly through the policy process as the 1980s wore on. The crime rate increased year on year until 1986–7, seemingly resistant to increased punishment and rising rates of imprisonment. But in one crucial respect, crime rates fell. The 1982 Criminal Justice Act had made provision for enhanced community penalties, and a Home Office conference concluded with a recommendation to target real resources on the hitherto neglected Intermediate Treatment schemes. Home Office Circular 42/1983 invited applications for funding and areas which benefited were able to foster community programmes for young offenders, diverting them from custody and monitoring crime rates locally. The schemes worked to good effect, rates of known juvenile offending falling rather than rising, giving substance to hopes that community programmes would indeed 'pay off' in terms of lower crime rates. Though the fall in juvenile offending later came to be discounted, as lacking credibility in the context of steeply rising crime rates, and the view gained ground, among the police and tabloid media, that the system disallowed them grounds for effective intervention with young offenders, for a time it bolstered confidence that such policies worked to some degree.[48] More imaginative 'social' forms of crime prevention were later to flow from studies of re-victimisation, by Ken Pease in particular.[49] His studies of burglary victims clearly showed that being victimised once disproportionally raised the risks of subsequent victimisation, with risk at its height the closer in time to the original break-in. 'Cocooning' the victim by alerting neighbours and upgrading security as soon as possible lowered rates of burglary quite significantly. Though other changes introduced locally added complexity to any direct equation between cocooning and crime rates, the research team found little evidence of the displacement of offences to adjacent areas, thus encouraging the view of Clarke and others that the removal of opportunity in one area or crime type did not automatically become 'displaced' to others – sometimes offending simply ceased.

This approach went far to encourage the Home Secretary and Home Office policymakers in their search for an alternative strategy to ever-increasingly resorting to penal measures in the face of rising crime. As David Faulkner[50] put it: 'Douglas Hurd became Home Secretary in 1985 . . . The movement towards the Criminal Justice Act 1991 began in earnest after the 1987 general election . . . Acknowledging the limited impact which the criminal justice system can on its own have on the general level of crime, other programmes were to be developed to prevent and reduce crime and its impact and to promote public confidence. They included compensation and services to victims; more attention to problems of racial discrimination and prejudice; a renewed emphasis on crime prevention, including the national organisation promised in the manifesto [soon to be established as Crime Concern]; and social action involving partnership to deal with such problems as drugs, alcohol, child abuse, opportunities for young people [later to be developed through the programme known as Safer Cities.]'[51]

Developments in crime prevention were arguably to have a lasting impact on trends in crime. The sea change in crime rates from the mid-1990s onwards has entailed a sustained fall, in sharp contrast to their 'rise and rise' more or less continuously since the mid-1950s, not only in Britain but also cross-nationally, both in terms of official police figures and those culled from victim surveys. Given the simultaneous increase in many socio-economic variables theorised as highly criminogenic, in particular the growth of economic inequalities and the 'winner-loser culture', the main alternative explanation of this trend, apart from increased imprisonment and 'tough on crime' community penalties belatedly making a lasting impact, has to be the formidable array of crime prevention measures developed from the 1980s on.

The prevalence of various forms of crime prevention has been more extensive in England than elsewhere, and they are by no means necessarily benign. 'Substantial reductions in domestic burglary and car crime have played a larger role in England than in comparable societies.'[52] Regrettably, the price to be paid for engineering a falling crime rate in a highly criminogenic society has gone far beyond stronger door and window locks and car immobilisers. Given the 'arms race' quality of the politics of crime control in England, it has entailed what, in Durkheimian terms, would be considered a burgeoning pathology of over-control. 'Gated communities', the highest rate of CCTV surveillance in the world, DNA samples retained by the police even if no grounds for prosecution are found: much crime prevention entails active exclusion and control, mainly highly stratified in social class terms. 'As a result, the "paradox of insecurity" has come to prevail as the price to be paid for the prevention of crime in everyday life: the more "secure" we are, the more insecure we feel.'[53]

This is not the place to discuss the relative merits of imprisonment vs. crime prevention as antidotes to crime, especially as it may well be argued that it is their interaction which jointly effected the notable fall in crime rates since the mid-1990s. However, received opinion, both governmentally and politically, as well as public, tends to the view that it was the 'Prison Works' U-turn of Michael Howard's term as Home Secretary which sparked the fall in crime rates since that date. The role of crime prevention, so important in the making of the 1991 Act, whose framers' primary intention was to reduce the prison population, has ironically thus been to reinforce the opposite effect in the longer term. The effects of contingency can also be seen here, as it was conceivably the impact of the 1989–92 recession which so steeply raised the level of unemployment, and thus the crime rate, after which the enforced exit from the European Monetary Union in 1992, and the economic recovery that entailed, greatly assisted in its reduction.

### v. *Informed Dissent*

As Lord Windlesham wrote in his 1987 *Responses to Crime*, 'it is important for the reductionist case to be argued and developed into a distinctive strand in the continuing debate on penal policy . . . The sound of critical voices insisting that imprisonment should be used only as a last resort, always questioning and pressing for cogent justifications, is conducive to a more broadly based, more knowledgeable and open process of policy formation. In the ringing words of the May Committee, "Closed institutions above all require open, well-informed discussion."'[54] Though Windlesham goes on to question the realism of such a case for drastic reductionism as that proposed by Andrew Rutherford in his *Prisons and the Process of Justice* (1984), given its insulation from the political climate, his overriding point stands. And in the 1980s, the proponents of a more liberal penal policy within the Home Office made good use of the contributions of penal reform and pressure groups to sustain parliamentary and public debate along reductionist lines.

The existence of an array of penal reform groups in Britain is unmatched elsewhere in the world. And in the 1970s and 80s new groups sprang up to enlarge the quite numerous body of such associations, centres and leagues already in being. The Prison Reform Trust was founded in 1982 to press for much the same goals, but more intensively,[55] as the oldest such group in Britain, the Howard League for Penal Reform, set up in 1921 from the 'amalgamation of the original Howard Association, founded in 1866, and the more militant Penal Reform League, formed in the wake of the Suffragette movement in 1907.'[56] Inquest, founded in 1981, was formed to press for a more democratic and accessible system of inquiry into unexplained deaths. The National Association for the Care and Resettlement of Offenders (NACRO), founded in 1966, developed under the aegis of Vivien Stern into a formidable force for the expansion of community alternatives to custody as well as making the case for penal reforms. Other groups with an impressive lineage are JUSTICE, a highly successful pressure group focused on criminal justice reform; LAG, the legal aid group in action since 1971; and a host of others, including victims groups, collectively represented by the most important, Victim Support, single-issue groups, and professional interest groups. The number presenting evidence to the Woolf Inquiry on the prison riots of 1990–1 amounted to 65. In part the reason for the upsurge in activity in the 1980s was the abolition of the Advisory Council on the Penal System after the 1979 Conservative electoral victory preceded a cull of NGOs, despite its minimal costs and impressive track record. It was, inter alia, the group which launched Barbara Wootton's Community Service Orders, a 'world first' and much copied abroad.

The 1970s also saw the emergence of a radical criminology, with a representative body, the NDC (National Deviancy Conference – formerly Symposium) founded in 1968 and holding regular conferences at York University. Out of this movement, which made contact with allied criminologists abroad, especially in Scandinavia, came RAP (Radical Alternatives to Prison), founded by Ros Kane, a Probation Officer, and PROP (Preservation of the Rights of Prisoners), founded by Geoff Coggan, a former prisoner, and Mike Fitzgerald, a criminologist. While the Howard League in particular was seen as, in Mick Ryan's phrase, 'the acceptable pressure group,'[57] RAP and PROP were regarded by the Home Office and the POA as an unwarranted distraction from the serious business of penal administration.

For example, both during and after the Hull Prison riot in 1976, PROP asserted its presence by publicly supporting the prisoners' cause and by aspiring to conduct its own inquiry with Home Office support, a claim to union status which infuriated the POA and was icily rejected by the Home Office.

Such groups by no means spoke with one voice – indeed, some were at odds with others, as in the case of those representing 'secondary' victims of homicide and the broader National Association of Victim Support Services (NAVSS), whom the former saw as too 'soft' on offenders.[58] In alliance, however, they could make a formidable case for change, as in the Parliamentary All-Party Penal Affairs Group (PAPPAG), a combination of penal reformers from all parties in both Houses of Parliament. Paul Cavadino, Deputy Director of NACRO, was its clerk throughout the 1980s, so knowledgeable and active an expert that in one debate in the Lords he was called a 'one-man Civil Service'.[59] That the 1980s ended with no larger a prison population than at its outset was due to some extent to the activism of these networks, though their proliferation was no guarantee of lasting success, as events after 1993 proved.

Two examples of reformist intent assisted in the counter-intuitive penal reform trend of the 1980s which culminated in both the 1991 Criminal Justice Act and the Woolf Report of the same year. The first was the creation of the Labour Party Campaign for Criminal Justice (LCCJ), a forum set up by Alex Lyon M.P.[60] in 1978 to promote greater debate within the Labour Party on criminal justice matters and to reform the system along more socially democratic lines. Participants were largely, though not exclusively, Labour Party members, including MPs, though few attended meetings at all regularly. No survey of membership was ever carried out but at its height numbered around 400, mainly academics, lawyers, JPs, researchers, probation officers and social workers, and at least one deputy prison governor. Harriet Harman, Deputy Leader of the Labour Party 2007–10 and Shadow Deputy Prime Minister 2010–15, was its first secretary. Apart from Alex Lyon, MPs included Clive Soley, Alf Dubs, Chris Smith and Barry Sheerman and, on occasion, Robert Kilroy-Silk, chair of PAPPAG. The then shadow Home Secretary, Roy Hattersley, only occasionally took part but lent his active support.

Meetings every month or so took place in the House of Commons in the era before standard security checks became *de rigeur*. There was an LCCJ presence at annual party conferences, and a few publications eventuated: on crime and penal policy; on crime prevention; on public order; and on police accountability.[61] The LCCJ programme for criminal justice policy under a Labour government following the 1992 election, which the Conservatives somewhat unexpectedly won, despite the recession of 1989–2, was a set of recommendations towards further penal reductionism, harm reduction in relation to drug abuse, and a greater emphasis on human rights.[62]

The LCCJ's influence on Labour Party policy in the 1980s was doubtless uneven, but it did provide backing for the Opposition's commitment to further movement away from custodial and towards community penalties. This stance gained weight from Roy Hattersley's seniority, and was a virtual precondition for Douglas Hurd and his successors as Conservative Home Secretaries to pursue the policies of the Home Office reformers, led by Sir Brian Cubbon and David Faulkner, to assemble a coherent basis for reductionism as a key priority. If the Labour Opposition had berated the government at any point for being 'soft on crime' or careless of the plight of victims, such a policy priority could hardly have been sustained. As it was, Labour were critical of the government for not being reductionist enough, a stance which lasted until after their fourth successive election defeat in 1992, at which point the new shadow Home Secretary, Tony Blair, began to rebrand Labour as 'tough on crime' and to distance the party from the policies it had espoused in the 1980s. The LCCJ now came to be chaired by Alun Michael, M.P., an ally of Jack Straw, who was soon to become shadow Home Secretary when Blair won the leadership contest after the death of John Smith in 1994. Its name was changed to the Labour Forum for Criminal Justice, a symbolic retreat from the campaigning role it had played under the chairmanship of Labour MPs Alex Lyon, Chris Smith, Clive Soley and Barry Sheerman. It ceased to exist soon afterwards.

The second example of what might be termed informed dissent in relation to orthodox penal policy was the Discussion Group assembled by David Faulkner, whose meetings were held at the London office of NACRO from 1981 until 1992. Those taking part were senior Home Office civil servants, Faulkner as Chair throughout and, at different times, Bill Bohan, Philippa Drew, Margaret Clayton, Mary Tuck and Arthur de Frisching. Academics taking part throughout were David Downes, Rod Morgan and Andrew Rutherford. The most influential as the decade wore on was Andrew Ashworth,[63] the key British advocate initially of ideas for a Sentencing Council and later of 'just deserts', the minimal version of retributive 'proportional' sentencing originating in the USA with the work of Andrew von Hirsch.[64] Others in the group included Cedric Fullwood, Chief Probation Officer in Manchester; Ian Dunbar, Governor of Wakefield prison; Roy King; and throughout Vivien Stern,[65] Director of NACRO and a doyenne of criminal justice reform. Roger Hood and Anthony Bottoms took part on occasion. The group met monthly to discuss policy matters usually in response to a paper written by either one of its members or a visitor invited specially for the topic concerned. Prison regimes formed the staple theme for the first few years of the group's existence but sentencing, which was seen as the key to penal reform, loomed larger as the decade progressed.

The decision to form such a group had been the result of Sir Brian Cubbon's encouragement of David Faulkner to pursue ideas for stabilising and if possible reducing the prison population, an aim endorsed by the recent report of the May Committee in October 1979. Faulkner was freed up, as it were, to discuss the issues involved with other than Home Office colleagues and in a setting other than the Home Office itself or a formal conference. It flew in the face of civil service protocol and several senior colleagues of Faulkner frowned on its very existence. It was seen as a hostage to fortune, spawning ideas which could prove combustible. To guard against this danger and assuage such anxieties, members of the group worked to Chatham House rules, which disallowed attributing views and opinions to specific individuals but which allowed ideas generated by the group to stimulate wider debate and discussion. Faulkner's exceptional independence of mind flourished in such a circle and arguably enriched in-house analysis of policy issues.

The eventual shape of key clauses in the 1991 Act were heavily influenced by Andrew Ashworth in particular. The strength of the Act lay in its clear focus on the principle of 'just deserts',[66] which Ashworth had been enunciating for over a decade and which had found its most influential expression in Andrew von Hirsch's *Doing Justice* (1976). The principle had been extensively discussed in a Home Office document of 1982, without apparently becoming adopted at that point as the basis for a major policy initiative.[67] It reaffirmed that the punishment should be proportional to the crime and the least severe consonant with just retribution. How far the backing this principle received in the discussion group influenced Faulkner in his growing commitment to it as the centrepiece of penal reform is a somewhat arcane question, but its acceptance as a key principle was arguably a major factor in its inclusion in the 1991 Act. In Faulkner's summary view, 'It is hard to say whether or how far the group had any direct influence on policy. The ideas and information we considered were all in the public domain, through government or the members' own publications, and similar ideas were being discussed in other settings. The group had no status or authority; and any ideas which emerged from it had to be tested in the ordinary policymaking process, including with ministers, but I think I can say that my colleagues and I were better informed, had a clearer understanding of the issues and were more confident in the arguments we used, than we might have been otherwise.'[68]

### vi. *The Comparative Dimension*

Comparative criminology, in the sense of cross-national analysis, had been more absent from than present in the study of crime and punishment for most of its history. Born comparative, especially in the exploration of the prisons and lazarettos of Europe by John Howard,[69] criminologists nevertheless tended to stay within the confines of a single society from that point on. Such parochialism is all the odder since penal administrators and policymakers were far keener to learn lessons from abroad. De Tocqueville and de Beaumont were despatched from France to study the penitentiaries of America, a spin-off of which was de Tocqueville's *Democracy in America*[70] (1835, 1840). Bentham's *panopticon* design for the model prison was much admired abroad, as was the Borstal system from its foundation in 1908. And international congresses were far from unknown up to and including those of the United Nations and the European Union today. Yet, with a few notable exceptions,[71] it was only in the 1980s that the study of crime control paid more systematic attention to the comparative dimension. That revival was in part due to the remorseless trend of penal expansion, itself due in large part, so it seemed, to the apparently endless trend in rising crime rates in the post-World War II era, despite full employment, diminishing poverty and the growth of the 'welfare state'.

Criminologists had drawn on cross-national data before the 1980s but in a different sense to the later analysis of comparative rates and trends in crime, deviance and control. The Royal Commission on Capital Punishment (1953) had analysed such data to test the proposition that the death penalty deterred people from homicidal acts. They found no evidence to support this widespread belief, a precondition for its abolition in the 1960s (see the relevant chapter above). Hermann Mannheim, the co-architect of British criminology with Leon Radzinowicz, drew widely on studies in different countries to furnish data relevant to testing theories of crime and delinquency causation.[72] And Radzinowicz wrote on the 'search for criminology' in different countries' institutes and universities.[73] Both the Mountbatten and Radzinowicz reports on regimes for long-term imprisonment drew on foreign experience in relation to the specific issues on which they had been required to report. Important as these studies were, they did not engage with the comparative linkages relating crime and punishment to variations in social structure, culture and political economy across different societies.

The comparative dimension in cross-national and penal studies resurfaced in the 1980s, with the work not only of academic criminologists but also of penal reform groups. The May Committee had drawn attention to the variations in imprisonment whereby England and Wales compared harshly with Sweden and the Netherlands, and to no apparent gain in crime levels or its reduction. And it was NACRO which hosted the lecture by Hans Tulkens, the Head of the Dutch prison service, on Dutch penal policy compared to that of England. Academic work followed that lead, with Downes's study focusing on contrasts between Dutch and English penal policy in the post-war period (1982, 1988); Rutherford on the American, Dutch and Japanese systems compared to that in England (1984); and John Graham (1988) on West Germany's success in reducing their prison population in the 1980s.[74] A plethora of studies was to follow, much of it centring on what was held to be 'the punitive turn' in punishment worldwide. The most prominent sign of growing interest in the relevance of 'abroad' in relation to penal policy was the production of, and publicity given to, the so-called 'league table' of rates of imprisonment by country around the world. It provided the basis for the penal reform lobby to claim that Britain 'headed the league table' of Western Europe in terms of rates of custody, that such a relatively disproportionate resort to imprisonment was unwarranted and that its scaling down should be given far higher emphasis in policy terms: prison prevention, as it were, should accompany crime prevention as key priorities. The terms of the debate were to bear fruit in the conferences at Leeds Castle in 1987 and Ditchley in 1989.

## vii. *The Policy Process: Momentum and Direction*

The 1980s were a decade in which criminal justice policy in general, but penal policy in particular, came to be influenced by the thinking and energies of David Faulkner. Faulkner had come to realise the unsustainability of pursuing separate and distinct departmental goals within the Home Office and between the Home Office and other ancillary ministries. For example, in a talk at Southampton

University (5 June 1984) he listed a number of 'problems of co-ordination and control' in criminal justice, such as the 'shift from a "policy" approach to a "management" approach[75] with the emphasis, as across all government spending, on "value for money".' As this shift was being put into operation, and being presented as not so much a policy in its own right as a priority that brooked no alternative, it would logically lead to more intensive scrutiny of the costs of the criminal justice system, growing as the crime rate itself was increasing year by year. Penal policy in particular had become a source of seemingly endless increases in expenditure as the biggest prison building programme for a century still failed to make an impact on prison 'over-crowding'.

Faulkner saw prison over-crowding as a symptom rather than a cause of the seemingly endless crises in the prison system. In 1987, in a talk to magistrates in Berkshire (28 October) he cited the over-use of prison, despite huge costs and increased overcrowding, as 'a dangerous and damaging situation' which has 'distorted' debate. 'The argument ought to have been on what scale, for what purpose and for what sort of offenders the ultimate sanction of imprisonment ought to be used. Instead it has been mostly about how we could reduce prison over-crowding . . . What ought to have been an argument of principle has become confused with arguments of expediency and cost, and the whole debate has become overlaid with cynicism, suspicion and unhealthy recriminations between the judiciary and the executive with the probation service placed awkwardly in the middle.'[76]

Nevertheless, in both this and numerous other talks, lectures and presentations over the decade, Faulkner stressed that there was some good news on which to build. 'Juvenile crime is not rising in the way that is commonly supposed.'[77] Victims and crime prevention have been given higher priority. Elsewhere he stressed the fall in juvenile detention as hopeful and that the much revised Police and Criminal Evidence Act of 1984 'may come to be regarded as one of the significant elements in the de-Orwellisation of 1984.'[78]

All in all, however, he saw the need for a unifying theme to the welter of change that was happening apace, largely for pragmatic if at times for principled reasons. The prison population needed to be reined in, not primarily to reduce overcrowding, but mainly to reconnect sentencing to a clear statement of principle. The basis for a fundamental rethink had existed at least since the 1980 cases of *Bibi* and *Upton* and the judgements of L.C.J. Lane in the Court of Appeal, which acknowledged the admissibility of prison overcrowding as a legitimate factor in sentencing.[79] 'Those judgements gave some grounds for hope that a dialogue might be established between the Home Office and the higher judiciary.'[80] Though early attempts to do so foundered on judicial suspicions and inaccurate press reporting, the idea later bore fruit in the conferences at Leeds Castle in 1987 and Ditchley in 1989.

The animating idea behind the need to engage in such a constructive dialogue was arguably a restatement of perhaps the oldest judicial concept of all, that of retribution. In his book *Doing Justice* (1976), the American legal scholar Andrew von Hirsch had argued that the principle of 'just deserts' should be revived and reformulated to displace deterrence and rehabilitation as the main consideration in sentencing. In 1987–88,[81] he joined forces with Andrew Ashworth to make the case for sentencing reform in England along those lines. The Advisory Council on the Penal System, in what became its last report, on maximum sentences for crime,[82] and the May Committee on the prison services in the UK in 1979, had both concurred on the need to reduce the prison population, the former by lowering maximum sentences to what were then the current maxima actually applied, and the latter by more general reductions, along the lines of comparable societies with substantially lower prison numbers than those of the UK, such as Sweden, the Netherlands and France. 'Just deserts' was becoming the focus of debate on sentencing reform, in particular as applied to the 'petty, persistent offender'.

Writing on the stock of knowledge at the time (and largely since) Andrew Rutherford commented: 'Remarkably little research has been conducted on the composition of prison populations. There has been no general prison population census in England, and the only detailed study was carried out in 1972 and based upon a ten per cent sample in the South East Region. The research found that 30 per cent of the sample of sentenced adult men could be described as petty or minor offenders.' A later study in 1983 found that 34 per cent of all persons received on sentence (excluding fine defaulters) were convicted of theft or related offences.[83] The earlier study by Charlotte Banks, and the subject of a Howard League pamphlet with Suzan Fairhead,[84] both former or current members of the Home Office Research Unit, in many ways broke new ground. Timothy Cook,[85] in his Foreword, wrote that it had 'Nothing sensational to report, it would seem, and nothing new for anyone at all familiar with the drifting, rootless petty thief or alcoholic. Yet it is as savage an indictment of present penal policies as it is possible to find, especially encouraging to those on the outside who have been trying to convince the Home Office of these findings for years and especially valuable in that these findings are those of the Home Office Research Unit itself.'

The problems posed for sentencers by 'petty, persistent offenders', though not the link to 'just deserts', were first aired as a priority in a NACRO seminar in 1979.[86] 36 participants were drawn from the Home Office, and practitioners across the array of criminal justice agencies. Several JPs and justices' clerks, but no judges, took part. Suzan Fairhead and Tony Marshall, both of the Home Office Research Studies Unit, analysed the needs of these offenders, whom they emphasised were not a homogeneous group, though many shared the problems of homelessness, alcoholism and poverty, a recipe for much petty offending. Imprisonment accentuated their problems: 'as the number of previous convictions increases, or the term of imprisonment increases, or both, the number with each of these disadvantages goes up.'[87] In one case cited, seven of 24 previous convictions were for the theft of milk. Mental illness was not, however, a factor in more than a few cases. Nevertheless, meeting elementary welfare needs for this type of offender would be far more humane and less costly than repeated terms of custody. Norman Tutt, of Lancaster University, addressed this issue, arguing for multi-agency co-ordination to tackle their problems, in part through a much-expanded network of probation hostels, drop-in centres and allied forms of community support.[88] Addressing the issue of sentencing the petty, persistent offender, Elizabeth Barnard and Anthony Bottoms focused on the single decision point relating to custody and what measures could 'facilitate decisions not to imprison'.[89] They analysed the pros and cons of several much-touted solutions. Statutory restrictions on imprisonment were unpopular with the judiciary and could be counterproductive, as occurred in the rise in detention centre and borstal orders following the abolition of the Approved Schools. Decriminalising such 'crimes without victims' as prostitution would affect very few and, if extended to the non-imprisonability of such groups as mothers with young children, could be seen as a 'licence to offend'. Mandatory suspended sentences would be seen as 'fettering the discretion of the judiciary' by both many judges and the press. Even the very cautious recommendations of the Advisory Council on the Penal System to reduce sentence maxima to actual sentencing practice was condemned as unduly restrictive. Sentencing guidelines were more popular with the judiciary, but only if sufficient exceptions were possible that could defeat the object of reducing custody substantially in such cases. They also risked too many appeals. Barnard and Bottoms gave due weight to the 'inevitability' of custody in the future as well as in the past, if offending continued. For many, it would be a case of deferring rather than eliminating imprisonment. The best way of delaying resort to custody, and delaying the escalation of previous convictions, arguably involved other elements entering the frame, such as reparation to the victim. However, the poverty of most petty, persistent offenders militated against that option. Overall, however, it was important to introduce options to reduce the 'last resort' to imprisonment being adopted too soon, and the experience of other countries, such as the Netherlands, showed real potential for that to be the case in Britain. It would appear that, at this point, 'just deserts' was not yet part of the policy options frame.

The Discussion Group at NACRO was just one forum at which the revival of interest in applying just deserts to sentencing was taken up by Faulkner. One of its two main proponents, Andrew Ashworth, was a regular member of the group and it was his advocacy 'not only there but as a prominent and even more influential figure at many other, more public events',[90] that mainly attracted Faulkner to the idea of focusing on just deserts as the key to sentencing reform as a means of reducing the size and scale of imprisonment especially for the petty, persistent offenders who were the mainstay of penal inflation. The principles of proportionality – the relative seriousness of the offence – and parsimony – the minimum penalty compatible with justice – combined to provide the basis for what became Clause 29 of the 1991 Act: that the main current offence should be the basis for the sentence, uncoupled from previous convictions – for which the penalty had already been paid – and other offences of lesser magnitude.[91]

An in-house discussion on the implications of the justice model as early as October 1982 had spelt out very clearly its strengths and problems, not so much in relation to sentencing and the size of the prison population but rather in relation to reformulating the basis for prison regimes and staff-prisoner relationships. A paper, 'The Justice Model and the Objectives of Imprisonment',[92] gave a generally highly favourable analysis of what a shift from the 'treatment' model to one characterised as the 'justice model' would entail. Emanating from the Directorate of Operational Policy, it spelt out in 14 pages the key justifications for its adoption:

-   'Under the justice model the only aim of imprisonment, indeed its only justification, is that it is a punishment that is appropriate, on a judicial assessment of just desserts (sic) to the offence. But the punishment derives entirely from the imprisonment – the deprivation of liberty – and not from the conditions of the incarceration.' (1–2)
-   Treatment and training must be entirely voluntary and with no element of compulsion, though opportunities should be provided as equitably as possible.
-   The inmate should retain as many of his rights 'as is consistent with his imprisoned status, and the procedures governing his condition, any necessary disciplinary proceedings and the like should meet high standards of equity and procedural propriety.' (2)
-   The justice model had till then been largely seen as preferable to the treatment and deterrence models due to the perceived inequity and disproportionality of these justifications for punishment. Yet the empirical basis for their deployment is simply not established. 'Thus while there is in theory an interesting issue about how far the claims of justice (or just desserts) should be sacrificed in the interest of achieving rehabilitation, in practice, in the current state of knowledge, that issue does not need to be addressed . . . This, for some depressing conclusion has profound implications not only for the justice model in relation to sentencing policy, but also in relation to the objectives of imprisonment, prison regimes and the role of staff.' (3)
-   For these reasons, parole is especially difficult to relate to the justice model: it amounts to 'a disguised form of re-sentencing' (4) in the light of assessments by staff and the Parole Board about likely *future* offending by the prisoner.
-   The justice model applied to internal prison management implies minimum standards governing conditions; the enhancement of rights and the duty of care to the greatest extent compatible with closed prison security; providing the resources and machinery to activate such rights; the acceptance of humane containment, in its fullest sense, as the main goal of the system, rather than corrective treatment or moral improvement as ends in themselves; and to enhance 'activities' for work, education and leisure as close as possible to what is available in the outside society.
-   The counter-argument that such a regime would lack moral purpose 'is a misconception. The model may be seen as envisaging a clear moral purpose, though one different from that articulated at the heyday of the treatment model. The aim would be to achieve – as an overriding and public objective – fairness and justice in all the everyday details of officer behaviour towards inmates. The Justice model thus becomes a rallying point for self-respect for staff, the standard by which its professionalism may be measured, a source

of clear guidance and a principle that inmates can certainly understand and (conceivably) respect.' (7)

- This need not involve a greater resort to court enforcement of such rights, but a framework to ensure their activation and enforcement is sorely needed now and would be equally urgent under the Justice model aegis.
- Much of the above approximates to the principle of 'normalisation'. This would not replace much of the 'most valuable remedial and social work – and sheer human befriending – which does take place in our establishments' (13). But it does offer a different framework for these principles to be upheld.

This paper was intended to elicit comments from other members of the Policy Directorate. The four on file took indirect issue with several points, the main ones being the problem of 'less eligibility' and an attempt to rescue the 'treatment model' by arguing that it had 'never been wholeheartedly tried'. More should be made of the overlap between the models, e.g. nothing about either conflicts with 'humane containment'.

The four rejoinders[93] did not reject the case for the 'justice model' but argued for further discussion and study, and awareness of the resource implications of its adoption as a new Rule One of the Prison Rules. Overall, the balance of the discussion was implicitly to reject the May Committee's case for 'positive custody' and to accept, again implicitly and without direct citation, the case for normalisation – that prison conditions should resemble as far as possible standards in the outside world – put by King and Morgan in evidence to that Committee and of Von Hirsch and Ashworth for a return to a modified 'just deserts'-based retributive model.

Faulkner's introductory paper to this in-house discussion did not focus in particular on the merits of the justice model, but it is remarkable how full a case was made for them in the paper by Quentin Thomas, and how early in the 1980s it was proposed for inclusion in the Home Office agenda. However, it was mainly drawn on in relation to prison management and staff-prisoner relations,[94] and not then given any priority in relation to sentencing, which only reappeared as a way forward in the 1990 White Paper[95] and after the dropping of the Sentencing Council concept following opposition by both the Home Secretary and the Lord Chief Justice. That was beginning to emerge as Faulkner's preference as a way of reining in penal expansion. For example, in talks to the Judicial Seminar in September 1983 and January 1984 he ranged widely over policy options but did not mention the 'justice model' at all. He did allude, however, to 'Andrew Ashworth's suggestion for a sentencing council (p. 12) after mention of "sentencing guidelines" as a subject for discussion'. Though the term 'proportionality' became code for 'justice model' later in the decade, that was not included at this point. Faulkner was concerned to point up the rapid growth of interest in relation to 'compensation, reconciliation and reparation between the offender and his victim. The victim support movement has gathered momentum to a very great extent in the last two or three years', avoiding the 'sensational news reports' or 'pressure for more severe penalties', 'as has tended to happen in the United States'. (p. 7) The later talk emphasised the shift from individual to 'system' thinking on policy; on crime prevention taking distinctive new forms, not just 'locks, bolts and bars', and the need to discuss principles of sentencing, drawing an explicit distinction between the independence of the judiciary in court and in a particular case, and the responsibility of the Home Office and government for legislation and possible changes in limits to judicial discretion. No mention was made of the 'justice model', only of possible discussion about a sentencing council. Given the sensitivity of the senior judiciary to any hint of a trespass on their independence, this topic had to be approached with immense caution.

The appointment of Douglas Hurd as Home Secretary in 1985 was taken by senior staff as a timely opportunity to remake criminal justice policy in general and penal policy in particular, linking that critical issue with other developments in crime prevention and community alternatives to custody. 1987 proved critical for the way forward on penal policy. At the 1987 conference at Leeds Castle in Kent, all departments within the Home Office combined to draw up an agenda for more substantial crime prevention and non-custodial sentencing powers, the groundwork for which had been laid at an all-day working seminar convened by Sir Brian Cubbon at Brighton just after the Conservatives were re-elected in 1987. The Leeds Castle conference established the cross-departmental planning framework and provided the basis for the Ditchley Conference two years later, unique for the range of participation by senior civil servants, the judiciary and politicians. The active support for these conferences by Hurd and his junior minister on penal policy, John Patten, was essential. In retrospect, this was the culmination of several years' orchestration of the direction of criminal justice and penal policy by Cubbon and Faulkner, the high point from which a more liberal approach was to be mounted. 'In June 1990, in one of his last speeches before being moved sideways to another part of the Home Office, he [Faulkner] referred to the decisions which had been taken at Leeds Castle three years earlier. "That was when Ministers decided that there must be a better way to deal with crime than by locking people up on the present scale."'[96]

The Home Office programme for the meeting on 28 September 1987 began to be formulated only a few weeks before the conference itself. A letter from David Faulkner (2.9.87) to his senior colleagues – Bill Bohan, John Chilcot, Christopher Train and Mary Tuck – sought ideas for what should be covered in Patten's 'wide-ranging presentation', the key agenda-setting speech of the conference. The overall themes he suggested were: i) a 'continued emphasis' on firm sentencing; ii) continued prison building 'to cope' with their growing population; iii) as the Parole Review, chaired by Lord Carlisle, was still awaited, nothing could change in relation to particular offences; iv) 'greater use of non-custodial' measures in relation to juveniles and young adults' without prejudice to (i) 'may entail the creation of new types of penalty e.g. by electronic tag, or v) 'Plan for some more positive initiative to start reducing the pressure on prisons by the end of the Parliament? For example, by legislative restriction on the use of custody in certain types of case and/or by a fresh approach to the Judiciary.' This last point was arguably the real agenda. In response, Bill Bohan, of the Criminal Policy Department, stressed the need for detailed international comparisons to be made, and that over-loading at all stages, culminating in the huge costs of prison overcrowding, made tackling this the most urgent priority. Chris Train, speaking for the Prisons Board, stated that despite overcrowding, Fresh Start was paying off and the Prison Offic-ers' Association were co-operating in its implementation.[97]

John Patten on 17 September sought comments from his key senior civil serv-ants on the outline draft of his presentation at Leeds Castle, planned to be the opening paper following a brief introduction by the Home Secretary. Despite some common ground, the paper as a whole contained much that was at odds with their own definition of the key problems and how to tackle them. His main points were:

1.   Crime, plus anger about and fear of it, 'are all increasing and need a decisive response'.
2.   There should be 'more punishment of the nastier and more persistent offend-ers' but also 'a more serious attempt to rescue the young offender . . . before it is too late'. Moreover, he stressed that more punishment for repeat and serious violence and domestic burglary offenders would lead to 25% more 'custodial sentences and sentence lengths'.
3.   Crime prevention should be publicised by a sustained campaign including the launch of a National Crime Prevention Organisation in early 1988, eight 'Safer Cities' schemes, other projects on the Five Towns model,[98] Neighbour-hood Watch guidelines and community programmes co-ordinating schools, housing, social services and social security, employment, etc.
4.   'Young offenders and young people': 'The time has come to make a more determined effort to keep young people out of trouble and, if in trouble, out of custody.' 'This is where our practice contrasts most significantly with that of other European countries.' It needs careful presentation to avoid the 'mug-gers' charter' jibe. Prevention and diversion programmes should be worked up and promoted with judges and magistrates. He would hope to reduce court and custody by 'x and y%' by 1991.

Faulkner's reply (18.9.87) focused on the positive aspects of crime prevention and reducing custody for young offenders, without alluding to the penally expansion-ist point 2. The strategy on crime prevention would benefit from such examples as the so-called '5 Towns' model:[99] 'Gone are the days when we saw a sharp dis-tinction between policies which aimed to "target harden" and those which were labelled "social crime prevention."' These complement each other, e.g. by good housing design, management and allocation policies.

The programme for young offenders and young people 'builds on successes already achieved.' The themes were the importance of personal and social respon-sibility, the need to link youth work with crime prevention more effectively, develop 'Safer Cities' and, more difficult, keep young people out of custody. The best example of what might be done is the gap between the measures taken in relation to 14–16-year-olds compared with 17–20-year-olds. In 1985 50 per cent of younger male offenders were cautioned compared with only 6 per cent of the older group. Custody was the sentence for only 6 per cent of the younger and 20 per cent of the older group. Even 'more dramatic' results emerged from comparing 16- and 17-year-olds: 16-year-olds are 'juveniles', 17s are 'young adults'. Yet twice as many 17-year-old persons were jailed compared to 16-year-olds, that is, there was much more success in diverting juveniles from custody. 'But a young person does not suddenly become a criminal at 17 . . . And, most significantly, this process of diverting juveniles from the criminal justice system has not resulted in any increase in juvenile offending: while recorded crime generally has been going up, crime committed by juveniles has remained steady and is now actually falling. What is now needed is a similar attack on young offenders: those in the age-group 17–20.'

What should be done?: 1. More, and more consistent, cautioning; 2. Probation should develop more non-custodial disposals, and ensure that they are known to the judiciary; 3. Via Probation, NACRO, etc., 'encourage . . . and fund the development of local strategies for dealing with young adult offenders *akin to those successfully developed for juveniles.'* (emphasis added); and 4. Make greater use of senior attendance centres.

This led to three main recommendations:

1. Such schemes should be better resourced and publicly backed.
2. We should legislate 'to abolish custody for 14-year-olds (except for section 53, perhaps in the current Criminal Justice Bill)'.
3. 'Raise the juvenile age limit from 17 to 18 in a later Bill.'

Also on 18 September, a draft programme was circulated by W. Fittall, Hurd's principal private secretary (PPS). Headed 'Programme for the Crime Strategy Seminar, Leeds Castle, 28 September 1987' the day was to begin at 9.30 with a five-minute introduction by the Home Secretary stressing its point as engaging in a 'free-ranging discussion' about criminal justice strategy over the lifetime of that Parliament. The first 70–80 minute session would be fielded by Patten and Faulkner speaking on 'Crime – General'; the second by Hogg and Chilcot on policing; the third by Caithness and Train on prisons; the fourth by Patten and Faulkner on criminal justice; and a final session on 'next steps'. Each session allowed twice as much time for discussion as for the talks.

Another preliminary to the conference was a letter from Patten (23.9.87) to all seminar participants, stressing the need to cultivate links with the judiciary: "We must continue to cultivate our relations with the higher judiciary. The ambition is to nudge the Judicial Studies Board towards wider vision and greater effectiveness and to establish some kind of contact with Presiding Judges, but there is considerable judicial resistence (sic)."

On 2 October, Fittall wrote a 13-page summary of the discussions at Leeds Castle. Patten had begun by stating 'Ministers should . . . be prepared, and perhaps even take credit for, a continuing increase in custodial sentences – perhaps up to 25% – over the period of the present Parliament. . . . It is important to ensure that the prison system could cope.' Such an aim ran counter to the motives of the senior civil servants and even the Home Secretary in assembling the meeting at all. 'With the judges in their present mood and with public and Parliamentary opinion as it was' there is no point now in 'attempting to substitute non-custodial alternatives on any significant scale.' He was 'sceptical about their value' except for young offenders. He closed by stressing the urgency of bringing situational and social crime prevention processes together.

Lord Caithness on prisons gave a sombre view of the critical state of the prisons and the trend towards increasing scale and overcrowding. Sir Brian Cubbon, in a letter a week later (8.10.87) referred to this talk, based partly on Caithness's trip to visit American prisons,[100] as a 'Domesday Scenario' for 1989. Overcrowding distorts and diverts 'activity and energies'. Building more prisons was no real answer. 'Something had to be done to stop the judicial ratcheting up of sentences.' All prison population predictions were 'gloomy'. There was a need to bring back rehabilitation. Fresh Start should re-energise work, training and education as the 'mainstay' of the system. Hurd, in discussion, agreed on the need for relief apart from building more prisons. However, he doubted or rejected the value of guide-lines, though 'beefing up' CSOs and probation should be profitable. According to David Faulkner,[101] it was the talk by Caithness which convinced Hurd, and converted Patten, to the need to think more radically about policies to reduce the prison population. They now saw its rapid growth as a source of alarm, bearing the potential for losing control of the prisons, and not only by prison riots. There was, however, 'no scope for a major reform of the criminal justice system within this Parliament', and Hurd at this point summarised the available options as: 1. Plan to develop 'tougher non-custodial penalties'; 2. Explore the supervised element of prison sentences in the community, linking with the Carlisle Committee and 3. Accommodate part of the remand population outside prisons, possibly by private security firms, on barges or former mental hospitals. In seeking greater co-ordination, he rejected the idea of a Ministry of Justice – 'too much upheaval' – but the Home Secretary, the Lord Chancellor and the Attorney General should meet regularly. In discussion, Sir Brian Cubbon asserted that there was 'general support for the idea of a Standing Conference [on Criminal Justice] to bring together on equal terms the judiciary, the bar, chief police officers, the probation service, Ministers and officials to discuss problems that affected them all.' In conclusion, he 'said that it [the conference] was, to his recollection, the first occasion of its sort . . . The Home Office could achieve few of its objectives without the help of others and this meant that establishing some sort of consensus was crucial.' Seeking the 'help of others' paved the way for the more ambitious conference at Ditchley two years later.

Faulkner was quick to capitalise on these conclusions. On 1 October, he wrote to Cubbon and other senior officials. The letter was headed 'Home Office Strategy: Sentencing, Prison Building and Prison Population.' He stated that Caithness had drawn attention to the looming problem of a 'prison population crisis' unless action was taken. 'This judgement was based upon the expected effect of the courts' developing sentencing practice as led by the Court of Appeal, the Lord

Chief Justice, the Presiding and Liaison Judges and the Judicial Studies Board; and on our current assessment of the progress of the prison building programme.' Any 'crisis would have to be dealt with or averted by action taken under the existing statutory powers.' No new criminal justice legislation was to be introduced before 1989 or in force before 1990, and might be crowded out by legislative pressure during the present Parliament [i.e. until 1992]. Various options identified at Leeds Castle, such as diversion with 'more positive' control, and the wider use of bail, were in hand, but either would not be enough or would meet much resistance. It was also possible to exploit L.J. Watkins' stress on magistrates imposing too many first custodial sentences, and the need to devise influences against that both in the lower and in the Crown Court. 'All this points to the need for the closest possible understanding between the various parts of the system and to the case for a standing conference and for effective and properly directed liaison at local level.'

The extent to which the Leeds Castle conference alerted ministers to the danger of allowing penal policy to drift was demonstrated at a meeting some six weeks later, held to review the options and take decisions on which to pursue. Faulkner's own account[102] is that the 'main issue in criminal justice..[was]..the precarious situation in prisons and the prospect of a continuing rise in the prison population . . . Ministers believed that although the money for more prisons might be available in the short term, the time might well come when it would no longer be possible to provide an ever increasing number of prison places for an ever expanding prison population. They had to consider whether there was any way of easing the pressure on the prison system that would be acceptable both to the judiciary and to public opinion.

The questions which we put to ministers were whether they should:

- Take no special position on sentencing and continue to handle situations as they arose;
- Expand prison capacity as necessary to match public and judicial demand for more severe sentencing;
- Exert some downward pressure on the rise in the prison population, and therefore on the sentencing of those not regarded as a threat to society.

Our preference was for the third, but I was concerned that we should present the choices and their implications as dispassionately as possible and without a recommendation of our own on the choice between them.' In the event, 'Ministers decided to take the third of the options we had presented to them'.[103]

A little later, on 18 November, Miss Jean Goose,[104] writing on behalf of Bill Bohan, to senior colleagues Rimmer and Sanderson, as part of the follow-up to the Leeds Castle conference, headed her letter 'Delaying the First Custodial Sentence'. Two arguments were identified: 1. The reoffending rate was far worse after custody than other penalties. Yet magistrates believe the earlier a prison sentence is imposed, the more effective it will be. Secondly, courts often sentence on an offender's record, giving a custodial sentence for a comparatively minor offence because of his record of previous convictions. This was brought out in a Panorama programme on sentencing earlier in 1987. 'Having seen that programme, L.J. Watkins commented to Mr. Faulkner on the need for that tendency to be counteracted.' This letter reflects Faulkner's hope that the facts would conceivably sway the judiciary away from the use of custody in such cases; and may also express the grounds for the reactivation of just deserts.

Leeds Castle galvanised the Home Office into a more urgent formulation and implementation of policies and programmes on several fronts. Following a meeting between Ministers and Divisional Heads on 20 October, a Programme of Work was despatched by Faulkner to Heads of Department on 21 October. The Safer Cities initiative was to be launched with Prime Ministerial backing. Syd Norris was due to report on The National Organisation on Crime Prevention. There would be a Ministerial Group, and a Standing Conference on Crime Prevention. Publicity would be greatly magnified.[105] A stream of papers were to be written by the end of the year: by Mary Tuck on 'Crime, Criminality and Crime Prevention'; by Douglas Hogg on drugs for discussion at the Ministerial Group; on sentencing prospects and their implications for the prison population; a paper on remands by 6 November. Discussions would be held on 'Managing the System', with exploratory discussions on the Standing Conference and Ministerial trilaterals with the Lord Chancellor's Department. There would be a Working Party on supervision and control, entailing a paper on sharpening up community service, by 6 November; the submission of a programme for young offenders, also by that date; and a Parole Review paper by the Working Party, to include its implications for prison regimes and drugs was planned for the end of February 1988. To cap it all, a Green Paper for discussion and a later White Paper were already on course and in view.

Hurd and Patten's conversion at Leeds Castle, not so much to the need for a radical overhaul of the system relating to the state of prison overcrowding, of which they were fully aware, but to the sheer urgency of the crisis that was unfolding, led them to engage with key constituencies in distinctive ways. As Lord Windlesham notes:[106] 'As with many attempted reforms there was no single target-group to be persuaded, but three markedly different ones. The first was the Conservative Parliamentary Party, whose support would be needed to carry the legislation. Then came the judiciary, who would determine the use made of any additional sentencing powers conferred upon them by Parliament; and finally the Probation Service . . . would be needed to supervise offenders in the community.' As a result, Hurd stepped up his contacts with the senior judiciary, in particular Lord Chief Justice Lane, and Patten initiated a series of lunchtime meetings with Tory MPs to broach the main outline of planned reforms to sentencing less serious offenders and gauge their likely response when they were asked to support the legislation involved. Faulkner had been given the go-ahead by Hurd to talk to Lord Justice Tasker Watkins about the prospects for judges accepting the government's lead in reducing levels of custodial sentencing.

The publication of the Green Paper *Punishment, Custody and the Community*[107] in July 1988 laid out, for the first time quite explicitly, the Home Office strategy for extending the same case for reducing the use of custody for adult offenders as had applied to juveniles earlier in the decade: that such a policy did not inevitably lead to a rise in crime rates but, at lesser cost, could even lead to their reduction. There was, however, one key difference. Whereas the non-custodial alternatives for juveniles had been community schemes of a supportive nature, those for adults had to pass the test of not appearing to be what Patten had earlier called a 'mugger's charter'. As a result, further restraints should be created to ensure their credibility as punishments in the eyes of both the judiciary and public opinion. This *quid pro quo* aroused the suspicions of the Probation Service and penal reformers alike that the reforms could engender the worst of both worlds: that the new measures would be used as alternatives to alternatives rather than to prison itself, and that they would be tougher and more readily breached, a recipe for yet more imprisonment in the process. At a conference on the Green Paper at the London School of Economics, for example, David Garland argued that the more punitive tone adopted to carry conviction with sentencers and the public would all too readily be taken as a call to more punitive sentencing. The Probation Service leaders discerned a shift in their role from 'befriending and assisting' the offender to a rigid correctionalism.[108]

'Despite its obvious nakedly political element, however, the idea of "punishment in the community" went much deeper than being a slogan under which non-custodial sentences could be sold to the public and to sentencers, and under which the government could confront the probation service. It provided the framework on which much of the 1991 Act was constructed. Once it was accepted that graduated loss of liberty was the connecting thread between imprisonment, the various non-custodial disposals and, by extension, fines, then it was possible to build a single conceptual "just deserts" framework within which all these forms of sentencing could be accommodated and made subject to consistent criteria. In that way, the idea of statutory sentencing criteria and the idea of "punishment in the community" fused together to form a genuinely robust core concept.'[109]

Hence, despite these resistances, ministers and their advisers remained convinced that the policy outlined in the Green Paper was the only realistic way forward. The main precondition for its adoption was to bond strongly enough with the judiciary to deal with the ever-present danger of their suspicions of an over-ambitious executive seeking to invade their preserve of judicial independence. The conference at Ditchley, in September 1989, was designed to allay those anxieties and foster stronger links across all those manning the component parts of the criminal justice system.

From March 1989 onwards, a stream of letters from the Home Secretary invited people from the highest levels of the criminal justice system to take part in the conference at Ditchley on 22–23 September. Hurd took great care to stress, as in his letter to LCJ Lane on 10 April, 'how Ministers and their Departments might strengthen our contacts with the leading figures in the criminal justice system and develop a more positive basis on which they can contribute to the development of the Government's criminal justice policy.' Present contacts are 'almost always on a bilateral basis' which, however useful, does not enable us 'to think strategically about the system as a system and I believe there is a case for an occasional less structured exchange of views.'[110]

The emphasis on 'system' thinking was expressed strongly in a paper dated 13/14 March which, though no author is named, was presumably by Faulkner, as he enclosed a copy with a letter, dated 4 August, to Raymond Potter, of the Lord Chancellor's Department, about Ditchley. Headed 'Management and Efficiency in the Criminal Justice System', it sets out the case against penal expansionism: 'The response of the system to some offences at present is more heavy-handed than can be shown to be effective in terms of justice, costs, public expenditure or crime reduction . . . If the response of the system can be made more proportionate and less costly without any loss of effectiveness, its efficiency will be improved . . . In the last five years, there has been growing acceptance of the need to manage the criminal justice system . . . *as* a system . . . A disproportionately heavy sentence is both expensive and unjust.' By this point, the term 'proportionate' had become code for 'just deserts', a bow to judicial sensitivities, as the very term connoted, in the context of sentencing reform, antipathy towards deterrence and rehabilitation as principles of sentencing.

As planning for the conference gathered pace, various cautionary notes were struck about some assumptions governing the elements of the main Home Office approach to sentencing reform. S.G. (Syd) Norris wrote to John Chilcot, Faulkner et al. on 25 August, less than a month before the conference, against too facile a use of the term 'system': 'judicial eyes may glaze at "recognisable criminal justice system . . .".' 'System' implies tight central management, but this is 'clearly incompatible with the constitutional arrangements and professional independence on which we rely to maintain the liberty of the subject.' Hence the need for 'trilateralism' as of mutual benefit. Peter Storr, Private Secretary to Douglas Hurd, wrote on 18 August to Faulkner to stress the need to prepare the Lord Chief Justice and Lord Justice Watkins about the importance of 'just desserts' ahead of Ditchley. It was not to be floated in the media beforehand but, after a pre-Ditchley meeting with them, an article in the Times would be helpful. Mary Tuck had earlier – on 9 August - raised doubts to Chris Nuttall about Faulkner's request for her to cover the crime reduction effects of parole in her speech. But she was unclear about what sources he had in mind. Neither Ditchfield's recent work nor HORS 38[111] 'quite make the point Mr. Faulkner wishes to make.' By the time of the conference, these issues had been ironed out. But the major concern over the judiciary's attitude to 'just deserts' remained the key background anxiety.

On 12 September, ten days before the conference, Raymond Potter wrote to Faulkner expressing concerns about the Lord Chancellor's chairing of the session on future legislation and policies. 'It is potentially the most difficult and controversial session of the Conference.' Patten was due to introduce the session, mainly on the proposed White Paper on Criminal Justice. 'The Government's proposals on custodial sentencing – the "Just Desserts" (sic) approach – are likely to be new to most of those present. They are likely to be controversial in themselves, particularly with the judiciary. The judges will be particularly sensitive to suggestions, implied or otherwise, that they should adopt the Government's policies on custodial sentencing. There is the danger that there will be a negative reaction if the Government's proposals – on custodial sentencing, community based sentences, juvenile justice and parole – are presented as a package to be taken as a whole or not at all. The issue will require careful handling if the judges are not to come to the conclusion that the Government will not implement the Carlisle recommendations on parole [which the judges favoured] if the "Just Desserts" approach is not embraced by them. They will be particularly sensitive to the suggestion that the relative cost of sentencing options is an important factor to be taken into account by sentencers in individual cases.'[112] A related concern was that discussion could well stray from the main points to topics that were being dealt with elsewhere, such as war crimes; the right to silence; video recorded evidence; murder and life imprisonment; Social Inquiry Reports; community penalties dismissed as ineffective; reclassification and mode of trial. They all merited discussion but not to obviate the main points.

In a paper three days later by Faulkner to the Home Secretary the point was reiterated: 'The discussion may prove quite difficult. Some of those present may wish to avoid the awkward and difficult questions listed in paragraphs 12 and 13, and talk about other things such as war crimes and murder.' Notwithstanding the implication that war crimes and murder were not awkward and difficult questions, the paragraphs concerned were expressly about 'the legislative framework for custodial sentencing, and what we have called the "just deserts" approach, outlined under the heading of "proportionality" (the expression "just deserts" will not be used at Ditchley)'. It was crucial to strike the right balance. 'The most sensitive aspect will obviously be the attitude and response of the judiciary. Ditchley will be testing in several respects. The judges have difficulty with the concept of policy development. They find it difficult to distinguish between interference with judicial discretion in dealing with individual cases and consultation on wider policies; and there is a degree of suspicion of the motives of any government proposals. For this and other reasons, we do not want to force the pace by pressing for specific conclusions on substantive issues. But we do not want the Conference to dissolve without our eliciting the views of the participants, particularly the judiciary, on immediate questions such as proposals for future legislation . . .' [underlining in the original].

On 18 September, four days before the conference was due to begin, Faulkner sent the Home Secretary a Draft Paper 'Proposals for Legislation on Parole and Sentencing' for him to approve and send to LCJ Lane for the preliminary talk between themselves, LJ Watkins and John Patten before the conference start. Having conveyed general agreement with the Carlisle Report on Parole, sentencing was to be introduced as based on a clear line between the sole responsibility of the courts for decisions in individual cases and the shared responsibility for sentencing policy. As a result of worrying inconsistencies of approach, especially in magistrates' courts, 'Ministers intend to bring forward proposals for a clearer framework of the sentencing, which would be applicable for custody, community penalties and financial penalties. The focus of the sentencing decision would be the seriousness of the offence and the punishment should be aimed primarily at retribution, denunciation and compensation. This is moving towards a form of proportionality in sentencing but avoiding the restrictions imposed by some of the U.S. legislation. It is in accordance with much recent guidance from the Court of Appeal.'[113] This stress on proportionality, code for just deserts, and the emphasis on retribution to signify that principle, implicitly derogated the importance of treatment, deterrence and incapacitation as of major relevance to sentencing. It amounted to the case for a revolutionary shift in sentencing policy and practice.

It was, however, at the expense of what had for some years been the main alternative policy for the proponents of penal reform. On the very eve of the conference, on 21 September, Faulkner sent a note for the Home Secretary headed 'Ditchley: Supplementary Notes', intended as briefings for possible questioning at the conference. These covered four topics, the first of which was 'Suggestions for mandatory sentences and a sentencing commission, and our reasons for rejecting them.' Mandatory sentences 'would be undesirable' as fettering judicial discretion. As for a Sentencing Council, 'we see no need for such a body. As envisaged by Professor Ashworth, it would be a constitutional nonsense, combining legislative, executive and judicial powers . . . The Sentencing Council as proposed by Professor Ashworth, would be made up of a senior judge, a circuit judge, a recorder, lay and stipendiary magistrates, a justice's clerk, a prison governor, a chief probation officer, a civil servant and an academic. There would be no difficulty in a body on these lines advising the Government on sentencing policy and maximum penalties, which the Government could then consider and put to Parliament in legislation.[114] However, Professor Ashworth envisages the Council would also draw up sentencing guidelines for the courts and statements of general principle to assist the courts in the exercise of their discretion. He suggests that the Council's declarations could be given legal force as subordinate legislation. Many people would see this as blurring the responsibilities of Parliament, the Government and the courts." In sum, implicitly, the removal of one *bête noir* would render the judiciary more receptive to what otherwise might be another, the priority to be given to 'just deserts'.

The conference at Ditchley Park[115] was unprecedented and remains unique for the involvement of the most senior ministers, civil servants, members of the judiciary, chief police officers and chief probation officers: in other words, the key players in the statutory criminal justice system. The status of the conference as a top-level authoritative gathering was implied by the absence of such ancillary players as the penal reform and charitable agencies, academics and the media. There were two overriding aims for the conference organisers in the Home Office: to embody the interdependence of the various component parts of the criminal justice 'system'; and to seek views on, and ideally support for, the sentencing reforms that were about to be unveiled. That this broke new ground is borne out by an experienced policymaker, Michael Moriarty, little having changed since his writing a decade earlier: 'Certainly there is not much mutual consultation between the judiciary and the executive on continuing aspects of penal policy – how, in a phrase, the system is operating. No doubt there are good constitutional and historical grounds for this: but perhaps the time is approaching for them to be re-examined. In some other European countries, the links are closer.'[116]

A later, undated and confidential document summarised the proceedings at Ditchley. After a brief introduction and welcome by the Home Secretary, Mary Tuck analysed the state of crime, its seven- to eightfold rise over the period since 1957, and the extent to which it was the preserve of young males. She argued that the key role of the criminal justice system was 'to mark the limits of tolerance of society at large' – it could not do much alone to reduce crime substantially. Mr. Malone-Lee did much the same for the resources of the criminal justice system, citing the near doubling of expenditure since 1979 and that its share of total public expenditure had risen from 3 to 4.5%. Over that period the prison population had risen by 14.6% and the numbers of prison officers by 45%. David Faulkner then addressed current issues and developments. Only in the past ten years had crime prevention and help for victims become government programmes. Expectations and responsibilities had burgeoned at every stage of the criminal justice process, explaining the growth in resourcing but sharpening the need for greater efficiency and effectiveness.

John Patten then addressed the key themes of 'future legislation and policies'. He began by stating that 'It was still difficult for people to accept punishment in the community as a "real" penalty'. He then defined the aims of penalties as (1) deterrence and incapacitation; (2) retribution and denunciation; and (3) rehabilitation and 'some reparation'. 'He also stated the need for fairness and proportionality.' Justice was 'best achieved by a combination of sufficiency and proportionality.' These terms bore flexible interpretation, but 'sufficiency' could be taken for 'parsimony'. This led to proposals on the use of custody with far-reaching implications. Courts were to be required to give custodial sentences only where the seriousness of the offence justified both the recourse to custody and its length. Moreover, 'increased severity would not be justified by previous convictions.' Also, Social Inquiry Reports from probation officers would be a precondition for a prison sentence and reasons were to be given in justification. Exceptions would be made for the 'most serious offences triable only on indictment', which somewhat weakened the proposal. Even so, a radical step was clearly envisaged. Its acceptance by a sceptical judiciary would be helped by Patten's rejection of a policy long opposed by them: '. . . there were no proposals for mandatory sentencing guidelines or a sentencing commission'. In discussion following Patten's paper, no serious objections were recorded, though 'there was some surprise expressed at the idea that persistent petty offending would never warrant a custodial sentence.' Such a policy would only work if it led to community penalties 'as severe as custody.'

Following a talk by Chris Nuttall, which focused on cross-national comparisons, especially with Canada, that highlighted the sheer variety of penal policy options, and by Sir Clive Whitmore, on the need for better information flow throughout the system, the final session consisted of comments by the Attorney General, the Lord Chancellor and the Home Secretary on 'future patterns and structure'. The Attorney General focused on the need for the three departments to pool their case for more resources. The Lord Chancellor focused on the need for better inter-departmental discussion. He had been surprised by the 'territoriality' of government departments and his discovery, on taking office, 'that there had previously been no regular trilateral meetings at Ministerial level.' The Home Secretary stated that, though prisons 'were emerging from crisis' [the prison population had fallen slightly over the past 12 months] there was still room for 'intelligent improvement' without new major policy or legislative change. The same applied to the police. Scope existed, however, for a new Criminal Justice Bill to include proposals about: 1. Parole and remission; 2. The right to silence; 3. Life sentences; 4. Private remand and escort services; 5. The organisation of magistrates courts; 6. Punishment in the community; and 7. Proportionality of sentences. The conference thus closed with the Home Secretary setting a formidable agenda to be followed up.

The conference was generally rated a success. In a 'note of first impressions' by Faulkner[117] it was described as 'successful and worthwhile'. However, at the preliminary meeting with the Lord Chief Justice (Lane) and the Deputy Chief Justice (Watkins), they 'were rather bemused by the "just deserts" approach to sentencing: it will need further work and more explanation.'[118] Yet 'they seemed to accept that the changes in parole would need to be accompanied by shorter sentences'. Patten's speech had been well received but 'doubts were expressed about the proposed requirement to bind over parents, and about the application of "just deserts" to persistent petty offenders.' It was 'evident throughout that sentencers still think of imprisonment as the only "real" punishment.' These reflections portended problems to come, and lent substance to Andrew Rutherford's[119] prediction that the proposed changes would be a bridge too far for the judiciary to accept.

One further postscript to Ditchley is of some note. Sir Clive Whitmore wrote to thank both Faulkner and Malone-Lee for amendments they had suggested to his Ditchley talk and enclosing a final copy which he was happy to have published.[120] His search for efficiency was exemplified in his point that Crown Court costs greatly exceed those of magistrates' courts, e.g. £300 compared with £122 for a guilty plea; £3,100 compared with £295 for a Not Guilty plea. The average cost in 1987/8 per defendant in the magistrates' courts was £45, in the Crown Court £390. While efficiency cannot be reduced to costs – 'the figure on top of the Old Bailey holds a balance, not a calculator' – they are still a major factor in relation to different parts of the system and their effects on each other. Major savings would flow from reducing committals from magistrates' to Crown courts. Overall, this was an important paper aimed at conveying the image of 'system' operations as worthy of analysis and reassuring judges that no derogation of their powers was involved in seeking to reform the system. He employed the metaphor of the criminal justice system as a convoy of ships, not a supertanker, which need to communicate by a 'modern information system' not by semaphore or loudhailer, and whose fuel supply is not infinite. Naval metaphors with their emphasis on landfall are innately less aggressive than the military 'war on crime' rhetoric of the more punitively minded politicians.

Having assessed the Ditchley conference as a success, insofar as the floating of 'just deserts' and greater co-ordination was received without strong opposition by the judiciary, and having established a sequence of conferences and talks to the various bodies that comprised the system, the next major step was to prepare the White Paper for a Criminal Justice Bill within the Parliamentary term. *Crime, Justice and Protecting the Public*[121] duly appeared in February 1990. It was animated by the Home Office's aim of steering sentencing policy and practice in a more penally moderate direction. The case against the over-use of imprisonment was strongly made, with resort to the phrase that imprisonment 'can be an expensive way of making bad people worse'.[122] Much cited in the media, the phrase worked in terms of 'getting the message across', though it perhaps unfortunately essentialised all prisoners as 'bad people' rather than people who had done bad things. Another solecism was the spelling of 'just deserts' throughout as 'just desserts', a minor slip in some respects but one which detracted from the otherwise eloquently expressed and well-constructed statement of purpose and intent.

Paragraph 2.7 in full conveyed those aims less abrasively:

> '2.7 It was once believed that prison, properly used, could encourage a high proportion of offenders to start an honest life on their release. Nobody now regards imprisonment, in itself, as an effective means of reform for most prisoners. If there is continued progress against overcrowding in prisons, the recent reforms should enable better regimes to be developed, with more opportunities for education, and work, and so a greater chance of turning the lives of some inmates in a positive direction. But however much prison staff try to inject a positive purpose into the regime, as they do, prison is a society which requires virtually no sense of personal responsibility from prisoners. Normal social or working habits do not fit. The opportunity to learn from other criminals is pervasive. For most offenders, imprisonment has to be justified in terms of public protection, denunciation and retribution. Otherwise it can be an expensive way of making bad people worse. The prospects of reforming offenders are usually much better if they stay in the community, provided the public is properly protected.'

Penal moderation was to be positively encouraged by the greater use of community penalties and by scaling down the length of sentences where custody was incurred. Crime prevention programmes and victim support were to be stepped up. Fines were to be related to offenders' means by the adoption of a 'unit fine' system, comparable to the use of 'day fines' in Sweden and West Germany, thus rendering fines more manageable for low-income and less derisory for high-income offenders and removing standard judicial reasons for their relative decline in use. Maximum sentences for most property offences, including theft, vehicle related crime, and non-domestic burglary were to be reduced. Social Inquiry Reports from the Probation Service would be a precondition for sentencing. Written reasons would have to be given by the court in cases where a custodial sentence was imposed, a measure that had proved effective in the case of young offenders since the 1982 Criminal Justice Act. Overall, the White Paper stressed the case for proportionality and 'just deserts' in sentencing, as against deterrence and rehabilitation, though without spelling out any specific methods that would achieve that aim. Court of Appeal judgements to that end were skilfully woven into the White Paper. In 1988–89, the prison population had, encouragingly, started to fall, from 49,949 to 48,610, suggesting that earlier measures to staunch its seemingly inevitable rise were beginning to work. However, deferring the challenge of defining precisely how to draft the 'just deserts' clause would ultimately present insurmountable difficulties.

What the White Paper spelt out in striking terms was the need to disregard deterrence as a principle to be accorded priority in most cases: '2.8 Deterrence is a principle with much immediate appeal . . . There are doubtless some criminals who carefully calculate the possible gains and risks. But much crime is committed on impulse, given the opportunity presented by an open window or unlocked door, and it is committed by offenders who live from moment to moment; their crimes are as impulsive as the rest of their feckless, sad or pathetic lives. It is unrealistic to construct sentencing arrangements on the assumption that most offenders will weigh up the possibilities in advance and base their conduct on rational calculation. Often they do not.'

The crux of the intended legislation is laid out in the next paragraph: '2.9 The Government's proposals therefore emphasise the objectives which sentencing is most likely to meet successfully in whole or in part. The first objective for all sentences is denunciation of and retribution for the crime. Depending on the offence and the offender, the sentence may also aim to achieve public protection, reparation and reform of the offender, preferably in the community. This approach points to sentencing policies which are more firmly based on the seriousness of the offence, and just desserts (sic) for the offender.' What this was intended to mean in practice was further clarified in 2.18: 'An offender can receive repeated financial or community penalties, if his offences merit that level of penalty. As the Court of Appeal has said, an offender should not be "sentenced for the offences which he has committed in the past and for which he has already been punished. The proper way to look at the matter is to decide a sentence which is appropriate for the offence . . . before the court" (**R v Queen** 1981). A good record may enable the court to reduce the sentence. The Court of Appeal has reaffirmed this principle on many occasions and has emphasised the seriousness of the offence before the court as the primary factor in sentencing.' At the same time, and in some respects as a *quid pro quo*, several forms of negative encouragement to adopt penal moderation were included in the proposals. Chief among these was the stiffening of requirements that offenders on probation could be made to serve. Probation was also – in a break with tradition – to become a sentence of the court rather than a choice made by the offender instead of a sentence. That change was quickly defined as a challenge to the overriding welfare role of probation officers, as distinct from a more strict correctional function. It was, however, a prerequisite for the sentence to link probation to other non-custodial measures, especially compensation to the victim. Another key concession to the fear of the proposals being labelled a 'muggers' charter' were the increases in sentence maxima for robbery, crimes of violence and drug offences; and, perhaps most tellingly, the exemption of the most serious cases from the restrictions placed upon the majority of standard list property offences. This has been seen as a development of bifurcationist policymaking[123] whereby moves towards penal moderation for the general run of 'petty, persistent offenders' are traded off against harsher measures for those offences deemed most dangerous, typically offences of violence and involving 'hard' drugs. In this case, the bifurcationist or 'twin track' strategy applied to the more moderate measures also, as the scope was to be widened for more demanding discretionary conditions attached to probation orders. The outcome reformers have both anticipated and warned against is that the harsher measures are duly enacted whilst the more moderate measures are ignored, leading to a 'ratcheting up' effect in terms of breach proceedings, reoffending and more, not less, resort to imprisonment.

Additional innovations to meet potential criticisms of the Act as unduly lenient were the introduction of new powers of curfew and of electronic monitoring, and of the power for courts to bind over parents to attend trials involving their children as well as to pay any fines their offences had incurred. It was not only public opinion in some vague general sense that had to be appeased: 'One of the most alarming features of criminal justice policy in the 1980s and 1990s has been the rise in influence of the media, particularly the written press. The need to explain and justify one's decisions to the media became as important as the content of the policies themselves . . . The most constraining influence exerted by the press during Hurd's period as Home Secretary and since was the rise of the populist tendency most vociferously represented by the *Daily Mail* . . . Closely allied with the populism of the press on criminal justice policy was the influence of the muscular or punitive brand of Conservatism . . . If Hurd was seen to be moving too far in a liberal direction or perceived as not handling an issue with sufficient firmness, the rumblings could be detected from the influential Conservative Home Affairs Committee.'[124] In this context, opening up the remand sector of the prison system to private sector management, a step he had previously regarded as both overly difficult and unprincipled, became pragmatically justified. Also, the policy could be seen as potentially cost effective, a useful counter to the increasingly vocal pressure from the Treasury to scale back the mounting costs of imprisonment.

Before the Act could be passed, however, the context was to change in ways which rendered it less rather than more likely to be sustainable. First, Douglas Hurd, by now a Home Secretary of real stature, was moved sideways to become Foreign Minister in October 1989. Nevertheless, his successor, David Waddington, although avowedly more punitive than Hurd, supported the passage of the Act through Parliament. Second, and more decisively, the retirement of LCJ Lane made way for a successor, LCJ Taylor, who was at best unsympathetic to the Act and at worst a hostile critic wedded to its abolition. Thirdly, and even more crucially, the crime rate rose by over 40 per cent in the four-year period 1989–92, stoking fears that juvenile offending in particular was 'out of control'.[125] Though the balance of evidence, both then and now, links the crime rises with the impact of massive deindustrialisation and rising inequality, the tabloid and much public response was to indict 'soft on crime' policing and over-lenient punishment.

Even so, its passage was relatively smooth. The Act was a weighty piece of legislation, perhaps necessarily so given the various items to be included. Of its 102 sections, two stood out as especially problematic. Section 29 set out the method whereby the 'just deserts' principle was to be upheld in court. The sentence was to focus on the principal offence and, if more offences were involved, the second most serious offence. Previous convictions were to be ignored unless they signified some career element in the offender's history. As originally enacted, this read:

'*Effects of previous convictions etc.*

(1)  An offence shall not be regarded as more serious for the purposes of any provision of this Part by reason of any previous convictions of the offender or any failure of his to respond to previous sentences.
(2)  Where any aggravating factors of an offence are disclosed by the circumstances of other offences committed by the offender, nothing in this Part shall prevent the court from taking those factors into account for the purpose of forming an opinion as to the seriousness of the offence.'

In a review of a study of the 1991 Act[126] the writer expressed 'healthy scepticism' regarding the government's 'mission' to reduce the prison population. 'This writer shares their concern over s. 29 of the Act which in subs (1) tells the sentencing court to ignore previous convictions in assessing "seriousness" and then in subs (2) promptly invites the court to take them into account when they constitute an "aggravating factor"'. Moreover, the government's somewhat naive faith in the powers of the Court of Appeal to control matters by way of guideline judgements is rightly called into question by the authors and by Professor Ashworth whom they quote at some length.' The Act thus faced on this clause a double range of attack both from its substantive critics, notably among the judiciary, but also from its substantive proponents, whose major objection was to what Ashworth termed, *inter alia,* its 'abysmal drafting':[127] 'Its effect was frequently mis-stated as "courts are not allowed to take account of previous convictions", whereas it was intended to reflect the common law principle that a good record may mitigate while a bad record should not lead to a disproportionate sentence.' This well-established principle was to be in effect overturned by the 1993 Act, which – following judgements contrary to its purpose in the Court of Appeal under Lord Chief Justice Taylor[128] – substituted: 'In considering the seriousness of any offence, the court may take into account any previous convictions of the offender or any failure of his to respond to previous sentences'.[129]

A further difficulty was posed by offences 'taken into consideration' (t.i.c.s), a problem dealt with formally but far too opaquely in 29:2 above. The fundamental difference between previous convictions and t.i.c.s in 'just deserts' terms was that the former had already elicited penalties which had been paid, whereas the latter had not. The 1988 Criminal Justice Act had amended sentencing criteria for young offenders to specify custody as appropriate only if an offence was 'so serious that a non-custodial sentence for it cannot be justified'. 'The Court of Appeal eventually held[130] that the phrase "for it" must mean that if a defendant was due to be sentenced on several counts at the same time, the sentencing court should consider them individually and could not give a custodial sentence if none of the individual offences was sufficiently serious to warrant it. This approach was considered by the framers of the 1991 Bill to be right on merits, since they feared that sentencing courts might give custodial sentences for several minor current offences taken together, in just the same way that they might "sentence on record" because of previous convictions.'[131] A deputation of judges led by Lord Justice Glidewell approached the Home Secretary, David Waddington, to persuade him to change this restrictive approach to multiple offences, but he would concede only that one more offence could be considered, making two in all. Lord Ackner, a Law Lord, later cited in debate the problem posed by the repeated theft from an employer of £100 a week by a person over a long period, which would if dealt with in totality merit imprisonment but who would escape custody if only two counts were dealt with. 'His description of just deserts as a "platitudinous policy" can now be seen as a sufficiently clear indication of the senior judiciary's attitude, though it is unlikely that its full implications were hoisted on board at the time.'[132] It is also arguable that the bill contained the makings of a counter to such critical examples, given the scope for Court of Appeal clarification which the framers relied on. The most damning criticism of the Act's newfound emphasis on just deserts was that by David Thomas, author of *Principles of Sentencing* (1970) which from its original and subsequent editions had come to be a *vade mecum* for the judiciary. 'The basic idea of desert theory, that the punishment of an offender should be proportionate to his crime, was hardly a new one: it had formed the basis of articulated judicial sentencing policy, with recognised exceptions, for many years. To lawyers it was recognisable as the basis of the tariff, itself a reasonably complex body of principle based on case-law and convention. The primary objection to the proposal to enact the principle into law was not that it was revolutionary but that it was redundant, and that the manner in which it was carried out would create more problems than it would solve."[133] What this indictment glosses over, however, is the main point of the proponents of the revival of just deserts: that petty, persistent offenders were routinely jailed for their record rather than their current offence, however trivial.[134]

The intellectual and legal case for just deserts in the drafting of clause 29 and related clauses could arguably have been strengthened further. In Ashworth's words: 'What I've heard from David Faulkner and others . . . is that when the draftsmen were given the task of drawing up the bill, they were given, among other things, three academic articles to read. And those three were one of Tony Bottoms' articles on community punishment, an article by Wasik and von Hirsch . . . on non-custodial penalties and how to make those fit within a desert perspective and how to avoid breachers going into prison . . . and my article as well.[135] The evidence is they didn't read much of them, I'm afraid."

What did the articles seek to convey? Wasik and von Hirsch emphasised the neglect of desert in relation to non-custodial penalties by comparison with the focus on custody and length of sentence. The main question was: how do non-custodial sentences compare in terms of severity? 'Banding' and 'ranking' non-custodial penalties in terms of severity entails a theory of what constitutes severity. For example, fines exact monetary loss but community service involves both that, by the imposition of unpaid labour, and the restriction on liberty by the constraint on the offender's time. Unit fines based on income are essential if fines, which most readily fit the rationale of desert, are to be 'readily calibrated in their comparative severities'[136] The adoption of unit fines is also crucial for the 'partial substitutability' of non-custodial penalties, which is a prerequisite for back-up sanctions to avoid automatic resort to custody in the event of breaches. The derisory treatment of unit fines in the judicial and media responses to their enactment reveals the gulf in understanding of what that part of the Act was meant to achieve: a greater degree of equity in financial penalties imposed on offenders of vastly different wealth and income. The measure, fundamental to the criminal justice systems of Scandinavia and Germany, nevertheless proved a bridge too far for the judiciary. Problems had been anticipated in training sessions prior to the Act coming into operation, but had been successfully surmounted. A key factor in their alleged unworkability once in general use had been a late change to the unit fine model based on Treasury rules. However, it would be hard to find a measure with greater potential for informed revision, rather than its abolition after only several months in operation.

The paper by Ashworth is a balanced analysis of the strengths and limits of the just deserts model, but argues for the priority it should be accorded in sentencing, for the coherence and consistency it lends to *principled* sentencing. His key point is the importance of proportionality as a 'core principle' in two senses: first, 'ordinal proportionality' is 'a correspondence between relative seriousness of behaviour and relative severity of sentence, on which various moral and political judgements must be brought to bear'; secondly, 'cardinal proportionality' 'requires that the absolute level of the penalty scale, both maximum penalties and actual sentence ranges, be not disproportionate to the magnitude of the offending behaviour.'[137] This provides a framework in contrast to the 'sentencing anarchy' inherent in the 'cafeteria' or 'smorgasbord' approach which assumes equity of choice between retribution, deterrence, rehabilitation and incapacitation in sentencing. According primacy to retribution, or just deserts, does not eliminate bringing other principles to bear when cases demand it, but should entail an 'orderly plurality of sentencing aims' within the just deserts model. Ashworth is crystal clear on the 'cardinal weakness' of just deserts: it can be invoked to justify more severe sentencing as readily as moderation. The case for moderation must be made on other grounds, of social, moral, and economic orders. 'Just deserts' is about justice, not – except as a fundamental assumption of any system of justice – its role in crime prevention. The latter is overwhelmingly governed by social norms and structures.

Bottoms' paper[138] grounded these considerations in a detailed examination of how probation and non-custodial penalties such as community service orders lend themselves to desert-based sentencing. Both are sanctions intermediate between custodial sentences for serious offences and nominal penalties for the non-serious, and link desert with social work principles. The background to 'current confusion' among magistrates in relation to different community options sprang from two sources: first, the proliferation of new sentences since 1967 – suspended and partly suspended sentences, Community Service Orders, and probation with day centre requirements – and the gradual erosion of the 'tariff/individualised dichotomy', the clear separation, analysed by David Thomas on the basis of Appeal Court judgements,[139] between sentences based on offence- and offender-based consid-erations. The then recent shift to offence-based tariff sentencing had been largely due to growing doubts about the efficacy of 'treatment' and the morality of sen-tencing more intrusively than the offence tariff normally indicated. In the USA, examples of injustice such as the 1967 case *In re Gault* had generated such unease that a slew of studies appeared critical of sentencing to prevent *future* offending, rather than passing sentence for the present offence. The most authoritative case for 'just deserts' sentencing by Andrew von Hirsch[140] had sparked much academic but little judicial interest in Britain and it was the case for greater coherence in sentencing which the three papers were concerned to make. His theory of sentenc-ing did provide a 'framework for considering the distribution of penalties (includ-ing non-custodial penalties), while also allowing departures from that framework in appropriate cases . . . An approach of this kind allows the sentencing system in the normal case, to "concentrate on proportionality and fairness" (Ashworth, 1989, p. 355)'.[141] A key point was that repeated non-custodial penalties should be repeatedly given for offences of 'intermediate gravity' – *not* the 'penal ladder' approach that deems successive offences should attract 'escalating sanctions'.[142] In 'just deserts' sentencing, the 'ladder' of offence seriousness should be matched by a 'ladder' of matching penalties. The problem of back-up penalties in the event of further offending of similar gravity should be for sentencing to remain within the band of 'intermediate sanctions' or one step up if still short of custody. The top band of pre-custody therefore needs to be used as sparingly as possible.[143] 'Within this essentially offence-based framework, the probation service's role would then be <u>effectively to manage within the community, using appropriate social work and other skills, those offenders who had been awarded certain intermediate sanctions by the courts.</u>'[144]

The earlier (Madingley) paper[145] was also replete with warnings against penal inflation. The search for 'realistic options' to enable sentencers to avoid impris-onment was criticised as mostly illusory as, however much they are 'heated up', they are always seen as 'less punitive than prison' - hence the danger of end-less escalation in the search for the ideal, 'tough' community sentence which, when breached, leads to even longer prison sentences. Nor do desert-based pen-alties, which should be the core of coherent sentencing, exclude rehabilitative aims: probation should remain infused by such social work values as respect for persons; care for persons; and hope for the future. 'There is nothing inher-ently contradictory in the idea of a social work agency exercising certain control functions.'[146] Hence, though seriousness of offence should replace the 'needs' of the offender in the treatment model whose high point had been the 1959 White Paper *Penal Practice in a Changing Society*, and despite the traumatic effect on the probation service of the short-lived 'Nothing Works' verdict on rehabilitative measures, there was scope for voluntary 'non-treatment' helping strategies in such a framework.

Taken together, these papers provided the basis for a thorough revaluation of the principle of desert in the sentencing process. But given the extent to which these principles were left implicit in the Act, especially in the drafting of section 29, the training of the judiciary would be a critical factor in its implementation. To Ashworth,[147] 'This was hailed as the most major piece of sentencing legislation since at least 1948 and . . . probably longer. And it was quite common for judges to be trained in new statutory changes. But this one required a proper programme of judicial training throughout, from the magistracy right up to the top. And in fact the judicial training . . . in those days did include Court of Appeal judges and High Court judges as well as the foot soldiers. . . . But the major training role was given to . . . David Thomas. And David Thomas thought the Act was misconceived, pointless because . . . this was teaching your grandmother to suck eggs because, in fact, the statute just said what judges had been doing for years. And that was absolutely wrong because, if you look at his own writings, he said the first thing a judge has to decide is whether this is a case for a deterrent sentence or a case for a rehabilitative one. It's there in his textbook . . . And where's proportionality there? Where's just deserts there? It's not there. This was a new emphasis, but of course David was a great master at taking apart legislative drafting and of course he had a field day with this one, because it was inadequate in so many respects . . . '[148]

Could the damage have been limited by timely revision of the offending clause 29? Ashworth had argued that this was indeed the case, and in 1992, in his *Sentencing and Criminal Justice*,[149] had reconstructed section 29 of the Act as yielding 'three propositions:

(i) That an offender's response to any previous sentence is not relevant to the seriousness of the present offence;

(ii) That any previous convictions the offender may have do not render the present offence more serious;

(iii) That the circumstances of any offence of which the offender has been previously convicted, or of any other current offence, may be relevant in assessing the seriousness of the present offence.'

Ashworth's main pointer to the reasons for the Act's drafting flaws is that the government's intention, clearly stated in the White Paper, was lost in translation. 'All that the Government intended to do . . . was to reiterate the principle of progressive loss of mitigation which had been declared in *Queen* and . . . other decisions . . . Only if there are identifiable "ceilings" in sentencing can the principle of progressive loss of mitigation [for first offences, gaps in offending over time, social circumstances etc.] be distinguished in practice from the cumulative principle of simply "adding on" for previous convictions.' [paren-theses added].[150] It was left to the courts, and especially the Court of Appeal, to draw this framework together, but in the event no more than a few months elapsed before Kenneth Clarke, the incoming Home Secretary, swept away the key clause, by then deemed by both some senior judiciary and popular media to constitute a 'rogues' charter'.[151] Despite the above *caveats*, Clarke interpreted the Act as introducing 'a new sentencing rule that the sentencing of criminals was to have no regard to the offender's previous convictions . . . I had not noticed this piece of legislation when it went through Parliament. I had been buried in the affairs of another department. Now that I did notice it, the lawyer in me was outraged, as were many judges and members of the public. I was traditional enough to believe that it was highly relevant to sentencing to know whether the person in the dock was a first offender or someone with many previous convic-tions.'[152] Such a precipitate jettisoning of the key clauses on sentencing in the 1991 Act forestalled any possible revision or reformulation of their meaning. Symbolising that potential were a quartet of studies by some of the Act's main proponents. *Materials on the Criminal Justice Act 1991* 'brings events up to date as at implementation of the Act in October 1992.'[153] Section 29 is vigor-ously defended by Paul Cavadino. 'Critics have suggested that section 29(2) is confusing and unclear. In fact, its construction and wording clearly indicate that it applies only when the circumstances of other offences *disclose* (i.e. shed light on) aggravating features of the *current* offence."[154] Examples include evidence of professional rather than opportunist burglary; racial motivation in an attack; deliberate targeting of highly vulnerable victims of theft; and repeated sales of adulterated food. 'To sum up: a court cannot regard an offence as more serious because it is one of a series; a court cannot regard an offence as more serious because the offender has done it before (even many times before); if the cir-cumstances of other offences shed light on *features of the current offence* which make it more serious, the court can take this into account. It is therefore submit-ted that section 29(2) of the Criminal Justice Act 1991 does not undermine the desirable principle laid down by section 29(1) that an offender should not be punished twice for the same offence.'[155]

Section 18 should have been far more straightforward. The 'unit fine' system, which applied only to magistrates' courts, was simply a way of expressing in numbers a proportion of an offender's income. It was to be that rather than a monetary amount unrelated to income which would be the basis for the fine. The 'day fine' system, in which fines were assessed in relation to the offender's daily earnings, had long proved eminently workable in several European countries, including Finland, Germany and Sweden. The new model had worked well in piloting exercises to test its efficacy.[156] However, just before the Act was imple-mented in 1992, a new set of criteria for income scales was introduced, more than doubling the maximum amounts to be paid by the most affluent offenders, which complicated the ease of translation into sentencing terms. Its unpopularity with courts was due to that late and ill-advised alteration rather than to any inherent and irremediable defect. 'Some absurdly heavy fines were (unnecessarily and perhaps provocatively) imposed as a result . . . Rather than correct the scheme, the Home Secretary (then Kenneth Clarke) decided to abandon it altogether.'[157] The two sets of problems in tandem rapidly led to tabloid attacks on a few outlandish sentences and the Act rapidly gained currency as unworkable. Ironically, even in its short period of operation, unit fines were beginning to produce the desired effects. 'Home Office monitoring showed that in the period following the implementation of the Criminal Justice Act 1991, the steady decline in the use of the fine in magistrates' courts was temporarily reversed, only to be resumed after unit fines were abolished by the Criminal Justice Act 1993 . . . Moreover, the average fine for the unemployed decreased (from £88 to £66) during the period that the unit fine was in operation, while it increased for those in employment (from £144 to £233).'[158] The new Home Secretary following the unexpected Conservative victory in 1992, Kenneth Clarke, had lost little time in giving notice that these alleged problems would be despatched at the earliest opportunity, which led to the Criminal Justice Act 1993. Both key clauses were replaced by what amounted to a reversion to the pre-1991 Act law. Thus perished the most sustained attempt in England and Wales to legislate for a markedly more moderate use of imprisonment. It was succeeded by two decades of an almost cavalier disregard for the scale of imprisonment, driven by a bipartisan penal populism, a disregard reined in only by anxiety about the costs of imprisoning twice as many prisoners in 2007 as were in custody in 1992. The 'three strikes and you're out' clauses of the 1997 Crime (Sentences) Act, enacted by the Conservatives but implemented by the incoming 'New Labour' government were the exact reverse of 'just deserts'. The Act provided for an automatic life sentence for a second serious sexual or violent offence; a minimum seven year sentence for third-time trafficking in class A drugs; and a minimum three-year sentence for third-time domestic burglary.

The short-lived nature of the two key clauses of the 1991 Act cannot be assigned to their poor draftsmanship alone, which could have been amended during its passage, or later, rather than hastily dropped. The major reasons were their unpopularity with a critical mass of the judiciary and the tabloid media. The judicial view had appeared more favourable at Ditchley than proved in reality to be the case. As David Faulkner himself has commented: 'The conference seemed to give broad approval to the approach which the government had proposed, although the judges' undoubted good will may have been mistaken for agreement to the policy and there may have been some wishful thinking.'[159] As a result, 'the first surprise for those managing the Criminal Justice Bill in 1990 was the marked lack of affection shown for it by the senior judiciary . . . Dr. David Thomas, who was closely involved in training judges in sentencing through the Judicial Studies Board, and whose views were therefore given special weight by judges, publicly attacked the Bill for the way in which it sought to apply "just deserts" principles . . . David Thomas denounced the Bill as the "biggest load of codswallop I have ever seen."'[160] Despite what was achieved at Ditchley, John Halliday, David Faulkner's successor, recalled that 'the reaction of the senior judges when they saw the draft of the CJ Bill was the first proper test of judicial reaction to the actual HO intentions, and they latched immediately on to the handling of previous convictions and concurrent offences. The language I heard on arrival in the HO . . . to the effect that "we had to stop sentencing on record" had not, I think, been made explicit to judges much if at all before the draft Bill appeared. The senior judiciary (and not just D. Thomas) were on to that straight away.'[161]

As stated above, salient developments that weakened support for the bill were the loss of Douglas Hurd to the Foreign Office, in October 1989, and the retirement of LCJ Lane who was succeeded by LCJ Taylor, a determined opponent of the bill. In a series of judgements by the Court of Appeal, LCJ Taylor reinstated deterrence and prevalence as key sentencing principles.[162] Hurd's successors, David Waddington and Kenneth Baker, whilst not opposed to the bill, lent it less effective support than Hurd would in all likelihood have mustered. Faulkner himself was moved in October 1990 to the post of Principal Establishment Officer, which carried responsibility for overall management of the human resources of the Home Office. John Halliday recalled: 'I vividly remember, around the time I was taking over from David Faulkner, a senior judge, who later became an even more senior judge, telling me privately: "John, you do realise, don't you, that most of my colleagues" (he was referring to the Circuit Bench and the High Court, and excluding himself) "consider the Home Office to be full of pinko-liberals who are obsessed with the size of the prison population and soft on crime."'[163] He added: 'The HO made enormous efforts to communicate the principled basis for the '91 Act, and its intended consequences for the use of custody, for example by organising special conferences involving all participants in the criminal justice process. With HO colleagues I recall buying totally into the just desert model . . . but I am not sure we were able to alter a widespread supposition in the judiciary that we were being driven by expediency.'[164] Even so, the Bill went through Parliament relatively unscathed[165], so that the scale and intensity of the opposition it encountered after the government's re-election in April 1992 came as a shock to its proponents. That, however, had as much, if not more to do with the rapidly changing politics of crime control, which we analyse in a second volume.[166] Nevertheless, as Ian Dunbar and Anthony Langdon assert:[167] 'Whatever its defects, however, the Act represented an unprecedented effort to establish a foundation for consistent sentencing principles and it deserved a better fate than the one that soon overtook it as a result of its own shortcomings and a significant change in the political background.'

Why that 'better fate' was to be denied was, in John Halliday's summation, ineluctably linked to the 'explosion in concern about crime' from 1992 onwards 'driven above all by public/police/media and political perceptions of young offenders being out of control.' The killing of James Bulger a year later came overwhelmingly to surmount rather than cause those fears. 'The dominant things for me were the front pages of the tabloid and other papers, parading pictures and stories about young people taking cars and driving them recklessly around housing estates at night, terrorising the neighbourhood; and the serious case published by police organisations, to the effect that the real volume of juvenile crime had been concealed by the official statistics, and the Home Office assumptions about

Recorded Crime, England & Wales, 1945-1997

*Figure 5.5* Crime rate, England and Wales, 1900–1997

*Source:* Criminal Statistics (various)

crime reduction, alongside reduced custody for juveniles, were simply wrong. I had a particularly difficult session in front of the Parliamentary Home Affairs Committee on all that and my strong feeling is that the Home Office was unable to sustain its belief that had underpinned its approach to the 1991 Act, i.e. that reduced custody for juveniles had been accompanied by lower levels of juvenile offending.

The belief that a successful reform of sentencing for juveniles could be replicated with equal success for adults through the 1991 Act was such a bedrock of Home Office thinking that its removal (rightly or wrongly) in the period after 1992 effectively undermined the whole structure. The need for a new policy was driven fundamentally (as I see it) by a wider and more complete loss of whatever faith there had been in the assumptions underlying the 1991 Act about how best to respond to juvenile offending, as well as a wider perception that crime was increasing and "out of control" . . . It was about then that the Daily Mail, on its front page, reported a belief in government circles that the Home Office was very much like what the senior judge had told me his colleagues thought of it a few years earlier, i.e. a department staffed by pinko-liberals who were obsessed by the size of the prison population and soft on crime. That front page is in my view an important indicator of the change in political wind.'[168]

In a sense, the fate of the 1991 Act was a supreme case of the wisdom of Harold Macmillan's celebrated phrase, when asked about the main difficulties facing governments: 'events, dear boy, events'. If the crime drop which began in the mid-1990s, both in Britain and in comparable countries, and which owed much to major investment in crime prevention measures, had occurred a year or two earlier, the main precepts of the Act could well have been handled far more constructively. It is also vital to register the stress on utilitarian thinking in the history of English criminal justice.[169] It may be that the 1991 Act's radical devaluation of previous convictions in sentencing, and its upholding of the current offence as its main determinant, was too anti-utilitarian to be acceptable. But the 'unit fine' concept perfectly combined just desert with utilitarian principles, and that too was swept away. In short, the 1991 Act, whatever the problems of drafting and the chance factors involved, foundered in part due to its accidental yet unavoidable 'bad timing'.

## Notes

1  Simon Bastow, 2012, 'Overcrowded as normal: Governance, adaptation and chronic capacity stress in the England and Wales prison system, 1979–2009', Ph.D. thesis, London School of Economics,: 92.
2  In his *Prisons and the Process of Justice*, 1984, London: Heinemann; and 1986, 2nd ed. rev., Oxford: Oxford University Press.
3  *Committee of Inquiry into the United Kingdom Prison Services*: 124.
4  From Thomas Guiney 2019 'Solid foundations? Towards a historical sociology of prison building programmes in England and Wales, 1959–2015', *Howard Journal of Crime and Justice, 58, 4: 459–74.*
5  Roy King and Kathleen McDermott (1989a) *The State of Our Prisons*: 108–9; see also their summary article 'Prisons: The Ever-Deepening Crisis' *British Journal of Criminology*, 1989(b), 29, 2, 107–128.
6  See King and McDermott, 1989b: Table 1, 113.
7  Ibid: 115.
8  Ibid: 118.
9  Ibid 118
10  Ibid: 121.
11  Ibid: 122.
12  Ibid: 124.
13  Ibid: 126.
14  See Cavadino and Dignan, 2007: 289–92.
15  Thomas Guiney, 2018, *Getting Out: Early Release in England and Wales, 1960–1995*, Oxford: Clarendon Press: Ch. 3: 55–78. Based on his 2015, *In the Shadow of the Prison Gates: An Institutional Analysis of Early Release Policy and Practice in England and Wales, 1960–1995*, Ph.D. thesis, unpubl., London School of Economics: 108 et seq.
16  Guiney, 2015: 156.
17  Cabinet meeting 2 December 1965, CAB 195/26.
18  Roy Jenkins, 1991, *A Life at the Centre*, London: Macmillan: 175.
19  See Paul Rock, 2019a, *The Liberal Hour*, London: Routledge, on the abolition of capital punishment, abortion and homosexual law reform. Despite his many positive attributes, Jenkins saw Soskice as lacking in practical political sense and as 'extremely indecisive'.
20  Hansard: HC Deb 12 December 1966, Vol. 738 col. 1502. Quoted in Guiney: 157.
21  Cavadino and Dignan, op. cit.: 290.

22  The term 'bifurcation' was first coined by Anthony Bottoms (1977) to denote a policy of tougher sentences for offences considered dangerous, in particular those involving violence, and a more lenient approach to those considered petty offences, especially minor theft.

23  H.C. Deb., Vol. 738, col. 66, quoted in Bottoms, 'The suspended sentence in England 1967–1978', *British Journal of Criminology,* 21, 1, Jan. 1981: 3.

24  2 Q.B. 29.

25  Sparks, Richard F., 1971, op. cit.: 83. See also his Table V, 2: 84.

26  Committee of Inquiry into the United Kingdom Prison Services Report (The May Committee) October 1979: 55, para. 3.55.

27  *The Howard Journal*, August 1987, 26, 3, 177–202.

28  Ibid: 177.

29  Quoted in ibid.: 196. Dr. David Thomas QC (1938–2013), Reader in Law, Trinity Hall, University of Cambridge, author of successive editions of *Principles of Sentencing* 1970. London: Heinemann. Thomas also influenced judicial training in England and Wales through his work with the Judicial Studies Board (now the Judicial College).

30  Michel Foucault, 1977, *Discipline and Punish: The Birth of the Prison*, London: Allen Lane. See also Stanley Cohen (1979) 'The punitive city: notes on the dispersal of social control', *Contemporary Crises*, 3. 8. 339–63.

31  In his *Responses to Crime, Vol. 2: Penal Policy in the Making*, 1993: 168, n. 65.

32  Parl. Debates, HL, 431 (5th Series), col. 948, 22 June 1982.

33  See, on this issue, Taylor, L., Lacey, R. and Bracken, D. (1979) *In Whose Best Interest?* Cobden Trust/MIND.

34  The 'tariff' was the informal scale of severity evolved by the judiciary based on considerations of deterrence or retribution. A group of criminologists and social work staff, mainly based at the University of Lancaster, were to the fore in exploring how the rehabilitative reforms of the 1969 Children and Young Persons Act had unwittingly snared in the criminal justice system children whose needs were often for welfare measures, or whose offending should be addressed by involvement in local community programmes rather than custody. See especially the key work of the so-called 'Lancaster School' in exposing the shortcomings of and proposing alternatives to this system: Thorpe, D.H., Smith, D., Green, C.J. and Paley, J.H. (1980) *Out of Care: The Community Support of Juvenile Offenders*, London: Allen & Unwin; and Andrew Rutherford (1986) *Growing Out of Crime: Society and Young People in Trouble*. Harmondsworth: Penguin.

35  See especially Denis W. Jones (2012) *Conditions for Sustainable Decarceration Strategies for Young Offenders*, Ph.D. thesis, London School of Economics, published electronically.

36  Lord Elton, Parliamentary Undersecretary of State 1982–87; Minister of State, Home Office, 1984–5.

37  Windlesham, 1993, op. cit.: 169–70.

38  Tim Newburn (2002) *Oxford Handbook of Criminology*, 3rd Ed.: 554.

39  Allen, R. 1991, 'Out of Jail: The Reduction in the Use of Penal Custody for Male Juveniles 1981–88', Howard Journal, 30, 330–52.

40  David Faulkner, CCBH Witness Seminar: The Criminal Justice Act 1991, 2010: 6.

41  Conceived at a Home Office conference in Brighton in 1987, Safer Cities was designed to develop 'partnerships' between local government and voluntary organisations, combining social and situational crime prevention measures. 'The approach would cover subjects such as town planning, architectural design and public transport as well as those associated with policing and law enforcement.' David Faulkner (2014) *Servant of the Crown: A Civil Servant's Story of Criminal Justice and Public Service Reform*, Hook: Waterside Press: 111. There was an unusually direct flow of ideas into such schemes from earlier criminological work such as Oscar Newman's concept of 'defensible space' and that by Pat Mayhew and Ron Clarke on situational opportunities for crime (see below). See also Faulkner's account of the impact of such studies on the

development of crime prevention policies in the Home Office in *Crime, State and Citizen,* 2001: 275–80.

42 Trevor Bennett (1989) 'The neighbourhood watch experience' in Morgan, R. and Smith, D. (eds.) *Coming to Terms with Policing,* London: Routledge. Initially a prolific success – 'within a decade of its establishment, over five million households were covered by one of over 100,000 schemes in England and Wales' (Newburn, T. (2007) *Criminology,* Willan: 568) – its popularity, at its greatest in the least crime-prone areas, waned as police resources proved too stretched for adequate monitoring.

43 R.V.G. Clarke (1980) '"Situational" crime prevention: theory and practice' *British Journal of Criminology,* 20. Clarke went on to be the Head of the Unit before moving to the USA to take up a Chair in Criminology at Rutgers University.

44 Oscar Newman, (1972) *Defensible Space: People and Design in the Violent City,* London: Architectural Press.

45 See, for example, the review by A.E. Bottoms, (1974), *British Journal of Criminology,* 14.

46 R.V.G. Clarke and P. Mayhew (eds.) (1980) *Designing Out Crime,* London: HMSO.

47 Op. cit.

48 See Denis Jones, *Conditions for Sustainable Decarceration Strategies for Young Offenders,* 2012, Ph. D. thesis, London School of Economics, for the view that, *inter alia,* criminologists failed to challenge this unwarranted dismissal and even supported it without demur.

49 Forrester, D., Chatterton, M. and Pease, K (1988) *The Kirkholt Burglary Prevention Project, Rochdale,* London; and Frenz, S., O'Connell, M. and Pease, K. (1990) *The Kirkholt Burglary Prevention Project, Rochdale: Phase II,* London.

50 D.E.R. Faulkner developed throughout the 1980s the role he had been allotted by Brian Cubbon (q.v.) at its outset of assembling for ministers what came later to be termed evidence-based options for the future of the penal system. His career at the Home Office from 1959 culminated as Head of the Criminal and Research and Statistical Departments 1982–90. After his retirement, he became a Fellow of St. John's College and a member of the Centre for Criminological Research at Oxford University. He has written three books analysing and reflecting on criminal justice policy since World War 2: *Crime, State and Citizen* (2001, 2nd ed. 2006) Winchester: Waterside Press; (with Ros Burnett) *Where Next for Criminal Justice?* (2012) Bristol: Policy Press; and *Servant of the Crown: A Civil Servant's Story of Criminal Justice and Public Service Reform* (2014), Hook: Waterside Press.

51 Brackets added. David Faulkner, 'The Criminal Justice Act 1991', paper given to the Centre for Contemporary British History (CCBH) Witness Seminar, 7 May 2010: 5, unpubl.

52 Adam Crawford, 2009, 'Situating crime prevention policies in comparative perspective' in A. Crawford (ed.) *Crime Prevention Policies in Comparative Perspective,* Cullompton: Willan: 25.

53 Robert Reiner, 2007, *Law and Order: An Honest Citizen's Guide to Crime and Control,* Cambridge: Polity: 115–16; Lucia Zedner, 2003, 'Too much security?', *International Journal of the Sociology of Law,* 31:1, 155–84. Cited in Downes, 2010, 'What Went Right? New Labour and Crime Control', *Howard Journal of Criminal Justice,* 49, 4: 395–6.

54 May Committee, op. cit.: 3; Windlesham, 1987: 229. The first of his four-volume *magnum opus.*

55 Martin Wright, Director of the Howard League 1971–82, stated the view that the Prison Reform Trust was 'probably founded because people felt that the Howard League wasn't doing enough.' (interview, 6.6.14)

56 Downes and Morgan 1997: 113; see also Ryan, 1978.

57 See his book of that title (1978), in which he compares the Howard League, RAP and PROP in their relation to the Home Office and the establishment in general.

58  Paul Rock (1998) *After Homicide: Practical and Political Responses to Bereavement,* Oxford: Clarendon Press.

59  *Parl. Debates,* HL, 529 (5th Ser.) col. 631, 4 June 1991. Cited in Windlesham, *Responses to Crime,* Vol. 2, 1993: 9n.

60  Alex Lyon (1931–1993) was called to the Bar in 1954 and became Labour MP for York 1966–83, Minister of State at the Home Office 1976–78. 'A man of marked principle', Lyon irked the Labour leadership in government, first in 1968 by voting against the Bill to severely restrict immigration by Kenyan Asians fleeing Uganda under Idi Amin. When James Callaghan became Prime Minister in 1978, Lyon 'was asked to leave the Government.' (obituary by Tam Dalyell MP, *The Independent,* 1 October 1993). His second wife, Clare Short, became Labour MP for Birmingham Ladywood 1983–2010, and Secretary of State for International Development 1997–2003. She resigned the party whip in 2006 to serve as an independent MP.

61  David Downes (1983) *Law and Order: Theft of an Issue* LCCJ/Fabian Society; David Birley and Jon Bright (1985) *Crime in the Community: Towards a Labour Party Policy on Crime Prevention* LCCJ; Ruth Allen (1985) *Public* Order LCCJ; and David Downes and Tony Ward (1986) *Democratic Policing,* LCCJ.

62  Sheerman, B., *Seven Steps to Justice,* 1992, Labour Party.

63  Andrew Ashworth is the Vinerian Professor of English Law Emeritus at the University of Oxford, a member of the Centre for Criminology and Fellow of All Souls College. His books include *Sentencing and Penal Policy,* 1983, London: Weidenfeld & Nicolson; *Sentencing and Criminal Justice,* 1992, London: Weidenfeld & Nicolson; (with Andrew von Hirsch (eds.) *Principled Sentencing: Readings on Theory and Policy,* 1992, Edinburgh University Press, 2nd and subsequent editions, Oxford: Hart; and (with Lucia Zedner) *Preventive Justice,* 2014, Oxford: Oxford University Press.

64  Three articles by Ashworth, Bottoms, and Wasik and von Hirsch were important influences on key clauses in the 1991 Act: see pp. 150–152.

65  Vivien Stern was Director of the National Association for the Care and Resettlement of Offenders (NACRO) 1977–96; Secretary General of Penal Reform International 1989–2006; and co-founder, with her husband, Professor Andrew Coyle, of the International Centre for Prison Studies, 1997. In 1999 she became Baroness Stern of Vauxhall, sitting as a cross-bench peer in the House of Lords. Her books include *Bricks of Shame: Britain's Prisons,* 1987, Harmondsworth: Penguin; *Creating Criminals: Prisons and People in a Market Society,* 2006, London: Zed Books; and *A Sin Against the Future: Imprisonment in the World,* 1998, Harmondsworth: Penguin.

66  Unfortunately misspelt as 'just desserts' in the Act itself. This misspelling had, however, recurred in many of the Home Office papers circulating in connection with the conferences held at Leeds Castle in 1987 and Ditchley in 1989, important steps towards the 1991 Act (see below).

67  An introductory presentation by David Faulkner and headed 'The Justice Model' was dated October 1982. In a later note, he states 'This had its origin in the Discussion group.' An earlier (13 pp.) paper entitled 'The Justice Model and the Objectives of Imprisonment' was a searching analysis of the contrast between the 'justice model' and the 'treatment model' favouring the former as the preferred model for the future. Unsigned and undated, it emanated from the Directorate of Operational Policy. Comments on its argument, generally supportive, were dated 12, 23, and 24 July 1982. [Source: The Faulkner Papers, file 4] [See below].

68  David Faulkner, 2014, *Servant of the Crown: A Civil Servant's Story of Criminal Justice and Public Service Reform,* Hook: Waterside Press: 83.

69  See the third edition of his *The State of the Prisons in England and Wales: With Preliminary Observations and an Account of some Foreign Prisons and Hospitals,* 1784: Warrington: W. Eyres.

70  De Beaumont, G. and de Tocqueville, A. (1833) *Du Systeme Penitentiaire aux Etats-Unis, et de son Application en France.* Paris.

71  For example, Emile Durkheim, *Suicide*, 1897, tr. 1952; Georg Rusche and Otto Kirch-heimer, *Punishment and Social Structure*, 1939.

72  Hermann Mannheim, 1965, *Comparative Criminology*, 2 vols., London: Routledge & Kegan Paul.

73  Leon Radzinowicz, 1961, *In Search of Criminology*, London: Heinemann.

74  Hans Tulkens, 1979, op. cit.; David Downes, 1982, 'The origins and consequences of Dutch penal policy since 1945: A preliminary analysis', *British Journal of Criminology*, 22: 325–62; 1988, *Contrasts in Tolerance: Post-war Penal Policy in the Netherlands and England and Wales,* Oxford: Clarendon Press; Andrew Rutherford, 1984 and rev. 1986, *Prisons and the Process of Justice*, Heinemann and Oxford University Press; John Graham, 1988, 'The declining prison population in the Federal Republic of Germany' *Home Office Research and Planning Unit Research Bulletin,* 24: 47–52.

75  David Faulkner, 'Criminal Justice: Problems of Co-ordination and Control', talk at the University of Southampton, 5 June 1984: 2.

76  Ibid: 3.

77  Ibid: 3–4.

78  Talk to the Judicial Seminar, 10 January 1985: 5.

79  *Begum Bibi* (1980) 71 Cr App R 360; *Upton* (1980) 71 Cr App R 102. Lord Lane LCJ, Lawton LJ and Straw LJ reduced a sentence of three years' imprisonment on Bibi, a Kenyan widow and mother convicted of importing two and a half kgs. of herbal cannabis, to six months.

80  David Faulkner, introductory address to the Witness Seminar on the Criminal Justice Act 1991: 4.

81  In 1993 he was appointed to a Visiting Fellowship at the Institute of Criminology at Cambridge University.

82  *Sentences of Imprisonment: A Review of Maximum Penalties* 1978, London: HMSO.

83  Andrew Rutherford, 1986, op. cit.: 187, note 43, citing 'A Survey of the South East Prison Population', *Home Office Research Unit Bulletin*, No. 5, 1978, pp. 12–24; and *Prison Department Statistics, 1983*, 1984.

84  Charlotte Banks and Suzan Fairhead, 1976, *The Petty Short-Term Prisoner*, London: Barry Rose and the Howard League for Penal Reform. Tony Parker, the prolific probation officer turned author, had written a widely acclaimed study of one such habitual prisoner, in *The Unknown Citizen*, 1963.

85  Timothy Cook, author of *Vagrant Alcoholics*, 1975, London: Routledge and Kegan Paul.

86  See *The Petty Persistent Offender: Proceedings of a Seminar held at NACRO on 26 June 1979*, London: NACRO. Chaired by Sir Arthur Peterson, Permanent Secretary at the Home Office 1972–77.

87  Suzan Fairhead and Tony Marshall, 'Dealing with the Petty, Persistent Offender: An Account of Current Home Office Research Unit Studies', in ibid, 1–9: 2.

88  Norman Tutt, 'Meeting the Welfare Need', ibid, 11–14. At the time of the seminar, 26 June 1979, Principal Social Work Adviser at the Department of Health and Social Security, later that year Professor of Applied Social Studies at Lancaster University.

89  Elizabeth Barnard and A.E. Bottoms, 'Facilitating decisions not to imprison', ibid, 17–27. At the time of the seminar, Elizabeth Barnard was a lecturer in criminology at Sheffield University, later that year Principal Organiser for NACRO. Tony Bottoms was Professor of Criminology at Sheffield University.

90  David Faulkner, personal comments.

91  See Ashworth 1983; von Hirsch 1976; and von Hirsch and Ashworth 1998.

92  Unsigned but almost certainly by Quentin Thomas, as comments by recipients were sent to 'Mr. Thomas'.

93  The authors were D. Atkinson; C.B. Stevens; Robin Duval; and Julian le Vay.

94  As, for example, in a talk given by Faulkner at the 1982 Prison Governors' Conference. See his *Servant of the Crown*, 2014: 64–66. The arguments anticipated the key theme of the 1991 Woolf Report (see Chapter 5 below).

95  *Crime, Justice and Protecting the Public* (Cm. 965) Feb. 1990.
96  Quoted by Rutherford 1996: 105.
97  Fresh Start was the major initiative introduced by Douglas Hurd to tackle the complex issues of institutionalised overtime and other matters relating to staff pay and career structures that the May Committee had not managed to resolve. Basically it involved a generous pay settlement in return for the POA's acceptance of new manning and working arrangements to obviate institutionalised overtime.
98  See below.
99  Demonstration projects in crime prevention which succeeded in lowering crime rates among young offenders.
100  Lord Caithness had visited the USA on behalf of Parliament (7–19 September 1987) to explore the lessons to be drawn from their experience of privatisation – nothing to be gained and some adverse effects; construction and design – nothing to make us change direction, though 'we were all reassured by new generation prisons' (see Ch. 4 above); the different federal, state and county systems; and electronic monitoring – generally a good thing as it dispenses with the 'sombre impression created by numerous keys'. The visitors included Margaret Clayton, who as Director of Services, Prison Dept., 1985–89, was mainly responsible for prison building design (see Ch. 4 above).
101  In conversation, 6 February 2013, and subsequently confirmed by email.
102  In a draft of the book on his career, *Servant of the Crown* 2014.
103  Op. cit.: Ch. 7 'Later Years 1987–1992', pp. 2–3.
104  Jean Goose was to play a critical role in drafting the pivotal Clause 29 of the Criminal Justice Act 1991 (see below).
105  'Product Image' was starting to figure strongly in the publicity plans. One theme 'in the PR campaign should be that of togetherness or of the good neighbour, bringing out that everyone had a role in crime prevention, not just Government.' But the 'active citizen' should be mobilised first. This approach was, arguably, needed politically as the Conservative government had earlier made a huge fanfare about tackling crime by sterner measures, yet the crime rate had continued to rise year by year.
106  In his *Responses to Crime* Vol. 2: *Penal Policy in the Making* 1993: 223.
107  Cm 424, HMSO.
108  David Garland in Huw Rees and Eryl Hall Williams (eds.) *Punishment, Custody and the Community: Reflections and Comments on the Green Paper*, Suntory Toyota International Centre for Economics and Related Disciplines/London School of Economics, 1989: 8–14.
109  Ian Dunbar and Anthony Langdon, 1998, *Tough Justice: Sentencing and Penal Policies in the 1990s*, London: Blackstone Press: 89. In a footnote to the penultimate sentence, they add: 'The formulation of a desert model for non-custodial disposals was due to Wasik and Von Hirsch in "Non-custodial penalties and the principle of desert", *Criminal Law Review*, p. 555 (1988), which is known to have influenced the framers of the 1991 legislation.' See below for further discussion on these points.
110  Material relating to the Ditchley conference is based on files made available for the official history by David Faulkner.
111  J.A. Ditchfield, Home Office research study not specified; the HORS 38 reference is to C.P. Nuttall et al (1977) *Parole in England and Wales*, Home Office Research Studies, number 38, HMSO.
112  Parenthesis added.
113  Para. 9, op.cit.
114  Indeed, this was precisely the role, if not the composition, of the Advisory Council on the Penal System, which ran from 1965–1979, but was not allowed to continue by the incoming Thatcher government.
115  Ditchley Park, a classic English country house in Oxfordshire, was developed in the post-war period as perhaps the leading venue for national and international conferences on policy issues.

116  M. Moriarty, 1977, 'The policy-making process: how it is seen from the Home Office' in N. Walker and H. Giller (eds.) *Penal Policy-Making in England*, Cambridge: Institute of Criminology, Cropwood Series No. 9.

117  4 pp., 26 September1989, to senior colleagues.

118  Quotation from what appears to be an earlier draft of the same note.

119  Then Reader in Law at the University of Southampton and the Chairman of the Howard League.

120  17 pp. long, and published, abridged, 1990: 'Managing the Criminal Justice System', *The Magistrate*, 46, 1: 4–5.

121  Cm 965.

122  Ibid: para. 2.7

123  See Bottoms' original use of the term (1977) 'Reflections on the renaissance of dangerousness', *Howard Journal of Penology and Crime Prevention*, 16, 2, 70–96; and Cavadino, Dignan and Mair (2013) *The Penal System: An Introduction*, London: Sage. 5th ed., 27–31.

124  Mark Stuart, 1998, *Douglas Hurd: The Public Servant*, Edinburgh: Mainstream: 182. Chapter 12, 'Watching One's Back: Reforming the Criminal Justice System' concerns his time as Home Secretary 1985–1990.

125  See, for example, Robert Reiner, 2007, *Law and Order: An Honest Citizen's Guide to Crime and Control*, on crime and neo-liberalism; Downes and Rock, *Understanding Deviance*, 2003, 4th ed.: 166–70, for a discussion of such topically related theories as the 'crisis of masculinity', the 'new underclass', etc.; and Stephen Farrall and Colin Hay (eds.), 2014, *The Legacy of Thatcherism*, British Academy/Oxford.

126  Roger Leng and Colin Manchester, *A Guide to the Criminal Justice Act 1991*, reviewed by anon., *Law Society Gazette*, 3 June 1992.

127  Andrew Ashworth, 'Sentencing', in Maguire, Morgan and Reiner (eds.) *Oxford Handbook of Criminology*, 1997, 2nd ed.: 1113. In interview (28 May 2014), Ashworth developed this point further: 'If you look at the White Paper, the White Paper is pretty clear about what its leading philosophy was, what it wanted to do, but that clarity evaporated in the drafting. And rather than saying that sentences should be proportionate to the seriousness of the offence as determined by harm and culpability, the usual things that desert theory said, the only word out of that that survived was seriousness. And that wasn't really enough to carry the big change in philosophy that was being put forward . . . Then if you turn over to the provision on previous convictions, section 29, that was the most involved and detailed and misconceived that you could come across.' Nevertheless, suitably revised, section 29 could have been made 'perfectly workable'. See Ashworth (1992) *Sentencing and Criminal Justice* London: Weidenfeld & Nicolson: 151–2.

128  And speeches by him: 'Criticism of the Act came to a peak in an address by the Lord Chief Justice of England, Lord Taylor, to the Law Society of Scotland. Congratulating the Scottish judiciary on the fact that the Act did not apply to Scotland, Lord Taylor CJ said that parts of the Act defied common sense and hoped that it would be reviewed and that sanity would be restored.' David Thomas, 'Sentencing Reform: England and Wales' 1995: 145.

129  As amended by section 66(6) of the Criminal Justice Act 1993. See Cavadino and Dignan 2002, third edition: 100 and 117n.

130  In *Davison* (1989) 11 Cr App R (S) 570.

131  Dunbar and Langdon, op. cit.: 94–5.

132  Ibid: 95.

133  David Thomas, 'Sentencing Reform: England and Wales' in C.M.V. Clarkson and R. Morgan (eds.) *The Politics of Sentencing Reform*, 1995, Oxford: Clarendon Press: 135.

134  Though John Halliday, later the main author of an important report on sentencing in 2001, '*Making Punishments Work,*', which sought to modify a renewed emphasis on

proportionality by greater attention to recent and relevant previous convictions, does not recall much if any evidence being adduced by advocates of desert theory at the time to show that increases in the prison population had been driven by 'sentencing on record'. (Personal comment, 2019). It was, however, defined by penal reformers as a staple rather than an increasingly important factor in sentencing. Analysts of the prison population, especially Ken Pease, had long stressed the scale of the change that would be needed to make a dent in its size by focussing on short-term prisoners. See his *Prison Population: Using Statistics to Estimate the Effects of Policy Changes*, 1980, Milton Keynes: Open University Press.

135 A.E. Bottoms, 1989, 'The Concept of Intermediate Sanctions and its Relevance for the Probation Service' in R. Shaw and K. Haines (eds.) *The Criminal Justice System: A Central Role for the Probation Service*, University of Cambridge: Institute of Criminology; M. Wasik and A. von Hirsch, 1988, 'Non-Custodial Penalties and the Principles of Desert', *Criminal Law Review*, 555–572; and A. Ashworth, 1989, 'Criminal Justice and Deserved Sentences', *Criminal Law Review*, 340–355.

136 Op. cit.: 567.

137 Op. cit.: 344.

138 Which developed themes addressed in an earlier paper by him: 'The Place of the Probation Service in the Criminal Justice System', in Central Council of Probation Committees, 1989, *The Madingley Papers II*, Cambridge: University of Cambridge Board of Extra-Mural Studies.

139 *Principles of Sentencing*, 1979.

140 Originally set out in his *Doing Justice* (1976) New York: Hill and Wang.

141 Bottoms, in Shaw and Haines (1989): 87.

142 Bottoms, op. cit.: 88–9.

143 Ibid: 92–3.

144 Ibid: 92; underlining in the original.

145 Not given to the drafters.

146 Bottoms, 1989, The Madingley Papers.

147 In interview (28 May 2014).

148 On this point, Graham Angel, a member of the drafting team, commented: 'It was almost entirely the judiciary. The opposition was vehement. It was very vehement . . . I wanted to mention David Thomas because we became caught in academic rivalry. Because we were influenced by Ashworth, David Thomas, who was the in-house academic for the senior judiciary, felt that his position was not exactly "under threat", but he took a different view. He was able to influence the senior judiciary to a considerable extent and that stoked up the hostility to a substantial degree.' Centre for Contemporary British History Witness Seminar, *The Criminal Justice Act 1991*, 7 May 2010, London: Birkbeck College: 59.

149 London, Weidenfeld and Nicolson: 151–2.

150 Ibid: 151.

151 See e.g. the Criminal Bar Association, August 1990, *The Times*, cited by Ashworth, op. cit.

152 Kenneth Clarke, 2016, *Kind of Blue: A Political Memoir*, London: Macmillan: 294.

153 Andrew Ashworth, Paul Cavadino, Bryan Gibson, John Harding and Andrew Rutherford (eds.) 1992, Winchester: Waterside: 5. The three preceding volumes, by the same editors with the addition of Peter Seago and Lorna Whyte, were *Introduction to the Criminal Justice Act 1991*, 1992, reprinted May 1993; *Criminal Justice Act 1991: Legal Points: Commentary and Annotated Guide for Practitioners*, 1992; and *The Youth Court*, 1992, reprinted February 1993, All Winchester: Waterside Press. The early reprints indicated a significant interest in its interpretation which outlasted its abrupt abolition, though the youth court survived largely unscathed.

154 Op. cit.: 62.

155 Ibid: 64.

156  Bryan Gibson, 1990, *Unit Fines*, Winchester: Waterside Press; and David Moxon, 1990, *Unit Fines: Experiments in Four Courts*, Home Office Research and Planning Paper No. 59, London: HMSO.

157  David Faulkner, 2014, *Servant of the Crown*, Hook: Waterside Press: 133.

158  Michael Cavadino and James Dignan, 2002, *The Penal System: An Introduction*, London: Sage: 129.

159  CCBH Witness Seminar: The Criminal Justice Act 1991, 7 May 2010, paper by David Faulkner: 8.

160  *Guardian*, 20 November 1990; cited in Faulkner, ibid: 10.

161  Personal communication, 2019.

162  As, for example, *Cunningham, (1993* 14 Cr App R (S) 444.*).*

163  Interview with John Halliday, 2015.

164  John Halliday, personal communication, 2019.

165  Dunbar and Langdon note: "Labour opposed the Bill's second reading but on grounds that had nothing to do with the points we have mentioned", largely concerned with the previous convictions issue. "The main Labour argument was that the Bill was inadequate and that it ignored such things as a code of prison standards and a sentencing council . . ." op. cit.: 96.

166  (forthcoming) D.Downes and T. Newburn, *The Politics of Law and Order*, Vol. 4 of this history.

167  Ian Dunbar and Anthony Langdon, op. cit.: 87.

168  Personal communication, 2019.

169  Paul Rock, 2019a, *The 'Liberal Hour'*, London: Routledge.

# 6    The Woolf Report and After

In the mid-1980s, a substantial change occurred in the pattern of disturbances in English prisons. In the 1970s and early 1980s, the worst rioting and serious disturbances took place in the dispersal prisons created as a result of the Radzinowicz Report on the imprisonment of long-term prisoners under conditions of maximum security. On 30 April 1986, however, prisoners at HMP Northeye, a category C prison, damaged the buildings so extensively by fire that the prison had to be evacuated and prisoners housed elsewhere. Riots took place on the same night at seven other prisons. This initiated a spate of disturbances across 40 prisons, including locals and remand centres. 'At a number of prison establishments control broke down . . . 45 prisoners escaped and there was a considerable amount of structural damage to buildings, 800 places were lost to the system, over 200 of them permanently.'[1] The Chief Inspector of Prisons called it 'the worst night of violence the English prison system has ever known.'[2]

The precipitating event for this spate of rioting was an overtime ban imposed by the Prison Officers Association which severely restricted evening regimes in prisons across the country. The POA action was in response to a dispute at HMP Gloucester where the Governor had 'locked out' prison officers on 27 April and ran the prison by other governor grades shipped in to support him from other prisons across the country. The fraught state of industrial relations in the prison service was thus the immediate cause of the disruption but the more fundamental source was the character of penal regimes and the pressure of steadily rising numbers.

These events were soon to be seen as the prelude to yet more serious developments in riotous assembly and mounting destructiveness in English prisons. 'What the events of 1986 and 1990 demonstrated was that all establishments were vulnerable to disorder and that remand prisoners were now as likely as sentenced prisoners to participate.'[3] The 'events of 1990' were the riot at Strangeways Prison, Manchester, followed by its occupation by prisoners, a state of affairs which lasted three weeks and which sparked lesser but still very serious disturbances at over 20 other establishments. Between 1986 and 1990, ministers had striven to address the seemingly best attested reasons for the rapidly deteriorating state of security and control across the prison sector as a whole: the ever-rising prison population and subsequent overcrowding. But events were to overtake their best endeavours, the main result of which was the Criminal Justice Act 1991 (see Chapter 5).

The report of the subsequent inquiry, chaired by Lord Justice Woolf and co-authored, in part, by the Chief Inspector of Prisons, Judge Stephen Tumim,[4] has achieved justifiably classic status as a record of the events themselves and their immediate causes, and as an analysis of the more fundamental underlying causes. Its 598 pages contain 12 key recommendations and 204 accompanying proposals. If the prison system, at least for a time, began to provide better living standards and more tangibly 'humane containment' than that of 1990, despite the doubling of the prison population it houses, that state of affairs can in large part be attributed to the impact of the Woolf Report. Though not without its critics,[5] it set a standard for advanced public inquiry into penal affairs that has not been surpassed.

## The riot at HMP Manchester

Strangeways Prison on 1 April 1990 held 1,647 prisoners, the largest in England and one of the largest in Europe. Well over a third were on remand, both adult and young prisoners either awaiting trial or sentence. Conditions were all too typical of an English local prison built in the Victorian era: heavily overcrowded, its Certified Normal Accommodation (CNA) of 970 inmates having a ratio of 1.69 to its actual population, insanitary and, despite some recent tangible improvements, provoking bitter criticism by inmates of most aspects of their prison experience as a whole.

As documented by the Woolf Report, there had been some warnings of trouble to come at the chapel service on Sunday morning 1 April 1990.[6] But there was nothing too unusual about that. Some precautions were taken, but not enough: seven extra officers were positioned in the vestry. However, when it came, it quickly mushroomed, with prisoners holding the chapel and some taking a route, evidently little known to the staff, to the roof.

When Brendan O'Friel, the governor, took control of the staff response, after coming in from time off, he devised a plan to retake the main prison. This strategy was overruled by the Deputy Director of Prisons, Brian Emes[7], a decision heavily criticised by Woolf as missing a good opportunity to retake control. As a result, the disturbances lasted a further three weeks. Emes had evidently overstressed the danger of staff being outmanoeuvred due to the nature of the physical layout which, in Woolf's view, he had not properly assessed. He should have backed O'Friel's judgement as the man on the spot. Friel's Plan B, to which he did agree, proved far less effective, retaking only the kitchen.

Poor communication figured heavily in the earliest stages of the riot which rapidly grew to the occupation of the prison by a small minority of prisoners. A senior prison officer had warned that trouble was 'brewing' in the following morning's chapel service, but his advice to station prison officers on the roof above the projection room was not followed (3.94) by an inexperienced duty officer. Although the warning was logged, it was not formally passed on as needed to the day shift duty governor. Reliance on informal communication proved fruitless.

This lack of co-ordination meant that prisoners rapidly took over the chapel, from which they expelled staff, from whom keys were stolen. In the general melee of fighting, confusion and horrendous noise, senior duty staff took the decision – wrongly according to Woolf – to evacuate the centre, which could have been held (3.143–4). The loss of the wings and the hospital left the prison effectively in the prisoners' hands. The plight of those Rule 43 prisoners still inside the prison (some had been transferred after evacuation) proved a nightmarish ordeal, with beatings and torture-like assaults taking place. One was stabbed in the side with scissors and thrown over the balcony onto the netting where objects were thrown on top of him. Other prisoners interceded and helped them to release – amazingly none was killed. Staff also acted, at times heroically, to release prisoners who requested it. Trust between staff and inmates paid off remarkably at times (3.213–4). At the same time, fires were started and slates and bricks rained down on staff from the roof (3.222). In that context, it was no mean feat to evacuate and transfer 1,289 prisoners without any escapes. Liaison between regional and national HQs worked well on this front, with Emes co-ordinating at the HQ end.

Day 2 of the disturbances began inauspiciously. Despite the remand centre being retaken relatively easily by the Control and Restraint (C and R) unit, a larger-scale plan jointly drawn up by the unit and O'Friel to retake the prison was rejected by Emes at national HQ. Woolf is severely critical of Emes's over-riding of O'Friel's wish to proceed as planned, stressing his great expertise and experience as governor as well as being 'the man on the spot' (3.263–4). Moreover, no direct communication had taken place between them except under poor circumstances – Emes had, at the key time, been at the Home Office to brief ministers, not at Prison Service HQ. He had received misleading reports of what was planned and vetoed it on risk of loss of life grounds. Woolf comments that O'Friel did not defend his plan strongly enough, but all the evidence suggests that 'whatever Mr. O'Friel had said during the conversation, Mr. Emes would have come to exactly the same decision.' (3.260) Emes failed to appreciate the breathing space the delay would give the defiant prisoners to strengthen their defences and the negative effect on morale of the staff. Yet Emes had himself been a prison governor of some considerable experience and his erring on the side of caution on risk of loss of life grounds was borne out by events, even though the long delay in retaking the prison reverberated throughout the entire system and sparked substantial, if lesser disturbances in twenty more prison establishments, five of which, in addition to Strangeways, were analysed as part of the inquiry. Overall, if one compares the retaking of Strangeways after the riot and lengthy occupation by prisoners with the loss of 96 lives at Hillsborough football stadium in April 1989, only one year earlier, followed by what were later found to be massive cover-ups and revelation of corrupt practices by the police, the concern to avoid loss of life must have weighed extremely heavily at the time.

The siege lasted another 23 days until the prison was retaken on 25 April. By 3 April, 85 prisoners were still at large in the prison. Over 1,500 had been evacuated and transferred elsewhere. By 4 April there had been two deaths, of one prisoner and one staff, following injuries and complications. 29 prisoners surrendered,

26 remained in the prison. Massive media coverage had been mounted, with prisoners trying to overcome staff blocking their access to them, a spur to rooftop occupations which could not be hidden from view. The cameras captured such symbolic displays as the prisoners singing 'We Have the Power', and mothers imploring their sons to come down from the roof for their own safety.[8] By the second week, 21 prisoners were still holding out. Emes rejected use of the army on the grounds that no threat to life existed and the disturbance had been contained. The occupation had settled into a war of attrition, with more prisoners surrendering, though seven were still at large on 16 April. The retaking of the kitchen on the second day had meant prisoners were substantially deprived of supplies of food and drink. Great anxiety about booby traps and structural damage involving collapse still led to caution against risk of further injury in a major attack. The third week thus began with a further decision by Emes and Alastair Papps, the Regional Director, against action to retake E Wing, the easiest to assault. The growing involvement of ministers and tactical discussions to retake the prison led to its achievement on 25 April. 'The final re-taking of the prison was rapid and successful . . . and its very success raises the question as to why an attack was not made earlier. After all, from the weekend of 13 April, there were no more than ten prisoners at large." (3.335) The most spectacular prison insurrection in British history was at an end, but debates about its causes, character and consequences were just beginning.

The set of consequences most commonly attributed to the occupation of Strangeways Prison, Manchester, in particular due to its sheer duration, was that it triggered similar, though less serious disturbances in over 20 other penal establishments, five of which were analysed in some detail by Woolf and his team of assessors. Glen Parva was a Young Offender Institute and Remand Centre near Leicester. Generally a well-run and spacious institution, it was 'an unlikely site for the next serious disturbance after Manchester'. (4.2) The key factor was seen as the cell-sharing of two would-be escapees, one of whom had been transferred from Strangeways after the riot, and who resented the greater distance this imposed between him and his family. They attacked an officer for his keys and the disturbances spread rapidly from that point on. It was contained and resolved without too much difficulty.

The riot at Dartmoor was an altogether more serious affair. If Strangeways was the spark, a plethora of underlying causes fuelled the flames. Two wings were taken over by prisoners and, as at Strangeways though in this case due to the governor, an intervention plan was called off. A prisoner started a fire which caused his own death. Over £3 million worth of damage was done. Large numbers of prisoners surrendered but one held out on the roof for a further six days. Dartmoor was notoriously forbidding and isolated. Long scheduled for closure, it was still the main category B prison for the south-west. Grievances abounded, not least the distance from prisoners' families, but overcrowding did not figure among them.

Riots at Cardiff, Bristol and Pucklechurch were also analysed in some detail by Woolf and his team. By contrast with Dartmoor, Cardiff was 'grossly overcrowded' (6.6) but staff-prisoner relations were good within a relaxed regime. The critical factor seems to have been the need to accommodate 50 prisoners transferred from Strangeways. A disturbance, not directly due to them, led to the overnight occupation of two wings, but the great majority of prisoners did not wish to get involved and the trouble subsided when access to the roofs was forestalled. Disturbances at Bristol were more severe, and were also triggered by transfers due to rioting, this time from Dartmoor. Despite grossly inadequate conditions, without the Dartmoor arrivals, Woolf doubted if such a major disturbance would have flared up – three wings were occupied, an officer was held captive and £3 million worth of damage resulted.

Apart from Strangeways, Pucklechurch Remand Centre was the site for perhaps the next most serious set of events in the aftermath of Strangeways. Recently built, and lightly overcrowded but with no transfers from other riotous prisons, the troubles seemed to have passed Pucklechurch by, due to a tightened regime for 12 days. A strong reaction to the nearby Bristol riot was to be expected, as many of the young male prisoners had personal contacts there. Relaxed on 21 April, on 22 April keys were grabbed from an officer and other prisoners were quickly unlocked. From small beginnings the disturbances became extremely serious. Roofs were occupied, missiles – slates, coping stones, fire extinguishers – were hurled at staff. Costs of £4–5 million were incurred, 35 prisoners and 41 staff were injured, some seriously: it was 'a shattering and terrifying experience'. (8.182) Minor errors – such as keys which, when stolen, gave inmates the run of large parts of the prison (8.188:8–9) combined with regime harshness – no workshop or vocational training, the stifling of young men's energies by lack of facilities and association periods too lightly abandoned – to stoke what came to be seen by Woolf as the prime reason for the riots in general: a potent sense of grievance and injustice.

### The Search for Causes and Remedies

The terms of reference for the Inquiry, following the appointment of Lord Justice Woolf to conduct it on 5 April 1990, were extended a few days later to take account of the disturbances at other prisons. They were: 'To inquire into the events leading up to the serious disturbances in Her Majesty's Prison Manchester which began on 1 April 1990 and the action taken to bring it to a conclusion, having regard also to the serious disturbances which occurred shortly thereafter in other prison establishments in England and Wales'. (2.4) These terms of reference were taken by Woolf to warrant a full-scale analysis of both the immediate and the more fundamental causes of the riots, an approach similar to that adopted by Lord Scarman in his inquiry into the Brixton riots a decade earlier.

In a key section termed 'the central problems of the Prison Service', which served as a unifying theme for the entire report, Woolf argued that riots were not isolated, one-off events but were generated by 'serious underlying difficulties' (1.142) What were they? Prisoners and pressure groups stressed insanitary, overcrowded conditions; negative regimes; lack of respect towards prisoners; the destructive effect on family ties and the inadequacy of visits; and the lack of independent redress for grievances. (1.143) Staff stressed the lack of staff and training; and isolation and poor leadership. Governors stressed lack of support from HQ. Some stressed poor co-ordination across the criminal justice system as a whole.

Woolf agreed that all these were relevant as contributory factors and causes but identified 'one principal thread' which linked them: 'It is that the Prison Service must set security, control and justice in prisons at the right level and it must provide the right balance between them.' (1.148) In what amounts to one of the most definitive statements of root causes in the analysis of social unrest, he stressed that all three are interdependent. Poor control in part stems from injustices in the system, leading to grievances which fuel disturbances. 'Justice, therefore, contributes to the maintenance of security and control.' (1.151) For example, escapes were narrowly averted but could equally have resulted. Lack of respect for prisoners was a clear factor in the troubles at Dartmoor and Pucklechurch.

What should be done to prevent repetitions of the riots? Recent important changes were the massive new building and refurbishment programmes, costing £450 million in 1990/91 alone. Secondly, two radical managerial reforms since 1987 were 'Fresh Start', to remedy the over-reliance on overtime pay – a reform which to Woolf had not really worked as yet; and in September 1990 a 're-organisation of management above establishment level', not spelt out but presumably the change in 1990 replacing line management by regional directors, responsible for around 40 prisons in each region, to area managers, which was intended to provide firmer oversight of operational performance in eight-ten prisons.

However, these changes did not address how 'prisoners and staff are treated.' (1.164) and the need to achieve the proper balance between security, control and justice. 12 steps to achieve that goal formed the report's central recommendations. These were:

i.  Closer co-operation between different parts of the criminal justice system, leading to a national forum and local committees. A Criminal Justice Consultative Council was needed as a forum to link the main departments of the system and other departments, such as Health, as required. (1.169–72);

ii. More visible leadership by a director general as operational head of the prison service. He should work to a 'compact' or 'contract' provided by ministers. During the riots, the existing director general took a back seat and the deputy director general took overall charge. In the recent reorganisation, there was no longer a deputy director general but the director general should be a much more visible leader. There was no need to resort to agency status to achieve this end. A 'compact' or 'contract' would spell out tasks and responsibilities. (1.173–78);

iii. Increased delegation of responsibility to governors: HQ should be more 'enabling' than hitherto, and support governors in their role rather than imposing it. (1.179);

iv. An enhanced role for prison officers: they should be better trained with prospects of accelerated promotion. 'Fresh Start' was not enough: there was also the need for 'contracts'. (1.180–82);

v. A 'compact' or 'contract' for each prisoner in relation to the prison in which he or she is held, reviewable every 12 months, and to be upheld by Boards of Visitors. (1.183–85);

vi. A national system of Accredited Standards, to be subject to judicial review once certified as achieved. (1.186–87);

vii. A new Prison Rule to limit numbers to a prison's CNA. Parliament to be informed if this is not adhered to. This would put an end to overcrowding, if properly managed. (1.188–91);

viii. A timetable to provide access to sanitation for all prisoners by February 1996: 'After overcrowding, the most destructive feature of the prison system at the present time is the lack of sanitation and the degrading process of slopping out which is its consequence.' Everyone agreed on this point but no date had ever been fixed for its eradication. February 1996 is the recommendation of HM Chief Inspector of Prisons (Stephen Tumim) which should now be binding. (1.192–93)[9];

ix. A better basis for prisoners to maintain family and community links via more visits and home leaves, and via 'community prisons' they could be held as near as possible to their homes. Such links are a key factor in reduced reoffending and are a big element in riots and disturbances due to prisoners transferred too far from their homes. (1.194–96);

x. By the same logic related to social relationships, prisoners and staff would be better served if prisons were divided into 'small and more manageable and secure units' of some 50/70, within prisons which should not exceed 400 in total. Larger prisons could be redesigned to operate two or more prisons within the same perimeter. Electronic locking would obviate the problem of keys fitting all locks, one of the main problems in existing prisons. (1.197–203);

xi. A separate set of aims and lower categorisation for remand prisoners are needed. There is a strong case for separate treatment and a real upgrading of conditions is long overdue. More bail is an obvious option. To encourage much needed reforms, a separate Statement of Purpose for remand prisoners is required. They should also be Category C rather than B unless a very strong case is made. (1.204–206);

xii. Improved justice and grievance resolution procedures. Boards of Visitors should lose their adjudicatory role to an independent Adjudicator and Ombudsman system. Prisoners should be given reasons for any decision affecting them. Serious criminal offences committed in prison should be heard by the normal criminal courts. All disciplinary offences should be dealt with by the Governor. (1.207–9)

All 12 should be regarded as elements of a package and achieved together. No doubt many would be costly but it is important to realise that many would *save* money, though that is not the main aim, by reducing disturbances, riot, damage and the overuse of custody.

In summarising the lessons to be learnt from the detailed analysis of the disturbances, Woolf was at pains to stress the watershed character of developments in the 1980s. 'The pattern of serious disturbances in English prisons has deepened and widened. Until 1986, large scale disturbances occurred mainly at training prisons and, in particular, at high security dispersal prisons. But the latest series of disturbances in April 1990 indicates that, with the exception of open and specialist prisons, no prison can be said to be immune from a substantial risk of involvement in prison disturbances." (9.17) Moreover, remand prisoners had figured seriously in all disturbances examined, except Dartmoor. 'It is quite wrong to assume that, because prisoners are on remand, they do not have the potential for creating serious control and security problems.' At Pucklechurch, young males on remand 'exhibited more hostility and aggression towards staff than was exhibited in other disturbances, other than possibly Strangeways and Bristol.' Too many were held in over-secure conditions. (9.6) It should now be clear that 'a further catastrophe of the scale of Strangeways could have brought the Prison Service to the verge of collapse', and constituted a threat to other parts of the criminal justice system. 'No-one should doubt the importance of achieving a more stable prison system than we have at present.' (9.18)

Having established the importance of security, control and justice to a stable prison system, Woolf went onto to analyse how best the balance between them could be achieved, though attention to each was also vital. 'Security' referred to preventing escapes; 'control' to preventing disruption; and 'justice' to humanity and fairness in relation to prisoners and the objective 'to prepare them for return to their community in a way which made it less likely that they will reoffend.' (9.19–20) Though significant improvements were needed to bolster security and control, the main deficit lay in relation to justice.

Above all, 'the disturbances demonstrate a need to pay more attention to justice within prisons'. Felt grievances were the key to the riots. Over-frequent transfers were a major cause of resentment and bitterness, especially at being removed far from families. Moves for control reasons were heavily implicated, and were therefore counter-productive. It was not the case that transfer automatically led to riots, but 'in all the cases studied, the precipitating incidents . . . involved those who had been recently transferred. Evidence on prisoners' need for predictable stability, such as the research by Bottoms, Hay and Sparks,[10] also showed that 'the incidents which at the start involved only a few inmates, spread because they found ready support from many more inmates . . . A transfer against the wishes of a prisoner is one of the most resented actions which the Prison Service can take. It is made worse when the prisoner feels he has been given no satisfactory explanation . . . and when the transfer results in his being further away from home.' (9.33–35) Conversely, prisoners 'will not join in disturbances in any numbers if they feel conditions are reasonable and relationships are satisfactory.' (9.37)

On security and control, Woolf rejected the case for a categorisation of control risks, to match that of security risks, on the grounds that no such equivalence existed. 'The evidence suggests that a prisoner who creates control problems in one prison, may behave with complete propriety in another.' (9.48) There was also great danger of injustice in imposing such a blanket categorisation. Other lessons to be drawn from the riots were:

- Security information reports must be completed and properly submitted to the governor;
- The disastrous effect of the loss of an officer's keys must be reduced;
- Staff must initially be expected to withdraw from the immediate scene of a serious disturbance;
- There should be security firebreaks to which staff can withdraw and hold;
- Physical security should be checked and, where necessary upgraded e.g. tools and building equipment should not be left 'lying about for rioters to seize';
- There must be improved methods of communication, and better contingency planning and training;
- Boards of Visitors should have a central role in contingency planning;
- The prison service should have the capacity to deploy water during a disturbance;
- Control and Restraint (C & R) techniques will need to continue to be reinforced and co-operation with the police maintained.

Most reports would have ended there with an appropriate summary and conclusion. The architecture of the Woolf Report was far bolder, reflecting Woolf's determination to spell out in great detail and with judicious force the importance of reconfiguring the penal system to take far more account of the neglected priority of justice, fairness and humanity in its structure and administration. The report was, after all, the culmination of three decades of cumulative demands for reform of the system after the hiatus of the war and immediate post-war period. Those demands had shifted from an emphasis on the scientific treatment of offenders in the Butler White Paper of 1959, *Penal Practice in a Changing Society*, to *inter alia* the case for the 'normalisation' of regimes which King and Morgan put to the May Committee in 1978, the case for 'decency' put by Rutherford and for 'tolerance' by Downes, based on what had proved possible in comparable societies, the schemes for and debates about penal reform tirelessly put by NACRO, the Howard League, the Prison Reform Trust, Justice and the Parliamentary All-Party Penal Affairs consortium, the opening of the Home Office to sentencing reform due to an unusually liberal generation of senior civil servants, and the potential for radical reform of the (then) impending Criminal Justice Bill. The work of the Cambridge criminologists, Bottoms, Sparks and Hay on the overriding importance of prisoners' sense of the *legitimacy* of the prison regime as a precondition for compliance and therefore order, was clearly implicit in Woolf's analysis, though their book which stressed the synthesising concept of legitimacy was published after the Report.[11] The Inquiry team not only invited submissions of evidence and interviewed relevant practitioners and professionals in the traditional way, but did so in uniquely open fashion, holding three day-long public seminars along with discussions at site visits to locations where riots had occurred.[12]

Hence, **Part II** of the Report, co-authored by Stephen Tumim, was a detailed exposition of how the changes recommended to ensure stability in the system applied to imprisonment, the buildings, management, staff, and the prisoners themselves.

**Section 10: Imprisonment** (pp. 239–64) stated the need to clarify its aims and methods, to reduce numbers and therefore overcrowding, and to see it as part of the criminal justice system. The May Committee had traced the loss of purpose to a loss of belief in rehabilitation and sought to replace it with 'positive custody'. But Rule 1 had not been rewritten along the lines suggested. Nevertheless, Rules 1 and 2 already suggested two key aims: (1) prisoners should be subject to minimal security; and (2) they should be encouraged to lead a good and useful life. The Prison Board's Statement of Purpose adds 'with humanity' (10.10), and Woolf would add *justice* in prisons as implicit in its purpose and as integral to the criminal justice system as a whole. Inhumane and degrading conditions constitute *injustice* (10.19). The responsibility to ensure justice in prison regimes was lacking. Moreover, generating bitterness fuels the likelihood of crime after release. The degrading state of the prisons accentuated both insecurity and loss of control, which then entailed ever more disproportionate use of resources on those fronts, leaving too few for support, training, education and welfare.

Remand prisoners were a forgotten but growing minority: up from 14% in 1975 to 22% in 1990, an increase due to increasing time held on remand. As many as 950 were remanded in custody for over six months in 1989 (10.51) so they were not short-term visitors only. They cannot simply be taken for granted as non-problematic – remand prisoners took an active part in virtually all the disturbances. The fact that they were held in worse conditions than the sentenced is 'a travesty of justice'. (10.58) Bail was a crucial issue. If it was withheld, no further damage should be inflicted on those remanded in custody. A separate Statement of Purpose was accordingly needed in their case. (10.63) They should be guaranteed, not simply granted, the fullest possible access to work, training, family visits and the like. The Prison Rules should be revised to fit the European model.

Increasing numbers lead inevitably to overcrowding which had, in Terence Morris's words, a 'mesmeric effect' on the prison service, diverting attention from the need to improve regimes and conditions. A much higher priority should be given through the criminal justice system as a whole to the need to reduce the numbers imprisoned in order to afford better conditions. Sentencing was the key to this end, leading Woolf to recommend the formation of two new bodies. A Criminal Justice Consultative Council should gather, analyse and disseminate up-to-date information on the state of and trends in prison conditions, especially for remands and specific minorities, such as mentally ill prisoners. This would not be a Sentencing Council but a conduit for better information flows between different parts of the system. Secondly, Local Committees should be established to do the same at local level. These would replace the then current Regional Liaison Committees and add a judicial representation and purpose. (10.185)

**Section 11: Buildings** (pp. 265–84) laid out 14 principles which should govern future developments in prison accommodation and architecture. These ranged from the glaringly obvious (which had nevertheless escaped attention in the past), such as the need for different units to have different keys or, ideally, electronic systems, to fundamental choices about conditions and location. Primarily, prisons should be based on units of some 50–70 prisoners numbering in all no more than 400. They should allow for flexibility and varied regimes within a prison. Harking back to the 1988 Prison Design Briefing System, and the influence of American 'New Generation' prison design, Mr. Lynch, the inquiry's architectural adviser, argued that small unit design can be a way of containing disturbances and simultaneously promoting better staff-prisoner relations.

A related principle was that, wherever possible, prisons should be *community prisons*, based on the need to respect prisoners' closest family and neighbourhood links. Staff and inmates alike relate better when from the same region, though the May Committee had disputed this assumption. A major gain would be avoiding the unsettling effects of transfer away from a prisoner's locality, a key factor in the disturbances. Localisation should be the overriding principle, though some specialist prisons like Grendon would be exceptions. (11.63) Even women could be accommodated within special units on this basis. Though Woolf had not addressed the reasons why women, who were held at even greater distances from their homes than men, due to their much smaller numbers, had taken no part in the disturbances, the principle was seen as just and desirable in its own right, and not solely as a riot prevention measure. Much the same could be said for the need to provide satisfactory facilities for visits, including adequate visitor centres, especially where no such facilities existed at all.

Another swathe of proposals related to hygiene, where Woolf adopted the principle that standards should be those of the community at large. There should be one prisoner to a cell, and no enforced cell sharing. Dormitory accommodation was undesirable, and breached both the (non-binding) European Prison Rules and the UN Standard Minimum Rules. In some countries, e.g. the Netherlands, this principle has real force. Similarly, most urgently of all, slopping out should be phased out and a target date set for its elimination. (11.95) Prisoners need access to hygienic sanitation at all times, which had been seen as a top priority by successive HMCIPs and penal reformers for decades. The date of February 1996 was fixed as the point for all prisons to comply with this requirement, a provision which, if unmet, would be a mockery of humanity and justice and one on which the UK was out of step with all other countries visited. (11.112) Insistence on this point was arguably Stephen Tumim's major contribution to the report[13] and in the event the requirement was largely met. However, the practical difficulties in some cases meant that the formal termination of slopping out fell and still falls short of the reality. In-cell sanitation still does not exist in some 2000 prison cells across 10 prisons and the replacement by electronic unlocking systems too often fails to work.[14]

Standards of hygiene should be no less than those accepted in the community. This principle was extended to cover kitchens, washing facilities and other amenities which were all too exposed to infestation by pests. A key change was that, on 1 April 1992, as a result of the 1990 Food Safety Act, 'prison establishments will be open to inspection by local authority and environmental health officers'. (11.119) Better arrangements should be made to dispose of packets of excreta dropped from cell windows, often in protest at the poverty of sanitary facilities. (11.120–1)

Overcrowding recurred as a major issue (see below). The Director General of the Prison Service was quoted as stating at one of the inquiry sessions 'that the life and work of the Prison Service have, for the last 20 years, been distorted by the problems of overcrowding . . . The removal of overcrowding is . . . an indispensable pre-condition of sustained and universal improvement in prison conditions.' (11.135) Then current trends and 10,000 more places could solve the deficit within two years, but Woolf stressed that this would not allow for uneven distribution and low standards. Moreover, strict controls over keeping to prisons' CNA should be introduced in a way that linked with parliamentary scrutiny and certification if it was exceeded by more than three per cent in any establishment.

Beyond a certain level, overcrowding not only increased the strain on prisons but extended disarray and unwanted costs to the rest of the criminal justice system. Police cells were generally a very expensive, fetid and cramped alternative when the Prison Officers Association adopts a CNA ceiling on prison receptions in the course of industrial action. This led to police cells being used for far too many prisoners for far too long a period: 'not a reasonable exercise of power.' (11.158) But one which forward planning would obviate, as would be provided by a body such as the proposed Consultative Council.

**Section 12: Management** (285–336) must confront a central and persistent paradox: high staff commitment to the service is combined with marked staff distrust between all levels, 'a remarkable dichotomy' (12.1). There is a perpetual sense that every crisis must lead to an inquiry which is a 'last chance' to put things right. The problem is solvable, given recent improvements in conditions and organisation, and given 'more visible leadership' (12.5) No more management changes were needed, save for a more developed 'contract' between the service and ministers. However, senior management reorganisation since 1979 and the May Report have not improved things and have led to an 'unsettled' atmosphere.

A key recommendation was that the director general should become less of a purely administrative and more of an operational head. The deputy director general post, now abolished, had undertaken that task and played a 'very authoritative role' during the disturbances (12.28) That should now be the responsibility of the director General, whose responsibilities should be threefold: 1. Operational Head of the Service; 2. Advising ministers on policy formulation and implementation; and 3. Developing co-ordination with other criminal justice agencies. Ministers should adopt a 'hands off' approach to their role in relation to the prison service, which would obviate (as recommended in their evidence by Louis Blom-Cooper and Terence Morris) the need for agency status. (12.57) Relations between HQ and establishments should tilt in favour of greater autonomy for the latter, including budgetary control. A Prison Service Planning Document should be drawn up, based on the need for more sophisticated indicators of performance and forward projections over five years, which would provide the basis for a 'contract' between the prison service and ministers. Despite objections, a Code of Minimum Standards should be perfectly manageable. Such Accredited Standards would provide a framework for prisoner 'contracts' to ensure progression throughout the sentence. However, Woolf equivocated on whether the term 'compact' should be used, as such provisions would not be legally enforceable.

Disruptive behaviour, so important as a cause of the Manchester riots, was not especially related to overcrowding in any direct way, but rather to the nature of the regime, as international comparisons showed. Disruptive behaviour can be reduced by system change. Where it nevertheless arises, it can be dealt with by transfer, either for up to a month to a local prison for 'cooling off' or to a local for up to six months; by segregation under Rule 43; or by allocation to a Special Unit for the Control of Disruptive prisoners. Prisoners subject to transfer or segregation should at least be given reasons in writing, as grievances are all too likely to result. Policy on allocation to Special Units had been reformulated by the 1983 Control Review Committee report, which had recommended diverse rather than uniform provision. [15] Three such units had been created at Hull, Parkhurst and Lincoln and a fourth was planned at Milton Keynes. However, 'at present Special Units make only a small contribution to the Prison Service's response to problems of control. They cater for a very small group of prisoners' (12.283–4), 34 in all in September 1990. Overall, though all such options are important enough to be retained and improved, they are not nearly enough to constitute a response to the problems of control posed throughout the penal system. The only real answer is to move to a small units policy in community prisons.

Several other important recommendations in this section were:

> that, following the evidence of Roy King's research on Oak Park Heights prison in Minnesota, a new maximum-security prison along 'new generation' lines should be built, facilitating small unit design. (12.304–5) Whitemoor Prison, due to open in 1991, may lend itself to this purpose;
>
> that remand prisoners should be housed as close to home as possible and normally be category C, not B as was then the case, a clear instance of over-security. They too should benefit from 'contracts' and induction programmes;
>
> that the stress on work, training and education was even stronger in the case of young offenders, who still amounted to 20% of the prison population despite recent reductions in the number aged under 17: down from over 4,000 receptions in 1979 to some 1,800 in 1989; (12.326)
>
> that prison is the perfect crucible for drug use and gambling, due to long hours of boredom. Apart from regime enhancements to reduce this root cause, 'drug-free' zones within prisons, as in the Netherlands, should be explored. A thorough review was also needed of policy towards HIV/AIDS, as those designated carriers were subject to regime deterioration, a disincentive to disclosure.

**Section 13: Staff** (337–370) are seen by Woolf and Tumim as subject to their loyalty being compromised by deep insecurity and fears for their personal safety, especially at weekends. 'Fresh Start', the major policy initiative to eliminate the excessive reliance on overtime, had if anything exacerbated rather than resolved this problem. Aimed at achieving a 15% reduction in hours worked, and then a further 9%, whilst only making up half that amount by extra recruitment, clearly required a great deal of trust if it was to succeed. In the event, despite the initial enthusiasm of staff for Fresh Start, it became very unpopular due to the way it was implemented, by playing up the attractive and playing down, or even mis-leading staff, about the increased work needed to achieve savings without more staff. No real allowance had been made for the very different needs of different prisons, blanket savings being made across the board. Regimes were thus not enhanced and even deteriorated. Staff shortages were blamed for the disturbances by half the staff letters to the inquiry. The Prison Governors' Association further criticised the effect of converting lost overtime into Time Off In Lieu (TOIL was the unintentionally ironic acronym) which fragments stability and security. Woolf and Tumim saw this evidence as a cause for 'serious concern'. (13: 78) They concluded that Fresh Start was needed, due to the distortions that ensued from massive amounts of overtime, but that it was implemented far too speedily and on the basis of misinformation to staff. Though there was no case for a return to the *status quo ante*, there was a great need to tackle concerns about the consequences of Fresh Start.

The problem of greatly reduced manning levels at weekends, when the dis-turbances started, and activities for prisoners are at a low point or even stopped altogether due to low staff numbers, thus remained to be dealt with. The loss of double-time rates had actually heightened the problem. TOIL therefore needed rethinking. A related criticism was that training should be improved. The POA evidence pointed to the situation in the Netherlands where five years' training as part of the career is normal. (13.109) In the UK, preliminary training of 13 weeks is adequate but no further in-service training is offered, e.g. on the implementation of Fresh Start. A host of specialist skills should also be provided, e.g. AIDS coun-selling. Moreover, staff facilities should be improved: abysmal conditions affect staff morale too. The idea of 'contract' was not specified but should be worked towards for staff. 'The evidence suggests that the Prison Service is . . . making bet-ter provisions for the health and fitness of inmates than it is for its staff.' (13:204) More should be done on this front.

The May Committee had well summarised problems of industrial relations which had become endemic. In 1989 a new Dispute Procedure for a 21-day 'cooling-off' period was no more successful than earlier interim measures. Yet it was not yet the time for making POA strike action illegal. Greater attempts on both sides to reach agreements prior to strike action could be made in the new context of Fresh Start. 'Apart from overcrowding . . . staffing levels are perhaps the biggest cause of industrial unrest.' (13:252) But the unions should drop their opposition to redress manning levels in the light of 'corporate objectives', just as the prison service should consult unions more in the future than in the past.

Concluding this section, Woolf and Tumim point to the huge increase in staff-ing levels: in 1947 the staff/prisoner ratio was 1:7; in 1989 it was 1:2.3. Yet no real commensurate improvement had occurred due to the persistence of bad conditions. They do not cite a major factor of regime change: in 1947 prisoners were far more likely than in 1989 to be locked in their cells, with extremely limited exercise and association time. Yet more staff were therefore needed if stability was to be achieved. There was also the need for 'dramatic change in relations between management and staff'. (13: 258) Vast amounts of TOIL had accrued to be honoured, and on that count too more staff were needed. But uniformed staff 'must appreciate they are already an expensive commodity' and better training will make them more so (13:259). They should acknowledge that by greater commitment.

**Section 14: Prisoners** (371–432) and what actions should best flow from their experience of imprisonment form the concluding and longest part of the analysis. Respect, responsibility and justice – or the lack of them – pervade all aspects of prisoners' lives. Though they have to be earned and upheld by both staff and prisoners, the context is all important. Incentives and disincentives are currently confused, and both Prison Rule 4 and Standing Orders need to be clarified to enable prisoners to know what goods and services they are entitled to, not as 'privileges' but as of right. (14.35) Petty discretionary rules should be avoided, such as prisoners being allowed to have a box of tissues in one prison but not another. (14.37) Such anomalies make the case for the 'contract'. The report backs the Control Review Committee's defence of incentives structured to give prisoners a sense of progression throughout their sentence. This should also apply to short-term and remand prisoners. Currently conditions in Category C prisons were in a worse state than those in Category B, a clear disincentive to improving conduct for recategorisation. By the same token, more use should be made of open prisons. Both are examples of costly over-securitisation.

A new Directorate of Inmate Programmes had been created to implement sentence planning ideas. Its new director was the former Deputy Director of the Prison Service, Brian Emes. He was hopeful that sentence planning could be introduced in 1991 for long-term (10 years or more) prisoners and for sex offenders. (14.60) Woolf was very much in agreement with the proposal in evidence of Paul Cavadino of NACRO that all prisoners should be involved as far as possible in three stages of assessment, initial followed by systematic assessment and post-release assessment. (14.61–83) Proper induction would involve a personal officer to each prisoner, 'contracts' for all prisoners, and sentence plans for all serving over 12 months. Such programmes had already been operative for young offenders since 1988. Release plans would involve co-ordination with Probation and other agencies about accommodation and employment, a role for which prison officers should receive training. In some respects, such a role change would endow prison officers with the welfare dimension to their job which they had long held had been denied them.[16]

**Education** had shown a 'remarkable improvement' in the previous decade. (14.85–7) Local Education Authorities provided teaching staff for prisons, the cost of which had risen from £10.85 million in 1985/6 to £21.2 million in 1989/90, with student hours rising from 5.56 million in 1987/8 to 7.75 million in 1989/90.

Good as this was, it was still not enough. Too many classes were cancelled due to industrial action and staff shortages. A Parliamentary Committee had called for a Prison Regimes Act to make access to education a right for every prisoner, and for it to be remunerated on a par with work (14.94–102), making bridges to work in the community after release.

**Work** was mainly provided by the Prison Service Industries and Farms (PSIF) with 16,000 employment places at an annual cost of £17 million. Industrial work predominated (11,000), 2,500 places were subcontracted to the private sector, 1,000 to laundry work and some 2,000 to farming. The farm sector supplied 75% of the milk and 85% of the eggs to prisons, the surplus being for sale. The PSIF was highly productive and should not be privatised, as that would entail profit superseding prisoners' training needs. Many inefficiencies were systemic and thus remedial, such as shorter hours leaving expensive plant idle due to lunch being taken too early at 11.00 a.m. and supper at 4.00 p.m. (16.00) to fit in with the staff working day.

Woolf and Tumim proposed an 'integrated approach' to work, training and education. 'This integrated approach has considerable implications for the selection and organisation of industrial and agricultural work in prisons . . . We recognise the need for some work of a simple nature, such as packing and assembly, or the knotting of strings into nets: but on our visits we have been as depressed as many of the prisoners to see intelligent and articulate prisoners, well able to perform really challenging work, kicking their heels in such workshops. This is more than just dampening to the morale of both prisoners and staff: it provides a sense of frustration and lack of worth which can only help contribute to an atmosphere of aggression in a prison.' (14.135) Much work is seen as 'slave labour' according to prisoners' letters to the inquiry. (14.136) Evidence from the Apex Trust encouraged Woolf to recommend the pursuit of links with outside organisations, both public and private, as is done by many overseas systems, including Germany and even the USA. Prisoners also welcome charity work as helping to make amends.

**Pay and Private Cash** levels are 'ludicrously low' compared to some other European countries. Average pay is £2.80 for a full week's work, yet it was just not possible to buy a reasonable basket of foods from the canteen for less than £8. Prisoners' pay was a common source of grievance and derided as 'pocket money'. Private cash therefore gains in importance but Woolf recommends no change to the system as it was, as this would make for inequality and exploitation among prisoners. The best policy was to raise prison pay quite substantially. To encourage greater responsibility, pay should be raised over the long term to £15 a week. The report goes so far as to suggest linking pay and work quality to earlier release. (14.173–4)

**Kit** remained an issue, as shabby and dirty clothing damages self-respect. The move to personal kit was a good step forward, but was as yet very unevenly permitted. The trend should be towards prisoners wearing more of their own clothing.

**Food** drew complaints for its poor quality in over one-third of letters from prisoners, more than any other subject for complaint. (14. 198) Described as monotonous and inedible, the faults lay in preparation and serving rather than in the basic ingredients. At a weekly cost per inmate of £6.71, the logistics of catering were clearly formidable, including the need to vary diets for minority religious groups. There was a need for better food inspection and communal dining. The timing of meals was very out of step with normal hours of eating – 11.00 a.m. for lunch, 4.15 p.m. for dinner (14.207), which should be changed until later, as was the case abroad. (14.213) Eating in cells was the major cause of food being inedible, the food being cold and tasteless due to the time taken for delivery.

**Family ties** are highly valued by prisoners and their disruption is a frequent source of grievance. The Prison Service recognises their importance and potential for improving success in life after release. Woolf agreed and recommended accordingly that: **visits** should be increased, from the then right to a minimum of one per month for half an hour only, and 15 minutes per day for the unconvicted, to one visit for an hour per week, in better conditions and with visitor centres provided for shelter and information prior to the visit. For remand prisoners there should be three of an hour per week. Travel costs for families should be met where needed; **home leave** is much valued by prisoners, but at present is too cautiously allowed, especially by comparison with other countries. It should be expanded and extended. It builds trust as well as being crucial for reintegration. Prisoners in remote locations, such as Dartmoor, should be granted more generous home leave wherever possible. **Family visits**, including conjugal visits, are especially important for long-term prisoners who are not yet eligible for home leave. 'If such visits were available, prisoners might be less likely to behave in a dangerous and disruptive way while in prison.' (14.248) Such arrangements exist abroad, in the Netherlands, Spain and Canada, which Woolf and his team had visited, so 'private family visits are no longer an unthinkable and eccentric exception.' (*idem*); **telephones** for normal use are common abroad, even in Rikers Island, New York City in the USA, so hardly 'the preserve only of "new generation" prisons, or of those prison authorities with the most liberal traditions.' (14.251). Cardphones facilitate the maintenance of family links and contacts. Their use is still far too restricted, however, especially for high-security prisoners; **censorship of correspondence** has been greatly reduced. In 1986 it was abolished in open prisons and in 1988 was reduced to a sample of 5 per cent in category C prisons. Elsewhere one statutory and one 'voluntary' letter are allowed for adult prisoners, two of the latter for young prisoners. More can be allowed where practicable and for various special circumstances, such as transfer. There is in Woolf's view a strong case for a great spread of the ban on censorship except where real grounds exist for suspicion as to purposes; **communication with prisoners** offers great scope for improvement regarding two-way communication via committees on which prisoners elect representatives. But Woolf, following Emes, prefers consultation via questionnaires and governors' meetings. (14.286)

**Remedies** recapitulates earlier themes and integrates them with the more detailed analysis of sources of grievance. It begins by restating the crucial dictum of the European Court of Human Rights: 'Justice does not stop at the prison doors.' Consequently, 'in spite of his imprisonment, a convicted prisoner retains all civil rights which are not taken away expressly or by necessary implication.' (see R v Board of Visitors of Hull prison, Ex Parte St. Germain [1979]) (14.289). Therefore, a prisoner is entitled to bring civil proceedings or judicial review against the Home Office. (14. 290) Other rights listed are the right to appeal to the European Court of Human Rights, the Prison Ombudsman or to petition Crown and Parliament. (14.292–4) Given the vulnerability of prisoners to 'arbitrary and unlawful actions', these rights are fundamental (14.294) and consequently satisfactory grievance procedures are essential. It follows that:

**Reasons for Decisions** should be given as a matter of good management, as it reduces the likelihood of grievances being the result of adverse decisions, often of a petty kind and easily explicable, e.g. gym cancelled due to staff illness. But this should be backed by a new prison rule to spell out the need for reasons to be given, in writing if the prisoner requests it, about transfer or parole decisions. The Parole Board now supports moves towards this policy. (14.306)

**Grievance Procedures** must be straightforward, expeditious, effective and independent. (14.309) The Jellicoe Report[17] in 1975 recognised that the independence of Boards of Visitors was compromised by their adjudicatory role. The Chief Inspector of Prisons Report of 1987, *A Review of Prisoners' Complaints*, had led to the establishment of the Prison Service Working Group in 1988. In April 1989 the Working Group's recommendations led to the abolition of certain restrictions on making complaints, e.g. the offence of making groundless complaints. (14.315) However, though some reforms preceded the 1990 disturbances, there was still no independent review system. Further reforms followed Working Group recommendations in September 1990. A five-step process should be involved: 1. Talk first to the wing/landing officer; 2. Make an oral statement which should be recorded in writing by the officer and dealt with on the same day; 3. Failing that, an application to the governor should be discussed with a senior staff officer; 4. A written complaint should be made; 5. If all else fails, an oral complaint could be made to the Board of Visitors.

Woolf and Tumim's proposals went considerably further. First, the principle of confidential access should be clarified. As it was, the complaint could be handed on to other senior staff, against whom the complaint may have been made. Full confidentiality clashed with the principle that staff should be informed of any complaint against them at the earliest opportunity. Such implications should be spelt out in advance to the complainant, who should be given the chance to withdraw. Secondly, there should be at least one meeting with the governing governor, and at the very least that governor should read the complaint. The scale of complaints numbered 290,000 in 1988 (14.317), so such a meeting could not be guaranteed. However, earlier stages should filter out the cases which are more easily dealt with. Thirdly, the Board of Visitors should advise and, if necessary, examine the case, but only go further if grounds exist, otherwise decline to take action on the prisoner's grievance. Fourthly, a Prison Ombudsman was vital, as gaps still exist and no truly independent element inheres in earlier stages. Otherwise, a Complaints Adjudicator system, reporting to Parliament annually, 'should make a Prison Ombudsman unnecessary'. (14.352) However, the Parliamentary Commissioner for Administration will still deal with the bulk of grievances, the route mostly taken by prisoners complaining of grievances to Members of Parliament. (14.353)

**Disciplinary Procedures** had resisted substantial change despite strong and mounting criticism over the previous decade. The Prior Report of 1984–5, 'the most authoritative source on the prison disciplinary system', had made 100 recommendations, of which the main ones were that governors should continue to deal with most offences against discipline; Boards of Visitors should lose their adjudicatory role; and that a new independent Prison Disciplinary Tribunal should hear the more serious cases, with panels chaired by experienced lawyers (14.363–4). A 1986 White Paper, *The Prison Disciplinary System in England and Wales*, had accepted all recommendations bar the need for lawyers to act as chair, thus bringing annual costs down from £0.9 million to £0.4 million. However, 'even this was not to be' (14.370). Boards of Visitors wanted to keep their adjudicatory powers, and saw no conflict of roles. 'Consensus' regarding the form the new tribunals should take was not achieved by the prison service, and therefore the system was retained largely unchanged, though Clerks of Justice would give advice to Boards of Visiting when adjudicating (14.371–3), and the list of disciplinary offences should be clarified.

Real problems, therefore, still remained. A questionnaire to Boards of Visitors by the Clerk to the Justices of Cardiff Court had shown that referral of a case to them meant a penalty higher than the governor's maximum. Also, they associated finding a case unproved with 'letting down the prison'. 'This is clearly not a satisfactory basis on which to conduct an adjudication.' (14.377) Yet Boards of Visitors could inflict a penalty, even after the 1991 Criminal Justice Act, of added days, previously loss of remission, greater than a magistrate could impose as a sentence. (14.382) Though this may not amount to a punishment greater than the original sentence, that is how prisoners see it. Boards of Visitors are seen as favouring the system come what may.[18] The *status quo* is, therefore, very unsatisfactory. Forfeiture of remission amounts to an extra 600–700 prisoners to the annual prison numbers. 'This is an astonishing extra burden on the prison service.' (14.401) And if such lengthy terms are involved, it is far better that they should be awarded by a court. (14.402)

Woolf and Tumim proposed instead 28 days maximum loss of remission as a penalty of the governor and abolition of the adjudicatory role of Boards of Visitors. And even then other penalties are greatly to be preferred, such as loss of facilities and amenities. But 'the problem at the present time is that a prisoner has little to lose apart from remission – that should not be the position in future.' (14.406) Serious criminal cases should go to the court. All their recommendations added up to the case for quite substantial reform with regard to grievance and disciplinary procedures.

The main body of the report was then brought to its conclusion by a recapitulation of the 12 major recommendations for change (see above, pp. 5–6) and 204 more detailed proposals for effecting a better balance between the three dominant principles of security, control and justice. As a whole, the Woolf Report achieved an exhaustive and masterly analysis of the most fundamental causes of the penal crisis that led to successive disturbances, culminating in the effective destruction of a major prison. It gave overriding importance to 'treating prisoners like human beings' and spelt out in full the principal requirements for that to be achieved. This reorientation of penal philosophy was to be seen by Sparks, Bottoms and Hay[19] as shifting the focus of analysis to the prisoners' acceptance of the *legitimacy* of the prison as a precondition for stability and order.

## The Problem of Overcrowding

For at least two decades prior to the Woolf Report, the staple theme in explanations of prison disturbances, especially in the 1980s, had been overcrowding. Yet it was by no means a key factor in all prisons most affected: Northeye had not been overcrowded, in 1986, nor Dartmoor in 1990. Two key problems with the overcrowding thesis, much as it contributed to the miseries of prison life in England and Wales, were first, that it distracted attention from other problems, such as injustices in the system – to Terence Morris, it played a 'mesmeric role'; secondly, it became normalised as 'manageable', encouraging the illusion that problems of mounting disorder were soluble by a combination of better crisis management and expanding building programmes.

Simon Bastow's research on the subject[20] focuses on what he terms 'chronic capacity stress' (CCS), i.e. coping with the persistent imbalance between what the system is equipped to accomplish and what it is required to do in practice. The prisons since 1945 have been expected to house numbers of prisoners higher, at times far higher, than their 'certified normal accommodation' (CNA), a surplus disproportionately borne by the local and remand prisons in order to protect the regimes for longer-term prisoners in training and dispersal prisons from overcrowding. Until the early 1970s, the percentage of prisoners held three-to-a-cell exceeded those held two-to-a-cell.[21] 'Doubling' began only in the mid-1960s, 'tripling' having been preferred due to fears of homosexuality. A certain fatalism is at root the source of CCS: the acceptance that those running the system can't change things, leading to what Bottoms[22] termed a state of permanent crisis. The system was rife with secondary conflicts feeding off CCS: the unions could exert acute leverage on the government by limiting the numbers of prisoners entering a prison to its CNA; squalid conditions could be explained by reference to overcrowding; riots and disturbances could be accounted for by the pressure of numbers, etc. Crisis intervention evolved into the case for New Public Management which in turn 'fed into and sustained CCS'.[23] To the dismay of the penal reform groups, CNA as a measure of capacity came in 1992–3 to be complemented by Operational Capacity (Op Cap), which was based on the pragmatic concept of what the prison 'could hold' as distinct from what it 'should hold'. 'CNA is a clear illustration that the system can sustain obsolescence despite widespread knowledge of the fact . . . Op Cap has been a device for normalising deviance away from what is "normal". This in turn has played a major role in shaping and sustaining the culture of coping and crisis',[24] complementing the shift to managerialism in the process. One signal result has been to centralise decision-making, a key indicator of which is that, in 1979, over 90 per cent of expenditure on prisons was spent by prison establishments; by 2009 that had dropped to 64 per cent. 'This ratio indicates the considerable bolstering of centralised control mechanisms' particularly since the move to agency status in 1993.[25]

To Bastow, chronic capacity stress is 'a function of governance dysfunction',[26] a product of conflicts, confusion and constraints about what the system is intended to achieve. CCS was magnified by the decline of the rehabilitative ideal, though that project never held sway at all convincingly. As one governor put it, 'many good things get sacrificed on the altar of overcrowding.'[27] For example, the directive to transfer 20 prisoners to make room for 20 more takes no account of adverse effects on their progress in drug therapy, counselling or educational course work. The coping and crisis culture sustained a higher prison population at the cost of a sense of inherent failure. Subsequent efforts to remedy this impasse lead to countervailing resistances, leading in turn to 'sustained obsolescence and redundancy': failure is reconfirmed. Ultimately, following Strangeways and the Woolf Report, managerialism lent legitimacy to the system by making some things work better: a more ordered and disciplined system emerged in the course of the 1990s and after. The pursuit of 'decency', better co-ordination and population management (Pop man) across the penal system paid off to some extent, raising the spectre of prisons becoming too successful and therefore encouraging their overuse. The rise and rise of the prison population since 1993 to date, which amounts to a doubling of scale despite a falling crime rate, has meant the recrudescence of 'normalising crowding'. It has also entailed a somewhat stunted revival of the rehabilitative ideal, in the form of an emphasis on success in reducing reoffending as the touchstone of penal success.

The problem with this approach to the explanation of overcrowding as both cause and effect of chronic capacity stress is that of functional analysis as a method: that it treats as a functional necessity that which is socially, economically and politically constructed. Bastow is well aware of 'constrained autonomy' and places it at the heart of his analysis. But learning to live with and adapt to a set of problems such that it becomes institutionalised as a way of life does not make it necessary or 'the best we can do'. Other countries have 'coped' without resort to overcrowding, and the prelude to Strangeways was ironically one in which the stress of overcrowding in the system as a whole was actually being reduced, as the prison population fell, albeit unevenly, from 50,000 to 42,000 between 1987 and 1990. As a result, the proportion of prisoners held three to a cell fell from over 10 per cent in 1987 to under two per cent in 1992, after which the strain was taken along with those held two to a cell falling from some 30 per cent to 16 per cent over the same period. When the prison population resumed its climb, it was soon followed by increasing 'doubling', though not 'tripling', of cell occupancy.

Woolf's analysis built on the need to move away from overcrowding as the pre-dominant problem, but his proposed remedies did depend on that reductionist trend being maintained. As we know, that was not to be the case. But the reasons were not to do with any 'functional' necessity, but with the loss of the political momentum that had favoured penal moderation and the resurgence of a belief in more aggressively punitive policies. Lord Woolf was adamant on that issue: 'The only thing which I think has been the tragedy is the political dimension meant there was no commitment to really tackling the problems that made it impossible for our Prison Service to move forward in the way it could . . . What I'm really saying is that they used the resources they had in the wrong way because they would not put a brake on the numbers.'[28]

## After Woolf

'The Woolf Report has created a legitimate expectation of major change.' So con-cluded the editors' introduction to a book of studies of the report and its impact by leading criminologists and practitioners, published three years after the report's own publication.[29] The report had struck a skilful balance between security and control, on the one hand, and justice and humanity on the other, enabling Woolf to avoid alienating the 'law and order' lobby as well as maintaining hopes that prisons would be reshaped. Woolf thus went well beyond the standard liberal agenda, offering a synthesis of measures which, though far from novel in them-selves, gained credence by what amounted to a radical analysis of why and how justice principles should animate prison life. Even so, and despite its overwhelm-ingly favourable reception, one year on from Woolf, the omens were not good. Resources were still too limited, governors remained frustrated at their lack of autonomy and evinced 'an enduring lack of confidence . . . in their relationship with Prison Service HQ[30] Even at the epicentre of the troubles, during the refur-bishment of Strangeways itself,' an opportunity to create small units was passed up in favour of increased security at the end of each landing in the roofs.

As a foremost authority on penal policy, Alison Liebling, later wrote:[31] 'His message was enthusiastically received but came to be widely misunderstood. Jus-tice became leniency, in some important places. Prison staff understood that order in prisons might depend on developing good relationships with, or "being nice" to, prisoners. Woolf's careful 600-page report was never read by prison officers. Nor by senior managers, or many others. His terminology cried out for careful reflection, but hardly received it . . . The question of what it might mean to opera-tionalise justice in the context of a prison was never addressed . . . "Being nice" is not the same as "being fair". These confusions and their consequences have made it much harder to develop and defend just criminal justice practices, or to humanise prisons.'

By contrast, Lord Woolf's view[32] is that 'Fortunately the Prison Service itself adopted the report . . . and welcomed it and, you know, I carried them with me on what I was recommending. And they still, to some extent, those who remem-ber the report, the older and more senior ones, still think it was the right way.

And so it's just that economics and politics were what undermined it. They've never kept the numbers down and so they didn't have the money for doing the other things.' As to why that should be, 'I'm afraid it was the adversarial political game and we go back, I must say, to Tony Blair. Tony Blair, probably rightly, thought the one thing the Labour Party must not appear as was soft on crime. And he was not going to let it happen because he was going to manage the prison system in a way which showed that Labour were tougher than the Tories and were going to be tougher than the Tories on crime. And I remember telling him, you know, you're to blame for Michael Howard.' When asked what he [Tony Blair] replied, he [Lord Woolf] said 'He didn't reply. He just wouldn't address it.'[33]

Ultimately, three points about the report and its impact emerge from these analyses:

1. The overall tenor of the report went some way to shifting the terms of the debate about the future of the prison system. The stress on justice and the primacy of the prisoners' sense of the legitimacy of the actual experience of imprisonment set new standards for policymaking.
2. Some specific and strong recommendations were taken up and acted upon: on sanitation, visitor centres and the need for a prison Ombudsman in particular.
3. However, the perhaps excessive reliance on 'contracts' and 'compacts', and the cap on CNA tied to parliamentary monitoring, were too legalistic, despite Woolf's *caveats,* to be sustainable as safeguards against the breaching of standards. The main casualties here were arguably Accredited Standards and their legal enforceability.

A huge opportunity to remake the prison system along more civilised lines was therefore largely missed, though Woolf remains a touchstone for evaluating standards of penal reform. This outcome was attributable in small part only to the inherent problems of the report itself. Far more reason for what went wrong lay in the combined effects of the sea change in the politics of crime control during Michael Howard's tenure of the Home Office and the untimely escapes from two maximum security prisons in 1994–5. The latter precipitated inquiry reports which reorientated the prison service to a renewed emphasis on the security of long-term prisoners at the expense of the reforms for which Woolf had argued across the penal estate. Charges of undue leniency in the background to the escapes became unfairly connected with his focus on justice. The political climate which had seemingly so favoured penal reform, in the context of a reductionist criminal justice policy, was rapidly eclipsed by an aggressive reaffirmation of penal populism, symbolised by Howard's assertion at the 1993 Tory Party Conference, that 'Prison Works'.

That transformation in the politics of law and order will be dealt with more fully in a separate volume. It was, however, exacerbated by the escapes from Whitemoor and Parkhurst prisons in September 1994 and January 1995, events which proved in many ways as awkward for the Home Office, and the Home Secretary in particular, who in part created the very conditions for his own embarrassment, as the escapes from Wandsworth and Wormwood Scrubs in the mid-1960s which had initiated half a century of changes in long-term imprisonment. The events of 1993–5 'raised difficult questions about the division of responsibility between the Home Secretary and the Director General in the New Agency but they also followed hard on the heels of a renewed and very deliberate politicisation of penal affairs initiated by the Home Secretary himself. This prior stance – and the general tenor of retrenchment and increased severity that went with it – seem to have conditioned the nature of the official response to the Whitemoor and Parkhurst incidents.'[34]

Howard's 'Prison Works' speech was a ferocious negation of the spirit of the 1991 Act which had already been neutered by the Criminal Justice Act 1993, a piece of amending legislation by his predecessor, Kenneth Clarke, which was in fact a wrecking measure. His statement that he did not 'flinch' from the idea that more people might, as a result, go to prison implied that those who had so opposed this policy acted from moral cowardice rather than the balance of evidence that 'prison could be an expensive way of making bad people worse.'[35] His assertion that regimes should be 'decent but austere' encoded the tightening of regimes and the pruning of entitlements. He also announced the commissioning of six new private prisons without reference to Woolf's priorities of 'community prisons', sustaining family links and enhanced training for both prisoners and staff.

This speech proved a landmark in the politics of crime control, as it signalled a new intensity to playing to the gallery of tabloid journalism and public opinion for electoral reasons which the Labour Party had begun to match. The escapes from Whitemoor and Parkhurst were thus, for both parties, a godsend, seemingly confirming that prison management, even in the highest security units, had been infected by a laxity born of liberal principles, on the one hand, or governmental incompetence, on the other. The escapes from Whitemoor occurred whilst the guards were playing Scrabble. The presumption of impregnability, which a recent but as yet unpublished report by HM Chief Inspector of Prisons, Stephen Tumim, had echoed, had become an article of faith which encouraged lapses from strict adherence to security procedures. Such faith was to be mocked by the ease of the escapes, even if all escapees were quickly recaptured, and by the subsequent discovery of Semtex explosive in one prisoner's property. Five of the six escapees were IRA prisoners, whose skill in challenging security arrangements was much stressed in the official inquiry report.[36] For example, CCTV cameras were seen by the prisoners as 'intrusive' on their privacy and were in some cases tilted away. Such instances revived old fears of the 1970s that staff were vulnerable to being psychologically manipulated, if not suborned, by sophisticated prisoners who, in the case of the IRA, could back up 'mind games' with implicit threats to the safety of their families as well as to staff themselves, if their demands were not met. However, as Sparks, Bottoms and Hay point out, such intimidatory tactics could be neutralised by deploying different staff for different tasks, a defence strategy which Woodcock fails to mention. Woodcock also makes much of staff acceding to the prisoners' complaint that security procedures took so much time that the two-hour visits were often curtailed. Yet prisoners were entirely within their rights to register this as a legitimate grievance. Long-term prisoners in particular value family visits, often involving lengthy, costly and time-consuming travel, a point made emphatically in the Woolf Report but entirely ignored by Woodcock. As a result, the Woodcock Report, by a panel significantly chosen to comprise, almost entirely, retired senior police officers, focused almost wholly on recommending much increased surveillance and search measures and severe limits on property rights which, again, to long-term prisoners were especially valued. To Sparks, Bottoms and Hay, the report spelt the end of the long history of the Radzinowicz stress on liberal regimes within maximum perimeter security. But poor management rather than flawed principles were arguably the main problem.

Much the same could be said about the escapes from Parkhurst. However, if the Whitemoor case played into Michael Howard's hands, that of Parkhurst ensnared him in an embarrassing clash of roles and responsibilities. Following hard on the publication of the Woodcock Report, the escape of three prisoners from the dispersal prison at Parkhurst on the Isle of Wight became the catalyst for a heated dispute over ultimate responsibility for the conditions facilitating the escape and for the nature of what should be done by way of sanctioning those held to blame. Again, the escapees were all recaptured, albeit some weeks later – a longstanding justification for siting maximum security prisons on the Isle of Wight was thus upheld – but the principle of how to allocate blame in the wake of the recent

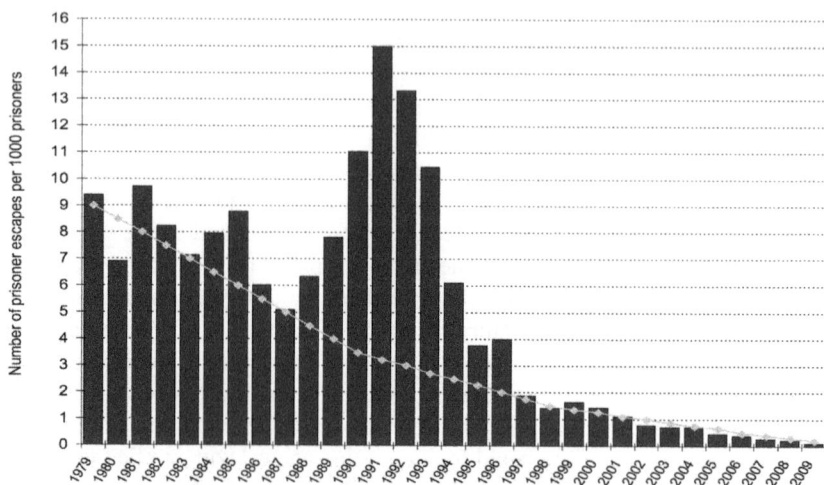

*Figure 6.1* Average annual number of prison escapes, per 1,000 prisoners 1979–2012

Source: Hansard electronic archive of written parliamentary answers and Prison Service annual reports.[37]

assignment of prison management and administration to a new agency, proved more lasting than the escapes themselves.

The three prisoners, two of whom were Category A, the third Category B, had escaped by contriving in the workshops to make parts of ladders long enough, when assembled, to surmount the security fence and outer wall, somehow evading the attention of staff both in the making of the escape equipment and then whilst slipping out of the workshops to make their escape on the early evening of 3 January 1995. It quickly became clear that the monitoring of top-security prisoners at both points, the workshops and the fences, had been impaired by slack procedures, notably not bothering to count prisoners at designated times, for which the governor, John Marriott, was ultimately responsible. However, pending further investigation of the incident, the appropriate course of action was that laid down in the new Code of Discipline drawn up by the new director general, Derek Lewis, appointed – from the world of business and not such traditional sources as senior Home Office civil servants – after Kenneth Clarke's decision that the Prison Service should attain agency status. The appropriate course of action was to transfer the governor to an alternative job while formal investigations were carried out.

'The following morning I briefed Howard ahead of his statement to the House. I told him what we had decided about Marriott and why. He exploded. Simply moving the governor was politically unpalatable. It sounded indecisive . . . If I did not change my mind and suspend Marriott, he would have to consider overruling me. His tone was menacing and I was left with no illusions about the possible implications for me . . . The risks to my personal position were serious, but the Code of Discipline was part of Marriott's employment contract, and I had a duty to interpret it fairly . . . Intervention in the decision by the Home Secretary would have been quite improper.' After much heated discussion, the Home Secretary agreed not to suspend Marriott. In the subsequent debate in the Commons following Howard's statement, he was asked by Gerald Kaufman, a leading Opposition front-bencher, 'Where does the buck stop?' 'After an indecently short interval, and without mature reflection, Mr. Howard uttered his now famous mantra for the first time: "I am responsible to Parliament for policy. The Director General . . . is responsible for operational matters."'[38]

Howard took his revenge in due course, dismissing Lewis from his post as director general in October 1996, after a period of turmoil leading up to and following the publication of the Learmont Report on the escapes from Parkhurst and on prison security in general.[39] A great deal, including Howard's ministerial career, hinged on how responsibility for the escapes would be allotted. Lewis emerged as both victim and unlikely hero of this period of transition. In his view,[40] with some justification, he had achieved 'dramatic improvements in security performance, except for the two high-profile escapes; achievement of virtually all the targets Howard had set us; only one riot; 12,000 more prisoners squeezed into the jails; the POA dealt with; a private sector established; and new home leave, drugs and privilege schemes successfully launched. Most notable of all was the 80 per cent reduction in escapes. I set out our plans for the future, emphasising how much was still to be done. It was a receptive audience, with one exception. Howard sat stony-faced and glassy-eyed throughout: it was either not what he wanted to hear, or his mind was on other things.'[41] Howard's body language may well have expressed his disbelief at Lewis's somewhat disingenuous claims for dramatically improved security on his watch: the escape of six of those designated most dangerous must outweigh that of the great majority, which were of far lesser consequence. A strong advocate of the new managerialism, agency status, and the market testing of private prisons, Lewis should have been the ideal director general for a neoliberal Home Secretary. But Lewis's principled refusal to accept Howard's preference for the immediate suspension of Governor Marriott after the escapes from Parkhurst set them at loggerheads. The escape route for Howard was the somewhat fictional separation of powers between the politician who decides 'policy' and the director general who is responsible for 'operations'. Howard's claim that the escapes and their aftermath were entirely operational matters, despite his determined attempts to influence such operations at crucial points, proved the grounds for his ultimate salvation and Lewis's downfall. Though the double standards were soon aired in the media, to the point where Jeremy Paxman's repetition of a question on this point twelve times on the public affairs BBC2 programme *Newsnight* attained epic status, the discreet silence of civil servants and ministers prevailed.

How far did the Learmont Report reflect this outcome? It has come to represent the *coup de grace* to any systematic implementation of the key proposals of the Woolf report. 'The unremitting emphasis on security at the expense of humanity in the Learmont Report was roundly condemned by the former Chief Inspector of Prisons Judge Stephen Tumim, who described it as "the road to the concentration camp" (*Guardian*, 28 October 1995).'[42] The American experience was drawn upon for its most punitive rather than its more liberal penal aspects. Echoing Mountbatten three decades earlier, Learmont called for a 'super- max prison' to hold the 200 'exceptional security risks' in the system. But he did so without Mountbatten's (and Radzinowicz's) insistence on a liberal regime within the putative totally secure perimeter that the Control Review Committee had seen as the potential offered by 'new generation prisons' in the USA. Instead, it would be the apex of a recalibrated six-fold security hierarchy, with the most difficult prisoners held in two Special Security Units' in Belmarsh and Whitemoor Prisons, 'denied many of the basic rights to which other prisoners are entitled including access to the library, gymnasium and chapel. They are also subjected to "closed" visits in which the inmate sits behind a glass barrier and communicates via a telephone or grill and, despite such intensive security, are also subjected to strip searches before and after every visit, supplemented by occasional even more intimate (and humiliating) "squat" searches.'[43] On this point, on security grounds, Lewis and Howard were as one. Learmont was initially inclined to reject such inhumane protocols but ultimately adhered to his own, Lewis's and Howard's, predilection for closed visits.[44] Lewis's dismissal, subsequently pronounced unfair by the courts, was thus not on a matter of principle so much as the *realpolitik* of saving the minister's neck. The reinstatement of security as the overriding principle of penal administration was thus effected at the expense of the more fundamental changes sought by the Woolf Report.

## In Perspective: The Fall of Penal Hope?

Whatever happened later, the 1991 Criminal Justice Act and the publication of the Woolf Report in the April of that year represented the culmination of a period of hope for liberal penal reform which could be dated back to 1959 or even far earlier. The belief that prison should be used as sparingly, and managed as justly and humanely, as possible, took on the aspect of achievable goals. That so signal an achievement should have proved so fragile invites the question: why and how did the reforms set out in the 1991 Act and, to a lesser extent, in the Woolf Report prove so precarious?

One authoritative answer is set out by Ian Loader in his view that the period after 1991 saw the fall of what one of his respondents termed the 'Platonic Guardians' who had dominated the course of criminal justice policymaking from the middle years of the twentieth century in England and Wales.[45] Drawing on published work and interviews with 40 retired senior civil servants from the Home Office, prominent figures in penal reform and pressure groups, past and present members of the Home Office research unit and senior academic criminologists, Loader depicts their shared culture of 'liberal elitism', the conviction that they should promote 'civilising values' in relation to criminal justice and penal policy, in particular seeking to rein in and contain 'public passions' that all too readily could inflame sentencing with punitive excesses. The coherence and ascendancy of this 'governing elite'[46] proved resilient in the face of two challenges to their legitimacy. The 'Nothing Works' 'moment of contention' in the early 1970s was surmounted by the timely arrival of an alternative rationale for avoiding unduly harsh responses to crime. Situational crime prevention, and its complementary social counterparts, seemingly confirmed the Enlightenment values of Cesare Beccaria, that certainty rather than severity of punishment was the more effective as well as the more civilised antidote to crime. The second critical challenge was the arrival of 'law and order' politics in the Thatcherite 1980s,[47] a prospect of punitive escalation largely averted – or, in the event, postponed – by the skill with which the alternatives were posed to successive Home Secretaries by senior civil servants in the Home Office, notably Sir Brian Cubbon and David Faulkner.[48] The third challenge, however, proved lethal. The turn to 'punitive populism' in the 1992–3 period, in which both major political parties pursued an electorally driven association with being 'tough on crime, tough on the causes of crime', wrested legitimacy from the liberal elite's allegedly wanton disregard for the costs and suffering inflicted on victims and society by crime and criminals. On this view, the 'Platonic guardians'' elitist cast could no longer accommodate the rising tide of public anger in the face of apparently endless rises in the rate and savagery of crime. A more democratic engagement with the public at large on the issue of responses to crime was called for as the only feasible alternative. There could be no going back.

It is difficult to disagree with the view that policies on crime and punishment should be conducted in as democratic, open and informed a way as possible. Indeed, Ian Loader and Richard Sparks have taken the initiative in calling for a 'public criminology'[49] to be far more of a priority for academic specialists in the field. However, to accept the self-appellation of 'Platonic guardians' (by a retired academic criminologist) is to equate 'liberal elitism' with non-, or even anti-democratic politics, as if democratic debate had been suppressed or avoided by those engaged in criminal justice policymaking in the latter part of the twentieth century. That is hardly sustainable in the light of the extensive efforts by, for example, the Woolf Inquiry team to engage in public debates with both participants on all sides and public seminars for interested parties. The Woolf Report is not, as it happens, cited as an example of 'Platonic guardianship'. But it more than fulfils many of its criteria, notably to promote 'civilised values' in relation to the extent and experience of imprisonment. Also at stake is the view that democratic principles are manifested by political moves to reverse the direction of change sought by the Woolf Report and the 1991 Criminal Justice Act. Yet, as at least one major American study has shown,[50] surges in public hostility to offenders are far more related to political campaigns than to changes in the crime rate. Moreover, 'public opinion', once informed more fully of the relevant evidence, has been revealed as markedly less punitive than its tabloid version allows.[51] It has also been shown that different versions of democracy and political economy are associated with major differences in penal policy[52] and responses to such extreme crimes as child-on-child homicide.[53] Two further points in this connection are, first, it is difficult to see how, without liberal networks making the running, in the teeth of majority opinion, capital punishment would have been abolished, homosexual relations legalised, abortion laws reformed and theatre and literary censorship greatly relaxed. Secondly, so-called liberal elitism was itself subject to democratising changes over the period in question. The Woolf Inquiry was a markedly more democratic process than the Mountbatten or Radzinowicz Inquiries, liberal as they had been in many respects. Sir Brian Cubbon was a far more democratic Permanent Secretary than Sir Charles Cunningham. In short, the view that the eclipse of liberal policymaking was due to its elitist character does not allow for the somewhat fateful role of events in the making of criminal justice policy.

Despite the reversion to security and control at all costs, the inspirational impact of the Woolf Report lasted into the new millennium. The 'What Works' agenda, which had begun to fill the motivational vacuum created by the 'Nothing Works' perspective, provided important grounds for innovation. 'In the first few years of my tenure as DG, the prison population grew slowly, and rehabilitative activity grew enormously.'[54] The Department of Health took over prisoners' healthcare, and the Department of Education took over teaching. The New Labour government greatly increased resources both for both prisons and Probation, as it embarked on the merging of the two key services into the new National Offender Management Service. Drug treatment was much expanded and cognitive behaviour programmes began to be set up. 'It was a time of optimism . . . Evidence began to emerge of us beginning to make an impact. Crucially, the proportion of prisoners going into employment after release leapt forward by about 10% in two years'.[55] There was even a move to relate the recommendations of the newly established Sentencing Guidelines Council to cap the size of the prison population at 80,000. The pursuit of the 'decency' agenda did seem for a brief period to be gathering fresh momentum.[56]

This renewal of constructive penal policy, along the lines spelt out by Woolf and the penal reform groups, proved all too short-lived. The upsurge in prison numbers, which had levelled out briefly from 1998 to 2001, resumed its seemingly inexorable rise, despite a fall in the crime rate. From 42,000 in 1991 numbers rose to 65,000 in 1998–2001 and then to 76,000 by 2004. The very acceptance by Martin Narey and the then Home Secretary, David Blunkett, of a 'cap' of 80,000 – which never occurred due to the resignation of Blunkett on a quite unrelated matter[57] - in itself testified to the acceptance of a prison population rate that was the largest in Western Europe and which, as Narey himself states, 'vacuumed up every penny we had'.[58] Ironically, David Blunkett himself unintentionally added to the numbers by his support for the Imprisonment for Public Protection Act of 2003 which added an open-ended indeterminate element to sentences for those designated very serious offenders, responsible for primarily violent and sexual crimes. Their release would depend on their completion of rehabilitative pro-grammes, whose resourcing was to prove woefully inadequate, thus adding several thousand prisoners to the population in future years who would normally have been released. In short, the failure to address the root problems of sentencing reform defeated many a best effort to humanise our prisons.

## Notes

1  *Report on the Work of the Prison Service 1986–87.* London: HMSO. November 1987. Cm 246. 1:2.
2  *Report of an Inquiry into the Disturbances in Prison Service Establishments in England between 29 April and 2 May 1986.* 16 July 1987.
3  Rod Morgan, 1994, 'An Awkward Anomaly: Remand Prisoners' in Elaine Player and Michael Jenkins (eds.) *Prisons After Woolf: Reform Through Riot*: 150.
4  *Prison Disturbances April 1990: Report of an Inquiry* by The Rt Hon Lord Justice Woolf (Parts I and II) and His Honour Judge Stephen Tumim (Part II). Feb.1991. HMSO: Cm 1456. L.J. Harry Woolf was appointed a High Court judge in 1979, promoted to Lord Justice of Appeal in 1986. He became a Law Lord in 1992, Master of the Rolls 1996–2000, when he became Lord Chief Justice until his retirement in 2006. Stephen Tumim (1930–2003) was the first judge to be appointed HM Chief Inspector of Prisons, 1987–1995.
5  See, for example, Joe Sim, 1994, 'Reforming the Penal Wasteland? A critical review of the Woolf Report' in E. Player and M. Jenkins, op. cit.: 31–45.
6  '. . . Sunday – a day associated with prison disorder across the decades due to reduced staff cover and the assembling of large numbers of inmates in chapel.' Review by Pamela Cox of *Inter-War Penal Policy and Crime in England: The Dartmoor Convict Prison Riot, 1932* by Alyson Brown (Palgrave, 2013). *Brit. J. Crim.*, 54: 157. The book compares certain aspects of the 1932 Dartmoor Riot with that at Strangeways in 1990.

7 Brian Emes was Governor of D Wing, Wormwood Scrubs in the late 1960s, transferred to Home Office P2 Division (treatment and training) 1970–75, Governor Leeds Prison 1975–6, Governor of Wakefield Prison 1976–9, 1979 moved to Home Office P5 (security) Division, Deputy Director General of the Prison Service 1987–91, Director of Prison Regimes and Planning 1991–2.

8 Their version of the 1982 hit song 'You Have the Power' by WAR. See the 2015 TV documentary *Strangeways: Britain's Toughest Prison*, directed by David Belton, for a vivid and perceptive account of how events unfolded.

9 In interview (1 April 2014) Lord Woolf credited Stephen Tumim for his role in ending 'slopping out' as a seemingly permanent fixture of British prison life: 'He had a great insight into the prison system and he was terribly committed to doing something about slopping out. And that was . . . his great mission.'

10 'Situational and Social Approaches to the Prevention of Disorder in Long-Term Prisons', referred to by the Report, was based on research at Long Lartin and Albany prisons. Its authors formulated a theory of 'social crime prevention' within prisons. which became the basis for the book by Sparks, Bottoms and Hay (1996) *Prisons and the Problem of Order*, Oxford University Press.

11 Sparks, R., Bottoms A.E. and Hay, W. (1996) *Prisons and the Problem of Order* Oxford: Clarendon Press.

12 In interview, Lord Woolf stressed how much he had learnt from his 'hugely impressive' core inquiry team, including John Lyon (Secretary, from the Lord Chancellor's Department) and, as Assessors, Gordon Lakes, CB MC who, until 1988, had been the Deputy Director of the Prison Service; Professor Rod Morgan, who had taught at Bath and Bristol Universities and conducted seminal research on penal policy and practice; and Mrs. Mary Tuck CBE who, until 1989, had been head of the Home Office Research and Planning Unit. In interview, Lord Woolf commented 'They trained me.'

13 According to Rod Morgan, one of the three assessors attached to the inquiry, Tumim had earlier reported on slopping out as a thematic inquiry in 1989 as HMCIP.

14 *'Slopping Out?' A Report on the lack of in-cell sanitation in Her Majesty's Prisons in England and Wales.* London: National Council of Independent Monitoring Boards, 2010.

15 See Ch. 3 above. The publication of the report was in 1984, not 1989 as stated by Woolf (12.281).

16 See in particular J.E. Thomas *The English Prison Officer since 1870: A Study in Conflict*, 1972, London: Routledge & Kegan Paul; also his evidence to the Inquiry.

17 Jellicoe, Earl (Chair) *Boards of Visitors of Penal Institutions: Report of a Committee set up by Justice, the Howard League for Penal Reform, and the National Association for the Care and Resettlement of Offenders* 1975 Chichester: Rose.

18 The Report (14.389) cites the research by Maguire and Vagg, 1984, as confirming this perception by prisoners.

19 Sparks, Bottoms and Hay (1996): op. cit.

20 Simon Bastow (2012) *Overcrowding as normal: Governance, adaptation, and chronic capacity stress in the England and Wales prison system, 1979 to 2009.* Ph.D. thesis, electronically accessible, Department of Government, London School of Economics. Published as *Governance, Performance and Capacity Stress: The chronic case of prison crowding.* Palgrave, 2013.

21 See fig. on 'overcrowding', Ch. 5, p. 1.

22 In his Introduction to Bottoms, A.E. and Preston, R.H. (eds.) (1980) *The Coming Penal Crisis* Scottish Academic Press.

23 Ibid: 49.

24 Ibid: 140–41.

25 Ibid: 69.

26 Ibid: Chapter 9.

27 Ibid: 210.
28 In interview, April 2014.
29 Elaine Player and Michael Jenkins (eds.) *Prisons After Woolf: Reform Through Riot*. London, Routledge. 1994: 28.
30 Ibid: 25.
31 Alison Liebling (2006) 'Prisons in transition', *International Journal of Law and Psychiatry*, 29: 423–4.
32 In interview, 1 April 2014.
33 Tony Blair was, at the time, Prime Minister and the occasion was the birthday celebration of one of Britain's most famous actors.
34 Richard Sparks, Anthony E. Bottoms and Will Hay, *Prisons and the Problem of Order*, Oxford University Press, 1996: 22–3.
35 Home Office (1990) *Crime, Justice and Protecting the Public*, Cm 965. London: HMSO: 4.
36 Sir John Woodcock (December 1994) *Report of the Enquiry into the Escape of Six* Prisoners *from the Special Security Unit at Whitemoor Prison, Cambridgeshire, on Friday 9th September 1994*, Cm 2741. London: HMSO.
37 Simon Bastow, 2012, op. cit.: 90.
38 Derek Lewis (1997) *Hidden Agendas: Politics, Law and Disorder*, London: Hamish Hamilton: 168–72.
39 General Sir John Learmont (October 1995) *Review of Prison Service Security in England and Wales and the Escape from Parkhurst Prison on Tuesday 3rd January 1995*. London: HMSO. Cm 3020.
40 In a speech to the annual conference of senior civil servants and politicians concerned with criminal justice and penal policy, at Chevening, the residence of the Foreign Secretary, on 28 September 1995.
41 Derek Lewis, op. cit.: 194.
42 M. Cavadino, J. Dignan and G. Mair (2013) *The Penal System: An Introduction*, London: Sage, 5th Edition: 199.
43 Ibid: 198.
44 Lewis, op. cit.: 185–7.
45 Ian Loader (2006) 'Fall of the "Platonic Guardians": Liberalism, Criminology and Political Responses to Crime in England and Wales', *British Journal of Criminology*, 46: 561–586.
46 Ibid: 563.
47 On this topic, see in particular Stephen Farrall and Will Jennings (eds.) *The Legacy of Thatcherism*, 2014.
48 Confirmed by Douglas Hurd in interview (11 November 2014): when asked if there were any particular officials whom he remembered as being of importance in the whole process, he replied 'Sir Brian Cubbon and David Faulkner . . . Brian Cubbon was a sort of umpire . . . in the sense that if he thought that the discussion was going too far one way and there were important factors not being taken into account, he used to speak . . . And David Faulkner was, in a way, the workhorse of the whole thing. I think he thought a lot about it and he had all the sort of parallels and historical facts at his disposal and he was a great help, a great help.'
49 Ian Loader and Richard Sparks (2010) *Public Criminology? Criminological Politics in the Twenty-first Century*. London: Routledge.
50 Katherine Beckett (1998) *Making Crime Pay: Law and Order in Contemporary American Politics*, Oxford University Press.
51 See, for example, M. Hough and J. Roberts (eds.) (2002) *Changing Attitudes to Punishment: Public Opinion, Crime and Justice*. Cullompton: Willan.
52 See, for example, M. Cavadino and J. Dignan (2006) *Penal Systems: A Comparative Approach*. London: Sage.

53  David Green (2008) *When Children Kill Children: Penal Populism and Political Culture*. Oxford University Press.
54  Martin Narey, 2012, 'Prisons, Brutality and Decency: Reflections on thirty years': talk at the Institute of Criminology, University of Cambridge, unpubl. He was Director General of the Prison Service 1998–2003, and Chief Executive of the National Offender Management Service (NOMS) 2004–5.
55  Ibid: 8.
56  See, in particular, Andrew Rutherford, 1993, *Criminal Justice and the Pursuit of Decency*, Oxford: Oxford University Press. Foreword by Lord Scarman.
57  His speeding-up of a visa being granted to his child's Nanny.
58  Narey, op. cit.: 9.

# 7 The Pursuit of Innovation

There have been few periods when those responsible for penal policy have *not* been in pursuit of innovation in some direction or other. For whatever reason – the forced ending of transportation, the arrival of a reformist Home Secretary, or the pressure of such events as high-profile escapes – remedies were sought in policy changes that inherently risked being ill-judged. A good example would be the mid-1970s conception of 'special' control units (see Ch. 3, 'Forcing the Issue'). Forward, long-term planning, drawing on the knowledge of those with relevant experience and expertise, could guard against such dangers. This chapter examines five important innovations which were aimed at steering the system in a more humane, knowledge-based and civilised direction: the Advisory Council on the Penal System, 1966–79; the Home Office Research Unit 1957–1993; the parole system, initiated in 1967; the independent Prison Inspectorate, set up in 1982; and the attempted redevelopment of Holloway into a therapeutic prison for women. A sixth innovation, so-called private prisons, was more specifically aimed at cost-efficiency and managerial effectiveness.

The wartime context encouraged such approaches, and it was during World War II that the Home Secretary, Herbert Morrison, conceived the idea of a standing body of relevant experience and expertise to advise the Home Office on criminal justice. In September 1944, with post-war reconstruction in prospect, the Advisory Council on the Treatment of Offenders (ACTO) was set up under the chairmanship of Mr. Justice Birkett. Its terms of reference were simply 'to assist the Home Secretary with advice and suggestions on questions relating to the treatment of offenders'. Its membership ranged widely from Margery Fry, the notable penal reformer, to Harold Laski, the LSE Professor of Political Science. Among its first tasks was to review the salience of the measures contained in the Criminal Justice Bill of 1938, discussion and debate on which had been delayed by the war. One key recommendation for a new form of institution for young offenders, which materialised as detention centres in the 1948 version of that bill, was studied and supported by ACTO. 'As in 1938, the essence of the legislation was to remove young people from prison but not from the prison system.'[1] Though ACTO was no radical force for change, it played a crucial role in shielding liberal reforms from what Leon Radzinowicz was later to term 'penal regression', by which he meant the erosion or abandonment of moderate penal policies.[2] Corporal punishment had been abolished by the 1948 Criminal Justice Act, but a substantial body of opinion in the Conservative Party persistently clamoured for its reintroduction. Matters came to a head in 1958 at the annual party conference. The Home Secretary, R.A. ('Rab') Butler 'deftly referred their claims to the expert, and non-political, Advisory Council on the Treatment of Offenders,'[3] whose firm rejection of the proposal[4] was based in part on empirical research findings on its ineffectiveness. In short, by the late 1940s and 50s, the establishment of advisory bodies was seen as a productive way of generating new, and despatching outworn ideas.

## The Advisory Council on the Penal System

The Advisory Council on the Penal System (ACPS) was a new Council in membership and terms of reference to its predecessor. 'By 1966 the earlier body was dormant, its last flicker of life being a report on after-care in 1963.[5] The report was not without influence, as it contributed to the transition of the probation service from a group of self-employed social case workers into a nationally organised and publicly funded service.'[6] What caused the hiatus in the existence of the advisory bodies was the establishment in 1964 of the abortive Royal Commission on the Penal System which was said to have foundered, after some 15 months of unproductive discussion, on the impossibly wide terms of reference, the Chairman (Viscount Amory)[7] lacking a grasp of the field, and the impatience of the new Labour government to move ahead with its criminal justice reforms without waiting for their report. The root cause, however, was arguably the incompatible views on the principles of punishment and treatment among its members. Three leading advocates of its dissolution, Professor Leon Radzinowicz, Barbara Wootton and Bea Serota,[8] agreed to membership of a re-formed advisory body, which could produce informed reports on specific topics without the lengthy process of compiling a Royal Commission report. The ensuing Advisory Council on the Penal System could pursue innovation without that encumbrance.

In the view of a later Home Office minister, Lord Windlesham, 'The distinction of its expert, and non-party political, composition coincided with a period when party ideology was relatively weak as a source of innovation. From its early days the ACPS was more than an independent group playing with new ideas. It became a clearing house in which proposals could be assessed and tested against a formidable corpus of knowledge and experience before being recommended for legislation or implementation in administrative practice. For a decade, under both Labour and Conservative administrations, the ACPS enjoyed unusual authority.' The use of the term 'ideology' is a little misleading in this summation, however. It is the case that, following the reformative accomplishments under the Labour government in 1964–67, building on the report written whilst still in Opposition, *Crime – A Challenge to Us All* in 1964, and taking in Frank Soskice's preparing the ground for Roy Jenkins' 1967 Criminal Justice Act, which followed the abolition of capital punishment in 1965, abortion and homosexual law reform in 1967, the momentum behind these great liberal reforms slackened. But that should not detract from the achievement preceding the ACPS of a startling legislative sequence of libertarian as well as liberal reform. Though enacted as private member's bills, the Labour government facilitated their passage by parliamentary time management.[9]

The reports of the ACPS between 1968 and 1978 were compiled independently of the Prison Department of the Home Office, whilst being resourced and assisted secretarially by their civil servants. The topics could emanate from the Home Secretary, the Home Office or the members of the ACPS themselves. Inquiries were delegated to subcommittees, whose chairs and members were decided on by the ACPS Chairman, Kenneth Younger. Published reports over the decade of its operation were as follows[10]:

*Detention of Girls in a Detention Centre* (1968) recommended and led to the closure of the only such centre then in existence.

*Regime for Long-Term Prisoners in Conditions of Maximum Security* (1968), which recommended the dispersal system rather than that of concentration in a single prison as recommended by Mountbatten. (See Chapter 2 on this subject.)

*Detention Centres* (1970) recommended their continuation pending a major review.

*Non-Custodial and Semi-Custodial Penalties* (1970) made several recommendations implemented in the 1972 Criminal Justice Act, the main innovation being the creation of Community Service Orders. Some recommendations not accepted included the establishment of an Enforcement Office to collect overdue fines, whose non-implementation arguably reinforced the reluctance of courts to fine rather than imprison petty, persistent offenders.

*Reparation by the Offender* (1970) recommended the power of the courts to make compensation orders, and for a criminal bankruptcy scheme. Both were implemented in the 1972 Criminal Justice Act.

*Young Adult Offenders* (1974) recommended a single custodial sentence ('the custody and control order') for offenders under the age of 21. Such a sentence, which entailed the abolition of detention centres, borstals having been closed down by the Criminal Justice Act 1982, was achieved in the 1988 Criminal Justice Act. 'Youth custody' was now at the end of the era of belief in the rehabilitation of young offenders by welfare and training. 'By the mid-1980s the punishment approach was supreme. The only deliberately punitive institutions within the prison system were exclusively for its youngest inmates.'[11]

*Powers of the Courts Dependent on Imprisonment* (1977) examined court and police powers in relation to offences punishable with imprisonment. A few changes were recommended, to no effect.

*The Length of Prison Sentences: Interim Report* (1977) recommended changes in judicial practice to reduce the length of prison sentences for non-serious offending.

*Sentences of Imprisonment: A Review of Maximum Penalties* (1978) recommended reducing maximum penalties, which were rarely passed, by some ten per cent, on the basis that sentence length would be scaled down accordingly. The change would have entailed legislation, and the recommendations were not accepted.

This was to prove the last of the APRC reports, and it was an unfortunate accident of bad timing that the committee was in abeyance at the point of an imminent general election. The APRC's term of operation needed to be renewed, and this was left to the post-election period. In the event, the incoming Tory government in 1979 under Margaret Thatcher began its administration with an attempt to roll back the state that entailed a cull of quasi-autonomous non-governmental organisations (QUANGOS), sweeping away in the process over a hundred such bodies. One curious ground for such action was that quangos were both costly and inefficient. Yet the ACPS was composed of people for their expertise on an unpaid public duty basis, earning no more than their travel and subsistence expenses. Lacking such bodies in large areas of legal responsibility, governments from this point on relied more and more on outsourcing inquiries to private consultancy firms whose charges were far from negligible, or on recruiting advisers not beholden to civil service obligations, such as the requirement to appear, if asked, before Parliamentary Select Committees. Louis Blom-Cooper, who had served on the ACPS throughout its life, wrote to Lord Windlesham:

> 'ACPS was dissolved because of the Conservative Government's distaste for independent advice. It was not axed because it was ineffective. Apart from its last report, every other report ultimately found its way either on to the statute book or to a change in penal practice . . . I am convinced that Ministers of both parties (up until 1979) and Home Office officials all valued the Council and would have argued for its retention.'[12]

In a detailed review of the role and work of the ACPS, commissioned by the National Association for the Care and Resettlement of Offenders (NACRO), Rod Morgan concluded that it had amply fulfilled its brief and recommended its reconstitution on a more permanent basis.[13] 'I take the view that advisory bodies should, in the light of the latest research and most comprehensive information, describe the assumptions on which current policies rest and should, whenever appropriate, provide an alternative perspective to established bureaucratic orthodoxy. An advisory body should force departments to think of policies which do not find a place within official attitudes even if they directly conflict with departmental philosophies and traditions.

Given this approach, the independence of a committee is vital. The good committee is one within which the membership is knowledgeable, well informed as to the exigencies and practicalities of policy in operation, but not weighed down by such considerations. The good committee should stress not operational expertise – many departments, including the Home Office, have well established research units – but informed imagination.'[14] Of the eight reports published by the ACPS, that on semi- and non-custodial penalties, chaired by Barbara Wootton, was – along with that chaired by Leon Radzinowicz, on maximum security prison regimes, discussed elsewhere – the most outstanding example of an inquiry fulfilling those criteria.

## Community Service Orders

'The idea of Community Service Orders (CSOs), as they became known, "floated" into Barbara's mind one day "on the commonsense basis that instead of sending people to prison it would be better to get them to do some useful work". She vaguely remembered that the Germans had some scheme of this kind. The German in question was "the Chocolate Judge", Karl Holzschuh of Darmstadt, who acquired a degree of fame in the 1950s for his practical suggestion that a child who had stolen sweets should make reparation for this crime by giving some to a local orphanage. He also enjoined a motorbike thief to join the local walking club, and a boy who had stolen milk from doorways to wash bottles in a dairy. He was a man after Barbara Wootton's own heart, rejecting the idea of punishment as ineffective retribution.'[15] The ideal opportunity to give shape to this idea came with the invitation to chair the ACPS subcommittee set up, following the request by the Home Secretary, Roy Jenkins, 'to consider what changes and additions might be made in the existing range of non-custodial penalties, disabilities and other requirements, which may be imposed on offenders.'[16] Alongside Barbara Wootton other members of the subcommittee with criminological expertise were Louis Blom-Cooper, Professor Gordon Trasler and Dr. (later Professor) Nigel Walker. The remaining, non-criminological members were Lady James, Mr. R.E. Millard, Lady Rothschild and Mr. George Twist. But all members agreed on the desirability of linking community service to the disposal of offenders.

As well as service to the community, the inquiry covered fines, deferment of sentence, senior attendance centres, disqualification and forfeiture, intermittent custody, such as weekend prison, and probation both with and without additional orders. The inquiry took over three years to complete, 39 meetings were held and visits were made around the country and abroad to gather information about the experience of such measures as the Swedish day-fine system, a version of which was recommended but not adopted until the 1991 Criminal Justice Act, when it lasted only several months. A key difference between the two countries was that in Sweden all incomes are publicly declared, a condition which in Britain was regarded as a violation of privacy. The committee was keenly aware that 'our assignment represents the first comprehensive enquiry into the adequacy of the existing powers of the courts to deal with offenders aged 17 and over without resort to custodial sentences.'[17] It recognised the 'need for innovation' in several respects: to give the courts new powers to develop alternatives to the deprivation of liberty; and to conduct such innovation by evaluative research and experiment. The cost factor should not be paramount but neither should it be ignored, with a ratio of 1:22 in the costs of supervising a probationer and imprisonment.

Community service was the 'most ambitious proposal of this report', one that 'breaks new ground in this country'.[18] It builds on the longstanding history of voluntary service. Examples of work that rested on voluntary effort cited to the committee included: 'constructing adventure playgrounds; clearing beaches and country paths; helping with reclamation efforts and restoring canals' and a host of other examples. 'In all cases, care is taken to ensure that the use of volunteers does not prejudice the position of paid employees: local Councils of Social Service each have a trade union representative among their members. In general, the work is such that if it were not done by unpaid labour it would not be done at all.'[19] The idea of such a sentence has 'appeal to adherents of different varieties of penal philosophy. To some, it would be simply a more constructive and cheaper alternative to short sentences of imprisonment; by others it would be seen as introducing into the penal system a new dimension with an emphasis on reparation to the community; others again would regard it as a means of giving effect to the old adage that the punishment should fit the crime; while still others would stress the value of bringing offenders into close touch with those members of the community who are most in need of help and support.'[20] Such community service would best be performed in association with volunteer non-offenders, in the hope that they would exert a beneficial influence, though this condition should not be rigidly adhered to. It would apply to the general run of offenders rather than those engaged in more serious and professional criminality, though it should not be confined to imprisonable offences: for example, some forms of traffic offending would be suitable for such a sentence. It could be imposed as a sentence in its own right or in combination with a probation order. And, rather than constituting a new supervisory agency, the processes of finding and monitoring suitable service tasks would best be undertaken by the existing probation and after-care service, whose resources should be strengthened accordingly.

Looking back, Barbara Wootton wrote: 'Some of the difficulties which we foresaw were discussed in the Report, but we frankly admitted that it would not be profitable to attempt to work out every detail on paper, and that "the only way of discovering whether schemes will work is to try them out". And tried out they quickly were. Within little more than two years of the publication of our report, the community service proposal . . . reached the statute book in the Criminal Justice Act of 1972 after a relatively uncontroversial, not to say enthusiastic, passage through Parliament.'[21] Though there were changes to the recommended detail of which she disapproved, especially the limitation of restricting CSOs to imprisonable offences, excluding the link to probation orders, and doubling the maximum length of the orders to 240 hours, the reaction that clearly stung her most was the 'trenchant criticism' from a leading criminologist, Roger Hood.[22] He had argued that 'the authors of the ACPS Report were . . . at fault because they "failed to provide any analysis of the case for its proposals in terms of criminological and penological knowledge", or "any convincing criminological argument' in support of them, and because they had "conducted no specific research". According to Hood, our proposals were founded on *assumptions* (his italics) about the reactions that we hoped might be evoked in offenders. Nor had we produced any basis for supposing that these proposals "would be at least as acceptable to the courts and *at least not less successful* (italics original) for whatever purpose imprisonment was being used". Such argument as the Council did produce (and even more the subsequent enthusiasm with which the community service proposal was greeted in Parliament) was simply condemned as "ideological" (a term nowhere defined by our critic).'[23]

In her, and the report's, defence, Wootton countered that, having been subject to terms of reference which enjoined them to consider *additions* to the existing range of non-custodial sentences, they were bound to rely on 'psychological and imponderable' data, in the absence of the body of 'criminological and penological knowledge' invoked, but not specified, by Hood. She might have added that, had such data existed, they would surely have been brought to the committee's attention by the two criminologists on the ACPS subcommittee handling the enquiry, Nigel Walker and Gordon Trasler. As it was, they were seeking to advance criminological knowledge. The report 'expressly recommended that the proposal should be regarded as experimental, and that the practicability of the whole idea should be tested in the first instance in a few pilot areas.'[24] In 1973 the piloted use of CSOs was set up in six petty sessional areas: Durham, Inner London, Kent, Nottinghamshire, Shropshire and south-west Lancashire. From these modest beginnings, the idea was taken up around the world. 'By the late 1970s, CSOs were being used throughout the UK, and the British scheme served as a model for those elsewhere, in Australia, Belgium, Czechoslovakia, Denmark, Finland, France, Germany, Greece, Italy, Luxembourg, the Netherlands, New Zealand, Poland, Portugal, Norway, Sri Lanka, Sweden, Switzerland, the USA and Yugoslavia.'[25] It had proved a 'world first'.

The Home Office Research Unit (HORU) monitored the use of CSOs from the outset, with early results showing a clear use of CSOs as an alternative to prison in at least a substantial minority of cases: 'One remarkable feature of the picture was the length of the previous criminal record of those directed to community service: three or four previous convictions were typical in every area. Moreover, of the 757 CSO cases in which full criminal records were available, 159 had already served at least one custodial sentence (excluding committals to approved schools), 120 between two and four, while 43 had been "inside" five or more times. Altogether it looks as if the courts must have welcomed the CSO as a godsend in the all-too-familiar situation in which they are faced with an offender who has been conditionally discharged, subsequently fined, and after perhaps more than one spell on probation, must now be sentenced for yet another offence. How often have not my colleagues and I concluded despairingly that in such cases a custodial sentence is unlikely to do any good – but what alternative was available?'[26] The fact that approaching half of those sentenced to community service had already been imprisoned confirmed the hopes of the ACPS and Parliament that a way had been found of dealing with the petty, persistent offenders who filled the local prisons to overflowing. Moreover, HORU had concluded its survey of the pilot schemes with an assertion that not only was the scheme 'viable' but that, despite some *caveats* concerning such issues as the reliability of certain supervisors, and the most appropriate kinds of work for different types of offender, they 'feel much more optimistic' than their list of doubts implies, and that at best community service is 'an exciting departure from traditional penal treatment'.[27]

But did it work? Two investigations by HORU[28] were somewhat inconclusive, confined as they were to the six pilot areas and lacking convincing control groups. Gordon Trasler summarised their effectiveness several years later: 'The experience of the first few years of CSOs has been encouraging: a majority of offenders complete the number of hours' work imposed under the order, the number of individuals reconvicted during the period of the order are broadly comparable with those for probation (as far as one can judge), and the recidivism rate following the completion of the terms of the order is certainly no worse than that for men discharged from prison.'[29] This was in itself a justification for Barbara Wootton of the entire scheme, much as she hoped for lower rates of recidivism for those so sentenced: 'If, however, recidivism after a CSO turns out to be at least not significantly *worse* than that following short sentences of imprisonment, it will be justified on economic grounds alone, because, as the Inner London report puts it, offenders "employed on tasks for the benefit of others . . . could have been sitting in prison cells, benefiting none, but each costing the nation between £30 and £40 a week and, perhaps, as much again to support their families.'[30] Less to her taste and convictions would have been the transforming of 'community service' into 'community punishment' by the 2001 Criminal Justice Act. As she had acknowledged, 'Hood's warning about the possible fading of initial enthusiasm is not without force. Much will depend here on the attitude of probation officers and magistrates.'[31] Or, more consequentially, on the 'tough on crime' strategy of a future New Labour government.

## The Home Office Research Unit

Innovation can emerge from unexpected quarters. The Home Office Research Unit (HORU) was set up to inform policymakers, test initiatives and monitor progress, but not specifically to formulate policies. 'In the early days not all the Unit's research officers appreciated that, however important the development of criminology as a social science, their job was to produce evidence relevant to the formation of policy.'[32] As it evolved, the research of HORU proved highly influential both in generating policies of crime prevention which transformed the criminal justice and penal systems, often in ways contrary to those its originators intended, and in major contributions to criminology.[33]

HORU was established in 1957, in the wake of the success accorded the Mannheim-Wilkins prediction study of borstal training[34] and following some decades of the case for some such unit having been made.[35] Leslie Wilkins provided the expertise to fulfil both in-house and academic interests in supporting such an investment.[36] For much of the 35 years of its operation, 'the Unit occupied a central role in British Criminology, not least because it was the largest employer of criminologists in the country – when I joined the Unit [in 1964] it had about 20 research staff and when I left [in 1984] this number had grown to more than

40.'[37] Ron Clarke, who briefly headed the Unit 1983–4, when he departed to a Chair in Criminology at Rutgers University in the USA, summarised its main tasks as '(a) to undertake an in-house programme of policy-relevant research (identified in consultation with Home Office administrative units); (b) to manage a programme of Home Office funded research in universities; and (c) to provide "on-tap" social science advice to administrators and ministers.'[38] To Clarke 'The Unit's outstanding achievement was its sustained production of an in-house programme of world class research . . . The main importance of the Unit's research lies in its programme, sustained over many years, on the reduction of recidivism and the control of crime.'[39] The Mannheim-Wilkins study set an example of rigorous empirical work which was sustained throughout the Unit's existence and became the hallmark of its high international reputation. It was symbolic of the sea change in penal policy that, having fulfilled all the criteria for excellence in contributing to 'evidence-led policy' over three to four decades, it was killed off as the politics of crime control changed shape to usher in a new era of penal expansion, in 1992.

While it is difficult to grasp quite what Clarke had in mind in regarding the 'reduction of recidivism' as the first of two claims to the importance of its work – if anything, it bolstered the 'Nothing Works' perspective on sentencing options – there can be no dispute about its massive contribution to our knowledge of crime prevention. Pat Mayhew's *Crime as Opportunity* (1976)[40] began a sequence of studies conducted by HORU researchers which within a decade had transformed the field in crucial respects. Situational crime control had, argued Ronald Clarke,[41] along with Mayhew its chief proponent, been utterly neglected by criminological theorists who assumed *dispositional* factors, to do with the offender's deep-rooted psychological, social, cultural and/or economic background, were the primary causes of crime and deviance. Such banal-sounding examples as the far greater incidence of vandalism on the top deck of buses without conductors testified to the crucial character of surveillance in shaping the incidence of crime. Earlier work by an American architectural theorist, Oscar Newman,[42] had linked far higher rates of crime with high-rise housing projects in the USA than with earlier low-rise estates, on the grounds that people's sense of belonging and involvement in the community were fractured by impersonal housing design. As a result, people were not only disinclined to intervene in acts of public crime and victimisation: they were unable to see it happening.

Newman's work attracted a great deal of critical interest but a British attempt at replicating his approach, by Alice Coleman, led to a barrage of criticism.[43] Her study of a new high-rise development in London was assailed for its architectural determinism and elementary methodological errors.[44] In general, however, situational control theorists proved adept at dealing with seemingly decisive objections to their approach. One such objection, that crimes were simply *displaced* from one type of site, target or method to others, if offenders were faced by blocked opportunities and/or enhanced surveillance, was rebutted by evidence that such deflection occurred in only a small minority of cases. As a result, situational crime prevention measures swiftly rose up the agenda for both national and local government in the teeth of remorseless rises in crime rates. Such measures as installing CCTV, steering locks in cars and stronger doors in public housing were manifestly more feasible than changing the psychic make-up of offenders or the socio-economic opportunity structures of entire societies.

Another approach altogether, which nevertheless partly sprang from and complemented situational crime prevention techniques, was what came to be known as social crime prevention. A celebrated example was based on the pioneering work of Ken Pease on re-victimisation. Pease had established that victims of burglary were significantly more likely than non-victims to be burgled again within a short period after the original offence. Reasons for such re-victimisation were manifold: offenders passed on to friends and associates details of the contents, layout and means of access to properties they had burgled. In a celebrated experiment on the Kirkholt estate near Liverpool, Pease and his team alerted neighbours when burglaries occurred, asking them to 'keep an eye' on the property involved.[45] This 'cocooning' had the effect of significantly reducing the rate of burglary on the estate, and without any apparent displacement effect on neighbouring estates. In the 1970s and 80s, a panoply of community schemes were rolled out by both central and local government, with varying effects. Neighbourhood Watch schemes were imported from the United States. Programmes such as 'Safer Cities' were developed with grant aid to local authorities from central government to mount offender employment programmes, experimental youth work and the like. 'Crime Concern' under its first Chief Executive, Nigel Whiskin, sought to co-ordinate local and charitable agencies to work to reduce reoffending along lines inspired by Oscar Newman's work. The National Association for the Care and Resettlement of Offenders became a force to be reckoned with in the field of community projects and social programmes to nurture work training and employment schemes for young and ex-offenders in the community. Difficult as it was to demonstrate the effectiveness of social crime prevention projects, it was assumed they were at least paying off by reining in rising crime at the margins.

Though it was hard to argue more positively for the success of such schemes in the midst of the post-Martinson, 'Nothing Works' era that lasted from the mid-1970s until the mid-1990s, the Home Office Research Unit played a key role in that regard. If the more progressive welfare and treatment projects were shown to have only negligible impact, the same held true for the tougher forms of punishment, in particular imprisonment and stronger policing strategies. Home Office researchers carried out a thorough deck-clearing operation in their empirical evaluations of custodial sentencing and police effectiveness. Steven Brody's *The Effectiveness of Sentencing*, published in 1976, was a landmark study of how little impact penal policies of incapacitation would make on rates of crime.[46] In a much-quoted summary, Roger Tarling[47] established that it would take a 25 per cent rise in the prison population to reduce the crime rate by one per cent. By the same token, a 250 per cent rise in the prison population would reduce the crime rate by 10 per cent, and a 500 per cent rise by 20 per cent. In the event, only the USA was prepared to pay that price, in both economic and human terms. Ironically, this statement coincided with Michael Howard's 'Prison Works' speech, ushering in the reversal of decades of policy aimed at reducing the prison population in England and Wales. The double irony is that this result could have been reached by other and vastly less costly means. A key example is that the striking fall in the US homicide rate since the early 1990s has been closely matched by that in Canada, where the markedly lower rate of imprisonment has remained much the same for the past 40 years.[48] Why the homicide rate should have fallen so strikingly, not only in the USA but in other countries which have made no such recourse to mass imprisonment, remains a mystery, though such attempts as have been made focus far more on social, cultural and historical trends rather than short-term criminal justice explanations.[49] Medical advances reducing death from serious injury offer one plausible approach, though that would predict a continuous fall rather than marked fluctuations in the homicide rate in the last seventy years.

The same logic was applied by HORU researchers to the assessment of policing. It had long been assumed that the answer to more crime was more police, at least as the basic element in crime control strategies. 'More bobbies on the beat' became a refrain in electoral politics, particularly in the Thatcher era of government. Growing investment in the technological armoury of policing had been a factor in criminal justice policymaking at least from the time of Frank Soskice as Home Secretary. Yet the growing number of studies evaluating the effectiveness of policing were generally negative in their conclusions. The most celebrated such study in Kansas City in the early 1970s found no fall in the crime rate resulted from investing in intensified police surveillance and patrols in some areas compared with areas where no such changes were made.[50] As Reiner comments: 'This and other research questioning police effectiveness in crime control was given much publicity by several influential Home Office publications in the 1980s.'[51] The cumulative effect of negative findings on the effectiveness of policing and imprisonment combined with positive results from crime prevention projects led the Home Office in 1983 to create a Crime Prevention Unit, the most tangible sign of a paradigm shift in thinking about crime control.

It is important to stress that this change in approach at both theoretical and policy levels was not achieved as a smooth process of what later became termed 'evidence-led policy'. Its advocates faced severe, often bitter criticism from both academic criminologists, who contested the view that opportunity mattered as much as, if not more than, the motivation to offend in the first place, and from orthodox practitioners and politicians schooled in a belief in the efficacy of policing and imprisonment in the 'war against crime'. As Ron Clarke, the main protagonist of situational crime prevention asserted: 'The main conclusion of the work on policing was that increasing the numbers of police officers would have little effect on crime rates. This was highly controversial and caused much embarrassment in the Home Office, arriving as it did soon after the Thatcher government gained power, having promised to strengthen the police force. The struggle to publish this report, which went through some 15 drafts, took place soon after I had become the Unit's Head and it contributed to my reluctant decision to leave. However, the report did succeed in making calls for more-of-the-same policing intellectually suspect and it permitted the CPU, and later the Police Research Group, to explore new policing directions.'[52] The fact that the research was published at all bears testimony to the view of John Croft, the Head of HORU 1972–83, that 'at no point was there any negative interference with the product of the Unit, attempts to influence the Unit's programme or suppress publication of research results.'[53] That did not preclude exhaustive redrafting to overcome possible political objections to publication. In the event, Clarke concludes that 'The bedrock of success was the assumption that every research report that the Unit produced should be published. How this assumption came to be, I do not know but, whenever questioned, it was resolutely defended by Tom Lodge and John Croft (successively the Unit's Heads from 1957 to 1982). The benefits of this principle were many – for the Home Office, publication exemplified transparency; it helped to ensure the quality of the research undertaken; it guaranteed that administrators paid close attention to the Unit's reports, which in many cases resulted in their support for potentially controversial implications; and . . . it demonstrated a commitment to evidence-based policy.'[54]

At the least, it could be claimed that the 'main importance of the Unit's research lies in its programme, sustained over many years', from the Mannheim-Wilkins borstal prediction study (1956) onwards, 'on the reduction of recidivism and the control of crime . . . The work culminated in Stephen Brody's report, *The Effectiveness of Sentencing* (1976), a major contribution to the "nothing works" debate. When the debate became public in this country, the Home Office was well grounded in the issues and was not an easy target of criticism.'[55] The term 'culminated' is a little odd, as this period was the prelude to some two decades of research by HORU and its offshoots which went far to transforming the field of criminology and criminal justice policy. HORU became positioned as a leading force in a rapidly changing criminological universe, in which dispositional theories, while still granted their due, were seen as playing a much reduced role in explaining trends and variations in the incidence of crimes. Nevertheless, a social dimension came to be added to the situational approach to crime prevention. The regeneration of high-crime estates was to emphasise tenant participation in their management,[56] as well as attending to stronger door and window locks and the installation of CCTV, entry phones and the like. The American theory of 'broken windows',[57] argued that such phenomena as unchecked litter, graffiti, dereliction and disrepair symbolised community deterioration. If not promptly dealt with, such signs of neighbourhood decay led to a downward spiral entailing an exodus of the respectable and an inflow of the disreputable. What began as a theory of policing priorities soon expanded to take in other forms of social intervention – 'multi-agency' teams combining police, social workers, probation officers, urban planners and youth workers gained credence. The British Crime Survey was inaugurated in 1981 and generated a data set annually which enabled researchers to gauge crime trends on a basis free from the exigencies of police statistics. The demographics of crime victimisation could now be mapped far more accurately.[58] 'Designing out crime' architecturally was but one strand in an array of social and situational measures to counter the opportunistic 'reasoning criminal'.[59] 'Routine activities' theory focused on another dimension of mundane life which criminologists had traditionally ignored. Sweeping social and techno-logical change held implications for generating rife opportunities for crime, on the one hand, and the removal of many constraints and controls against it, on the other. For example, the increase in women working outside the home removed their presence as 'capable guardians'.[60] Burglary was the more likely as a 'rational choice' than would otherwise have been the case. Example after example was given of similar chains of cause and effect. These approaches shared the overrid-ing emphasis on the primacy of the situational over the dispositional, and yielded ready solutions to the bulk of 'standard list' property crimes that could be defined as opportunistic rather than 'professional' or 'organised'. A wealth of technical solutions were at hand that could be and were formulated and implemented by central and local government departments to reduce crime levels, from so-called 'target-hardening', such as vehicle steering locks, and electronic surveillance to more social processes of crime prevention, such as 'cocooning' victims of burglary, to fend off re-victimisation, and 'mentoring' young offenders. At the same time, huge increases occurred in the upgrading of private security on both domestic and business premises. Such extensive investment in crime prevention owed much to Home Office policies, though in Clarke's view the opportunity was missed to undertake more thoroughgoing programmes: 'Some criminologists such as Jan van Dijk, Nick Tilley and Graham Farrell are now arguing that these improvements in security provide the best explanation for the worldwide declines in crime that have occurred during the past couple of decades. Assuming they are correct, this constitutes the third missed opportunity for the platonic guardians – they could have claimed that their policies had produced the decline in crime.'[61] More than that, such recognition might have forestalled the credit claimed for that decline by the proponents of the revival of penal expansionism, not least that ushered in by Michael Howard's 'Prison Works' speech in 1993, a theme to which we return in analysing the politics of crime control.

Despite the many virtues and undoubted successes of situational crime con-trol,[62] its unabashed utilitarianism has severe limits.[63] It has tended to understate the problems of the displacement of criminal activity to other targets, sites, meth-ods and types of offence. Computer crime has entailed illegal downloads by the million which go unrecorded as crime and which the police are ill-equipped to handle, a trend which coincides with the remarkable drop in crime rates. Indeed, computer and digitally processed financial frauds are disowned by the police as a matter for the banks.[64] Juvenile shoplifters and rowdy youth remain the 'low-hanging fruit' more readily dealt with by the criminal justice system. The sociological con-cern to discern the character and meaning of criminality is simply ignored, as is the problem of explaining maturation out of crime. As Stan Cohen remarked, the rational choice approach leaves the offender with nothing *but* choice, stripped as he or she is of any other attributes. The sharp decline in violent crime, including homicide, has been sustained now for over two decades, but is scarcely addressed by the situational approach. That said, virtually all sociological theories predicted a continual escalation in violence, especially in the context of sharply increasing inequality, and the extent to which governments wedded to neo-liberalism do not so much facilitate as cower in the face of the power of the financial corporations. The alternative explanation offered by Steven Pinker based on Norbert Elias's celebrated 'civilisation' thesis, is that the substantial falls in violence mark the resumption of long-standing civilising developments, following four decades during which rates of violent crime substantially rose, mainly due to a false dawn of permissiveness.[65] Reiner criticises Pinker for caricaturing 1960s youth culture in a negative, and that of the 1990s in a positive light to make his case that the former led to a rise, the latter to a fall in violent crime. Yet the 'gangsta' rap of the 1990s, along with lurid video games and internet porn, can be cited as incitements to violence beyond anything the 1960s had to offer. Pinker dismisses this as 'media-savvy, ironic, postmodern'.[66] There is no concrete evidence that this isn't enhanced *de-civilisation* rather than re-civilisation, apart from the fall in crime and violence itself – a circular argument.[67] All approaches harbour major problems, but the fact remains that situational crime prevention in both theory and practice, as developed in the Home Office Research Unit, constituted an innovation of signal importance in crime control both in this country and around the world.

## The Parole System

The pursuit of innovation in the criminal justice system of England and Wales is well exemplified by the development of parole as the means of securing early release for those prisoners deemed worthy of it. Early release had long been part of the system, but it had taken the form of 'remission', a fixed proportion of the sentence which needed to be served only if a prisoner's misconduct led to its forfeiture in whole or in part. Remission had grown out of the 'ticket of leave' principle developed during the system of transporting prisoners to the colonies, first to America and then, after the American War of Independence in 1776, to Australia. Transportation was brought to an end in 1868, following decades of increasingly rebellious protest by the rapidly growing number of legal emigrants.[68] Convict labour played a vital role in establishing the economic basis of life in the new colony, a novel element being that of assignment to a master acting as the government's agent of control. 'The convict who had been given a ticket-of-leave no longer had to work as an assigned man for a master. He was also free from the claims of forced government labour. He could spend the rest of his sentence working for himself, wherever he pleased, as long as he stayed within the colony . . . The ticket lasted only a year and had to be renewed, and it could be revoked at any time. It was an effective way of fostering conformity and self-help while keeping the convict on a leash.

Ticket-of-leave men could be denounced by anyone, and thus they lived in some uncertainty . . . One lost one's ticket, Governor King proclaimed in 1804, by being idle, or insolent to "any officer, soldier or Constable," or charging too much for out-of-hours work. But fragile as it was, the ticket-of-leave was craved by every convict in the colony and regarded by most of them as a natural right, a goal that one struggled toward and was entitled to. It played an immense role in the moral economy of colonial life. The worst thing a master could do to a convict servant was to keep him from getting his ticket-of-leave."[69] It is salutary to recall how many of the hopes and fears of prisoners undergoing modern parole systems were presaged in those of the ticket-of-leave system.

It was, however, to be more than a century before the formal system of parole was enacted by the Criminal Justice Act of 1967. The long period of delay, compared with its much earlier introduction in such comparable societies as the U.S.A. and the Netherlands, was due to the popularity with penal administrators of the system of remission. The Director of Convict Prisons, Sir Joshua Jebb, believed that penal servitude should be structured 'so as to keep alive "an invigorating hope and a salutary dread at every stage of the progress of the prisoner"'. Jebb favoured a system of remission of sentence as the best means of sustaining the "invigorating hope" in the heart of every convict but until 1857 his advice went unheeded by the Home Office. The passage of the 1857 Penal Servitude Act finally led to the establishment of a formal scheme whereby sentences of three years were subject to one-sixth remission for good behaviour, the proportion gradually increasing so that sentences of fifteen years or more were subject to one-third remission. Eligibility for remission depended on a system of good marks and conduct badges which gave public recognition of a prisoner's progress towards eventual early release on a ticket of leave.'[70] The system remained wedded to this principle for much of the following century. Changes were introduced in 1891 that fixed remission for male convicts to one-quarter and for female convicts to one-third of their sentence. In 1898 the recommendation by the Gladstone Committee that remission should be extended to ordinary prisoners, who had been convicted of less serious offences, was put into effect. Equity and rehabilitative hopes combined to justify the change, though convicts were liable to recall for any 'misconduct' before the end of their sentence term, anticipating the later parole system of recall for breach of the licence, whereas prisoners were free from the day of their early release.[71] In 1940, under war-time exigencies, and pressure on prison places, remission for both groups was increased to one-third, and remained at that level until 1987, the abolition of penal servitude in 1948 having abolished the convict licence. Why, given the relatively straightforward operation of remission, was it felt necessary to couple it to a system of parole?

The Criminal Justice Act 1967 'can be considered an archetypal product of the rehabilitative paradigm that dominated penal policy in the 1960s.'[72] Home Office documentation reflected the momentum built up by penal reformers that saw parole as 'an idea whose time had come'.[73] For example, the influential Labour Party Study Group chaired by Lord Longford had recommended, among its many proposals for radical reform of the criminal justice system, the 'extension of powers of Prison Department to release on licence borstal trainees who have served a quarter of their sentences to include prisoners serving any sentence of imprisonment; and setting up of the Parole Board to advise the Home Office on the exercise of this power.' The report argued bluntly: 'We doubt the value of keeping men in prison after they have learnt their lesson; at this point the cost of continuing to keep them in prison is no longer justified.'[74] The group drew on the last report of the Advisory Council on the Treatment of Offenders (ACTO),[75] whose terms of reference did not include early release principles, but who recommended sweeping changes to prisoners' aftercare, notably by amalgamating responsibility for the diverse aftercare agencies within the Home Office, with its own inspectorate, training board and central council, and a greatly expanded Probation and Aftercare Service. These and allied proposals gave substance to the White Paper, *The Adult Offender*, in 1965, which formed a major part of the 1967 Criminal Justice Act.

A novel justification for the parole system in the White Paper was the belief, for it was little more, that some, though by no means all, long-term prisoners experienced a 'recognisable peak' in their 'training', at which they 'may respond to more generous treatment but after which, if kept in prison, they may go downhill'. Their release 'under supervision, with a liability to recall if they do not behave', would therefore be a risk worth taking to enhance their chances of becoming 'decent citizens'. The 'recognisable peak' thesis chimed strongly with the rehabilitative spirit of the times and gave Sir Frank Soskice a plausible rationale for a system of parole boards which would include academic expertise as well as legal and lay members. 'When the issue returned to the Home Affairs Committee on the 22 September 1965 Soskice was able to update the Committee and strengthen his case by confirming that his consultation with the formative Royal Commission on the Penal System and senior judiciary had been encouraging (TNA: CAB 134/2001). Furthermore, a national conference with Prison Governors in August 1965 had indicated strong support for the initiative, most notably as a useful tool of discipline and control: *"every Governor I have consulted has emphasised that if he could hold out to prisoners in his charge the hope of an earlier release on parole, subject to licence, towards improved behaviour and in conducting his prison . . . it would also very greatly strengthen his hand in influencing them. It would, in the view of prison governors, lead to a large number of prisoners abandoning a life of crime on their release under licence and returning permanently to society as useful citizens."* (TNA: CAB 134/2001)'[76]

Soskice drove the liberal agenda forward despite being dogged by ill-health. Harold Wilson and the Cabinet took some persuading to treat criminal justice as a priority, given their wafer-thin majority and the difficulties they faced in fending off devaluation: 'As the prospects of a Criminal Justice Bill dimmed, the Home Office changed tack and sought permission first from the Cabinet Home Affairs Sub-Committee in November 1965 (TNA: CAB 134/197) and then from Cabinet on 2 December 1965 to publish a White Paper entitled the Adult Offender (TNA: CAB 128/39/83). In the minutes from Cabinet it was noted that:

The Home Secretary said that Government might be liable to incur criticism from liberal opinion if they did not soon make a distinctive contribution to the reform of the penal system; and, since there was no immediate prospect of introducing a Criminal Justice Bill, it was proposed that a White Paper on the Adult Offender should be published as a counterpart to the White Paper on young offenders which had been published in August.'[77]

The prioritisation and formulation of clear policies on parole, youth justice and the abolition of capital punishment,[78] whatever caveats may persist about the legacy of mandatory life sentences for murder, constitute a formidable defence of Soskice's achievements during his 18-month tenure of the Home Office, against criticisms of his record as negligible, especially by comparison with his successor, Roy Jenkins.[79] Soskice also convinced the Treasury that the extra expense involved in establishing the parole system would be offset by savings on a reduced prison population. The Probation and After-Care Department in the Home Office was persuaded to accept the need to combine a new parole system with the long-established remission framework. 'The fusion of parole onto the existing system of remission stands out as one of the defining features of early release in England and Wales.'[80] The main anomaly was that those refused parole were later released on remission with neither supervision nor being subject to recall on breach of licence, to both of which those prisoners viewed as lower risks worthier of earlier release were subject.

Such was the enthusiasm within the Home Office for the proposed innovation that by 1 October 1965, in response to a series of questions by Brian Cubbon, then Principal Private Secretary to the Home Secretary, as to how the system would work in practice, Norman Storr, an Assistant Undersecretary, described the proposed system in detail. Moreover, it resembled extremely closely in form and substance the proposals that were eventually included in the draft Criminal Justice Bill published in December 1966.[81] First, all prisoners serving determinate sentences would be eligible for parole after serving 12 months or one-third of their sentence, whichever was the longer. Secondly, parole would be discretionary, not automatic. Thirdly, parolees would be released on licence under the supervision of a probation officer. Fourthly, until the date of remission, parolees would be subject to recall for breach of their licence. Fifthly, the Home Office Research Unit estimated that approximately 3,000–3,500 prisoners 'would immediately qualify for consideration with a further 400 receiving a positive release recommendation. (TNA: PCOM 9/665)

To all intents and purposes this memorandum set out the fundamental planks of the parole system that would subsequently be introduced by the Criminal Justice Act 1967. Like many liberalising measures from this era parole is commonly associated with the progressive reforms of Roy Jenkins . . . Here we have clear evidence that its origins lay firmly in the much-maligned Home Office of Frank Soskice and his Permanent Secretary Sir Charles Cunningham . . . It is almost certain that the proposed scheme had been in gestation far longer, perhaps in preparation for a likely Labour government or as part of the Home Office's own policy development processes.'[82] Despite, or because of, this and other unsung achievements, Jenkins was scathingly critical of Soskice's record in office. '. . . he was a remarkably bad Home Secretary. He had practically no political sense and an obsessive respect for legal precedent. In addition he was extremely indecisive.'[83] It was Jenkins, however, who most eloquently stated the case for parole, in tandem with suspended sentences and other reforms in the 1967 Criminal Justice Act: 'These reforms revolve around the single theme, that of keeping out of prison those who need not be there.'[84] This encapsulation of the penal welfare principle with that of reducing the prison population was perhaps the post-war apex of the hopes for rehabilitation in a penal context, and it provided the rationale for the system which would last for two decades, despite the failure of the reforms to curb the rising prison population.[85]

The limits to the likely success of parole in relation to prisoner numbers were in some respects built in from the start. The stipulation that parole was aimed at long-term prisoners, in part due to the 'recognisable peak' thesis, restricted its operation to those serving three years or more. The Parole Board and its network of Local Review Committees (LRCs) had a strictly advisory role. Their operation was subject to 'the twin assault from different wings of the political spectrum which attacked parole as either being "soft on criminals" at a time when the crime rate continued to rise or, alternatively, too arbitrary and lacking in basic procedural fairness safeguards necessary to ensure that all prisoners were considered equally on the basis of reliable, relevant information.'[86] Indeed, Lord Hunt, the first Chairman of the Parole Board who, as the conqueror of Mount Everest echoed the earlier appointment of Earl Mountbatten of Burma to head the inquiry into prison security, complained scathingly about the 'scandalous' state of documentation on which the LRCs were meant to evaluate the case for a prisoner's parole. Jenkins and Callaghan clearly shared a preference for 'men of action' to symbolise integrity of judgement on contested ground. 'The quality of prison documentation improved significantly following the introduction of parole as prison authorities were forced to take prisoners' after-care arrangements seriously.'[87]

'Penal policy in the 1970s was shaped by the unravelling of penal welfarism.'[88] Rehabilitative claims for the prison and parole system became increasingly exposed to adverse research findings and withering criticism of human rights deficits. The May Committee report in 1980 clung to the notion of 'positive custody' in a last ditch attempt to salvage a continued role with affinities to 'treatment and training' but the pressure to replace it with genuinely 'humane containment' as the real alternative to squalid 'human warehousing' gained ground. The hiatus in political reform was replaced by pragmatic, Home Office driven preparing the ground for change. Michael Moriarty played a key role in committee work on earlier parole and extending eligibility, which were agreed by the Home Office and the Parole Board in 1975. Roy Jenkins, in his second term as Home Secretary, had stressed the dangers of the prison population, already standing at 40,500, reaching 42,000, notably in a speech to NACRO on 31 July 1975, and curbing the rise in the prison population was confirmed as a key feature of parole strategy. However, these minor changes had only a small and temporary effect, creating the pressure for parole eligibility to be extended to prisoners serving less than 18 months, three-quarters of the prison population.[89] Home Office officials had worked hard at engendering a tripartite understanding between the judiciary, legislature and executive about the best means of reining in or reducing the prison population. An extension of parole eligibility to short-term prisoners was preferred to a blanket increase in remission or the introduction of partly suspended sentences. The 1982 Criminal Justice Act, section 33, reduced the minimum period of eligibility for parole from 12 months to six months. 'Interestingly, this final provision did not feature in the original copy of the Bill. The reform that was to have the single largest impact upon the prison population in the 1980s was only incorporated into the Bill at Report Stage (Commons) following considerable pressure from PAPPAG [the Parliamentary All-Party Penal Affairs Group] supported by a number of penal affairs groups outside of Parliament (HC Deb 12 May 1982 vol 23 cc777–780).'[90] While the government and the other parties accepted that, and allied amendments, without demur, it implies that William Whitelaw's savaging at the Tory Party Conference in 1981 had led him to withhold that measure, perhaps in order to facilitate another clause 32, never acted on then or later, granting the Home Secretary emergency powers to release non-violent offenders up to six months before their remission date in the event of a penal crisis becoming unmanageable.[91]

Leon Brittan succeeded Whitelaw as Home Secretary after the 1983 general election. Perhaps determined to avoid the fate of his predecessor at the party conference referred to above, who had in effect been accused of being soft on crime, not least by a handcuff-waving Edwina Currie, yet needing to resolve the burgeoning penal crisis by relieving the sheer pressure of numbers, Brittan pursued a policy of full-blown bifurcation. Such policies had been a discernible trend in penal politics since the onset of the decline in penal-welfarism.[92] They entailed a liberal approach to petty non-violent offenders and a substantially tougher approach to more serious, especially violent offenders: 'a bifurcated policy allows governments to get tough and soft simultaneously.'[93] Brittan changed the parole system in three important respects. First, he activated s.33 of the 1982 Criminal Justice Act from 1 June 1984. 'The effect of this was that whereas before only those serving a minimum sentence of nineteen-and-a-half months could in practice attract parole, now those serving as little as ten and a half months were able to benefit. It meant that 2,500 more prisoners were out on parole at any one time.'[94] By contrast, those imprisoned for over five years for crimes of violence, sexual offences, arson or drug trafficking would be released only within a few months of the end of their sentence. A third change affected 'lifers convicted of the murder of police or prison officers, terrorist murderers, sexual or sadistic murderers of children, and murders by firearm in the course of robbery. Such persons would now expect to serve at least twenty years in custody, and other murderers, outside these categories, might merit equal treatment to mark the seriousness of the offence. The Home Secretary's statement made it clear that, although he would consult with the Parole Board about how these new policy objectives would be achieved in practice so that the Board's role was maintained, he had not consulted the Board in advance of the announcements. It was also made clear that the policy would be retrospective, and thus prisoners with release dates already identified were suddenly faced with the devastating destruction of their expectation of freedom. The policy changes were promptly challenged in the courts by four prisoners (two lifers and two serving fixed sentences) affected in this way, but the Home Secretary's right to alter his policy was upheld, finally, in the House of Lords.'[95] The retrospective character of the change provoked a barrage of criticism which foreshadowed later challenges to the Home Secretary's rights to increase sentences, and indeed to have the final say in the case of the release of lifers, which led ultimately to their repudiation by the European Court of Human Rights.

The scope for extensions of the parole system to staunch the rising prison population proved in the event to be far more limited than had been hoped by both the Home Secretary and the Home Office. The discontent of the judiciary with the potential for sentences to be overridden was paralleled by a growing clamour for 'truth in sentencing' by key sections of the media and 'public opinion'. The prison population reached 51,000 by early 1987, with almost 19,000 two or three to a cell. Deteriorating conditions were remarked on by HMI reports. Riots and occupations increased, and Northeye prison was damaged in 1986 to the point of temporary closure (see chapter on the 1991 Criminal Justice Act). There was now a double crisis of both prison and parole systems running out of control: the former due to increasingly widespread unrest and the second due to longstanding anomalies threatening judicial backlash. The effects of Brittan's bifurcatory measures made liberalisation much harder. Not only was there 'fierce criticism of the effect of the Brittan policy on long-term and life sentence prisoners.'[96] But also Douglas Hurd – Brittan's successor in 1985 – had no scope left to use parole as a way out of the prison population crisis.[97] In 1987 Hurd authorised an inquiry, chaired by Lord Carlisle, to radically overhaul the parole system, 'in particular to resolve the anomaly which had arisen from the reduction in the minimum period of imprisonment to be served. This anomaly had resulted in the custodial part of many prison sentences – those between 12 months up to and including two years – becoming much the same (about eight months). The judges had found this situation deeply objectionable, and in their concern to have it corrected they may have acquiesced more readily than they might otherwise have done in the sentencing proposals as they had been set out in the Green and White Papers.'[98]

The Carlisle Report,[99] published in 1988, rectified the anomaly at a stroke by abolishing remission, a system which had survived so long mainly because its automatic character had meant it was relatively simple for the prison authorities to operate. However, to forestall its abolition leading to a surge in the prison population, the committee felt the need to incorporate a two-stage framework to what otherwise could have been a single point for eligibility to be activated:

1    All prisoners sentenced to less than four years would be released on licence after half their sentence.
2    Prisoners sentenced to four years or more would have to serve half their sentence (instead of only one-third as before) before becoming eligible for parole. Those granted parole would then be released on licence, others would be released on licence after serving two-thirds of their sentence.
3    In both cases time would be added for any offences committed in prison.
4    All prisoners sentenced to twelve months or more would be liable to have the unexpired part of their sentence added to any new sentence imposed if they were convicted of another offence.

'The intention and the effect was to make the whole of the sentence . . . "count" in the sense that the prisoner would be subject to restrictions for the full term of the sentence including the portion which might be served in the community. The Carlisle Committee's aims, consistently with those which now informed the Government's criminal justice policy as a whole, were among others to provide for a greater degree of consistency, and to introduce a greater degree of openness, fairness and procedural justice into the decision-making process.'[100]

However, despite the committee's best efforts, the effect of the recommended reforms, enacted almost unchanged in the Criminal Justice Act 1991, and as predicted by several critics of the Carlisle Report, was somewhat to reduce the numbers achieving early release. 'Carlisle favoured two key principles: first, the idea of *parsimony* in the use of custody, and second, the notion of *real time* custodial sentencing (i.e. "truth in sentencing"). Unfortunately, however, without a reduction in the sentences passed by judges, these two principles inevitably clashed with each other, leading to a slightly uneasy compromise which came into being with the passing of the Criminal Justice Act 1991. It has been estimated that – contrary to Carlisle's desire for parsimony in punishment – the 1991 reforms overall actually added about 1,000 prisoners to the total prison population (Hood and Shute, 1996: 86).'[101] The parole reforms, which were designed to complement the 'just deserts' principle underlying the 1991 Act, made it even more imperative that custodial sentencing was moderated. In the event, that was not to be. (See chapter on the 1991 Act).

## The System of Prison Inspection

Just before 8 a.m. on the morning of 13 December 1995, David Ramsbotham, the newly appointed Chief Inspector of Prisons, arrived at the gates of Holloway Prison, the largest women's prison in the country, to join his team to conduct the first, and unannounced, prison inspection of his term of office. The next day he returned to announce his suspension of the inspection for six months and, having consulted his team of prison inspectors, and informed the governor of his reasons for the decision, he went to Prison Service headquarters to do so with the director general, Richard Tilt.[102]

Why had he taken so dramatic a step? His reason, which made all the more impact as his former military career had involved sites of pain and suffering, was that he and his team 'had been utterly appalled by the treatment of and conditions for prisoners, highlighting the filth, the absence of activities and the wholly inadequate medical arrangements . . . What I had seen in Holloway was an affront to human decency that was wholly unworthy of a civilised society. If my experienced professional inspectors were as shocked as I, a complete outsider to prisons, who had seen a number of appalling sights in my military career, what did this say about the standards of those in the Prison Service who were responsible for the situation? I had never before encountered so many deeply unhappy or emotionally damaged people for whom so little was being done.'[103]

The catalogue of neglect he had encountered on the aborted inspection included outside yards and inside corridors, stairwells, lavatories and washrooms strewn with food, clothing, sanitary towels, excrement and other rubbish; high rates of bullying and self-harming; complaints unanswered and unacknowledged;

association time out of cell frequently cancelled, thus in effect barring mothers from phoning their families and children – all of which and more had for months been issues alerted to Home Office ministers by the Board of Visitors. 'In sum, overcrowded Holloway was being badly managed. Little or nothing was being done beyond containing prisoners, who were not treated in accordance with the rules. Worst of all, neither government ministers nor Prison Service Headquarters appeared to have made any plans to rectify the situation.'[104] Moreover, the prison medical centre and mental hospital, at that point still not part of the NHS, was described by medical inspectors as a 'disaster area'. The single most scandal-ous revelation, which reverberated nationally when reported on the news media, occurred when the chief inspector met seven women in the mother and baby unit:

> '. . . a few generalities were exchanged about how long they had been there and whether they were visited. But nothing prepared me for what came next.
> "Do you think that it was right that I was in chains?" asked one woman.
> "Chains when?" I asked.
> "When I was having him," she said, pointing to her son.
> "Are you telling me that you were in chains while you were in labour?" I asked.
> "Yes", she replied.
> "So was I", said one or two others.
> "Am I hearing correctly?" I asked the governor.
> "It's security requirements," she replied, going on to detail under exactly what regulation.
> . . . Another described how embarrassing it was to have to go to the lavatory on the end of a long chain, and attached to a male officer because there were not enough female officer escorts.

I can only describe my initial reaction to the Health Care Centre as one of intense disgust.'[105] Nevertheless, the then Minister of Prisons, Ann Widdicombe, defended the shackling of pregnant women prisoners in hospitals outside the prison to prevent their escape, citing a number who had done so.[106] Jack Straw, the Shadow Home Secretary, countered that no woman prisoner in labour had achieved this feat.

The route to so excoriating an inspector's view of a prison, and one that was made public at the time, had not been won lightly. In a sense, it marked a return to times past. Prison inspections began in 1835. The first prison inspectors 'were statutory agents of central government, enforcing compliance with prison legisla-tion by the local authorities, which at that time were responsible for all but the con-vict prisons. The first inspectors, however, achieved more than that: they shaped prison policy. Their published reports were voluminous, detailed and trenchant. They developed systematic ideas about the desirable shape of prison regimes and converted ministers to their cause.'[107] Yet when central government assumed con-trol of all prisons in 1878, they dispensed with the inspectorate altogether. It was only revived much later, in attenuated form, senior staff conducting inspections on behalf of the Prisons Board, their reports a tool of management and strictly confidential. Mountbatten's report in 1966 sought to strengthen the inspectorate by signalling the need for a chief inspector to be granted more independence and higher status. But it was only when the May Committee in 1979, which took on a recommendation by the House of Commons Expenditure Committee of 1980, that it was guaranteed more independence and, against Home Office advice, the acceptance that reports should be published. In this regard the Home Office did not so much pursue innovation as attempt to shackle it.

Nevertheless, the Home Office proceeded to draw up a framework for such an inspectorate that ensured its integrity and has so far stood the test of time. 'The terms of reference having been announced, we still had to convert the May Committee's rather vague recommendation into an understanding about the chief inspector's relationship with the Prison Department and with prison establishments and their boards of visitors. In consultation with colleagues, I drew up a 'charter' which said that the inspectorate's main occupation would be the regular inspections of establishments, concentrating on such matters as the morale of staff and prisoners; the quality of the regime; the condition of the buildings; questions of humanity and decency; and whether the establishment was giving value for money.'[108] Most crucially, despite forebodings that appointments should avoid persons with backgrounds in the law and the military, on the grounds that they would be too legalistic or militaristic, in the event the post came to be filled by people who defied such assumptions. 'Bill Pearce, the chief probation officer for Inner London, was offered and accepted the post but sadly became ill and died soon afterwards. Later appointments – a prison governor in an acting capacity (Bill Brister), a diplomat (Sir James Hennessey), judge (Sir Stephen Tumim), a general (Sir David, now Lord, Ramsbotham) and a human rights lawyer (Anne Owers) – showed that assumptions should never be made on a basis of professional (or any other) stereotypes.'[109]

The Criminal Justice Act 1982 created the office of Her Majesty's Chief Inspector of Prisons, the title emphasising the element of independence that transcended simple renewal. Successive chief inspectors have been determined to fulfil that role. 'In the 1980s, largely as a result of the tenacity and plain speaking of the two successive Chief Inspectors, Sir James Hennessey and Judge Tumim, the inspectorate became increasingly relevant as an instrument of penal reform. A continuous stream of trenchant reports, all of which were published causing periodic embarrassment to the Prison Department, constituted a significant strand in the changing climate of public opinion. Personalities count, and Tumim in particular brought to a hitherto lacklustre public office a colourful personality and arresting turn of phrase which served him well in attracting attention to numerous defects in need of remedy.'[110] Tumim's major achievement was arguably his determination to press for in-cell sanitation by the stated date of 1994 as part of the myriad recommendations for reform in the Woolf Report on Prison Disturbances of 1991. Windlesham's eulogy might well be extended to Tumim's successors, though they increasingly faced the worsening climate for penal reform following the 'Prison

Works' edict of Michael Howard in 1993, which signalled a sea change in sentencing policy and practice, along with a massive shift of resources to security measures following the Learmont and Woodock Reports (see the chapter on the 1991 Criminal Justice Act), and a doubling of the prison population from 42,000 in 1990 to 85,000 by 2010. Though it is beyond our period of study, the full force of the change was only felt after the 30 per cent cut in the staffing and resourcing of prisons after 2012 under the 'austerity' programme of the Conservative-Liberal coalition. By this point, even full-bloodedly critical inspectorate reports fell on seemingly deaf ministerial ears.

## Afterword

The above examples of the pursuit of innovation in penal policy have on the whole painted a picture of the Home Office in a good light, barring the Prison Department's neglect of the state of Holloway Prison in the mid-1990s, and others no doubt for male prisoners could be similarly found. The Home Office and the Prison Department defence would logically be that prisons, unlike any other institution including schools, hospitals and public housing, have no control over the numbers they are meant to accommodate, their length of stay or the levels of funding to meet their needs. That is a matter for the judiciary and the politicians who determine sentencing policy and financial resourcing respectively. In general, however, the capacity of the Home Office civil servants to pursue innovation and to travel, albeit slowly, in the direction of the more liberal and humane policies and practice is, on balance, well borne out for this period. The most notorious of Home Office characteristics, secrecy and a resistance to open scrutiny, have arguably lessened over time as the culture of in-house closure was challenged by both internal debate and external pressures. As an American criminologist remarked, in a review of a study of British and American prison discipline: 'It will come as no surprise to connoisseurs of the English Home Office that they were unfailingly obstructive in providing any access to their institutions. The Scots were more forthcoming.'[111] The fieldwork involved had, however, been undertaken in 1973–4, the peak period of cover-up suspicions around the creation of the Special Control Units in Wakefield and, abortively, Wormwood Scrubs (see Ch. 2). A year or two earlier, Stan Cohen and Laurie Taylor had broken the academic self-denying ordinance to respect Home office ground rules and publish, without permission, their study of the experience of maximum security imprisonment at Durham Gaol.[112] A decade earlier, Terence and Pauline Morris had been refused permission to publish a chapter of their landmark study of Pentonville Prison because it dealt with prisoner unrest at the execution of a prisoner. The suppressed Chapter 14, 'The Prison Under Stress' dealt with staff and prisoner attitudes towards capital punishment, reactions to the executions within the prison, and within ten days of each other, of Joseph Chrimes and Ronald Marwood. Disturbances and demonstrations outside the prison on the day of the execution of Marwood – a local boy who had killed a policeman – were widely reported. Those inside the prison provoked a reaction from the governor and staff which the Home Office were clearly determined to avoid publicising:

'On 11 May, an attempt was made to discuss the events of the evening of 7 May. The Governor's reaction was to become furious. He said that stories of violence and brutality on the part of the staff were a "gross libel" and that prisoners were telling lies.

"Force had to be used. There were ugly scenes outside as well. You forget that there are <u>evil,</u> <u>wicked</u> men in here".

He was not concerned to deny that prisoners had been handled with some force, but rather to justify the situation by arguing that they had justly deserved all they received. He went on to say that he felt that the research was hostile to the prison staff and that because prisoners were coming to the research with complaints it was "prejudicial to good order and discipline". As he developed this theme he became increasingly angry and stormed from one end of the room to the other. He said he would endeavour to exclude the research at any time when <u>he</u> thought fit: he did not intend to give reasons.'[113] It should be added that the governor was an opponent of capital punishment who had been profoundly depressed by two executions taking place over a ten-day period in his prison. Given this context, Stanley Cohen and Laurie Taylor a decade later decided to 'publish and be damned' – at least by the Home Office – when it came to both the research – for which they had received no prior permission – and the publication of their findings and analysis of prisoners' experience of maximum security imprisonment in Durham Prison.[114]

From the mid-1970s on, however, the legal framework applied to custody began a period of incremental change. 'Until recently, prisoners [in Britain] had effectively no rights except the right to live and breathe. Everything else was a privilege, which could be withdrawn by administrators.'[115] Prisoner militancy, partly supported by PROP, led in turn to a rise in staff militancy, led by the POA. Riots and occupations at Hull in 1976 and Gartree in 1978, and at other top-security and even local prisons in the 1980s, whose 'brutal suppression . . . led to what were, for Britain, amazing innovations: prison officers were convicted of abusing their authority, and punishments inflicted by the "Visitors" were over-turned by external courts . . . At the same time, prisons came increasingly under the view of the courts, above all the European Court of Human Rights, which has gone far towards beginning in England the same kind of changes which the federal courts undertook in the United States in the 1960s.'[116] Prison conditions were not, however, improving: if anything, they had deteriorated under the pressure of rising numbers and subsequent overcrowding. Research by King and McDermott proved the point with data that dismayed both Home Office civil servants and ministers.[117] Penal reform pressure groups began to proliferate, such as the Prison Reform Trust, set up in 1981, alongside the Howard League, Justice and NACRO. The Parliamentary All-Party Penal Action Group (PAPPAG) pursued a largely critical but constructive path towards criminal justice policy. By the end of the 1980s, innovatory measures to curb penal expansion and pursue genuinely humane containment were increasingly influential. That countermeasures in the form of 'Prison Works' in Britain, and mass imprisonment and 'Supermax' prisons in the United States, gained ascendancy was substantially due to fundamental changes on the politics of crime control, the subject of the following volume.

## Women's Imprisonment and the Redevelopment of Holloway

Barbara Wootton once wrote, with characteristic irony: 'If men behaved like women, the courts would be idle and the prisons empty.'[118] Paradoxically, the relatively lower and less serious forms of female criminality diminished the pressure to take account of their special needs in the criminal justice sphere. And the numbers involved in custody were remarkably low. In the 1960s and early 1970s, women prisoners numbered around a thousand, roughly 3 per cent of the total for both sexes. In 1972, for example, almost half the average population were held in two prisons, Holloway, a local prison in North London (305) and Styal, in the Midlands, the only closed prison for women (183). The rest were held in two open prisons (Askham Grange and Moor Court), three remand centres for women and girls (Low Newton, Pucklechurch and Risley), three closed borstals for girls (Bullwood Hall, and small numbers within Holloway and Styal) and an open borstal for girls at East Sutton Park.[119] The most crucial deprivation for women prisoners was their greater consequent remoteness, compared with male prisoners, from family, especially children, and friends. Visiting was far more likely to face their generally poorer families with the greater expense in the time, effort and money involved in travel for prison visits, sometimes involving journeys across half the country. Though some concessions were made in relation to clothing, home visits and mail,[120] no substantial effort was made until the late 1960s to devise a regime better adapted to the needs of women prisoners.

As the previous section documented, in 1995 the problems of Holloway, the oldest and largest women's prison for a century or more, had become a grotesque travesty of humane containment. But this was not the result of decades of neglect. In the intervening period, Holloway had been the focus for a highly ambitious programme of transformation from a fortress-like prison to a lightly controlled, though still secure, treatment centre.[121] The initiative flowed from within the still vibrant culture of liberal reform which permeated certain echelons of the Home Office in the wake of the programme outlined in the 1959 White Paper *Penal Practice in a Changing Society*. The success of the establishment of Grendon Underwood as a psychiatrically oriented prison encouraged the pursuit of innovation in relation to women prisoners, long associated by penal reformers with unduly backward and repressive forms of custody. The relevant division, P4, also contained officials who worked on young offender establishments, among whom the spirit of Alexander Paterson was held to be lasting. The times seemed opportune for a major reform of women's imprisonment.

The main proponents of reform in the case of Holloway were Joanna Kelley and Kenneth Neale. Joanna Kelley had long experience of running a women's prison, having been Assistant Governor at Holloway 1947–52, Governor of Askham Grange 1952–59, and Governor III, again at Holloway 1959–66 before moving to the Prison Department of the Home Office as Assistant Director (Women), 1966–74. 'On promotion to Assistant Director, "I thought this was a wonderful opportunity . . . I shall spend my time getting Holloway changed and so I did". She considered the building of Holloway prison to be ill-suited to the application of a scientific criminology and a therapeutic regime. Its design was irredeemably punitive and "if you are very punitive in your regime you're much less likely to heal minds". It was quite evident to others around her in the still infant division that Joanna Kelley had arrived with an object . . . Ken Neale remarked, "Joanna Kelley was the powerhouse of the whole thing and she was a very dominant figure".'[122]

Ken Neale had spent his earlier career in the African Colonial Office and transferred to the Home Office in 1967 to head the new division P4, which mainly concerned responsibility for women's prisons. Accustomed to visiting 'outstations' to gauge problems at first hand, and applying that method to prisons, he found Holloway to be 'an affront to civilisation . . . it was so utterly unacceptable to put women and children in these conditions that it had to go'. He even escorted Treasury officials doubting the urgency of the case for change to see the situation for themselves. He and Joanna Kelley made a formidable alliance in convincing the newly formed P4 division to make the redevelopment of Holloway a major priority.

What they had in mind was the transformation of Holloway from a Victorian fortress-like, and inappropriately secure, prison to a modern, scientifically conceived centre for the rehabilitation of women offenders. Joanna Kelley had based her approach to that subject on a plethora of overwhelmingly psychological and psychiatric studies of female offenders, a strongly positivistic emphasis on the individual offender's mental state which, due to the dearth of sociological studies on female offending, lacked a corresponding social dimension. That imbalance had largely prevailed in relation to male offenders in Britain, though the 1960s saw the beginnings of a much more sociological criminology, largely inspired by and adapted from the more developed American sociological tradition. In relation to female criminality, however, and despite Barbara Wootton's root-and-branch castigation of psychiatrically based approaches to its explanation in general,[123] the model still upheld in the cause of the redevelopment of Holloway was that of Grace Pailthorpe, a pioneering exponent of a casework approach to female imprisonment in the 1930s: 'Pailthorpe employed a battery of diagnostic and clinical tests to measure the psychology of women in prisons (including Holloway) and in Preventive and Rescue Homes. Her two-hour interview explored a subject's:

> Reactions to the present situation, her emotional mobility, her moods, the way in which she was disposing of the present situation in which she found herself, viz. By projection, negativism, evasion, etc., her mannerisms (e.g. the childish antics of *dementia praecox*), habit spasms, tremors, blushing, sweating; her affects – self-reproach, self-pity, self-complacency, etc. – and

moods were all noted. Her history of depressions and states of excitement were all gone into minutely, with special regard to periodicity and relation to menstruation.'

. . . In an argument that presaged plans for Holloway formulated forty years later, she recommended the replacement of unscientific and irrationally-administered prisons for women by a diagnostic 'central clearing station system' to which 'patients' should be sent in, 'be fully investigated, physically and psychologically, and treatment allocated.'[124]

In the 1950s and 1960s, the psychiatrisation of explanations of both male and female criminality led to what was termed the dominance of the 'medico-legal' model, at the expense of social, cultural and economic perspectives. The contestation of that model was the catalyst for the formation of countervailing approaches, in particular those whose exponents gathered to found the National Deviancy Symposium (later Conference) in 1969. The shift in perspective in relation to male criminality was not, however, the case with that of females, leading Carol Smart to argue[125] that the subject had been relatively neglected by male criminologists. As a result, the explanation of female criminality proved far more resistant to change. Even the work of Lombroso and Ferrero, in their 1895 study *The Female Offender*, is not 'an antique intellectual curio, but a living body of thought, setting an agenda that is still operative: the subordination of women to the view that female crime is biological destiny, a view long since dispelled in the case of men.'[126]

Hence, 'without a "recognisable conceptual framework" and "usable criminological perspective", lacking a self-conscious academic community to sustain it, but nevertheless possessing copious statistics, the criminology of women in the 1960s tended to collapse into a small agglomeration of piecemeal empirical studies that fed on the numbers supplied by standard tests . . . They were diagnostic in character, expressed in a language that focussed on pathological symptoms and factors. They were, in short, fragmented lists of clinical components that were categorised, quantified and ranked.'[127] By a crucial analytical slippage, 'although it was almost invariably shown that pathological symptoms characterised only a minority of women prisoners, it was nevertheless the symptoms of the minority that were allowed to saturate descriptions of the whole. By a kind of interpretive legerdemain, the "abnormality" of a few attained much greater significance than the "normality" of the many . . . and it was abnormality which writers proceeded to discuss amidst what Carlen would much later call the "mounting academic claims that women criminals are abnormal women".'[128]

How did this approach translate into the planning of the 'new' Holloway? First, the times were propitious. Rehabilitation as a, if not *the*, key objective of imprisonment had been progressively instituted in the penal system by the appointment of psychologists and psychiatrists in a number of establishments, not least Holloway, since the early 1950s. Secondly, by the late 1960s, fresh and rebuilding had been forced upon the Home Office by the crisis of security and control following the escapes of Biggs and Blake. Since women prisoners were not seen as presenting high security risks, the argument could be made for rehabilitative measures as a priority in their case. Thirdly, the important precedent of launching the first therapeutic prison at Grendon Underwood had been hailed as a successful experiment in the humane treatment of selected male prisoners. 'In effect, it was planned that Holloway, the women's prison, and Grendon, by then exclusively a men's prison, would be twin therapeutic institutions.'[129]

The case for the 'new' Holloway had been spelt out by Ken Neale and Joanna Kelley in 1968 in a statement of P4 intentions, *Prison Policy: Women and Girls*.[130] Its first priority was to be the 're-development of Holloway beginning with the construction of a central hospital and psychiatric unit'. It was to be a 'larger, comprehensive, versatile and secure hospital'. 'Joanna Kelley wrote to Ken Neale, "I think we should work on the principle that Holloway is to be a large hospital, treatment oriented, with a small prison, and not as at present, vice versa." The prison should be redeveloped on site as a collection of sixteen small units, each housing about forty prisoners, each as far as possible a separate entity, and for the most part concentrated in a hospital block and hospital administration.'[131] Skilfully steered through the key committees and with little by way of real opposition, the proposals were announced as government policy by the Home Secretary, James Callaghan, on 16 December 1968:

> 'Following a review of the custodial arrangements for women and girls, I have decided upon a programme to re-shape the system of female penal establishments in England and Wales. The current total of 800 women and girls in custody has not varied significantly over the last quarter of a century, and is not likely to change markedly in the foreseeable future. Most women and girls in custody require some form of medical, psychiatric or remedial treatment. The main feature of the programme is therefore to demolish the existing prison at Holloway and redevelop the site by stages. This will permit the building of an establishment that will be basically a secure hospital to act as the hub of the female penal system. Its medical and psychiatric facilities will be its central feature and normal custodial facilities will comprise a relatively small part of the establishment.'

As Rock comments, amid the general acceptance or acclaim for the policy, 'no one came forward in the late 1960s to question the assumption that women required medical or psychiatric treatment.'[132] But the plan evolved by the P4 Project team over the next few years was not for some chillingly clinical, highly regimented mental hospital but a much more community-like series of small units centred around a village green-like open space. The forbidding architecture of the Victorian-era prison would be replaced by low, 'curvy' walled and variegated buildings. 'The new Holloway was a schematic repudiation of the old. The wings and their centre were turned inside out: where there had been a controlling hub, there would be an empty green; where there had been constraint and surveillance, there would be freedom . . .'[133] It was a highly original conception for humane betterment.

Implementing that conception, however, was not to be. Difficulties came thick and fast. Many arose from the inherent problems of simultaneous demolition and building afresh on site. The complex phasing agenda whereby one part of the old prison was demolished to clear the way for the new was subject to delays arising from industrial disputes, key components, damp affecting windows throughout and security issues involving civilian staff. Myriad issues arose with the neighbouring land-use owners and local authorities, all of which put completion beyond the planned date of 1977 until 1984, seven years late. By then, the momentum driving rehabilitative projects had been diminished, if not extinguished, by the adverse impact of research of the 'nothing works' era. Treasury stringency was reasserted and the 'new Holloway was stretched and altered to become neither a medically-orientated establishment nor a conventional secure prison, and the forces for change were both internal and external'.[134]

The main external change was the unanticipated growth in both the number of convicted female offenders, and a concomitant increase in the number sentenced to longer prison sentences, and a consequent perception that women prisoners were becoming 'much more "normal" than was expected in, say, the late 1960s'.[135] Reinforcing the view that a significant change was occurring were cases of female terrorists, notably Leila Khaled, a Palestinian, and the two 'Price sisters', involved in an IRA bombing campaign. Though none were held there, that merely emphasised that 'the old and the new Holloway were patently not equipped to undertake the long-term secure confinement of dangerous women.'[136]

It was at this stage that the Treasury began to impose spending restrictions, reflecting national economic crises epitomised by the 1973 miners' strike, the consequent three-day week, and a huge increase in oil prices. 'In 1974, it was agreed to lower ceilings and narrow corridors in the new establishment for reasons of economy, a decision that was to have surprisingly profound consequences. David Faulkner called it the one particular thing he regretted about the design'.[137] As the 1970s wore on, disillusionment also set in about the overriding psychiatric mission. Hospital and psychiatric facilities were severely reduced, leaving Holloway as a curious amalgam of being neither a secure nor a treatment-oriented prison. By 1977, 'staff had forebodings about the small units and their need for heavy supervision, the short corridors and their difficult sight-lines, the dog-leg bends and their threats of ambush, and the windows with their large areas of plain glass . . . Thereafter followed a sustained period of *anomie* attended by violent vandalism, assaults, graffiti, fire-setting, barricading and yet more window-breaking.'[138] This 'Dantean' atmosphere persisted and even worsened into the 1980s. The major problems arose from 'confused space' – the coexistence of a minority of 'very violent' women and gloomy corridors were a recipe for fear and anxiety among other prisoners and even staff; and surveillance, the whole point of the *panopticon* concept which had been inverted by the 'new Holloway' plan, was architecturally designed down, if not out. Mounting concern among prison staff led the Prison Officers' Association to condemn the prison's design as 'a failure'. Morale suffered, and rates of sick leave and absenteeism soared by the mid-1980s.[139]

The classic staff response to fears of loss of control was its reassertion by *force majeure*. 'Locking out' was a form of 'work-to-rule' whereby the local POA refused to accept any women prisoners above certified normal accommodation (CNA). The result was that some women prisoners were held, at times for several weeks, in the even greater confinement of police cells. 'Locking-in' resulted from an overtime limit imposed by the POA which meant prisoners were often confined to their rooms for 23 hours a day, with severe cuts to free association time. This practice, begun in 1978, lasted well into the 1980s. Staff-prisoner conflicts multiplied as a result. Such problems were intensified in C1, a unit for the most 'highly disturbed' women, which developed a reputation for crazed and aggressive behaviour redolent of Gothic horror fantasy. Physical squalor, noise, high rates of attempted suicide, self-mutilation and violence were beyond the scope of under-resourced medical and discipline staff, whose own lines of accountability were blurred and contested. 'C1 became known as a terrible place, to be described almost surrealistically, in the language of dream and nightmare.'[140] This transformation of Holloway from a putative treatment centre to scenes akin to an eighteenth-century bedlam led to mounting pressure from penal reform groups, strengthened since 1983 by the newly formed Women in Prison group, founded by Chris Tchaikovsky, herself an ex-prisoner, the media and Parliament for something to be done. The result in December 1984 was the Holloway Project Committee, whose report in 1985 recommended sweeping changes to its staffing, management structure, the location of C1, and its regime. Its acceptance by the Home Secretary, Leon Brittan, carried the weight needed for substantial extra resourcing.

The implementation of the report's recommendations was the main task for the newly appointed governor, Colin Allen. He had an unusual combination of the qualities needed to effect real change, demonstrating in the process that, with good, humane management, charismatic leadership and more resources, the original plan for the new Holloway proved, for a time, to be workable. Medical staff were strengthened and given a clear mandate to take charge of a relocated C1. The multiple functions of the prison could be clarified and properly administered. As the atmosphere improved, rates of assault, self-harm and rule-breaking fell substantially. Most importantly, prisoners were no longer confined to their cells for 23 hours a day. Governor-staff relations improved markedly with better arrangements for officers' views and the POA to be taken into account. Yet underlying problems on this front proved too severe for this regeneration to be sustained. In 1988, following a power struggle with the POA over manning levels for key tasks, the Prison Department, fearing a national backlash over the implementation of Fresh Start, in effect backed down. Colin Allen moved to the Prison Inspectorate, and the scene was set for the kind of deterioration in conditions that David Ramsbotham and his inspectorate team condemned as outrageous in 1995.

What were the underlying problems that came to defeat the aims of the plan for the new Holloway, when those for Grendon had proved both durable and effective?[141] Major differences were that Grendon prisoners were both selected and self-selected to 'fit' the varied therapeutic regime. There was no claim to be able to accept any but those deemed capable of benefiting from the treatment strategies available. Secondly, prisoners were transferred there for a period related to their response to treatment. Thirdly, they were not the most high-risk, category A, or their equivalent in control terms though, comparing 1971–72 receptions by offence with those of 1987–88, 'Grendon's population has become increasingly weighted away from shorter-term recidivist property offenders in favour of long-term prisoners serving sentences for offences of sex and violence.'.[142] Fourthly, Grendon was a smaller, single-purpose (if 'multi-functional') prison, with a smaller average population than that of Holloway, whose numbers varied greatly as the course of redevelopment proceeded and whose population came to stand at over 400. Holloway had no such parameters as Grendon and the planned changes were arguably overambitious and misconceived from the start, based as they were on the assumption that *all* women prisoners were in need of therapy rather than social support under conditions of humane containment. As Genders and Player comment: 'Woolf distinguished between the old discredited model of rehabilitative treatment, whereby offenders were sentenced to imprisonment *for* rehabilitative treatment, and the new rehabilitative approach. This is based upon providing opportunities for prisoners to address their offending behaviour and to prepare themselves for release within an environment which promotes individual responsibility and prevents 'a creeping and all-pervading dependency by prisoners on the prison authority'.[143] Unfortunately, the redevelopment of Holloway faced difficulties which prevented that transition.

### Private Prisons

The so-called privatisation of prisons, unlike the five innovations above, did not emanate from Home Office ministers or civil servants. Their agenda in the 1980s was to address the burgeoning prison numbers and other penal crises by such policies as sentencing reform, the development of specialised units to deal with troublesome long-term prisoners, and industrial conflict resolution. Private prisons unexpectedly emerged, *inter alia*, as a way of dealing with the power of the POA in the mid-1980s. Despite an awareness of their operation in the USA as an alternative to state-run prisons for minimum security prisoners, it had not been proposed at all seriously for this country. Two prime developments combined to promote it from the outlandish to the status of worth serious consideration by the Select Committee on Home Affairs and their report of 1987. These were, first, the rapid evolution of what came to be called neo-liberal political economy, the market-led sale of services built, managed and owned by the public sector. The sale of national utilities – notably gas, then electricity and water – to private corporations and investors was on such a scale that a former Conservative Prime Minister, Harold Macmillan, likened it in 1985 to 'selling the family silver'. The sale of local authority homes to their tenants at a significant discount proved electorally popular. What went largely unnoticed at the time was the prohibition against local authorities using the proceeds to build new homes for those in need of affordable housing, as it is now called, a prime reason for the marked increase in homelessness, and the selling-on of newly bought council homes to so-called 'buy-to-let' *rentiers*, a substantial cause of the huge increase in the price of housing to buy or rent. At the time, however, it was not regarded as feasible for prisons to be not only built by private sector firms but also managed by them. Only the Adam Smith Institute (ASI), a prominent proponent of privatisation across the public sector, made a strong and detailed case for market-led alternatives to be extended to the penal sphere. The second development, seized on by the ASI, was the growing problem of industrial conflict caused, in the view of the government, by the intransigence of the Prison Officers' Association in relation to pay and conditions of work. 'Working closely with John Wheeler[144] and other Conservative MPs, it made representations to the Home Office and held seminars on the subject.'[145] The problem of 'producer dominance' could only be tackled by introducing private sector competitiveness into the penal realm.

Private prisons had long been seen as discredited by their history. 'The avaricious turnkey portrayed by Hogarth (in *The Rake's Progress*, 1733–4) was not a contractor selling a service to the state, but a publicly appointed official who made most of his income by extracting fees from his prisoners. The natural consequence of this system of finance was that prisoners who had money (and owing to the intricacies of eighteenth-century debt laws such prisoners were not uncommon) could live in considerable comfort, while those who had none lived in the most dreadful squalor. . . . the idea that profit and punishment do not mix was established much earlier and more strongly in Britain than in the USA.'[146] The rejection of Bentham's proposal for a private-contractor 'Panopticon' by a parliamentary committee in 1810 was on the reformist grounds that exploitation would outweigh reformation. Following the abolition of fee-taking by gaolers in 1815, private commercial principles survived in limited fashion in prison industry and in juvenile institutions. The potential for prison industry profitability was progressively curtailed by the growing resistance of both employers and trade unions to the possible undercutting of their markets by prison labour. This meant that increasingly prison work became limited to such notoriously mind-numbing work as sewing mailbags. Juvenile institutions, from the Victorian industrial and reformatory schools that were state-subsidised but philanthropically run, to the approved schools that replaced them in the 1933 Children and Young Persons Act, acquired a somewhat tarnished reputation. 'Whatever we think of the ideal of loving Christian discipline which inspired (Mary) Carpenter, the reality of life in the schools was dismal. Tens of thousands of children were incarcerated for years, most for trivial offences, in conditions which were at best spartan, at worst horrifically brutal.'[147] Despite reforms such as the establishment of the Children's Branch of the Home Office in 1913, and the strengthening of powers of inspection, periodic scandals, such as that concerning excessive corporal punishment at Court Lees Approved School in the mid-1960s,[148] meant the system could never quite shake off the unsavoury parts of its past.

The most recent precursor for such a policy is usually claimed to have been the outsourcing of the detention of suspected illegal immigrants, by a Labour government, from Home Office-run centres to Securicor in 1970, a private security firm which provided both the security staff and the management of the centres. But the responsibility for immigrant detention, which throughout lay ultimately at the door of the Home Office Immigration and Nationality Department, had previously been that of the airlines serving Heathrow and Gatwick airports.[149] The transfer of responsibility from one commercial organisation to another is somewhat distinct from the transfer of control from the public sector to private agencies. It was nevertheless cited by the government's Green Paper on *Private Sector Involvement in the Remand System*[150] as an 'important precedent for the contracting-out of custodial duties, (para. 47)' leading Stephen Shaw of the Prison Reform Trust to suggest that the precedent was in some ways a worrying one.[151] 'He pointed to the lack of staff training – seven days on the general work of Securicor and just one day on their duties at the centre – and their lack of accountability."[152] Though each centre was inspected daily by a Home Office official, there was no Board of Visitors or equivalent, and questions in Parliament were restricted by 'commercial confidentiality'. Those concerns, along with incidents of staff brutality, anticipated the criticisms made by those opposed to privately run prisons, though in the event they have so far proved little different from state-run prisons. The main fear, however, especially among penal reform groups, was that the introduction of the profit motive into prison management would stimulate the growth of a 'prison-industrial' complex comparable to that discernible in the USA.

It was to the USA that the Adam Smith Institute (ASI) had turned for evidence that private prisons not only worked, but worked substantially better, and at lower cost, than state prisons. The ASI, founded in the USA by two British intellectuals in 1978, extolled free-market versions of social policy. 'Many of these were promoted as part of the "Omega Project" launched by the ASI in 1984, and it was in the *Omega Report on Justice Policy* that the idea of private prisons made its British debut.'[153] Three years later in 1987 its author, Peter Young, advanced his claims for private prisons more boldly, stating as a 'surprising' fact that there are '*greatly improved conditions for prisoners* in all the US private jails . . . perhaps the most compelling argument for prison privatization is therefore the humanitarian one."[154] (author's italics). The evidence failed to match the claims, however. Cost comparisons were described as 'almost useless' by a fellow ASI exponent of the case for private prisons.[155] The case for greatly improved standards and conditions in US private jails rested on four case studies, of three jails and a prison, only one of which could be said to have improved at all. Nevertheless, the ASI case for US private prisons as a success story proved influential in right-wing Westminster circles. Michael Forsyth, a Conservative MP, took the initiative in promoting the idea within the party. By August 1986 the Conservative Study Group on Crime embraced the idea in a report entitled *Prisons*. Even the Prime Minister, Margaret Thatcher, who usually left specific matters of law and order to ministers, explicitly endorsed fact-finding visits to the USA by the Home Office Minister of State, the Earl of Caithness, and by the House of Commons Select Committee on Home Affairs.[156]

By this point, prison privatisation in some form was firmly on the government's agenda, a process characterised by pragmatic as well as ideological motives. Lord

Windlesham, a leading Conservative peer and former Home Office minister, grasped the significance of private prisons in relation to his long-held belief that separate remand prisons, for accused persons awaiting trial, was an elementary right: they should not be forced to experience the conditions of full-blown imprisonment. 'The motivation was to rectify a situation that was fundamentally wrong; not to promote the idea of privatisation . . . In 1987 it was timely to join in a public debate that already had begun. But how best to bring the proposal to the notice of ministers? After reflection, I decided to aim high and to approach the Prime Minister . . . In a letter sent to the Prime Minister on 23 July I summarised the case for separate provision, enclosed the article on remand prisoners which I had written for *The Times*, and concluded:

> ". . . your own response, together with the Home Secretary's willingness to look to the private sector to expedite the construction of new prisons, encourages me to think that the Government may now be in a position to make a determined effort to lift the burden of supervising remand prisoners off the shoulders of the police and the prison service in a way I have outlined".'[157]

The letter was copied to Douglas Hurd at the Home Office and William Whitelaw, then Leader of the House of Lords and Lord President of the Council (and a former Home Secretary). In her lengthy response, 'in the drafting of which the hand of the Home Office could be detected', on 12 August 1987, Margaret Thatcher replied that 'The Government is fully committed to making greater use of the private sector wherever this helps Departments like the Prison Department of the Home Office to get better value for money. We know that the private sector is involved in the day to day running of prisons as well as in constructing them for example in the United States, and we shall have a clearer picture of this after Malcolm Caithness has made his tour of American prisons in September. To that extent our minds remain open. But, as you yourself say, there would clearly be many problems to resolve before we could contemplate similar developments in this country . . . At present the balance of the argument seems to be against moving in this direction, and that is why Douglas Hurd told the House of Commons on 16 July that he did not believe there was a case for handing over the business of keeping prisoners safe to anyone other than Government servants . . ." On those grounds, of the problems of security, legal responsibilities and accountability, even privatising court escort arrangements was rejected in favour of exploring 'the creation of a special grade of escort officer to assist the police with escort duties.'[158]

'The letter went on record in Whitehall as an authoritative statement of policy from the highest level of government.' How then did it become feasible to move from this situation to one where, four years later in the Criminal Justice Act of 1991, the capacity to privatise *any* prison was enacted? In Windlesham's words, 'by the spring of 1988 the traditional orthodoxy was beginning to weaken.'[159] Faced by a prison population rising to over 50,000 in mid-March, Hurd announced a crucial change of approach to the engagement of the private sector in prison building; a Green Paper would be published on its potential for involvement in 'all aspects of the remand system'; and private consultants would take part in working on practical implications.[160] The first move of signal effect, following the introduction of the issue by the Adam Smith Institute, was the decision by the Select Committee on Home Affairs to examine the state and use of prisons as the subject for its report in the 1986/87 parliamentary session. 'As part of the investigation the committee exercised its power to travel abroad by visiting a number of prisons and non-custodial sentencing schemes in the United States. The issue of privatisation was not specifically included in the Committee's remit, and according to Gerry Bermingham, one of the two Labour members who went on the American trip, it was only when they found that their timetable included visits to two establishments run by the Corrections Corporation of America (CCA) that they realised that the issue was on the agenda . . . It was the work of CCA, however, which was to feature prominently in the committee's report.'[161]

That report, and the associated public hearings and media coverage of the topic, in which evidence gathered on the committee's visit to America loomed large, ensured that the potential for prison privatisation was thrust onto the political agenda. Though the report, *Contract Provision of Prisons,* was only three pages long, it asserted boldly that contract provision of penal establishments: 1. relieves the taxpayer of the immediate burden of having to pay their initial financial cost; 2. dramatically accelerates their building; and 3. produces greatly enhanced architectural efficiency and excellence (para. 1). The report began by stating that 'During our visit to the USA we focused part of our attention on prisons and youth custody institutions operated (and in some cases built) by the Corrections Corporation of America.' Ryan and Ward comment: 'The ambiguous phrasing and repeated use of the plural neatly conceal the fact that they only actually saw one private prison.'[162] The dominant Conservative members of the committee played down or disclaimed the existence of any evidence critical of the state of private prisons in the USA, despite the Howard League producing a copious assemblage of such material in evidence to the public hearings. In short, despite the Committee having been deeply divided on the subject, an apparently unanimous, all too brief report was published which extolled the American experience as a virtually unqualified success story. The CCA's achievement was described by the Chair of the committee, Sir Edward Gardner, as 'stunning'.[163] John Wheeler[164] 'emerged as the most forceful advocate of "contract management" in the committee's public hearings',[165] and linked the resort to private prisons with the rise of legal action against state authorities for their failure to maintain minimum standards. Legally enforceable minimum standards were also being sought by penal reform groups,[166] not least by PAPPAG, of which Wheeler was a leading member, but – as the evidence submitted by the Howard League showed – the extent of privatisation in the United States remained 'embryonic' and 'marginal'. Moreover, evidence to the committee by the Prison Officers' Association (POA), which had also mounted a visit to the USA to gather first-hand evidence on private prisons, gave a far more critical picture of the establishments they saw. Notwithstanding their incentive to stave off the resort to privatisation in Britain, they visited more adult penal establishments than the MPs and found 'damning' evidence of poor conditions in three, of which one – CCA's Houston Processing Centre for suspected illegal immigrants – were worse than any in Britain.[167] Overall, 'nowhere in the *Minutes of Evidence* is there a word of support for privatisation from anyone except the Conservative MPs themselves.'[168]

Media coverage of the issue, given the generally pro-Conservative stance of the English press, was far from uniform in assessing the costs and benefits of prison privatisation. Reportage in the *Times* and the *Telegraph* furnished examples of critical coverage of actual conditions and regimes. Leader writers, however, took an almost uniformly positive approach to the issue, even in left-of-centre papers such as *The Guardian* and *The Independent.* The state of British prisons was deemed to be so dire that any attempt at radical reform would be worth trying. The broadcast media were even-handed in their coverage, and only one programme, a *Panorama* investigative report, struck a decidedly critical note. Nevertheless, 'what evidence there is tends to suggest that Home Office civil servants supported the Home Secretary's stonewalling on this issue; and the announcement of a Green Paper on privatisation in the remand system – a consultative rather than a policy document – seemed to confirm this view . . . Such activities kept opponents of privatisation on their guard, but nothing prepared them for the strong pro-privatisation flavour of the Green Paper which was finally published in July 1988. Though formally presented as a discussion document, it leaves the reader in little doubt that the government is determined to go ahead and involve the private sector in the building and/or management of both new remand prisons and more secure bail hostels, as well as contracting out escort services for those awaiting trial.'[169]

By contrast, Lord Windlesham, who played a significant role on this issue by urging the Home Office and the Prime Minister to take the step of enacting the Green Paper's proposals, tended to disregard the overstatement of the evidence for privatisation, viewing it as arguments that typified 'the quintessential Thatcherite outlook which already had led to such far-reaching changes in other fields of policy.'[170] A seminar held over dinner at the Carlton Club in October 1988 seemed to make the question of its enactment a foregone conclusion. The attendance, in Windlesham's words, who was presumably present, exemplified 'the overlap between Party political and commercial interests . . . The event was organised as one of a series by the Club's Political Committee, and a former Lord Chancellor, Lord Havers, agreed to preside. There were four main speakers: Gardner, John Hosking (Chairman of the Magistrates' Association), Jeremy Hanley MP (a member of the Home Affairs Committee who had visited private prisons in the United States), and the director of criminal justice planning for an American architectural practice. A ministerial contribution was made by Douglas Hogg, Parliamentary Under-Secretary at the Home Office. Several past and present Conservative MPs attended . . . A member of the staff of the Prime Minister's Policy Unit, which was keeping a weather eye open and was later to intervene, was there with a watching brief.'[171] Also present were Douglas Hurd's special advisers, Edward Bickham and his successor David Lidington, the sole link with the Home Office at the dinner. 'The ground was prepared by a discussion paper sent out in advance outlining ways of improving the quality of the Prison Service, with an emphasis on the private sector', though its authorship is not cited by Windlesham. 'The Adam Smith Institute and the Centre for Policy Studies both had staff members or advisers at the seminar, while a distinctively non-Tory flavour was added by the participation of a small but vocal group of academic criminologists.

The private sector was out in strength. As well as the new consortia, representatives of several other construction businesses were present, together with virtually all of the principal security firms. One of CCA's rivals from the United States also sent a representative. After the seminar, a detailed policy paper was drafted and circulated to all who had attended. Copies were sent to the relevant ministers and their special advisers, the Cabinet Office and the Policy Unit at 10 Downing Street.' Authorship again is not given nor are the academic criminologists named. However, the proponents of penal privatisation had undoubtedly raised their game by holding such an event. Even so, 'despite the urging of enthusiasts for privatisation to go further and faster, whether for commercial or ideological reasons, the Home Office was not prepared to raise the stakes beyond remand prisoners and court escorts. The way had been carefully prepared and the new policy could after all, Hurd now decided, be presented as an experiment.'[172]

Hurd now staked out what had become the new centre ground in the prison privatisation debate, withstanding the pressures from the right of his party to go further than the new remand centres and court escort duties to the mainstream prison sector, and those from the Left and the Labour Opposition, along with Liberal Democrats, who took such events as the Carlton Club seminar to herald the onset of a British 'penal-industrial complex', with a vested interest in penal expansionism. Such concerns were shared by at least some senior civil servants. Looking back on his time at the centre of Home Office planning, David Faulkner wrote: 'I did not see any serious problem about contracting-out specific functions within prisons, such as catering, education or treatment for drug addiction, provided that the prison itself stayed under public management . . . but outsourcing a whole prison was another matter. I was most concerned that those competing for contracts would become powerful and politically influential companies which would press for new prisons to be built and more people to be sent to prison in order to increase their profits and benefit their shareholders. I was not yet concerned about the effects of the "market state" on relationships and values . . . but I was unsure whether the Prison Service would have the skills in commissioning that it would need if it was successfully to negotiate contracts with commercially sophisticated and perhaps unscrupulous providers.'[173]

American critics had already made the case against privatisation on that ground, and Hurd's argument on the need for controlled experiment was more in keeping with Home Office caution. In the debate[174] on the proposals that followed the report of the private consultants, he proposed three strong defences against any dereliction of due standards of prisoners' safety and public security. These were that 'each contract should be subject to permanent on-site monitoring by a Government official (later named a controller) to be appointed by the Home Secretary. The official would have under his direct control the exercise of disciplinary sanctions over prisoners and the hearing of complaints. He agreed with the views expressed by most of the respondents to the Green Paper that contracted-out remand centres should have boards of visitors and be subject to inspection by Her Majesty's Inspectorate of Prisons.'[175] Though the statement elicited a predictably hostile response from Roy Hattersley, the Shadow Home Secretary, Hurd planned for legislation to that effect to follow in due course after further investigations into the logistic and cost implications of any such policy.

With Hurd's move to the Foreign Office in October 1989, a hiatus developed under his successor, David Waddington. A fall of several hundred in the remand prisoner population, combined with the 'coming on stream' of several new prisons planned under Whitelaw and Brittan in the early 1980s, reduced the pressure for immediate action, and the pragmatic case for privatisation. Waddington also had to deal with the major legacy of the Hurd era embodied in the second Green Paper of 1988, on punishment in the community and the primacy of sentencing policy reform (see Chapter on the 1991 Criminal Justice Act), the White Paper following in February 1990. 'No visionary by nature, he [Waddington] lacked the inclination to go ahead with what was likely to prove a time-consuming and controversial policy in the absence of compelling practical reasons to do so. Yet he could not afford to resile altogether from his predecessor's policy.[176] Sensing the need to recover momentum, Windlesham put down a Parliamentary Question for Written Answer in the House of Lords:

> 'To ask Her Majesty's Government whether the legislation forecast in the White Paper, Crime, Justice and Protecting the Public (Cm 965), will include proposals to provide a legal framework to permit the contracting out of remand centres and escort services to and from court as indicated in the Home Secretary's statement of 1 March 1989 (HC Deb col. 277) on private sector involvement in the remand system.'[177]

He wrote further to David Mellor, Minister of State for prisons, whose reply, on 20 March 1990, 'showed the indecision that prevailed'. The reason for any delay was given as 'that the Home Secretary and I are currently considering a report on the outcome of the further investigations which Douglas Hurd called for in his statement of 1 March [1989]. These included two parallel exercises to compare the costs of public and private provision of remand centres and of escorting and court custody services.' Windlesham replied that since legislation was pending, the opportunity should be grasped to secure such a power, whether or not it was implemented immediately. In a second reply, on 12 April 1990, Mellor basically reiterated the case for caution, given the likely strength of the opposition it would unleash. 'For some months the proposal hung in the balance. After being advised by the Department that a detailed study had confirmed that no substantial savings in cost could be anticipated, Waddington eventually came down against including a power to contract out certain remand prisons in the forthcoming legislation.' However, just when it seemed that the issue had been dropped, possibly for good, 'Waddington took the precaution of enquiring whether the Prime Minister assented to the conclusion he had reached so hesitantly. The answer was emphatic: she did not . . . Shortly afterwards draftsmen were instructed by the Home Office to add the necessary provision to the Bill which was already taking shape.'[178]

The final and unexpectedly complete victory for the proselytisers of a measure which had lacked any support from Home Office ministers and senior civil servants at the outset came when an 'amendment to the Criminal Justice Bill at Report Stage in the House of Commons enabled the Secretary of State by order to extend the power to contract for the running of new establishments containing remand prisoners to new prisons holding sentenced offenders, or existing prisons, or both . . . This provision was enacted as Section 84 of the Criminal Justice Act 1991.'[179]

Throughout the entire process, a crucial development, of much longer standing, was the worsening state of industrial relations in the prison sector of the criminal justice system. Prison officers had come to regard themselves as uniquely disprivileged, their role stripped of its welfare component by the induction of social workers and probation officers into the penal realm, yet their responsibilities for security both enlarged and undermined by more dangerous prisoners, especially of the IRA, those serving life terms for homicide and the growing number of those convicted of armed robbery. Their sense of grievance burgeoned in the 1970s due to the growth of radical protest groups organised to improve the state of the prisons, if not abolish them altogether, such as PROP (Preservation of the Rights of Prisoners) and RAP (Radical Alternatives to Prison). The Prison Department of the Home Office was seen as a more remote and bureaucratic authority than the Prison Commission that it replaced in 1963, as the Commission had more members with direct experience of prison governorship. Such grounds for conflict were articulated through their increasingly vocal trade union, the Prison Officers Association (POA), whose demands for increased pay and allowances had prompted the formation of the May Committee of Inquiry into the Prison Services of the United Kingdom, which reported in 1979 (see Ch. 3).

The pay settlement following the May Committee Report did not assuage the POA's demands. Modest gains seemed derisory by comparison with the generosity of the pay awards recommended for the police made at the same time by the Edmund-Davies Committee which the newly elected Conservative Government under Mrs. Thatcher accepted in full. The result was to encourage pay increases by indirect means, such as court escort duties and higher rates of overtime earnings which, by the mid-1980s, had become roughly one-third of the prison officers' pay bill. Moreover, the tactics of the POA became increasingly militant. Though careful to avoid outright strike action, which in their case, as with the police, was formally illegal, they adopted work-to-rule strategies which, when extensively followed, could render prisons virtually inoperative. For example, the prison staff could refuse to accept any new prisoners exceeding their Certified Normal Accommodation (CNA), making the use of police cells inevitable, despite the severe constraints on their facilities and resources.

Douglas Hurd, coming to the office of Home Secretary in September 1985, regarded this situation as intolerable and supported the Home Office solution, *Operation Fresh Start*, the major achievement of Christopher Train as Director

General of the Prison Service 1985–91. This offered prison officers a better basic pay deal in return for much-reduced overtime. The POA accepted with reservations, but the context of industrial relations had been transformed radically by the defeat of the Miners' Strike 1984–5, in effect the breaking of the power of the once-mighty labour movement. The scene was now set for the government to accept, despite Douglas Hurd's initial rejection of the idea, and the then outright opposition of the Labour Party and the trade unions, the Home Affairs Committee's proposal for an experiment in the private management of prisons, whose staff would be debarred from trade union membership.

The first contract for a prison to be privately run was for Group 4 to manage a newly constructed prison, HMP Wolds, for 320 remand prisoners, in April 1992. Blakenhurst and Doncaster Prisons followed in 1994, the latter to hold over a thousand prisoners, managed by Premier Prison Services, which were jointly owned by the American Wackenhut Corrections Corporation and the British firm Serco. These were contractually managed but, following Michael Howard's announcement that 'Prison Works' in October 1993, a commitment to privatise some 10 per cent of the prison system in England and Wales led to a plan for six new penal institutions to be funded by the government's Private Finance Initiative (PFI), on the basis of 25-year contracts for their finance, design, building and operation. In 1996, a White Paper proposed a further 12 prisons for the new millennium. All told, these would provide 9,600 new places for prisoners. The prospect of the incoming Labour Government decommissioning or simply blocking new private prisons, in line with their previously declared rejection of their rationale, was quickly dispelled by the new Home Secretary, Jack Straw, who declared, on 8 May 1997: 'If there are contracts in the pipeline and the only way of getting the accommodation in place very quickly is by signing those contracts, then I will sign those contracts.'[180] A year later he announced his own U-turn on pre-election policies by stating at a Prison Officers' Association conference that 'in future all new prisons in England and Wales would be privately constructed and run (although the Prison Service was now also to be allowed to tender for the contracts when current contracts expired). The threat of privatisation was also to be used to promote reform in "under-performing" public prisons.'[181]

Despite misgivings, and recognition of the extent to which any cost savings have been made at the expense of the labour force – through lower rates of pay, holiday leave, and sickness entitlements than in public sector prisons – there is still a general consensus on findings that, even if private prisons are no better than public, they are also no worse. Critics of prison policy and conditions as severe as Rod Morgan have asserted that 'contracts have been used to breathe life back into the rehabilitative ideal and stimulate cross-fertilisation of practice between state and privately-managed institutions . . . The government pursued privatisation primarily to tackle restrictive staff practices, and thus high costs, in a state-run system not reputed for its innovative or effective management. By this test the success of the initiative does not rest only on the relative unit costs of contract-out compared to state-run institutions . . . but rather in the degree to which practices in state-run prisons are transformed by the threat of privatisation and the need to tender against contractor-. . ."[182] A later such analysis finds variations within the private sector as important as those in the public sector. 'The best private prisons are among the better prisons in the system, providing an environment for prisoners that is safer and more respectful than almost all comparable public sector establishments . . . However, the opposite is also true: the least good private prisons are chaotic, dangerous and disrespectful . . . It is significant too that, regardless of quality, the 'feel' in private prisons tends to be relatively 'light' compared to the public sector . . . Thus a significant weakness of the privatisation 'experiment' is that, by deliberately diminishing the power of uniformed staff and exerting greater control over the workforce, it weights the balance of power between prisoners and staff sometimes excessively towards the former. The risks of this imbalance are all the greater if prisons are run at very low cost.'[183]

Liebling and Crewe concluded that there is no warrant in evaluations so far that so rapid an expansion of private prisons is justified, a conclusion shared by David Faulkner, who added: 'My fear that politically powerful contractors would argue for the greater use of prison sentences did not materialise, but the more subtle consequences of large scale involvement by international corporations, the influence they can bring to bear, their long-term effects on relationships and dynamics, and the costs of operational or financial failure, are still uncertain.'[184]

## Conclusion

The pursuit of innovation in criminal justice policy, as in other fields, is usually viewed as the prerogative of Members of Parliament, in particular government ministers, working to a mandate won in national general elections on the basis of a programme set out in election manifestos. Manifesto promises and commitments are born of responses to the needs and demands of diverse constituencies, shaped by family, class, gender, ethnicity and so on, but also by the advocacy of interest and pressure groups, ranging from the judiciary, the police, and prison staff to the Howard League, Liberty, NACRO and other highly informed and vocal groups, who in turn are influenced by 'events', crises of varying intensity and matters of scandal and concern. By contrast, civil servants, even of considerable seniority, are usually seen as, at worst, Machiavellian schemers, of the sort satirised, and traduced, in the comedy series 'Yes, Minister', or as the proverbial 'faceless bureaucrats' who ruin lives by taking 'unaccountable' decisions affecting powerless citizens. At best they are seen as somewhat robotic and passive public servants dutifully carrying out orders from their political masters.

The reality is less dramatic and more complex. As these case studies have shown, civil servants, working within the limits of their administrative roles, can and do generate policy initiatives, at times of great significance, as in the development of crime prevention policies in the 1980s and 90s, and the work that went into shaping the systems of parole and the prison inspectorate. Indeed, of the six cases studied above, only private prisons emerged and became reality without much effort or even despite resistance from Home Office administrators. The ACPS, HORU, and the systems of parole and prison inspection were all achievements that rested significantly on the experience and expertise of civil servants who were actively engaged in creative as well as instrumental tasks. The liberal culture which prevailed at senior levels was in the ascendant for several post-war decades, if not the entire century prior to the reversal of penal policy under Michael Howard and the ensuing 'arms race' of 'populist punitiveness'. The so-called 'platonic guardians' of that culture had to cede substantial ground to that reversal of policy, but their achievements, despite setbacks, such as the abortive redevelopment of Holloway, drawbacks and cutbacks, were still notable.

## Notes

1 Andrew Rutherford, 1986, *Growing Out of Crime*, Harmondsworth, Penguin: 52.
2 Leon Radzinowicz, 1991, 'Penal Regressions', *Cambridge Law Journal*, 50, 3, 422–444.
3 Lord Windlesham, 1993, *Penal Policy in the Making*, Vol. 2 of his 4 vol. *Responses to Crime*, Oxford: Clarendon Press: 73.
4 Advisory Council on the Treatment of Offenders, 1960, *Corporal Punishment: Report*, Cmnd. 1213, Home Office, London: HMSO.
5 Advisory Council on the Treatment of Offenders, 1963, *The Organisation of After-Care*, Home Office, London: HMSO.
6 Windlesham, op. cit.: 104.
7 Derick Heathcote-Amory had held the Ministry of Pensions, 1951–3; the Board of Trade, 1953–4; Agriculture, 1954–8; and had been Chancellor of the Exchequer, 1958–60. Created a peer as Viscount Amory, 1960.
8 Mrs., later Lady, Bea Serota had chaired the Children's Committee of the London County Council, 1958–65, and was granted a life peerage for services to children in 1967. Minister of State (Health), Department of Health and Social Security, 1969–70. Founder Chair, Commission for Local Administration, 1974–82.
9 See the relevant chapters in Paul Rock, 2019a, *The 'Liberal Hour'*, on the key reforms.
10 Summarised in ibid: 146–8.
11 Rutherford, op. cit.: 66.
12 Lord Windlesham, op. cit.: 150–51.
13 Rod Morgan, 1979, *Formulating Penal Policy: The Future of the Advisory Council on the Penal System*, London: NACRO. Professor Rod Morgan lectured at the Universities of Bath and Bristol on crime and criminal justice. He had co-authored with Roy King *A Taste of Prison: A Study of Trial and Remand Prisoners*, 1976, London: Routledge. Their evidence to the 1979 May Committee on the prison service was published in 1980 as *The Future of the Prison System*, Farnborough: Gower. He went on to hold, both part-time and full-time, 'almost every post it is possible to hold' in the criminal justice system, not least as Chief Inspector of Probation 2001–4 and Chair of the Youth Justice Board 2004–7, having been a member of the Woolf Inquiry team, 1990–91. (Wikipedia).
14 Ibid: 22.
15 Ann Oakley, 2011, *A Critical Woman: Barbara Wootton, Social Science and Public Policy in the Twentieth Century*, London: Bloomsbury Academic: 272–3.
16 Non-Custodial and Semi-Custodial Penalties: report of the Advisory Council on the Penal System, London: HMSO: v.
17 Ibid: 2.
18 Ibid: 12.
19 Ibid: 12.
20 Ibid: 13.
21 Barbara Wootton, 1978, *Crime and Penal Policy*, London: Allen & Unwin: 122–23.

22 Roger Hood, 1974, 'Criminology and Penal Change: A Case Study of the Nature and Impact of some recent Advice to Governments'. In his (ed.) *Crime, Criminology and Public Policy: Essays in Honour of Sir Leon Radzinowicz*, London: Heinemann: 375–417.

23 Wootton, op. cit.: 126.

24 Ibid: 127.

25 Oakley, op.cit.: 274, citing Ken Pease, 1985, 'Community Service Orders', *Crime and Justice*, 6: 51–94, p. 58.

26 Wootton, op. cit.: 127–28.

27 Ibid: 128.

28 Home Office Research Unit, 1975, *Community Service Orders*, Report No. 29; 1977, *Community Service Assessed in 1976*, Report No. 39, London: HMSO.

29 Gordon Trasler, 1986, 'Innovation in Penal Practice' in Philip Bean and David Whynes (eds.) *Barbara Wootton: Social Science and Public Policy – Essays in her Honour*, London: Tavistock: 234.

30 Wootton, op. cit.: 132, citing the Inner London Report on the first two years' working of the community service scheme, n.d., p. 28.

31 Ibid: 132.

32 John Croft, 'CCBH/LSE Ideas: The Home Office Research Unit', 2010, unpubl.: p. 5. John Croft was the Head of HORU, which from 1981 was renamed the Home Office Research and Planning Unit, 1972–83. CCBH/LSE refers to the Centre for Contemporary British History Witness Seminar on the Home Office Research Unit, which was held at the London School of Economics on 14 May 2010.

33 See also Ch. 2, vol. 1 of this history.

34 Herman Mannheim and Leslie Wilkins, 1955, *Prediction Methods in Relation to Borstal Training*, London: HMSO.

35 See Leon Radzinowicz, 1999, *Adventures in Criminology*, London: Routledge: 444.

36 A social statistician at the Home Office, Wilkins's work at this period included his influential *Delinquent Generations*, 1960, London: HMSO, which argued that the rising rate of delinquency was in part caused by the exigencies of war-time childhood; and *Social Deviance: Social policy, action and research*, 1964, London: Tavistock, which argued that the over- or mis-control of deviance generated a 'deviancy amplification effect' rather than conformity. This theory was embraced and built on by the rising generation of 'new deviancy' theorists who in general, and somewhat unfairly, regarded Home Office-based research with deep suspicion.

37 R.V.G. Clarke, 2010, 'The Home Office Research Unit – an insider's view", unpubl., CCBH/LSE Witness Seminar: 3. Dates in brackets added.

38 Ibid.

39 Ibid: 4.

40 P. Mayhew, A. Sturan and M. Hough, 1976, *Crime as Opportunity*, Home Office Research Study No. 34, London: HMSO.

41 R.V.G. Clarke, 1980, 'Situational Crime Prevention: Theory and Practice', *British Journal of Criminology*, 20.

42 Oscar Newman, 1972, *Defensible Space: People and Design in the Violent City*, London: Architectural Press.

43 Alice Coleman, 1985, *Utopia on Trial: Vision and Reality in Planned Housing*, London: Hilary Shipman.

44 See, for example, Bill Hillier, 'City of Alice's Dreams, *Architecture Journal*, 39, 9 July 1986.

45 Forrester, D., Chatterton, M. and Pease, K., 1988, *The Kirkholt Burglary Prevention Project, Rochdale*, London

46 Steven Brody, 1976, *The Effectiveness of Sentencing*, Home Office Research Study No 35, London: HMSO. See also S. Brody and R. Tarling, 1980, *Taking Offenders out of Circulation*, Home Office Research Study No. 64, London: HMSO.

47 Roger Tarling, 1993, *Analysing Offending: Data, Models and Interpretations*, London: HMSO.

48 Cheryl Webster and Anthony Doob, 2007, 'Punitive Trends and Stable Imprisonment Rates in Canada', in Michael Tonry (ed.) *Crime, Punishment and Politics in Comparative Perspective*, Chicago: Chicago University Press.

49 See especially Andrew Karmen, 2000, *New York Murder Mystery: The True Story Behind the Crime Crash of the 1990s*, New York: New York University Press; and Steven Pinker, 2011, *The Better Angels of Our Nature: Why Violence Has Declined*, New York: Viking.

50 Kelling, G., Pate, T., Dieckman, D. and Brown, C., 1974, *The Kansas City Preventive Patrol Experiment*, Washington, DC: Police Foundation.

51 Robert Reiner, 2007, *Law and Order: An Honest Citizen's Guide to Crime and* Control, Cambridge: Polity: 203–4. Cited are R.V.G. Clarke and M. Hough (eds.), 1980, *The Effectiveness of Policing*, Farnborough: Gower, and, 1984, *Crime and Police Effectiveness*, London: HMSO; P. Morris and K. Heal, 1981, *Crime Control and the Police,* London: HMSO.

52 R.V.G. Clarke, 2010, op. cit.: 4.

53 John Croft, 2010, *CCBH/LSE Ideas: The Home Office Research Unit*, p. 3. Unpubl. Supplement on the CCBH seminar on that topic.

54 Clarke, op. cit.: 2010: 6.

55 Ibid: 4.

56 Anne Power, 1981, 'How to Rescue Council Housing', *New Society*, 4 June.

57 James Q. Wilson and George Kelling, 1982, '"Broken Windows": The Police and Neighborhood Safety', *The Atlantic Monthly*, March.

58 M. Hough and P. Mayhew, 1983, *The British Crime Survey*, London: HMSO.

59 D. Cornish and R.V.G. Clarke, 1986, *The Reasoning Criminal*, New York: Springer Verlag.

60 Cohen, L.E. and Felson, M., 1979, 'Social Change and Crime Rate Trends: A Routine Activity Approach', *American Sociological Review,* 44: 588–608.

61 Clarke, op. cit. 2010: 8.

62 See, for example, R.V.G. Clarke (ed.) 1997 *Situational Crime Prevention: Successful Case Studies*, Albany: Criminal Justice Press (2nd rev. ed.)

63 See D. Downes and P. Rock, 2011, *Understanding Deviance*, Oxford University Press, 6th ed., 247–255, for a more extended critical commentary.

64 For sceptical views on the trends, see D. Downes, 'What Went Right? New Labour and Crime Control', Howard Journal of Criminal Justice, 49, September 2010, 394–97; and Marian Fitzgerald, 'The curious case of the fall in crime', London: Centre for Crime and Justice Studies website, 13 April 2014.

65 For a grounded analysis of the 'permissive society', see Tim Newburn, 1992, *Permission and Regulation: Law and Morals in Post-war Britain*, London: Routledge.

66 Steven Pinker, 2011, *The Better Angels of our Nature: Why Violence Has Declined*, London: Allen Lane: 153–4.

67 Robert Reiner, 2016, *Crime: The Mystery of the Common-Sense Concept*, Cambridge: Polity Press, 172–3.

68 Robert Hughes's *The Fatal Shore: A History of the Transportation of Convicts to Australia, 1787–1868*, London: Collins Harvill, 1987, is the most eloquent and riveting study of this penal experiment and experience.

69 Hughes, op. cit.: 307–8.

70 Stephen Livingstone and Tim Owen, *Prison Law*, 1999, 2nd Edition, Oxford University Press: 329–30.

71 Ibid: 330–31.

72 Thomas C. Guiney, *Getting Out: Early Release in England and Wales, 1960–1995*, Oxford: Oxford University Press, 2018: 91. Based on his Ph. D. thesis, *In the Shadow of the Prison Gates: An Institutional Analysis of Early Release Policy and Practice*

*in England and Wales, 1960–1995*, 2016, London School of Economics. See also the chapters above on the liberal reforms of the 1960s and on the making of the 1991 Criminal Justice Act.

73　Ibid: Ch. 3.

74　Labour Party Study Group, *Crime – A Challenge to Us All*, June 1964, London: Labour Party: 75, 43.

75　The Advisory Council on the Treatment of Offenders, 1963, *The Organisation of After-Care*, London: HMSO.

76　Guiney, op. cit.: 74.

77　Ibid: 75.

78　See the relevant chapters above on the history of its abolition.

79　See, for example, Terence Morris, op. cit.: 142, note 16 'Soskice had been appointed by Wilson in 1964 but he was a sick man and made no mark upon penal affairs nor on the Home Office generally.'

80　Guiney, op. cit., 2016: 132. See also his 2018: 184.

81　Guiney, op. cit., 2018: 76.

82　Ibid: 78, citing Allen, L., 2004, 'A Young Home Secretary' in Adonis, A. and Thomas, K. (eds.) *Roy Jenkins: A Retrospective*, Oxford: Oxford University Press: 78; and Williams, M. 1972, *Inside Number 10*, London: Coward, McCann and Geoghegan.

83　Roy Jenkins, 1991, *A Life at the Centre*, London: Macmillan: 175.

84　Speech to the Commons, 12 December 1966.

85　See in particular the chapter on 'The Making of the 1991 Criminal Justice Act'.

86　Livingstone and Owen, op. cit.: 334.

87　Guiney, op. cit.: 95.

88　Guiney, op. cit., 2016: 211. See also relevant chapters above.

89　Guiney, op. cit., 2018: 110–15.

90　Ibid: 141.

91　William Whitelaw was Home Secretary 1979–83. Having introduced a tougher, more militaristic regime in detention centres early in his tenure of office, he acknowledged its ineffectiveness on the basis of research by the Home Office Research Unit, which he commissioned, and adopted a more moderate policy aimed at reining in the rise of the prison population. He was ennobled in 1983 and became both Leader of the House of Lords and a stabilising influence on the leadership style of Margaret Thatcher.

92　The term *bifurcationism* was coined by Tony Bottoms in his prescient (1977), 'Reflections on the Renaissance of Dangerousness', *Howard* Journal *of Criminal Justice*, 16: 70–96.

93　John Pitts, 1988, *The Politics of Juvenile Crime*, London: Sage: 29.

94　Livingstone and Owen, op. cit.: 336.

95　Livingstone and Owen, op. cit.: 335–36.

96　Ibid: 338.

97　Guiney, op. cit.: 226.

98　David Faulkner, 2001, *Crime, State and Citizen: A Field Full of Folk*, Winchester: Waterside Press: 115.

99　*The Parole System in England and Wales: Report of the Review Committee*, 1988, Cm 532, London: HMSO.

100　Faulkner, op. cit.: 115–16.

101　Michael Cavadino, James Dignan and George Mair, 2013, *The Penal System: An Introduction*, 5th edition, London: Sage: 238, citing Roger Hood and Stephen Shute, 1996, 'Parole Criteria, Parole Decisions and the Prison Population: Evaluating the Impact of the Criminal Justice Act 1991', *Criminal Law Review*, 77–87.

102　David Ramsbotham, 2003, *Prisongate: The Shocking State of Britain's Prisons and the Need for Visionary Change*, Ch. 1 'HMP Holloway. 13–14 December 1995', London: The Free Press: 1–25. For the historical context, see Paul Rock, 1996, *Reconstructing a Women's Prison: The Holloway Redevelopment Project, 1968–88*, Oxford: Clarendon Press; and the following section of this chapter.

103 Ibid: 23, 24–5.

104 Ibid: 8.

105 Ibid: 18–19.

106 The *Independent*, 10 January 1996.

107 Rod Morgan, 'Her Majesty's Inspectorate of Prisons', in Mike Maguire, Jon Vagg and Rod Morgan (eds.) 1985, *Accountability and Prisons: Opening Up a Closed World*, London: Tavistock: 106. Cited are O. MacDonagh, 1977, *Early Victorian Government*, London: Weidenfeld; and S. McConville, 1981, *A History of English Prison Administration, 1750–1877*, London: Routledge and Kegan Paul.

108 David Faulkner, 2014, *Servant of the Crown: A Civil Servant's Story of Criminal Justice and Public Service Reform*, Hampshire: Waterside Press: 59.

109 Ibid: 60.

110 Lord Windlesham, 1993, *Responses to Crime, Volume 2: Penal Policy in the Making*, Oxford: Clarendon Press: 156.

111 Phillip Jenkins, review of *Inside Justice: A Comparative Analysis of Practices and Procedures for the Determination of Offenses Against Discipline in Prisons of Britain and the United States*, by Bayard Marin; *Journal of Criminal Law and Criminology*, Vol. 76: 786–788.

112 Stan Cohen and Laurie Taylor, 1972, *Psychological Survival: The Experience of Long-Term Imprisonment*, Harmondsworth: Penguin.

113 Terence and Pauline Morris, 'The Prison Under Stress', unpubl. Chapter 14 in the original typescript of their *Pentonville: A Sociological Study of an English Prison*, London: Routledge and Kegan Paul, 1963: 513–14.

114 Stanley Cohen and Laurie Taylor, 1972, *Psychological Survival: The Experience of Long Term Imprisonment*, Harmondsworth: Penguin.

115 Jenkins, op. cit.: 787.

116 Ibid.

117 Roy King and Katherine McDermott, 1989, 'British Prisons 1970–1987: The Ever-Deepening Crisis', *British Journal of Criminology*, 29: 107–28.

118 Barbara Wootton, 1959, *Social Science and Social Pathology*, London: Allen & Unwin

119 *Report on the work of the Prison Department, 1972*, London: HMSO, Cmnd. 5375: 82–84.

120 Paul Rock, op. cit.: 51.

121 Paul Rock, op. cit., 1996: provides the most illuminating and comprehensive analysis and account of the 1968–1988 period of attempted innovation.

122 Rock, op. cit.: 58.

123 Wootton, 1959, op. cit.

124 Rock, 1996, op. cit.: 69–70, citing G. Pailthorpe, 1932, *Studies in the Psychology of Delinquency*, London: HMSO: 12–13 and 97.

125 In her *Women, Crime and Criminology: A Feminist Critique*, 1976, London: Routledge & Kegan Paul.

126 D. Downes, P. Rock and E. McLaughlin, *Understanding Deviance,* 7th ed. Oxford: Oxford University Press: 269.

127 Rock, 1996, op. cit.: 71 and 73.

128 Rock, ibid: 74; citing Pat Carlen, 'Women's Imprisonment: Current Issues', *Prison Service Journal*, April 1988, 70: 8.

129 Rock, ibid: 88, note 47. The best study of Grendon is Elaine Genders and Elaine Player, 1995, *Grendon: A Study of a Therapeutic Prison*, Oxford: Oxford University Press.

130 *Prison Policy: Women and Girls,* P.D. 4 Study No. 1, Prison Department, Home Office, Oct. 1968.

131  Rock, ibid: 93.

132  Rock, ibid: 106–7. A sole exception was Ann Smith of Radical Alternatives to Prison.

133  Rock, ibid: 143.

134  Rock, ibid: 175.

135  Rock, ibid: 180, note 14, quoting from a 1979 internal paper.

136  Rock, ibid: 185.

137  Rock, ibid: 195. David Faulkner had been the head of P4 at an early stage, 1970–74.

138  Rock, ibid: 228–9.

139  Rock, ibid: 259–61.

140  Rock, ibid: 285.

141  See Genders and Player, 1995, op.cit.

142  Ibid: 16.

143  Ibid.: 4, citing para. 14.13 of the Woolf Report. See also Elaine Player, 2010, 'Prisons'
     Policy: The Redevelopment of Holloway Prison'.

144  '. . . an unusually influential back-bencher. As a former Assistant Governor in the
     Prison Service, Wheeler was well informed, moderate in outlook, and generally sym-
     pathetic to the Home Secretary's policies. His role was pivotal, since he occupied
     concurrently the Chair of the House of Commons Select Committee on Home Affairs
     and the reformist Parliamentary All-Party Penal Affairs Group . . . He was to prove
     the Home Secretary's staunchest ally. Hurd consulted him regularly, listened to what
     he had to say, and respected his judgement on the state of Parliamentary opinion, in
     the House as a whole as well as on the Tory benches.' Windlesham, 1993, op. cit.: 224.

145  Lord Windlesham, 1993, op. cit.: 292, citing Peter Young, 1987, *The Prison Cell: The
     Start of a Better Approach to Prison Management*, Adam Smith Institute: 4.

146  Ryan and Ward, 1989, op. cit.: 62.

147  Ibid: 64–5.

148  *Administration of Punishment at Court Lees Approved School: Report of an Inquiry*,
     1967, London: HMSO, Cmnd. 3367.

149  Mick Ryan and Tony Ward, 1989, *Privatization and the Penal System: The American
     Experience and the Debate in Britain*, Milton Keynes: Open University Press: 67–8.

150  London: HMSO, 1988. Cmnd 434.

151  S. Shaw. 1987. *Conviction Politics,* London: Fabian Society; 'Private Prisons: who
     guards the Securicor guards? *AMBOV Quarterly*, July 1985: 4.

152  Ryan and Ward, op. cit.: 68.

153  Ibid: 45.

154  Peter Young, 1987, *The Prison Cell*, Adam Smith Institute: 38. Quoted in Ryan and
     Ward, op. cit.: 46.

155  C.H. Logan, 'Proprietary prisons' in L. Goodstein and D.L. MacKenzie (eds.) *The
     American Prison: Issues in Research and Policy*, New York: Plenum.

156  Ryan and Ward, op. cit.: 47, whose sources wrongly stated Lord Glenarthur as the
     junior minister involved.
     See Lord Windlesham, 1993, op. cit.: 280–81.

157  Windlesham, op. cit.: 276–77.

158  Ibid: 278–79.

159  Ibid: 286.

160  Ibid: 286, citing *Parl. Debates*, HC, 130 (6th ser.), cols. 1084–5, 30 March 1988.

161  Ryan and Ward, op. cit.: 48.

162  Ibid: 53. The Committee had also written a separate and much fuller report, *The State
     and Use of Prisons*, on such topics as the need for minimum standards in prison and
     the electronic tagging of offenders in the USA.

163  Ibid: 49.

164  John Wheeler M.P.

165  Ryan and Ward, ibid.

166 See, for example, Larry Gostin and Marie Staunton, 'The case for prison standards: conditions of confinement, segregation, and medical treatment' and Silvia Casale, 'A practical design for standards', in Mike Maguire, Jon Vagg and Rod Morgan, *Accountability and Prisons: Opening Up a Closed World*, 1985, London: Tavistock.

167 Ryan and Ward, ibid: 51–2.

168 Ibid: 52.

169 Ibid: 57–8. The Green Paper cited is *Private Sector Involvement in the Remand System*, 1988, London: HMSO. Cm. 434.

170 Windlesham, op. cit.: 292.

171 Ibid: 288–9. It is worth noting that Windlesham retained the plural in alluding to the private prison visits of the Select Committee, whereas only one adult prison was involved.

172 Ibid: 289–90.

173 David Faulkner, *Servant of the Crown: A Civil Servant's Story of Criminal Justice and Public Service Reform*, 2014, Hook: Waterside Press: 151.

174 *Parl. Debates*, HC, 148 (6th series), cols. 286–7, 1 March 1989.

175 Ibid: 290.

176 Ibid: 294.

177 *Parl. Debates*, HL, 517 (5th. ser.), col. 1238, 2 Apr. 1990.

178 Windlesham, op. cit.: 295–97.

179 Ibid: 298, note 80.

180 Prison Reform Trust, *Private Punishment: Who Profits?*, 2005, London: Prison Reform Trust Briefing: 4.

181 Tim Newburn, *Criminology*, 2007, Cullompton: Willan: 701.

182 Rod Morgan, 2002, 'Imprisonment' in Mike Maguire, Rod Morgan and Robert Reiner (eds.) *The Oxford Handbook of Criminology*, 3rd ed., Oxford: Oxford University Press: 1148.

183 Alison Liebling and Ben Crewe, 2012, 'Prison life, penal power and prison effects' in Maguire, Morgan and Reiner, (eds.), *The Oxford Handbook of Criminology*, 5th ed., Oxford University Press.

184 David Faulkner, 2014, op. cit.: 152.

# 8   Conclusion

This history has been mainly concerned to address key issues in penal policymaking from 1959, a year notable for the optimistic White Paper *Penal Policy in a Changing Society*, and which we chose as the starting point for the entire period covered by our history, to 1997, a point by which Michael Howard's 'Prison Works' speech in 1993 had come to symbolise a lasting change of direction for both major political parties in affirming penal expansion as a bulwark against rising crime. Until that point, however, a different policy consensus had come to prevail, which consisted of, at least, two components. First, that prisons should offer, as far as governmentally set resources allowed, humane containment and a rehabilitative agenda. And secondly, to achieve that goal, as well as being desirable in its own right, the prison population should be reined in, or even reduced, without infringing on the independence of the judiciary in its choice of sentence and remand in custody decisions.

One main conclusion to be drawn from the history of imprisonment is that historical inevitability offers no explanation of its character or extent. There is no immutable relationship between trends in crime rates and imprisonment. In England and Wales, crime rates doubled between 1919 and 1939, while the prison population remained stable. And, though seldom drawn on, the period from the 1870s until World War II was one of substantial decarceration.[1] During much of this period, the rate of imprisonment per 100,000 in England and Wales was below that of the Netherlands.[2] By contrast, the post-World War II period in England was one of almost unbroken penal expansion. As a consequence, conditions worsened in significant respects, despite periodic spurts in building new prisons. Attempts by Home Office policymakers and some ministers, notably Soskice and Jenkins under Labour, and Whitelaw and Hurd under the Conservatives, to provide sentencers with convincing community alternatives to custody, failed for various reasons to live up to expectations. Their efforts culminated in the 1991 Criminal Justice Act which was based on a recasting of sentencing in terms of a more stringent interpretation of 'just deserts'. This fell foul of a critical mass of judicial opinion which rejected two of the innovative pillars of the Act: a radical revaluation of the role played by previous convictions in sentencing, and the linkage of fines to offenders' incomes. Even the sole major success story of decarceration in this period, the substantial drop in juvenile rates of imprisonment following the

1982 Criminal Justice Act, proved unsustainable after the 'Prison Works' era succeeded that of liberal reformism.

A second main conclusion, reflecting the above, is that individual ministers, not their party of allegiance, proved the more influential in determining criminal justice policy in general and penal policy in particular. 'Rab' Butler as Home Secretary was to the fore in giving precedence to rehabilitation rather than deterrence in the 1959 White Paper *Penal Practice in a Changing Society.* Butler famously detested the punitive mood all too apparent at Tory Party conferences.[3] However, largely due to the major and lasting reforms of the 1960s, the decriminalisation of homosexuality and abortion, and the ending of capital punishment and literary censorship, as well as the introduction of parole, Labour was associated with liberal policies across the board in the criminal justice field. But this was in some ways quite erroneous. James Callaghan as Home Secretary in 1969 rejected the Wootton Report's recommendation for the possession of small amounts of cannabis to be a non-custodial offence, a recommendation that fell short of decriminalisation.[4] Between 1974 and 1979, Labour oversaw the much harsher treatment of juvenile offenders than envisaged by the Children and Young Persons Act 1969 that they had formulated and enacted.[5] There was no simple relationship between party, policy and minister. William Whitelaw followed the logic of the May Committee by instigating a new and costly policy of new prison building, 14 in all, but argued that this was essential to improve conditions and reduce overcrowding. He upheld the Committee's case for a truly independent Prison Inspectorate, which was established in the Criminal Justice Act 1982. 'In the 1980s, largely as a result of the tenacity and plain speaking of the two successive Chief Inspectors, Sir James Hennessy and Judge Tumim, the inspectorate became increasingly relevant as an instrument of penal reform.'[6] Having announced a tougher policy on detention centres, he set up a committee to monitor their effects, which were grounds for abandoning that policy a few years later. He appointed Lord Scarman, a 'typical Whitelaw man, and the antithesis of a Thatcher man'[7] to report on the Brixton riots of 1981. And, as noted above, the 1982 Criminal Justice Act, following informed debate led by the Parliamentary All-Party Penal Affairs Group (PAPPAG) chaired by Baroness Faithfull, a Tory peer, introduced criteria, based on stricter non-custodial guidelines, which the judiciary should meet if a sentence of imprisonment for young offenders was to be imposed. Initially rejected by the government, it was recast more stringently by the Lords, and accepted on its return to the Commons.[8] Whitelaw's achievement, especially following the hostile reception his allegedly 'wet' approach to law and order received at the Conservative Party conference in 1981, was to hold the more punitive wing of the party at bay.

Following the brief tenure of the Home Office by Leon Brittan, mostly associated with his introducing retrospective restrictions on parole for violent and sexual offenders, Douglas Hurd came to evolve the closest fit between ministers, Home Office policymakers, and other components of the criminal justice system, including the judiciary, in the process of determining penal policy. Genuinely alarmed by the prison riots of 1985–6, which were taken to be real signs of the government losing control of the prisons, Hurd and his ministerial team were presented by his most experienced policymakers with what were in effect three choices: cracking down, muddling through or 'to exert some downward pressure on the rise in the prison population, and therefore on the sentencing of those not regarded as a threat to society'.[9] They chose the third option, setting in train the process which led to the 1991 Criminal Justice Act, an instance of a Home Secretary heeding the advice of senior civil servants at a time when they were in the ascendant. Though ill-fated, it represented the climax of decades of experience and expertise that saw sentencing as the key to penal reform.

The third main conclusion must therefore be that there were, in this period, myriad routes to criminal justice policymaking. While ministers and parliament were the ultimate decisive influence in most cases, senior civil servants were experienced policymakers who were highly active in defining terms, influencing agendas and setting priorities. They were of course in many respects reacting to events, media coverage, often intense pressure group activity, penal reform group campaigning and individual cases. But they also sought to uphold certain principles and pursue long-term policy goals. In-house units, such as the Home Office Research and Planning Unit, conducted research, and sponsored projects in higher education and other research institutes, which originated important developments, notably in crime prevention, but also critically, for example in relation to the presumed automatic benefits of more policing and penal incapacitation.[10] Reports by the Advisory Council on the Penal System, until 1979, and the Prison Inspectorate after its recreation in 1982, proved independent sources of informed debate and policy ideas. Community Service Orders, widely copied throughout the world as potential alternatives to custody, emanated from the Wootton Report of 1970. Reports by HM Chief Inspector of Prisons gave graphic accounts of the appalling underside of prison life.

Another side of Home Office life was the capacity to miss the opportunity to regard humane containment as a valuable end in itself. In this way the short-lived control unit disaster, as it came to be seen, was the outcome of fears that staff would be unable to avoid manipulation by troublesome prisoners, a risk that could have been neutralised by staff training and rotation. As it was, a highly repressive regime was installed which proved self-defeating, enmeshing the Home Office in a welter of 'cover-up' charges. By contrast, the redevelopment of Holloway largely failed due to the attempt to combine adherence to the 'treatment' model for *all* female prisoners, unlike the regime at Grendon which selected only those thought most likely to benefit, with a newfound priority to house those deemed highly dangerous, following the unexpected emergence of female terrorists. The philosophy of 'treatment' propounded in the 1959 White Paper went basically unchallenged in official discourse until the 'Nothing Works' era of the 1970s overcorrected for its limitations. Even so, the May Committee retained it in its concept of 'positive custody'. In the 1980s, the dominance of either 'treatment' or 'non-treatment' receded in importance, tending to be succeeded by a more pragmatic approach, with 'treatment' best seen as a choice that prisoners should be allowed to make but non-coercively.

Another Home Office blind-spot was the tendency to resist the 'human rights' approach that prisoners came to recognise as a way of gaining ground in the struggle to convert 'privileges', such as minimum standards of food, clothing and sanitation, into legally enforceable rights, a trend which gathered pace after the UK's accession to the European Union. Following the May Committee report, the Prison Department began to ease rather than discourage media and academic access to prisons, recognising that public awareness of the state they were in would encourage more generous resourcing. It was on these two fronts that the case came increasingly to be made, in the 1980s, both within the Home Office and by penal reform groups, for prisons to be made to pass the 'human decency' test by spending more on better conditions for fewer prisoners.[11]

A fourth main conclusion, therefore, is that although Home Office policymakers aimed, within severe resource restraints, to move beyond 'human warehousing' to 'humane containment', they resisted the adoption of a 'human rights' agenda and adhered for far too long to a system defined by Woolf as lacking the essential balance between security and control, on the one hand, and justice and moral legitimation, on the other. Developments since 1993 have greatly worsened that fundamental imbalance.

Why should this have been so? Penal policy does not take place in a vacuum, and the wider context has prompted some detailed inquiry into possible causal matrices. The best attested includes research on the links between levels of imprisonment and varieties of democratic capitalism. The more neo-liberal economies seemingly generate higher levels of imprisonment, ranging from England and Wales producing the highest levels of imprisonment in western Europe to the USA's attaining a state of mass imprisonment over the past few decades.[12] It is not simply that high and increasing rates of inequality generate high crime rates which are then met with corresponding increases in imprisonment. Trends in welfare are also implicated in types and levels of penal custody. Welfare capital is inversely related to penal capital.[13] A seminal study by Beckett and Western of inter-state trends in welfare and penal expenditure in the USA concluded 'In the 1990s, states with less generous welfare programs feature significantly higher incarceration rates, while those with more generous programs incarcerate a smaller share of their residents. . . . We conclude that the contraction of welfare programs aimed at the poor and the expansion of penal institutions in the 1980s and 1990s reflect the emergence of an alternative mode of governance that is replacing, to varying degrees, the modernist strategy based on rehabilitation and welfarism.'[14]

The same causal matrix is to be found in the case of England and Wales, though with a delay in the onset of the move to a penal shift from welfarism, due to the effect of ministerial and Home Office attempts in the 1980s to moderate the resort to custody for the petty, persistent offenders who overcrowded the jails. The onset of the 'Prison Works' era in 1993 saw the resumption of penal expansion more as a matter of conviction that it would prove essential to control crime rather than its reluctant acceptance as a matter of necessity to house rising numbers in custody. The falling crime rate after 1994 until recently seemed to confirm that approach. It is worth bearing in mind, however, that crime rates can rise and fall regardless

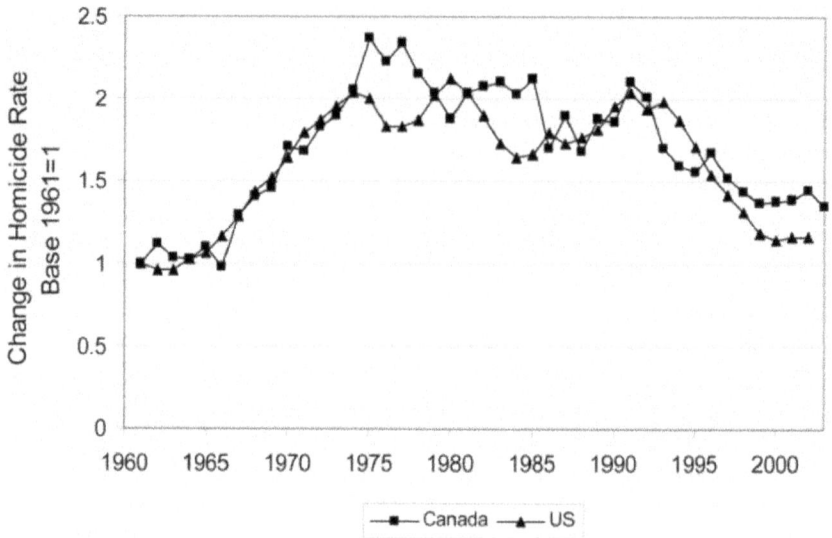

*8.1* Changes in homicide rates, Canada 1961–2003 and United States 1961–2002

Change in homicide rates, Canada (1961–2003) and United States (1961–2002). For each country, the figure plots changes from 1961. Each year's homicide rate (homicides per 100,000 residents) was divided by that country's 1961 rate (Canada, 1961 rate, 1.28; United States, 4.8). Source of data: Dauvergne (2004) and Pastore and Maguire (2004).[16]

of the size of the prison population, as occurred in the USA and Canada in relation to homicide over the past few decades.[15]

Homicide rates fluctuated in both countries with remarkable similarity, despite the Canadian prison population remaining remarkably stable whilst that in the USA reached mass imprisonment levels. Yet it is not the case, as Webster and Doob remark, that Canada was lacking in punitive voices. The difference between the two nations lay in the protective measures which Canada evolved as a bulwark against their ascendancy. These include, in particular, and by contrast with the USA, the insulation of the judiciary from populist pressures. Mainly, however, the culture of the judiciary in Canada is seen as strongly resistant to reducing penal moderation. In England judicial culture is markedly ambivalent on this score: having been receptive to the moves towards greater penal restraint in the 1980s, the judiciary adapted swiftly to the 'Prison Works' ethos of the 1990s. A key difference lies in the appeal of alternative narratives to that paradigm. The Canadian model was sustained by the development of cognitive behaviour therapies in the 1980s and 90s, in which Canada played a leading role.[17] Its appeal in Britain and the USA was blunted by the growing dominance of what David Garland termed the 'culture of control', two key elements of which are the reinvention of the prison as a purely incapacitative form of punishment, and a perpetual sense of crisis as overwhelming any attempt to moderate penal measures.[18]

As a result, the issue of political choice must be addressed: how far and in what ways has criminal justice policymaking hinged on developments in the political realm. Given the fiercely upheld character of judicial independence in England and Wales, politicians and their civil servants are famously wary of breaching the separation of powers principle. Nevertheless, the judiciary are bound to enforce the laws enacted by parliament, and governments also have the duty to legislate in the best interests of justice. That duty extends to the formulation of criminal justice policy, a process which includes taking account of what may be gauged as public opinion about the character of crime and punishment. It is far from obvious how different publics will respond to even the most heinous acts. For example, it seems inevitable that the killing of a child, even by other children, will provoke a profound desire to punish those responsible. The sea change in criminal justice policy in England can be seen as stemming from a collective reaction of horror to the killing of two-year-old James Bulger by two ten-year-old boys. Yet a comparable case in Norway generated a quite different response, one in which the boys responsible for the killing of a young girl were extended rehabilitative support.[19] The complexities and signal importance of the politics, and political economy, of crime control in England and Wales is the subject of the second volume on the history of penal policy in this period.[20]

## Notes

1 Important exceptions are Garland, 1985, op. cit, Rutherford, 1986, op. cit. and Wilson, 2014, op. cit.
2 Downes, 1988, op. cit.
3 Windlesham, 1993, op. cit.: 20.
4 Ann Oakley, op. cit.: 267.
5 Cavadino and Dignan, 1997, op. cit.: 251.
6 Windlesham, 1993, op. cit.: 156.
7 Hugo Young, 1989, *One of Us: A Biography of Margaret Thatcher*, London: Macmillan: 234.
8 Windlesham, 1993, op. cit.: 168–72.
9 David Faulkner, 2014, *Servant of the Crown: A Civil Servant's Story of Criminal Justice and Public Service Reform*, Winchester: Waterside Press: 125.
10 See especially the works cited by Brody, Clarke, Hough, Mayhew and Tarling cited in Ch. 6.
11 Arguments for this combination by academic criminologists and penal reformers were notably made by King and Morgan, 1980, op. cit.; Andrew Rutherford, 1993, *Criminal Justice and the Pursuit of Decency*, Oxford: Oxford University Press; and Vivien Stern, 1987, *Bricks of Shame: Britain's Prisons*, Harmondsworth: Penguin.
12 D. Garland (ed.) 2001, *Mass Imprisonment: Social Causes and* Consequences, London: Sage; M. Cavadino and J. Dignan, 2006, *Penal Systems: A Comparative Approach*, London: Sage; N. Lacey, 2008, *The Prisoners' Dilemma: Political Economy and Punishment in Contemporary Democracies*, Cambridge: Cambridge University Press; and M. Tonry (ed.), 2007, *Crime, Punishment and Politics in Comparative Perspective*, Chicago: Chicago University Press.
13 B. Western, 2006, *Punishment and Inequality in America*, New York: Russell Sage; D. Downes and K. Hansen, 2006, 'Welfare and Punishment in Comparative Perspective' in S. Armstrong and L. McAra (eds.) *Perspectives on Punishment: The Contours of* Control, Oxford: Oxford University Press: 133–54; D. Downes, 2012, 'Political

economy, welfare and punishment in comparative perspective', in S. Snacken and E. Dumortier (eds.) *Resisting Punitiveness in Europe? Welfare, human rights and democracy*, London: Routledge: 23–34; T. Lappi-Seppala, 'Explaining national differences in the use of imprisonment', in Snacken and Dumortier (eds.) op. cit.: 35–72.

14  K. Beckett and B. Western, 2001, in Garland (ed.), op. cit.: 46.

15  C. N. Webster and A. N. Doob, 2007, 'Punitive Trends and Stable Imprisonment Rates in Canada' in M. Tonry (ed.) op. cit.: 297–369.

16  Fig. 4 in ibid: 306.

17  T. Newburn, 2007, *Criminology*, Cullompton, Willan: 861–4.

18  D. Garland, 2001, *The Culture of Control: Crime and Social Order in Contemporary Society*, Oxford: Oxford University Press.

19  D.A. Green, 2008, *When Children Kill Children: Penal Populism and Political Culture*, Oxford: Clarendon Press.

20  Downes and Newburn, forthcoming, provisional title, *The Politics of Law and Order in England and Wales, 1960–1997*.

# References

Abse, L., 1973, *Private Member*, London: Macdonald.

Adonis, A. and Thomas, K. (eds.), 2004, *Roy Jenkins: A Retrospective*, Oxford: Oxford University Press.

Advisory Council on the Treatment of Offenders, 1960, *Corporal Punishment: Report*, Home Office, London: HMSO, Cmnd. 1213.

Advisory Council on the Treatment of Offenders, 1963, *The Organisation of After-Care*, Home Office, London: HMSO.

Advisory Council on the Penal System, 1968, *The Regime for Long-Term Prisoners in Conditions of Maximum Security*, (the Radzinowicz Report), Home Office, London: HMSO.

Advisory Council on the Penal System, 1970, *Non-Custodial and Semi-Custodial Sentences*, (the Wootton Report), Home Office, London: HMSO.

Advisory Council on the Penal System, 1978, *Sentences of Imprisonment: A Review of Maximum Penalties*, Home Office, London: HMSO.

Allen, L., 2004, 'A Young Home Secretary' in A. Adonis and K. Thomas (eds.).

Allen, Ruth, 1985, *Public Order*, London: Labour Campaign for Criminal Justice.

Allen, Rob, 1991, 'Out of jail: The reduction in the use of penal custody for male juveniles 1981–88', *Howard Journal of Criminal Justice*, 30, 1: 30–52.

Alper, B.S., 1968, 'Borstal Briefly Re-Visited: Recollections and Some Related Reflections', *British Journal of Criminology*, 8, 1, 6–19.

Anon., 1982, 'Britain's Control Unit Terror' in *Britain's State Within the State: A News Line Investigation*, London: New Park Publications.

Anon., 1992, review of Leng, R. and Manchester, C., *A Guide to the Criminal Justice Act 1991*, Law Society Gazette, 3 June.

Ashworth, A., 1983, *Sentencing and Penal Policy*, London: Weidenfeld & Nicolson.

Ashworth, A., 1989, 'Criminal Justice and Deserved Sentences', *Criminal Law Review*, 340–55.

Ashworth, A., 1992, *Sentencing and Criminal Justice*, London: Weidenfeld & Nicolson.

Ashworth, A., 1997, 'Sentencing' in M. Maguire, R. Morgan and R. Reiner (eds.) *The Oxford Handbook of Criminology*, 2nd ed., 1095–1136.

Ashworth, A., Cavadino, P., Gibson, B., Harding, J, Rutherford, A., Seago, P. and Whyte, L., 1992, *Introduction to the Criminal Justice Act 1991*, Winchester: Waterside Press.

Ashworth, A., Cavadino, P., Gibson, B., Harding, J., Rutherford, A., Seago P. and Whyte, L., 1992, *Criminal Justice Act 1991, Legal Points: Commentary and Annotated Guide for Practitioners*, Winchester: Waterside Press.

Ashworth, A., Cavadino, P., Gibson, B., Harding, J. and Rutherford, A., 1992 (eds.) *Materials on the Criminal Justice Act 1991*, Winchester: Waterside Press.

Ashworth, A. and von Hirsch, A., (eds.), 1998, *Principled Sentencing: Readings on Theory and Policy*, 2nd ed., Edinburgh: Edinburgh University Press.

Ashworth, A. and Zedner, L., 2014, *Preventive Justice*, Oxford: Oxford University Press.

Bailey, V., 1987, *Delinquency and Citizenship: Reclaiming the Young Offender, 1914–1948*, Oxford: Clarendon Press.

Banks, C. and Fairhead, S., 1976, *The Petty Short-Term Prisoner*, London: Barry Rose and the Howard League for Penal Reform.

Barnard, E. and Bottoms, A. E., 1979, 'Facilitating decisions not to imprison', in NACRO, *The Petty Persistent Offender*: 17–27.

Bastow, S., 2012, *Overcrowding as Normal: Governance, adaptation and chronic capacity stress in the England and Wales prison system, 1979–2009*, Ph. D. thesis, Department of Government, London School of Economics, unpublished but electronically accessible. Published, 2013, as *Governance, Performance and Capacity Stress: The chronic case of prison crowding*, London: Palgrave.

Bean, P. and Whynes, D. (eds.), 1986, *Barbara Wootton: Social Science and Public Policy – Essays in her Honour*, London: Tavistock.

Beckett, K., 1998, *Making Crime Pay: Law and Order in Contemporary American Politics*, Oxford: Oxford University Press.

Beckett, K. and Western, B., 2001, 'Governing social marginality: Welfare, incarceration, and the transformation of state policy' in D. Garland (ed.).: 35–50.

Behan, B., 1958, *Borstal Boy,* London: Hutchinson.

Bennett, T., 1989, 'The neighbourhood watch experience' in R. Morgan and D. Smith (eds.) *Coming to Terms with Policing*, London: Routledge.

Benney, M., 1938, *The Truth About English Prisons*, FACT Number 12, London: Kemp Hall Press.

Birley, D. and Bright, J., 1985, *Crime in the Community: Towards a Labour Party Policy on Crime Prevention*, London: Labour Campaign for Criminal Justice.

Bottoms, A.E., 1977, 'Reflections on the renaissance of dangerousness', *Howard Journal of Criminal Justice*, 16: 70–96.

Bottoms, A.E., 1981, 'The suspended sentence in England 1967–1978', *British Journal of Criminology*, 21, 1: 1–26.

Bottoms, A.E., 1987, 'Limiting Prison Use: Experience in England and Wales', *The Howard Journal of Criminal Justice,* 26, 3: 177–202.

Bottoms, A.E., 1989, 'The Place of the Probation Service in the Criminal Justice System', in Central Council of Probation Committees, *The Madingley Papers II,* Cambridge: University of Cambridge Board of Extra-Mural Studies.

Bottoms, A.E., 1989, 'The Concept of Intermediate Sanctions and its Relevance for the Probation Service' in R. Shaw and K. Haines (eds.) *The Criminal Justice System: A Central Role for the Probation Service*, Cambridge: Institute of Criminology.

Bottoms, A.E., 1991, 'The Control of Long Term Prisoners in England: Beyond the CRC Report', in K. Bottomley and W. Hay (eds.), *Special Units for Difficult Prisoners*, University of Hull: Centre for Criminology and Criminal Justice.

Bottoms, A.E. and Preston, R. H., (eds.), 1980, *The Coming Penal Crisis*, Edinburgh: Scottish Academic Press.

Bottoms, A. and Light, R. (eds.), 1987, *Problems of Long-Term Imprisonment*, Aldershot: Gower.

Bottoms, A.E. and Stevenson, S., 1992, 'What Went Wrong?: Criminal Justice Policy in England and Wales, 1945–70' in D. Downes (ed.) *Unravelling Criminal Justice: Eleven British Studies*, London: Macmillan: 1–45.

Boyle, J., 1977, *A Sense of Freedom*, Edinburgh: Canongate.

Boyle, J., 1984, *The Pain of Confinement – Prison Diaries*, Edinburgh: Canongate.

Brody, S., 1976, *The Effectiveness of Sentencing*, Home Office Research Study No. 35, London: HMSO.

Brody, S. and Tarling, R., 1980, *Taking Offenders Out of Circulation*, Home Office Research Study No. 64, London: HMSO.

Brown, A., 2007, 'The Amazing Mutiny at Dartmoor Prison', *British Journal of Criminology*, 47, 2, 276–292.

Brown, A., 2013, *Inter-War Penal Policy and Crime in England: The Dartmoor Convict Prison Riot, 1932*, London: Palgrave.

Burt, C., 1925, *The Young Delinquent*, London: University of London Press.

Cabinet Notebook, 30/11/67 – 20/6/68, CAB/195/29.

Callaghan, J., 1987, *Time and Chance,* London: Collins.

Canter, D., 1987, 'Implications for "new generation" prisons of existing psychological research into prison design and use', in Bottoms and Light (eds.) 214–227.

Canter, D. and Ambrose, I., 1980, *Prison Design and Use Study: Final Report*, Guildford: Department of Psychology, University of Surrey (mimeo.).

Carlen, P., 1988, 'Women's Imprisonment: Current Issues', *Prison Service Journal,* 70.

Carrell, C. and Laing, J. (eds.), 1982, *The Special Unit, Barlinnie Prison: Its Evolution through its Art*, Glasgow: Third Eye Centre.

Casale, S., 1985, 'A practical design for standards', in Maguire, Vagg and Morgan: 97–105.

Cavadino, M. and Dignan, J., 1992, *The Penal System: An Introduction*, 1st ed., London: Sage.

Cavadino, M. and Dignan, J., 2002, *The Penal System: An Introduction*, London: Sage.

Cavadino, M. and Dignan, J., 2006, *Penal Systems: A Comparative Approach*, London: Sage.

Cavadino, M. and Dignan, J., 2007, *The Penal System: An Introduction*, 4th ed., London: Sage.

Cavadino, M., Dignan, J. and Mair, G., 2013, *The Penal System: An Introduction*, 5th ed., London: Sage.

Centre for Contemporary British History, Witness Seminar, 2010, *The Criminal Justice Act 1991*, London: Birkbeck/King's College: unpublished.

Centre for Contemporary British History, Witness Seminar, 2010, *The Home Office Research Unit,* London: Birkbeck/King's College: unpublished.

Clarke, K., 2016, *Kind of Blue: A Political Memoir*, London: Macmillan.

Clarke, R.V.G., 1980, '"Situational" crime prevention: theory and practice', *British Journal of Criminology*, 20.

Clarke, R.V.G. and Mayhew, P., 1980, *Designing Out Crime*, London: HMSO.

Clarke, R.V.G. and Hough, M., 1980, *The Effectiveness of Policing*, Farnborough: Gower.

Clarke, R.V.G. and Hough, M., 1984, *Crime and Police Effectiveness*, London: HMSO.

Clarke, R.V.G. (ed.), *Situational Crime Prevention: Successful Case Studies*, 2nd rev. ed., Albany: Criminal Justice Press.

Clarke, R.V.G., 2010, 'The Home Office Research Unit – an insider's view', London: CCBH Witmess Seminar, unpublished.

Clayton, M., 1989, 'Managing the Prison Building Programme', *Prison Service Journal,* No. 76 New Series, October: 9–12.

Cohen, L.E. and Felson, H., 'Social change and crime rate trends: a routine activities approach", *American Sociological Review*, 44: 588–608.

Cohen, S., 1974, 'Human Warehouses: The Future of our Prisons?'. *New Society*, 30, 632, 14 November.

Cohen, S., 1979, 'The punitive city: notes on the dispersal of social control', *Contemporary Crises*, 3, 8: 339–63.

Cohen, S. and Taylor, L., 1972, *Psychological Survival: The Experience of Long-Term Imprisonment*, Harmondsworth: Penguin.

Coleman, A., 1985, *Utopia on Trial: Vision and Reality in Planned Housing*, London: Hilary Shipman.

Cook, T., 1975, *Vagrant Alcoholics*, London: Routledge & Kegan Paul.

Cooke, D. J., 1989, 'Containing violent prisoners: an analysis of the Barlinnie Special Unit' *British Journal of Criminology*, 29, 2: 129–43.

Cornish, D. and Clarke, R.V.G., 1986, *The Reasoning Criminal*, New York: Springer Verlag.

Cox, P., 2014, review of A. Brown, 2013, *British Journal of Criminology*, 54, 1: 156–60.

Coyle, A., 1987, 'The Scottish experience with small units', in Bottoms and Light, op. cit.

Crawford, A., 2009, 'Situating crime prevention policies in comparative perspective', in A. Crawford (ed.) *Crime Prevention Policies in Comparative Perspective*, Cullompton: Willan.

Croft, J., 2010, 'The Home Office Research Unit' in CCBH Witness Seminar, 2010, unpublished.

De Beaumont, G. and de Tocqueville, A., 1833, *Du Système Pénitentiaire aux Etats-Unis et de son Application en France*, Paris. Tr. and abridged by W. B. S. Taylor, 1833, *Origin and Outline of the Penitentiary System in the United States of North America*, London.

Derbyshire, A., 2000, 'Architects and the Prison Experience' in Fairweather and McConville (eds.): 55–60.

Ditchfield, J., 1990, *Control in Prisons: A Review of the Literature*, Home Office Research Study, 118, London: HMSO.

Downes, D., 1982, 'The Origins and Consequences of Dutch Penal Policy since 1945: A Preliminary Analysis', *British Journal of Criminology*, 22: 325–62.

Downes, D., 1983, *Law and Order: Theft of an Issue*, London: Labour Campaign for Criminal Justice/Fabian Society.

Downes, D. and Ward, T., 1986, *Democratic Policing*, London: Labour Campaign for Criminal Justice.

Downes, D., 1988, *Contrasts in Tolerance: Post-war penal policy in The Netherlands and England and Wales*, Oxford: Clarendon Press.

Downes, D., 1998, 'The Buckling of the Shields: Dutch Penal Policy 1985–1995' in R. Weiss and N. South (eds.) *Comparing Prison Systems*, Amsterdam: Gordon and Breach, 143–74.

Downes, D., 2010, 'What went right? New Labour and crime control?', *Howard Journal of Criminal Justice*, 49, 4: 395–96.

Downes, D., 2012, 'Political economy, welfare and punishment in comparative perspective' in Snacken and Dumortier (eds.): 23–34.

Downes, D., Hobbs, D. and Newburn, T. (eds.), 2010, *The Eternal Recurrence of Crime and Control: Essays in Honour of Paul Rock*, Oxford: Oxford University Press.

Downes, D. and Hansen, K., 2006, 'Welfare and Punishment in Comparative Perspective' in S. Armstrong and L. McAra (eds.) *Perspectives on Punishment: The Contours of Control*, Oxford: Oxford University Press: 133–54.

Downes, D. and Morgan, R., 1997, 'Dumping the 'hostages to fortune'? The politics of law and order in post-war Britain', in M. Maguire, R. Morgan and R. Reiner (eds.) *The Oxford Handbook of Criminology,* Oxford: Clarendon Press: 87–134.

Downes, D. and Morgan, R., 2012, 'Waiting for Ingleby: The Minimum Age of Criminal Responsibility – A Red-Line Issue?' in J. Peay and T. Newburn (eds.) *Policing: Politics, Culture and Control – Essays in Honour of Robert Reiner*, Oxford: Hart.

Downes, D. and Rock, P., 2011, *Understanding Deviance: A Guide to the Sociology of Crime and Rule-Breaking*, 6th ed., Oxford: Oxford University Press.

Downes, D., Rock, P. and McClaughlin, E., 2016, *Understanding Deviance: A Guide to the Sociology of Crime and Rule-Breaking*, 7th ed., Oxford: Oxford University Press.

Dunbar, I., 1985, *A Sense of Direction*, London: HM Prison Service.

Dunbar, I. and Langdon, A., 1998, *Tough Justice: Sentencing and Penal Policies in the 1990s*, London: Blackstone Press.

Dunbar, I. And Fairweather, L., 2000, 'English Prison Design', in Fairweather and McConville, (eds.): 16–30.

Durkheim, E., [1897] 1952, *Suicide: A Study in Sociology*, tr. by G. Simpson, London: Routledge & Kegan Paul.

Edwards, A. and Hurley, R., 1997, 'Prisons Over Two Centuries' in *The Home Office, 1782–1982*, London: HMSO: 33–40.

Fairhead, S. and Marshall, T., 1979, 'Dealing with the petty, persistent offender: an account of current Home Office Research Unit studies' in NACRO, 1979, *The Petty Persistent Offender*: 1–9.

Fairweather, L., 1989, 'Prisons: A New Generation?', *Prison Service Journal,* No. 76, October: 26–31.

Fairweather, L. and McConville, S., (eds.) 2000, *Prison Architecture: Policy, Design and Experience*, London: Architectural Press.

Farbstein, J. and Wener, R.E., 1982, 'Evaluation of Correctional Environments', *Environment and Behavior*, 14, 671–94.

Farrall, S. and Jennings, W. (eds.), 2014, *The Legacy of Thatcherism: Assessing and Exploring Thatcherite Social and Economic Policies*, Oxford: oxford University Press/ British Academy.

Faulkner, D. 2001, *Crime, State and Citizen: A Field Full of Folk*, Winchester: Waterside Press.

Faulkner, D., 2010, *The Criminal Justice Act 1991*, Centre for Contemporary British History Witness Seminar, London: Birkbeck/Kings College: unpublished.

Faulkner, D., 2014, *Servant of the Crown: A Civil Servant's Story of Criminal Justice and Public Service Reform*, Hook: Waterside.

Faulkner, D. and Burnett, R., 2012, *Where Next for Criminal Justice?*, Bristol: The Policy Press.

Fitzgerald, M., 1977, *Prisoners in Revolt*, Harmondsworth: Penguin.

Fitzgerald, M. and Sim, J., 1979, *British Prisons*, Oxford: Blackwell.

Fitzgerald, Marian., 2014, 'The curious case of the fall in crime', London: Centre for Crime and Justice Studies.

Forrester, D., Chatterton, M. and Pease, K., 1988, *The Kirkholt Burglary Prevention Project, Rochdale,* Home Office, Crime Prevention Unit, London: HMSO.

Foucault, M., 1977, *Discipline and Punish: The Birth of the* Prison, London: Allen Lane.

Fox, L.W., 1934, *The Modern English Prison*, London: Routledge.

Fox, L. W., 1952, *The English Prison and Borstal Systems: An Account of the prisons and Borstal systems in England and Wales after the Criminal Justice Act 1948, with a historical introduction and an examination of the principles of imprisonment as a legal punishment*, London: Routledge & Kegan Paul.

Frenz, S., O'Connell, M. and Pease, K., 1990, *The Kirkholt Burglary Prevention Project: Phase II*, Home Office, Crime Prevention Unit, London: HMSO.

Fry, M., 1946, 'The Borstal System' in L. Radzinowicz and J.W.C. Turner, (eds.) *Penal Reform in England: Introductory Essays on Some Aspects of English Criminal Policy*, 2nd rev. ed., London: Macmillan. First ed. published in 1940, London: P. S. King.

Garland, D., 1985, *Punishment and Welfare: A History of Penal Strategies*, Aldershot: Gower.

Garland, D., 1989, 'Critical Reflections on the Green Paper', in H. Rees and E. Hall Williams, eds.: 4–18.

Garland, D. (ed.), 2001, *Mass Imprisonment: Social Causes and Consequences,* London: Sage.

Genders, E. and Player, E., 1995, *Grendon: A Study of a Therapeutic Prison*, Oxford: Clarendon Press.

Gibson, B., 1990, *Unit Fines*, Winchester: Waterside Press.

Goodstein, L. and MacKenzie, D.L. (eds.), 1989, *The American Prison: Issues in Research and Policy*, New York: Plenum.

Gostin, L. and Staunton, M., 1985, 'The case for prison standards: conditions of confinement, segregation, and medical treatment', in Maguire, Vagg and Morgan (eds.): 81–96.

Graham, J., 1988, 'The declining prison population in the Federal Republic of Germany', *Home Office Research and Planning Unit Research Bulletin*, 24: 47–52.

Green, D., 2008, *When Children Kill Children: Penal Populism and Political Culture*, Oxford: Oxford University Press.

Guiney, T.C., 2018, *Getting Out: Early Release in England and Wales, 1960–1995*, Oxford: Clarendon Press. Based on his Ph. D. thesis, 2016, *In the Shadow of the Prison Gates: An Institutional Analysis of Early Release Policy and Practice in England and Wales, 1960–1995*, London School of Economics, electronically accessible.

Guiney, T.C., 2019, 'Solid foundations? Towards a historical sociology of prison building programmes in England and Wales, 1959–2015', *Howard Journal of Crime and Justice*, 58, 4: 459–74.

Gunn, J., Robertson, G., Dell, S. and Way, C., 1978, *Psychiatric Aspects of Imprisonment*, London: Academic Press.

Gunn, J. and Robertson, G., 1987, 'A Ten Year Follow-Up of Men Discharged from Grendon Prison' *British Journal of Psychiatry*, 151: 674–78.

Hillier, B., 1986, 'City of Alice's Dreams', *Architecture Journal*, 39, 9 July.

Hobhouse, S. and Brockway, A.F., (eds.), 1922, *English Prisons Today: Being the Report of the Prison System Enquiry Committee*, London: Longmans.

Home Office, 1959, *Penal Practice in a Changing Society: Aspects of Future Development (England and Wales),* London: HMSO, Cmnd. 645.

Home Office, 1965, *Report on the Work of the Prison Department, 1964*, London: HMSO, Cmnd. 2708.

Home Office, 1967, *Administration of Punishment at Court Lees Approved School: Report of an Inquiry*, London: HMSO, Cmnd. 3367.

Home Office, 1968, *Prison Policy: Women and Girls*, P.D. 4, Study No. 1, Prison Department.

Home Office, 1973, *Report on the Work of the Prison Department, 1972*, London: HMSO, Cmnd. 5375.

Home Office, 1977, *Report of an Inquiry by the Chief Inspector of the Prison Service into the cause and circumstances of the events at H.M. Prison Hull during the period 31 August to 3 September 1976*, London: HMSO 453.

Home Office, 1979, *Committee of Inquiry into the United Kingdom Prison Service Report*, (the May Committee), London: HMSO, Cmnd. 7673.

Home Office, 1984, *Managing the Long Term Prison System: the Report of the Control Review Committee*, (the Langdon Report), London: HMSO.

Home Office, 1985, *New Directions in Prison Design: Report of a Home Office Working Party on American New Generation Prisons*, (the Platt Report), London: HMSO.

Home Office, 1987, *Report of an Inquiry into the Disturbances in Prison Service Establishments in England between 29 April and 2 May 1986*, London: HMSO.

Home Office, 1987, *Special Units for Long-term Prisoners: Regimes, Management and Research*, A Report by the Research Advisory Group on the Long-term Prison System, London: HMSO.

Home Office, 1987, *Report on the Work of the Prison Service 1986–7*, London: HMSO, Cm. 246.

Home Office, 1988, *Private Sector Involvement in the Remand System*, London: HMSO, Cm. 434.

Home Office, 1988, *Punishment, Custody and the Community*, London: HMSO: Cm. 424.

Home Office, 1988, *The Parole System in England and Wales: Report of the Review Committee* (the Carlisle Report), London: HMSO, Cm. 532.

Home Office, 1990, *Crime, Justice and Protecting the Public*, London: HMSO: Cm. 965.

Home Office, 1991, *Prison Disturbances April 1990: Report of an Inquiry by the Rt. Hon. Lord Justice Woolf (Parts I and II) and his Honour Judge Steven Tumim (Part II)*, (the Woolf Report), London: HMSO, Cm 1456.

Home Office, 1994, *Report of the Inquiry into the Escape of Six Prisoners from the Special Security Unit at Whitemoor Prison, Cambridgeshire, on Friday 9 September, 1994*, (the Woodcock Report), London: HMSO: Cm. 2741.

Home Office, 1995, *Review of Prison Service Security in England and Wales and the Escape from Parkhurst Prison on Tuesday 3 January 1995*, (the Learmont Report), London: HMSO, Cm. 3020.

Home Office Research Unit, 1975, *Community Service Orders*, Report No. 29, London: HMSO.

Home Office Research Unit, 1977, *Community Service Assessed in 1976*, Report No. 39, London: HMSO.

Hood, R., 1965, *Borstal Re-Assessed*, London: Heinemann.

Hood, R., 1974, 'Criminology and Penal Change: A Case Study of the Nature and Impact of some Recent Advice to Governments' in his (ed.) *Crime, Criminology and Public Policy: Essays in Honour of Sir Leon Radzinowicz*, London: Heinemann.

Hood, R. and Shute, S., 1996, 'Parole Criteria, Parole Decisions and the Prison Population: Evaluating the Impact of the Criminal Justice Act 1991', *Criminal Law Review*, 77–87.

Hough, M. and Mayhew, P., 1983, *The British Crime Survey*, London: HMSO.

Hough, M. and Roberts, J. (eds.) 2002, *Changing Attitudes to Punishment: Public Opinion, Crime and Justice*, Cullompton: Willan.

House of Commons, 1910, *Debates*, 5th series, Vol. 19, 1353–4, 20 July.

House of Commons Expenditure Committee, 1980, *The Reduction of Pressure on the Penal System*, London: HMSO, Cmnd. 7948.

Howard, J., 1784, *The State of the Prisons in England and Wales: With Preliminary Observations and an Account of Some Foreign Prisons and Hospitals*, 3rd rev. ed., Warrington: W. Eyres.

Hughes, R., 1987, *The Fatal Shore: A History of the Transportation of Convicts to Australia, 1787–1868*, London: Collins Harvill.

James, E., 2016, *Redeemable: A Memoir of Darkness and Hope*, London: Bloomsbury Circus.

Jellicoe, Earl (Chair), 1975, *Boards of Visitors of Penal Institutions: Report of a Committee set up by Justice, The Howard League for Penal Reform and the National Association for the Care and Resettlement of Offenders*, Chichester: Rose.

Jenkins, R., 1991, *A Life at the Centre*, London: Macmillan.

Jones, D.W., 2012, *Conditions for Sustainable Decarceration Strategies for Young Offenders*, Ph. D. thesis, London School of Economics, electronically available.

Karamalidou, A., 2017, *Embedding Human Rights in Prison: English and Dutch Perspectives*, London: Palgrave Macmillan.

Karmen, A., 2000, *New York Murder Mystery: The True Story Behind the Crime Crash of the 1990s*, New York: New York University Press.

Kelling, G., Pate, T., Dieckman, D. and Brown, C., 1974, *The Kansas City Preventive Patrol Experiment*, Washington, D.C.: Police Foundation.

Kenyon, W.H., 1965, 'The escape of Biggs and three others from Wandsworth prison, 8 July, 1965', HO278/10; P.E. 8; IPE 100/1/15.

King, R.D., 1991, 'Maximum-Security Custody in Britain and the USA: A Study of Gartree and Oak Park Heights', *British Journal of Criminology*, Spring, 31, 2: 126–52.

King, R.D., 1999, 'The rise and rise of supermax: an American solution in search of a problem', *Punishment and Society*, 1 (2), 163–86.

King, R.D. and Morgan, R., 1976, *A Taste of Prison: A Study of Trial and Remand Prisoners*, London: Routledge & Kegan Paul.

King, R.D. and Elliott, K., 1977, *Albany – birth of a prison, end of an era*, London: Routledge & Kegan Paul.

King, R.D. and McDermott, K., 1989 (a), *The State of our Prisons*, Oxford: Clarendon Press.

King, R.D. and McDermott, K., 1989 (b), 'Prisons – The Ever-Deepening Crisis', *British Journal of Criminology*, 29, 2, 107–128.

King, R.D. and Morgan, R., 1980, *The Future of the Prison System*, Farnborough: Gower.

King, R.D. and Resodihardjo, S.L., 2010, 'To max or not to max: dealing with high risk prisoners in the Netherlands and England and Wales', *Punishment and Society*, 12, 65–84.

Labour Party Study Group, 1964, *Crime – A Challenge To Us All*, London: Labour Party.

Lacey, N., 2008, *The Prisoners' Dilemma: Political Economy and Punishment in Contemporary Democracies*, Cambridge: Cambridge University Press.

Lappi-Seppala, T., 2012, 'Explaining national differences in the use of imprisonment', in Snacken and Dumortier (eds.): 35–72.

Leigh, D., 1980, 'How Ministry hardliners had their way over control units', *Guardian*, 8 April.

Lewis, D., 1997, *Hidden Agendas: Politics, Law and Disorder*, London: Hamish Hamilton.

Liebling, A., 2002, 'A "liberal regime within a secure perimeter"?: dispersal prisons and penal practice in the late 20th century' in A. Bottoms and M. Tonry, (eds.), *Ideology,*

*Crime and Criminal Justice: A symposium in honour of Sir Leon Radzinowicz*, Cullompton: Willan.

Liebling, A., 2006, 'Prisons in transition', *International Journal of Law and Psychiatry,* 29, 5: 422–30.

Liebling, A. and Price, D., 2001, *The Prison Officer*, Leyhill: Prison Service Journal.

Liebling, A. and Crewe, B., 2012, 'Prison life, penal power and prison effects' in M. Maguire, R. Morgan and R. Reiner (eds.), *The Oxford Handbook of Criminology*, 5th ed.: 895–927.

Livingstone, S. and Owen, T., 1999, *Prison Law*, 2nd ed., Oxford: Oxford University Press.

Loader, I., 2006, 'Fall of the "Platonic Guardians": Liberalism, Criminology and Political Responses to Crime in England and Wales', *British Journal of Criminology,* 46: 561–586.

Loader, I. and Sparks, R., 2010, *Public Criminology? Criminological Politics in the Twenty-first Century*, London: Routledge.

Logan, C.H., 1989, 'Proprietary prisons' in Goodstein and MacKenzie (eds.).

London, J., 1903, *The People of the Abyss*, London: Isbister.

McConville, S., 1981, *A History of English Prison Administration, 1750–1877*, London: Routledge & Kegan Paul.

MacDonald, C. and Sim, J., 1977, *Scottish Prisons and the Special Unit*, Edinburgh: Scottish Council for Civil Liberties.

McDonagh, O., 1977, *Early Victorian Government*, London: Weidenfeld.

McDonald, L., 1982, 'Theory and Evidence of Rising Crime in the Nineteenth Century', *British Journal of Sociology*, 33, 3, 404–420.

MacNicol, J., 1987, 'In Pursuit of the Underclass', *Journal of Social Policy*, 16, 3, 293–318.

Maguire, M. and Vagg, J., 1984, *The 'Watchdog' Role of Boards of Visitors*, London: Home Office.

Maguire, M., Vagg, J. and Morgan, R. (eds.), 1985, *Accountability and Prisons: Opening Up a Closed World*, London: Tavistock.

Mannheim, H., 1939, *The Dilemma of Penal Reform*, London: Routledge.

Mannheim, H., 1965, *Comparative Criminology*, 2 vols., London: Routledge and Kegan Paul.

Mannheim, H. and Wilkins, L., 1955, *Prediction Methods in Relation to Borstal Training*, London: HMSO.

Mathiesen, T., 1973, *The Politics of Abolition: Essays in Political Action Theory*, Oxford: Martin Robertson.

Mayhew, H., 1851–61, *London Labour and the London Poor*, 4 vols., London: Office.

Mayhew, P., Sturan, A. and Hough, M., 1976, *Crime As Opportunity*, Home Office Research Study No. 34, London: HMSO.

Morgan, R., 1979, *Formulating Penal Policy: The Future of the Advisory Council on the Penal System*, London: NACRO.

Morgan, R., 1985, 'Her Majesty's Inspectorate of Prisons' in M. Maguire, J. Vagg and R. Morgan (eds.).

Morgan, R., 1994, 'An Awkward Anomaly: Remand Prisoners' in E. Player and M. Jenkins (eds.) *Prisons After Woolf: Reform Through Riot*, London: Routledge.

Morgan, R., 2002, 'Imprisonment: a brief history, the contemporary scene, and likely prospects' in M. Maguire, R. Morgan and R. Reiner (eds.), *The Oxford Handbook of Criminology*, 3rd ed.: 1113–1167.

Moriarty, M., 1977, 'The policy-making process: how it is seen from the Home Office", in N. Walker with H. Giller (eds.) *Penal Policy-Making in England: Papers presented to the Cropwood Round-Table Conference, December 1976*, Cambridge: Institute of Criminology, University of Cambridge.

Morris, P. and Heal, K., 1981, *Crime Control and the Police*, London: HMSO.

Morris, T., 1989, *Crime and Criminal Justice since 1945*, Oxford: Blackwell.

Morris, T., 1970, 'Humanity and security', *Observer*, 1 March.

Morris, T. and P., 1963, *Pentonville: A Sociological Study of an English Prison*, London: Routledge & Kegan Paul.

Morris, T. and P., 1963, 'The Prison Under Stress'. Suppressed chapter from *Pentonville: A Sociological Study of an English Prison,* Unpublished.

Morris, T., 1966, 'How to stop jailbreaks', *Observer*, 12 June

Morris, T., 1971, 'Mountbatten betrayed', *Observer*, 28 March.

Moseley, S.A., 1926, *The Truth About Borstal*, London: Cecil Palmer.

Mountbatten, Earl, 1971, 'Prison: A Human Problem', speech at the AGM of NACRO, University of York, 3 April. Mountbatten archive, University of Southampton, MB1/N84A.

Moxon, D., 1990, *Unit Fines: Experiments in Four Courts*, Home Office Research and Planning Report, No. 59, London: HMSO.

NACRO (National Association for the Care and Resettlement of Offenders), 1979, *The Petty Persistent Offender: Proceedings of a Seminar held at NACRO 26 June 1979*, London: NACRO.

Narey, M., 2012, 'Prisons, Brutality and Decency: Reflections on thirty years'. Talk at the Institute of Criminology, University of Cambridge, unpubl.

National Council of Independent Monitoring Boards, 2010, *'Slopping Out? A Report on the lack of in-cell sanitation in Her Majesty's prisons, England and Wales,* London.

Newburn, T., 1992, *Permission and Regulation: Law and Morals in Post-war Britain*, London: Routledge.

Newburn, T., 2002, 'Young people, crime, and youth justice', in M. Maguire, R. Morgan and R. Reiner (eds.) *The Oxford Handbook of Criminology*, Oxford: Oxford University Press: 531–578.

Newburn, T., 2007, *Criminology*, Cullompton: Willan.

Newman, O., 1972, *Defensible Space: People and Design in the Violent City*, London: Architectural Press.

Nuttall, C.P., 1977, *Parole in England and Wales,* Home Office Research Study, No. 38, London: HMSO.

Oakley, A., 2011, *A Critical Woman: Barbara Wootton, Social Science and Public Policy in the Twentieth Century*, London: Bloomsbury Academic.

Pailthorpe, G., 1932, *Studies in the Psychology of Delinquency*, London: HMSO.

Parker, T., 1963, *The Unknown Citizen*, London: Hutchinson.

Parker, T., 1970, *The Frying Pan: A Prison and its Prisoners*, London: Hutchinson.

Parry, G., 1975, 'Fear on prison control units', *Guardian*, 15 April.

Paterson, Alexander, 1911, *Across the Bridges: Life by the South London Riverside*, London: Edwin Arnold.

Paterson, Arthur, 1911, *Our Prisons*, London: Hugh Rees.

Pease, K., 1985, 'Community Service Orders', *Crime and Justice*, 6: 51–94.

Pinker, S., 2011, *The Better Angels of Our Nature: Why Violence Has Declined*, New York: Viking.

Pitts, J., 1988, *The Politics of Juvenile Crime*, London: Sage.

Platt, T.C., 1987, 'New Directions in Prison Design' in A. Bottoms and R. Light (eds.).

Player, E., 2010, '"Prisons" Policy: The Redevelopment of Holloway Prison' in Downes, Hobbs and Newburn (eds.): 95–113.

Player, E. and Jenkins, M. (eds.), 1994, *Prisons After Woolf: Reform Through Riot*, London: Routledge.

Power, A., 1981, 'How to Rescue Council Housing', *New Society*, 4 June.

Prescott, J., 1977, *Hull Prison Riot: Submissions, Observations and Recommendations of Mr. John Prescott, M. P., Hull East. Presented to Mr. G. W. Fowler, Chief Inspector of the Prison Service*, unpubl.

Price, D., 2000, 'The Origins and Durability of Security Categorisation: A Study of Penological Pragmatism *or* Spies, Dickie and Prison Security' in G. Mair and R. Tarling (eds.) *British Criminology Conference [1999]: Selected Proceedings, Vol. 3.* British Society of Criminology.

Prison Reform Trust, 2005, *Private Prisons: Who Profits?*, London: Prison Reform Trust.

PROP (Preservation of the Rights of Prisoners), 1978, *The Public Inquiry into the Hull Prison Riot*, London: PROP.

Rackham, C. D., 1940, 'The Probation System', chapter VIII in L. Radzinowicz and J. W. C. Turner (eds.) *Penal Reform in England: Introductory Essays on some aspects of English Criminal Policy*, London: P.S. King, 115–126.

Radzinowicz, L., 1961, *In Search of Criminology*, London: Heinemann.

Radzinowicz, L., 1991, 'Penal Regressions', *Cambridge Law Journal*, 50, 3: 422–444.

Radzinowicz, L., 1999, *Adventures in Criminology*, London: Routledge.

Radzinowicz, L. and Hood, R., 1990, *The Emergence of Penal Policy in Victorian and Edwardian England*, Oxford: Clarendon Press.

Ramsbotham, D., 2003, *Prisongate: The Shocking State of Britain's Prisons and the Need for Visionary Change*, London: The Free Press.

Randle, M. and Pottle, P., 1989, *The Blake Escape: How We Freed George Blake and Why*, London: Harrap.

Rees, H. and Hall Williams, E. (eds.), 1989, *Punishment, Custody and the Community: Reflections and Comments on the Green Paper*, London: London School of Economics.

Reiner, R. 2007, *Law and Order: An Honest Citizen's Guide to Crime and Control*, Cambridge: Polity.

Reiner, R., 2016, *Crime: The Mystery of the Common-Sense Concept*, Cambridge: Polity.

*Report of the Departmental Committee on Prisons*, 1895, (the Gladstone Report), Parliamentary Papers, LVII.

*Report of the Committee on Children and Young Persons*, 1961, (the Ingleby Report), London: HMSO, Cmnd. 1191.

*Report of the Inquiry into Prison Escapes and Security*, 1966, (the Mountbatten report), London: HMSO, Cmnd. 3175.

Robertson, G., 1999, *Crimes Against Humanity: The Struggle for Global Justice*, London: Allen Lane.

Rock, P., 1996, *Reconstructing a Women's Prison: The Holloway Redevelopment Project, 1968–1988*, Oxford: Clarendon Press.

Rock, P., 1998, *After Homicide: Practical and Political Responses to Bereavement*, Oxford: Clarendon Press.

Rock, P., 2019a, *The Liberal Hour*, London: Taylor & Francis.

Rock, P., 2019 (b), *Institution Building*, London: Taylor & Francis.

Ruck, S.K., 1951, *Paterson on Prisons: Being the Collected Papers of Sir Alexander Paterson, M. C., M. A.*, London: Frederick Muller.

Rusche, G. and Kirchheimer, O., 1939, *Punishment and Social Structure*, New York: Columbia University Press.

Russell, C.E.B. and Rigby, L. M., 1906, *The Making of the Criminal*, London: Macmillan.

Russell, C.E.B. and Rigby, L. M., 1908, *Working Lads' Clubs*, London: Macmillan.

Rutherford, A., 1986, *Prisons and the Process of Justice*, 2nd rev. ed., Oxford: Oxford University Press. 1st ed., 1984, London: Heinemann.

Rutherford, A., 1986, *Growing Out of Crime: Society and Young People in Trouble*, Harmondsworth: Penguin.

Rutherford, A., 1993, *Criminal Justice and the Pursuit of Decency*, Oxford: Oxford University Press.

Ryan, M., 1978, *The Acceptable Pressure Group: Inequality in the Penal Lobby – a case study of the Howard League and Radical Alternatives to Prison*, Farnborough: Saxon House.

Ryan, M., 2003, *Penal Policy and Political Culture in England and Wales*, Winchester: Waterside.

Ryan, M. and Ward, T., 1989, *Privatization and the Penal System: The American Experience and the Debate in Britain*, Milton Keynes: Open University Press.

Shalev, S., 2008, *A Sourcebook on Solitary Confinement*, London: Mannheim Centre for Criminology, London School of Economics.

Shalev, S., 2009, *Supermax: Controlling risk through solitary confinement*, Cullompton: Willan.

Shaw, G.B., 1946, *The Crime of Imprisonment*, New York: Philosophical Library.

Shaw, S., 1985, 'Private Prisons: who guards the Securicor guards?', *AMBOV Quarterly*, July.

Shaw, S., 1987, *Conviction Politics*, London: Fabian Society.

Shaw, S., 2000, 'Prison architecture and the politics of reform' in L. Fairweather and S. McConville (eds.): 150–158.

Sheerman, B., [1992], *Seven Steps to Justice: Proposals for Reforming the Criminal Justice System*, London: Labour Party.

Sillitoe, A., 1959, *The Loneliness of the Long-Distance Runner*, London: W. H. Allen.

Sim, J., 1994, 'Reforming the Penal Wasteland? A critical review of the Woolf Report', in E. Player and M. Jenkins (eds.): 31–45.

Smart, C., 1976, *Women, Crime and Criminology: A Feminist Critique*, London: Routledge & Kegan Paul.

Smith, M.K., 2001, *the encyclopedia of informal education*, www.infed.org/

Snacken, S. and Dumortier, E. (eds.), 2012, *Resisting Punitiveness in Europe? Welfare, human rights and democracy*, London: Routledge.

Sparks, R.F., 1971, *Local Prisons: The Crisis in the English Penal System*, London: Heinemann.

Sparks, R., Bottoms A.E. and Hay, W., 1996, *Prisons and the Problem of Order*, Oxford: Clarendon Press.

Stedman Jones, G., 1971, *Outcast London: A Study of the Relationship Between Classes in Victorian London*, Oxford: Clarendon Press.

Stern, V., 1987, *Bricks of Shame: Britain's Prisons*, Harmondsworth: Penguin.

Stern, V., 1998, *A Sin Against the Future: Imprisonment in the World*, Harmondsworth: Penguin.

Stern, V., 2006, *Creating Criminals: Prisons and People in a Market Society*, London: Zed Books.

Stevenson, S.J., 1996, 'Official responses to escapes from and crises of control in English prisons, 1945–74', unpubl., mimeo.

Stuart, M., 1998, *Douglas Hurd: The Public Servant*, Edinburgh: Mainstream.

Sutherland, E., 1934, 'The Decreasing Prison Population of England', *Journal of Criminal Law and Criminology*, 24: 880–900.

Tarling, R., 1993, *Analysing Offending: Data, Models and Interpretations*, London: HMSO.

Taylor, I., Walton, P. and Young, J., 1973, *The New Criminology: For a Social Theory of Deviance*, London: Routledge & Kegan Paul.

Taylor, L., Lacey, R. and Bracken D., 1979, *In Whose Best Interest?*, Cobden Trust/MIND.

Thomas, D.A., 1970, *Principles of Sentencing*, London: Heinemann.

Thomas, D.A., 1979, *Principles of Sentencing*, 2nd ed., London: Heinemann.

Thomas, D.A., 1995, 'Sentencing Reform: England and Wales', in C.M.V. Clarkson and R. Morgan (eds.) *The Politics of Sentencing Reform*, Oxford: Clarendon Press.

Thomas, J.E., 1972, *The English Prison Officer Since 1850: A Study in Conflict*, London: Routledge & Kegan Paul.

Thomas, J.E., 1980, 'Managing the prison service' in R. D. King and R. Morgan, op. cit.

Thomas, J.E. and Pooley, D., 1980, *The Exploding Prison: Prison Riots and the Case of Hull*, London: Preservation of the Rights of Prisoners (PROP).

Thorpe, D.H., Smith, D., Green, C.J. and Paley, J.H., 1980, *Out of Care: The Community Support of Juvenile Offenders*, London: Allen & Unwin.

Tonry, M. (ed.), 2007, *Crime, Punishment, and Politics in Comparative Perspective*, Chicago: Chicago University Press.

Trasler, G., 1986, 'Innovation in Penal Practice' in P. Bean and D. Whynes (eds.), 1986: 229–44.

Treasury, 1967, 'Prisons – Measures to arise from the Mountbatten Report on Prison Security and from the increase in number of prisoners', T 353/8, File No. 2HG 28/66/04.

Tulkens, H., 1979, *Some Developments in Penal Policy and Practice in Holland*, Chichester: Barry Rose, for London: NACRO.

Tutt, N., 1979, 'Meeting the welfare need', in NACRO, *The Petty Persistent Offender*: 11–14.

Von Hirsch, A., 1976, *Doing Justice*, New York: Hill & Wang.

Von Hirsch, A. and Ashworth, A. (eds.), 1998, *Principled Sentencing: Readings on Theory and Policy*, 2nd ed., Oxford: Hart.

Wasik, L. and von Hirsch, A., 1988, 'Non-Custodial Penalties and the Principles of Desert', *Criminal Law Review*, 555–72.

Webb, S. and B., 1922, *English Prisons Under Local Government*, London: Longmans.

Webster, C. and Doob, A., 2007, 'Punitive Trends and Stable Imprisonment Rates in Canada', in M. Tonry (ed.) *Crime, Punishment and Politics in Comparative Perspective*, Chicago: Chicago University Press.

Wener, R.E. and Olsen, R., 1980, 'Innovative Correctional Environments: a User Assessment', *Environment and Behavior*, 12, 478–93.

Western, B., 2006, *Punishment and Inequality in America*, New York: Russell Sage.

Wilde, O. [C.3.3.], 1898, *The Ballad of Reading Gaol*, London: Leonard Smithers.

Wilde, O., 1905, *De Profundis*, London: Methuen.

Wilkins, L., 1960, *Delinquent Generations*, London: HMSO. Home Office Research Unit report, No. 3.

Wilkins, L., 1964, *Social Deviance: Social Policy, Action and Research*, London: Tavistock.

Williams v Home Office, 1981, *All England Law Reports*, Queen's Bench Division, 1151–1161 and 1211–1248.

Wilson, D., 2014, *Pain and Retribution: A Short History of British Prisons, 1066 to the Present*, London: Reaktion Books.

Wilson, J.Q. and Kelling, G., 1982, '"Broken Windows": The Police and Neighbourhood Safety', *Atlantic Monthly*, March.

Windlesham, Lord, 1987, *Responses to Crime*, Oxford: Clarendon Press.

Windlesham, Lord, 1993, *Responses to Crime, Volume 2: Penal Policy in the Making*, Oxford: Clarendon Press.

Windlesham, Lord, 1996, *Responses to Crime, Volume 3: Legislating with the Tide*, Oxford: Clarendon Press.

Windlesham, Lord, 2001, *Responses to Crime, Volume 4: Dispensing Justice*, Oxford: Clarendon Press.

Wootton, B., 1978, *Crime and Penal Policy*, London: Allen & Unwin.

Wootton, B., 1959, *Social Science and Social Pathology*, London: Allen & Unwin.

Young, H., 1989, *One of Us: A Biography of Margaret Thatcher*, London: Macmillan.

Young, P., 1987, *The Prison Cell: The Start of a Better Approach to Prison Management*, London: Adam Smith Institute.

Zedner, L., 2003, 'Too much security?', *International Journal of the Sociology of Law*, 31, 1: 155–84.

Ziegler, P., 1985, *Mountbatten: The Official Biography*, London: Collins.

# Index

Note: Page references in *italic* refer to figures.

Milton Keynes UK
Ingram Content Group UK Ltd.
UKHW022017090823
426625UK00027B/417

9 780367 653996